ANTONIO L RAPPA

D1559487

GLOBALIZATION

WITHDRAWN

An Asian Perspective on Modernity and Politics in America

Marshall Cavendish
Academic

© 2004 Marshall Cavendish International
(Singapore) Private Limited

Published 2004 by Marshall Cavendish Academic
An imprint of Marshall Cavendish International
(Singapore) Private Limited
A member of Times Publishing Limited

Times Centre, 1 New Industrial Road,
Singapore 536196
Tel:(65) 6213 9288
Fax: (65) 6284 9772
E-mail: mca@sg.marshallcavendish.com
Website:
http://www.marshallcavendish.com/academic

ISBN: 981-210-418-6

A CIP catalogue record for this book is available from
the National Library Board (Singapore).

Printed by Times Graphics Pte Ltd, Singapore
on non-acidic paper

**London • New York • Beijing • Shanghai
• Bangkok • Kuala Lumpur • Singapore**

For Angie, George, and Quentin

Contents

Preface   vii

Acknowledgements   xii

Chapter 1   1
Introduction

Chapter 2   43
Fascinating America

Chapter 3   73
American Globalization and Asia

Chapter 4   145
Economy

Chapter 5   182
War

Chapter 6   208
American Popular Culture

Chapter 7   248
Norms and Values

Chapter 8   280
End Thoughts: The Business of Thinking Broadly

References   303

Author Index   313

Subject Index   316

Preface

Modernity is the study of interrogatives that surround the meaning of life in the world today. A central paradox of American globalization is that the governments voted into power do not implement the kinds of policies desired by the American voters. There is a widening gap between the person who stands for elections and the person who ultimately occupies the elected office. American voters have therefore been continuously misled by many of their governments, from the US presidents right down to the congressional representatives. The reason why the "buck" metaphor came about was because everyone kept passing it around. Some political scientists have called for a change in the electoral system. Other legal experts want the Electoral College removed. Still others prefer that there are modifications made to include more representatives into the Houses of Congress. Are there problems with government? Certainly. Consider the fact that many American legal experts and independent interpreters of the law throughout the US continue to question the outcome of the 2000 Presidential elections. Even the Judiciary has come under question from these experts. American government is at the heart of the central nervous system of the most powerful business, political and military nation the world has seen since 1989. If America gets its government wrong, the rest of the world is affected at some level. If American government makes a mistake, Americans get punished. If some of the best and brightest people on the planet are concentrated in America and America is at the forefront of modernity, we cannot afford to allow America to make any more mistakes. This book is about opening up the truth of the past and the present so that the problems in business, government, and culture can be resolved before it brings America down, before it brings the rest of the world down along with it. Think about the trillion dollar American economy and its impact on world trade. Not many people would like to go back to living off the land, and living in decaying urban caves.

The central metaphor in *Globalization: An Asian Perspective on Modernity and Politics in America* is "The Ship of Fools" constructed out of Michel Foucault's use of the metaphor in his work on *Madness and Civilization*. However, contrary to what Foucault had originally described as a vessel for lunatics who were rejected by society, *The Ship of Fools* metaphor in this book represents the metaphor for the kind of modernity that appears to have developed since the Industrial Revolution in the West. This modernity engulfs the entire philosophical, political, social, economic, religious, and cultural dimensions of Western nations from Europe to the Americas.

The framework for this book is designed around the historical, social, cultural, and normative perceptions of American government at home and abroad. The book is divided into several chapters that explore the central metaphor and the themes of hope, optimism and progress in modernity. It also takes on a slice of modernity as viewed from Asia. To what extent should Americans remain interested in businesses and investments in Asia? What are the pitfalls and obstacles of the past and the present that lurk in Asia? This book has been written to help us understand the meaning of globalization as a slice of Western modernity. It uses the American case as the primary vehicle for exploring the subtleties and nuances of the politics of globalization.

WHAT IS GLOBALIZATION?

Think about a world without email. No Internet access. No hand phones, cable television, or MTV Music Awards. A world where people actually look up at the sky. Everyday. Where the nearest post office is ten miles away. The nearest neighbor is five miles away. A world without weather channels, sports channels, digital calendars, PCs, Macs, palmtops or PDAs. Think about a world where air travel is still too expensive. Where you remember the last city you visited, and where all your relatives and the people in the town showed up to watch the train run into the station. A world where the pace of life is so slow that everyone watches the sun set, and then spends the next two hours looking up at the night sky. A world where there is no constant electricity supply, no threat from the ozone layer, environmental damage, or watches with GPS navigational devices. No fast food. No second car. No cheap foreign imports. No Nintendo GameCube, Play Station, X-Box, or Home DVD Home Entertainment Systems. No Accenture, Accura, Barney, Casio, Dell, Lexus, LG, Microsoft, Nike, Nickelodeon, Nokia, Oakley, Prada, Sponge Bob Square Pants, or Swatch.

If you can imagine such a world, then you are thinking about a world *without* globalization.

I began writing this book because of the questions that arose out of several undergraduate and master's courses that I teach in globalization, politics, and modernity at the National University of Singapore. I kept getting the same interrogatives from them such as: what is the difference between globalization and Americanization? Are we really global simply because we consume goods and services produced by different countries under different systems and cultures within a short span of time by people we are likely never to meet in our life? What is political about globalization? How can anyone survive the politics of globalization? What will America do next? When will the next Vietnam War return to Asia?

Looking at the various texts that are available, one finds that most of them raise important and similar ideas about globalization. Most of these books include economic and political dimensions and tend to separate their conceptual frameworks from their practical illustrations. My students and I discovered that there were many issues and items that these texts could not explain. Some texts seem to be very concerned about specific items in globalization such as fast food, environmental damage and green politics, or business development and human management strategies. Many of these texts also seem to ask more questions than providing answers. Many texts also raise questions that do not seem to point us in a direction which clarifies. At other times, some books suggest solutions that appear to cloud global issues rather than make them more lucid.

A participant at a political theory conference in Illinois recently asked me what I thought about the nature of globalization. I replied, "there was none." That is the beauty and perhaps the horror of it all. You can't really second guess meaning and content in globalization. What we can do is try to analyze the patterns that emerge from different ways in which individuals, communities and states respond to the forces of global economics, politics, and culture. We are interested here in how America has risen and fallen and risen again in this global sea. And how globalization tends to be about a struggle. Not a religious struggle nor a Marxist revolutionary struggle, but a struggle to make the world more complete, more predictable, more manageable, and more meaningful. Answering questions on globalization often entails the expectation of more questions. Interrogatives are indeed part of the meaning of globalization. However, we might be able to say with some degree of confidence that globalization is a series of experiences that has never been felt in previous centuries to the same depth and extent that it is today's modernity.

I wrote this book because I was also unhappy with the different approaches and themes that various books, articles, reviews and commentaries on globalization have provided so far. Most texts are either too full of academic jargon or too full of accusations of corruption and nepotism. They provide too little statistical data and have an overt reliance on quantitative analyses that usually end with simplistic conclusions and deductions that would blunt Ockham's Razor. Now someone else can be unhappy about this book. That's life.

Globalization tends to be confusing, not only for students in the humanities and social sciences but also for scholars and the general reading public. The confusion is demonstrated in the lack of agreement among scholars about the definition of globalization. But while globalization and its processes may be complex, it would be naïve to think that the best answer or solution is the simplest one. It is not. If it were, all those academics that have come up with simple solutions to the complexities of globalization would be able to retire and build their own Platonic Academy or Aristotelian Lyceum dedicated to philosophy and natural science. In late modernity, higher institutions of education are emphasizing Life Sciences, Earth Sciences, alternative food sources, water research, stem cell research, the use of nanotechnology and nanobacteria.

Let us call a spade a spade. If globalization presents us with complex problems, let us not pretend that we have the antidote for its problems or the best solutions for its challenges. Rather, let us begin our understanding of globalization in terms of Heidegger's notion of technology. This is technology that is defined as man's attempt to control his environment. And globalization by extension is the use of technology to enhance human life. This means that globalization often demands all its participants—citizens, individuals, communities and organizations of democracies and authoritarian states—to partake in corrupt behavior for the larger good. It may require honest citizens to close an eye to corporate greed and malfeasance if only to take home a small piece of the pie, to keep that paycheck coming or to keep that cushy job. Globalization may require state bureaucrats to sell off trade secrets, employ creative and crafty accounting strategies to waylay the unsuspecting tax official, or bribe foreign government officials to get the job done. Let's not pretend that anyone in politics is innocent and has nothing but lamb's blood on their hands. Let us assume that all who partake in politics are willing and able to bend the rules and keep their collective ethical conscience clear whether it's a wealthy billionaire CEO giving an expensive gift to a politician's daughter for future political "considerations" and kick-backs, or a trusted personal banker who needs an opportunity to improve her financial portfolio.

Man is by nature, as Aristotle believed, a political animal. However, there is something particularly essentialist about this Aristotelian claim. This problematic phrase should be treated as such because man is not only a natural being but both an unnatural and a supernatural one, as Nietzsche believed. Nevertheless, if we understand man as being temporarily grounded by his biological self, and by his desire and greed for power, and *taint* this with the brilliance of speaking truth to power as Foucault suggested, then we have reached an important compromise. And in order to survive in this globalized world of technological dependence and control, one has to play by formal rules and informal norms—or forever remain quiet about never "making it big." There appears to be set of very fine lines that continue to crisscross that abstract divide between permitted behavior and rule-bending and impermissible behavior and rule-breaking. It would appear to be true that globalization is political because it is an extension of man's nature. If we are able to tentatively accept this premise, we can then begin our understanding of why there is indeed "a politics of American globalization." And that is how we might begin to embark on our journey for understanding globalization in terms of modernity and politics in America today.

Acknowledgements

I am deeply thankful to Professor Joel B. Grossman, Professor Benjamin Hermalin, Professor John Quelch and Emeritus Professor Deane E. Neubauer for their intellectual thought, earnest criticism, and sincere advice. I also thank the two anonymous readers for their comments on the manuscript. Some of the readers of this manuscript had serious reservations about the controversial political and business issues that were raised in the book while others preferred deeper readjustments to be made away from the postmodern method of overlapping arguments that requires a kind of pendulous return to previous ground. The book demands the reader's attention. That is true.

I also have tried to resist the temptation to write in a linear fashion that forces a conclusion at the end. I chose to view these criticisms positively and inclusively. All errors and omissions are solely my responsibility.

I would like to thank Aryeh Botwinick, Joshua Cohen, J. Peter Euben, Amy Gutmann, Joseph LaPalombara, Anne Norton, and Marshall Sahlins for their words of encouragement and more importantly, for their profound sense of theory.

I remember and cherish the important role that approximately 159 undergraduate and graduate students played at the National University of Singapore (NUS) in my courses on "Contemporary Issues in Political Theory," "Globalization's Impact on Society and Culture," and "The Politics of Globalization" from the academic years 2000/2001 to 2004/2005.

I also thank my colleagues in the Department of Political Science, my colleagues from the other departments in the Faculty of Arts and Social Sciences at the National University of Singapore, and the editors from Marshall Cavendish Academic, Anthony Thomas, Roy See, and Joe Ng.

Eight years ago, I promised to dedicate one book to each of the six scholars who signed off on my doctoral committee. This book is dedicated to one of them, Henry S. Kariel, a philosopher, teacher and Nietzschean theorist, who passed on in the summer of 2004.

CHAPTER 1

Introduction

The Greek historian Herodotus saw the world as a means of understanding the discovery and acquisition of new lands and cultures through intergenerational transformation.[1] His was a world of opportunity and inestimable space. In a more recent text, J. Peter Euben argues that Greek tragedy represented the political context for classical thought as it anticipates modern struggles with freedom, justice and tolerance.[2] The world that Euben describes is far less spacious and more catastrophic than the one written and described by Herodotus.

This book presents a similar blend of tragedy and optimism in a rediscovery of the politics of American globalization. This book neither claims an epistemology of global proportions nor does it agree with the argument that American hegemony equals neo-Imperialism. Any book that can make such a predictive claim would be best thought of as being relegated to the American science fiction section of Borders Bookstore. Or the dustbin of the Ages. Rather, this book unravels several ideas that impinge on the complexities of American globalization. It supports the successes of American globalization with critical pauses along the way as a means of opening up the reasons for these successes. There can be no wealth without poverty, no freedom without transparency, no rights without struggle, and no values without norms. We are after all, in the global business of world politics whether we like it or not.

There is a politics of globalization because of the unequal distribution of power. Human beings seem to be both attracted and repulsed by power. They possess a quality and proclivity for politicizing issues. As long as there is power to be gained or deployed, dispensed or resisted, there will be politics. There is a politics of American globalization because America is very much a subset of global movements in information, technology, commerce, investment capital, trade, finance, banking, and services. Not the other way round. America appears to be the culprit for many reasons because it is vocal, loud, and internationally present. American politicians have also led their citizens down the garden path with rose-tinted spectacles. There are many things that are hidden from public America because the political system of overlapping checks and balances (for example, term limits and regularly scheduled elections) force politicians to devote much of their time towards re-election issues in order to retain the power of office. Americans themselves share divergent views of the politics of globalization. This is in part because the American Dream metaphor lends itself to different plausible interpretations, very much like Kant's belief that the interpretation of the object or thing is predominant and lends itself to subjectivity, rather than the thing itself determining the interpretation. The word "globalization" can also be potentially differentiated for every country in the world. The use of the word "American" is a point of reference that informs the title of this book, and not a suggestion that American globalization is globalization. Neither is the use of the word "America" to mean the United States of America in any way meant to marginalize Canada, Mexico, and the other countries in North America and Latin America. The politics of American globalization has never been written. And this book might be seen as an original survey of the material things that encapsulate American modernity. This area of research is also important because America has severely (and severally) impacted the modern world in so many ways as to make it both fascinating and horrifying as more data is revealed through the media and the Freedom of Information Act.

There is a central paradox in American politics. This puzzle has something to do with neoliberalism, the American domestic politics, American war motifs, American popular culture, the American economy, and the problems of American government. The paradox or puzzle involves the relationship between the American citizen's obligation to the State and the state's responsibility to the American Citizen. The State has failed in several areas in terms of responsibly dealing with the trust it has received from Americans. The reason, as shall be seen, is in the political institutions and the political system. It is a paradox that Americans have known for years but no one has publicly uttered.

OVERVIEW

Chapter One introduces the basic themes of the book: "tragedy." "hope," "optimism," "progress," "mimicry," and the "American Dream." It looks at the main assumptions involved in the major debates in globalization.

The chapter also surveys the literature on globalization and politics, and suggests two examples of what might be considered as representing the positive stream of globalization books, and another that represents the negative stream of globalization. It also examines the ideas behind American domestic politics, globalization and Americanization, globalization and religion, and an analysis about the globe. It develops the political, economic, and historical platforms for understanding the rest of the book. In a conservative sense, this chapter posits the theoretical framework of the book in terms of the kind of style that is used to differentiate between the spaces, which are the interstitial politics, of American modernity.

Chapter Two: Fascinating America analyzes the contradictions and complementarities that make American globalization worth researching. This chapter explains why America is so important to the rest of the world and how its importance might be tempered for the international public good. The chapter illustrates the integral complements within the American neoliberal system and highlights some contradictions within the American polity that do not seem to be synchronous with the most powerful nation on earth at the turn of the 21st century.

Chapter Three is a historical comparison of American global interests in Asia and explains the advantages of investing in Asia with a special focus on countries that have specific value and meaning for America and Americans. This is a particularly long chapter because it conveys the central thrust of the view from Asia itself, but does not singularly claim to be the best view, as in a view that is aesthetically pleasing and morally perfect. This chapter also examines the responses and issues across several larger and some smaller Asian counties *vis-à-vis* their ties to American politics and modernity.

Chapter Four details the economic aspects of American globalization and the impact of its economic activities on the rest of the world. A special point of emphasis here is the work on MNCs and their management. This is because globalization is not purely about reconciling the social needs and demands from the impoverished masses and the restrictions raised by the wealthy elite in their defense of neoliberal rights. This chapter deals with the business of American business and uses the story of the Panama Canal and the meaning of "Outsourcing" to distinguish the interlocking of politics, business, and labor in achieving MNC status.

The chapter also inspects the successful stories of several American CEOs as a segue into the modernity of American businesses.

Chapter Five is titled *War*. Pax Americana is built on America's ability to defend and protect its interests locally and overseas. The foreign and domestic policies of several administrations are used as a clue to American military might. The position that America has achieved in late modernity is not only due to technological supremacy or brute force. If it were merely technological supremacy of arms, then there are many other advanced nations that could lay claim to being a superpower. Neither is America's position a result of brute force because if this were true, the People's Republic of China, India, or the Russian Federation would fit the mold. Rather, it is the consistency of the neoliberal rhetoric contained within foreign and domestic policies coupled with the Military Industrial Complex that have made Pax Americana what it is in late modernity. Military power is the foundation of America as a Superpower. American military hegemony is a serious responsibility that when taken lightly bestows untold death and destruction. This chapter highlights the main problems hidden within the recesses of American military power and reveals the single most predatory problem that faces America today as a global power.

Chapter Six illustrates how important *American Popular Culture* is to our understanding of the politics of American globalization in terms of the sociology of leisure and the psychology of escapism. This area of research has been omitted by every book on the politics of America's global role. The chapter shows why American idioms, American images, and American idols continue to be attractive not only to the West but also, all over the world. This is the politics of mimicry *par excellence*. Part of the power of American globalization's politics is the highly successful cultural idioms that have evolved at least since 1776. This chapter also shows how these genuine American inventions are themselves important cultural stake-points for all Americans in modernity.

Chapter Seven is about the *Norms and Values* that dominate a vital aspect of globalization that has been left out by most writers on globalization. In describing and explaining the meaning of *Norms* and *Values*, the chapter serves a complementary function to the major themes of the book.

Chapter Eight proffers some end thoughts with the general argument that no single definition of American globalization will suffice, nor any particular theory or school of thought, in comprehensively showing the "what," "how," and "why" of globalization, politics and modernity in America. The conclusion also reveals that the current strength of America's politics of globalization will gradually erode to be replaced by a new a startling paradigm that does not involve American dominance.

MODERNITY AND LATE MODERNITY

Modernity and late modernity can assume several hermeneutical forms. These center on the work of critics like Schlomo Avineri, Arjun Appadurai, Zygmunt Bauman, Ulrich Beck, Jane Bennett, Hans Blumenberg, Aryeh Botwinick, Judith Butler, Noam Chomsky, Joshua Cohen, William E. Connolly, J. Peter Euben, William Faulkner, Anthony Giddens, Alvin Gouldner, Amy Gutmann, Jurgen Habermas, Martin Heidegger, Louis Hartz, David Harvey, Fredric Jameson, Charles Larmore, Scott Lash, D. H. Lawrence, Jean Francois Lyotard, Hebert Marcuse, Marshall McCluhan, R. K. Narayan, Deane E. Neubauer, Neil Postman, Mario Puzo, Roy A. Rappaport, Richard Rorty, Marshall D. Sahlins, Carlos Santana, Michael J. Shapiro, Judith N. Shklar, Tony Smith, Charles Tilly, Gianni Vattimo, Stephen K. White, Tennessee Williams, and Zhang Yimou. There are very many more scholars of equal intellectual girth whom I have not read sufficiently to address here and will leave it to the reader to expand the list. There appear to be three main forms of defining modernity. One way is through a genealogical looking glass from a contemporary perspective. This would mean that everything in the past that can be recalled or re-constructed might be compared either erroneously or deliberately with contemporary life. The second common form for defining modernity is through the use of relative platforms. That every age has its own modern and traditional periods and ought to be understood as such. Hence we have knowledge that could potentially be based on a series of overlapping modernities. A third form for defining modernity is chronological. This means that it tends to use dates and years as a marker of beginnings and endings. I like to use this form to explain to new students of modernity. If this form is used, then we might argue that modernity's characteristics became particularly apparent and prominent in the Industrial Revolution of the West. Late modernity is marked at around the time of the PC and Information and Communications revolutions in the late 1970s and early 1980s. Readers are requested to use think about the possibilities associated with all three forms of modernity that they encounter in this book.

DOMESTIC POLITICS

American politics impacts globalization. But this is achieved with different levels of intensity and only in many parts of the globe, and not most of its parts. It is not unthinkable for a national plan, economic strategy, and global philosophy that is crafted by American Republican Senators or an American Democratic President that has an immediate, pervasive and widening impact. It does not. This is because history, counter-canonical history, and revisionist histories are inaccurate predictors of the modalities of political life. And American history has shown itself to be a complex mixture of ideological norms and propagandistic values that have gained increasing predominance since the end of the 19th century on the world political stage. Modern America's search for global control since World War I has demonstrated the extent of its global reach. Yet, despite the international prominence of America, the greatest impact that America has had for the past two hundred years is on its own domestic politics. While the trend is for America to think of itself more often than it thinks of the rest of the world, it is also true that America thinks of itself by "out-thinking" the rest of the world. For this we need to understand its domestic politics because American domestic policies influence the nature of America's response to globalization and the world.

American globalization is defined as all those activities involving multinational business corporations headquartered in one of the fifty US States that provide goods and services for America and the rest of the world. American MNCs may principally serve a domestic market, but make its products in several countries overseas. This also counts towards globalization activity. If an American company is based in Arlington, Texas or Casper, Wyoming, but outsources its backroom operations to New Delhi in India or to Bangkok in Thailand, it is considered part of American globalization. If a company overseas purchases an American franchise and has an American customer base, it is American globalization. If a company uses American technology, information, and communications in its daily business activities, it is considered part of American globalization. American globalization is informed and moderated by the US government and to a lesser extent by the governments of host countries where the MNCs are landholders and labor employers. An Act of the European Parliament may have an effect on American globalization, especially now after the May 1, 2004 celebrations of European unity in Dublin. Police action against local

6

saboteurs on Bintan Island, Indonesia, may affect an American subsidiary located there. This is also part of American globalization. Acts of Congress, executive pronouncements, and Congressional committees may have an effect on American global companies.

Decisions made within the federal and state systems of courts, the political views of US judges, and the costs of legal action in the US system of civil law also an impact on the conduct of American globalization. For example, George W. Bush might not have become president if not for a bureaucratic deadline involving Florida State law. He won the first US election in history by not having the largest number of votes despite the agreement by all nine US Supreme Court justices that machine ballots were inferior and imperfect. The Supreme Court clearly wanted the American public to know that the Florida deadline was more important than democracy. In spite of the Florida Supreme Court's decision, the five conservative justices of the nine-member US Supreme Court decided that American red tape was more important than the need to allow the final 175,000 voters in Florida to express their democratic right of *political choice*. The unanimous decision of the Rehnquist Court was a conservative one made by Republican-biased Supreme Court judges. It was one of the sloppiest Supreme Court decisions ever made by the conservative Rehnquist mini "Ship of Fools" comprising himself, Scalia, Thomas, O'Connor, and Kennedy. To think that 265 million Americans were split so neatly as to give Bush a "final" 537-vote difference is not only questionable and unbelievable, it is also not credible. The domestic political arena of America could have waited till January 6, 2001 as stipulated by Florida State law. There was no hurry. In spite of *Burroughs v. United States* (1934), the December 9, 2000 stoppage of the Florida recount and the December 12, 2000 verdict effectively strengthened the case for US businesses and Corporate America; the same businesses and corporations that Republicans own and protect with their lives and their professions.[3]

But what does this mean for globalization? In the short run it appears to have created a better situation with regards to US corporate taxes but in the long run it has placed someone in a position of extreme power who has appointed people who have cost American lives in Iraq. American global business practices are also subject to the former Immigration and Naturalization Service (INS) now known as the US Bureau of Citizenship and Immigration Services (USCIS), the Drug Enforcement Administration (DEA), the Internal Revenue Service (IRS), the

Department of Defence (DoD) and a whole host of other bureaus and departments that make the US (America) one of the most densely bureaucratized places in the world.

There is also only a superficial sense of difference between the Democratic Party and the Republican one. Over the past fifty years, the primary distinctions between the two parties have all but completely evaporated. It is better to think of the Democrats and the Republicans in terms of their "position" on the political spectrum. In other words, it is better to think of the senators, representatives and elected judges as either Conservative or Liberal in political outlook.

The first type prefers big business, free trade, less government intervention in America (but not overseas) private sector, pro-life, and prefers incremental change. Liberals on the other hand are usually pro-choice, and emphasize minority rights over business rights, prefer more government intervention and larger kinds of community differences acting within a non-violent arena. These are gross representations of what Conservatives and Liberals are in daily political life. For example, there are situations where you can mix up all of the above characteristics and end up with either a Republican or a Democratic political view. There are also many shades of differences within the parties themselves. If acting in concert, the party may give an impression of overall unity although this is not quite the same unity as that found in parliamentary-type governments modeled on the Westminster system in Europe, Asia, Africa, and the Pacific since 1945.

There are also shades of difference within the party caucuses as politicians behave differently as individual representatives of the people and as collective representatives of the Nation. As an individual representative, a politician may emphasize a greater willingness to change over a given policy or to provide leadership on another issue. As a collective representative, she may or *may not* (legislatively) act in the same manner. There are also differences within the parties themselves in terms of seniority and rank. This cuts across conservative, radical and right-wing members of the same party. This is why it is better to think of the two parties as generally possessing the same characteristics and the capacity and resources to reinvent themselves to adapt and take a stand on virtually any political and non-political issue, to politicize or depoliticize any political or non-political issue, and to issue warrants of political rhetoric at appropriate times.

There are currently over 3.5 million Americans living overseas, mostly in Canada and Mexico. Why? The whole problem began with the *16th Amendment* to the *US Constitution* that provides for the Federal Government to collect *Income Tax*. This has resulted in the evolution of the IRS as into one of the most tax-efficient systems in the globalized world.

American global businesses come under the protection and control of US laws including ones involving Anti-Trust legislation. This means that "wise" American investors and corporate managers summarily create different pockets overseas in tax shelters such as the Bahamas. With the exception of insurance, reinsurance, banks, or trust companies, the Bahamas is where international business companies (IBC) can be formed to provide a tax shelter for profit. So what do you do when you have insurance, re-insurance, banks, or trust companies and want to open an IBC in the Bahamas? Just don't use the forbidden names. This only requires a minimum authorized capital of US$5,000 upon approval for incorporation of foreign companies. While off-shore bank accounts are useful, they can't really compete with the proximity and tropical attraction of the Bahamas and its fabled beaches of pink sand. The biggest selling point is the absence of a US-Bahamas double taxation agreement.

Many Americans work overseas under the US Department of State, the Departments of the Army, Navy and Air Force. However, a significant number of ordinary, non-military and non-sate employed Americans (about 1.05 per cent of all Americans) live on expatriate terms outside the US. Why? Because money accrued to individual work and profits in the United States can be comfortably and legally 'sheltered' in the Bahamas, Barbados, Berlitz, the Cayman Islands, Gibraltar, Singapore, and Switzerland. These Americans live overseas in order to fully realize their version of the American Dream. This serves to lower the incidence of tax from x per cent to (close to, or exactly at) zero. And if you use your credit cards, corporate, personal or other wise, the credit card's bank doesn't really care where the money comes from as long as you remain a customer in good standing. The Bahamas and other tax shelters have been used for decades by American companies seeking greater global opportunities to expand by taking advantage of IBC status that offers its shareholders exemption from all income taxes, capital gains tax and corporate taxes, inheritance, succession and gift taxes, stamp duties, and foreign exchange control regulations. Some Americans have even given up American citizenship in order to enjoy a slower pace of life with the profits realized from sheltered investments gleaned over a decade to 30 years.

Neoliberal capitalists feel that the profits derived from honest, hard work by American companies in the US and the rest of the world ought to go to the shareholders and not get raked in by Uncle Sam for fighting politically damaging wars in the Middle East that result in greater global hatred of America and Americans.

Consider the *Articles of Confederation*. These were constructed to protect, in a large part, the present and future of American businesses and property rights of the early Seaboard States from the aggressive colonial control of Great Britain. But as a result of breaking away, the new states had to pay for everything themselves. About 230 years later, the cost of American government has become the highest in the world. How does one survive modernity when the actual costs of governance exceeds OMB estimates by hundred millions in unaccounted funds? Notice that according to the US Bureau of Public Debt, the total US deficit runs over US\$7 trillion increasing at an increasing rate currently standing at over US\$1.58 billion per annum before adding the future costs of the current Second Gulf War. The average debt owed by each American on paper is US\$24,248. There is certainly a politics of American globalization because a large part of the deficit is due to American provisions of free international public good (such as "peace" and "stability") and the total cost of the Cold War program (1955–1989). Does the world owe America a favor?

While the rest of the book and the *Chapter* on *War* analyze the numbers that construct the politics of American globalization, it is also important to note some history here. The Founding Fathers' fear of the absolutism of King George led them to construct the two basic principles of American governance, i.e., a system of shared powers, and a system of checks and balances. In terms of political theory, much of the problems that American businesses face today are directly traceable to these two political fundamentals. The first reason is that the principle of shared powers is not about equally shared powers between the three arms of government. This is because the US executive branch really has only one person-in-charge, the President. While the House of Representatives has 435 seats, the US Senate has 100. This makes a total of 535 (different) individuals who have different terms of elected office and much lower access to the national media than the Chief Executive. *535 individuals who have to share power*. And the US Supreme Court has nine judges appointed by the President. How can power possibly be 'equally shared' when the size of these parts are grossly unequal in the first place?

The second principle of a system of checks and balances tends to emphasize the "checks" and not the "balances." This leads to a potentially disastrous situation where there are so many rules and regulations, that most Federal and State employees don't really read the manuals but merely follow their senior staffers and learn on-the-job. Because there are so many regulations it becomes virtually impossible to develop a professionally competent bureaucratic service. Despite the lack of a truly competent service, the old adage that the system is so well designed that even a monkey could run the US government is mostly untrue. And seems to be a relic from the unfinished work of Left-leaning Socialists keen on the return of the failed Communist Party of America. In reality, very crafty monkeys appear to have been running the *Ship of Fools*. The US government is riddled with presidential appointees, recalcitrant staffers from previous administrations, and those appointed out of political favor and support. All of them have a huge array of personal networks and contacts across America in retail, construction, education, financial services, management consultancies, banking, law, social work, and virtually every industry and in each profession. Every other person seems to want to get something out of Uncle Sam, from the big corporations to the small individual investors. And because America is a land of mixture. A land of multiple sensations where unethical workers, wheeling-dealing types, natural disasters and financial catastrophes co-exist and often distract the activities of honest Americans. Apart from the Weberian nightmare of the iron-cage syndrome, there are also problems with various grouses and gremlins like the "imperial presidency," "court packing," and "congressional grandstanding" to name a few. The problem of bureaucratic neutrality has resulted in Big Government being perceived as callous, unbending, and overwhelming. This is why it is better for us to understand American politics in terms of political personalities, political issues, recent legal history, and the norms and values that determine the place on the political spectrum from Conservative to Liberal, and from the "Left' to the 'Right" rather than simply ingest Senator (R)'s or Congressperson (D)'s political rhetoric, logical arguments, and "charts and graphs" debates on CSPAN.

Globalization is not beyond the reach of every one, but neither is globalization's reach able to touch everyone and everything. Perhaps one way of understanding globalization is to see it as a process rather than a goal. Once one is convinced of this starting point, accepting the idea of globalization as belonging to everyone and simultaneously belonging to no one is more easily attained. There are rational reasons for this paradox as seen in the competing array of challenges that the globe throws up every day. And the variegated responses that are designed to match these challenges. There is a politics of globalization because it is a process that involves the complex borrowing, sharing, stealing, and copying of ideas, visions, concepts and norms of technology's uses. Globalization is more than the human control of the external environment as Martin Heidegger suggested in the early 20th century, perhaps to the chagrin of Hannah Arendt. Neither is globalization the Panopticonian vehicle that acts to chauffeur the current worldwide democratic transformation in a forward and linear motion as Fukuyama and his supporters would be apt to believe.

Globalization involves all these different ideas and more. It is not moving only forward and back but also sideways and upwards. And globalization is reversible. Globalization is not an irreversible process, as some liberal economists insist, that is sweeping away the residues of resistance, be they national or regional. And with the end of the Cold War the world is not breaking up into rival economic blocs as some neo-mercantilists have argued. Instead globalization and regionalism are complementary processes. They occur simultaneously and feed on each other, thus leading to growing tensions between economic regionalism and economic multilateralism.[4]

But politics as we know it through the millennia is much more than the question of irreversibility. Alas, we are unable to completely learn from the past or else we could, inter alia, summon the greatest philosophers of each Age to envision their map of their world. And to paint a picture of their world *in situ*. What would be the result? We would see that globalization has in effect taken on an enlarging series of cartographic experiences overlapping, questioning, interrogating, rejecting and informing the preceding periods. The earliest Chinese philosophers saw the world as being inscrutably centered on China. The ancient Hindu philosopher kings thought that the world was best understood as unchallengeable but profound karmic interventions. The great Greek heroes of our own philosophical age saw the world as being divided between barbarians and civilized men. Later, some medieval Christian philosophers viewed the world as being symbolically four-cornered and flat. At every age and in every age there was talk and discussion about the world. As students of philosophy, alive and well today, we need to take cognizance of the fact that we are dispossessed of sufficient life to seek out the ends of globalization. And must quickly retreat to the places that support discernible patterns of what we can observe about our past and present futures. Less we forget. For the first quarter of the 21st century, there is significant data to support an assurance that there is likely to be an increase in Total World Output in trade. Additionally, sub-epistemological increases in human knowledge of food production vis-à-vis population growth[5] are also likely in terms of the volume of trade, commercial activities, and the value of global stock markets as Philippe Jorion and William N. Goetzmann have previously discovered. But this scenario is only likely if and when centers of economic production (that range from small farms and family holdings to multinational outsourcing powerhouses that pressure other conglomerates to perform and compete) perceive each other as complements rather than as lepers sharing the same leprosarium within the same leper colony.

On Assumption

There can be no single school of thought that explains globalization. I do not support any single anarchic, realist, structural, Marxist, neoMarxist, or liberal interpretation of the world and invite readers to create alternative critical modes of reading globalization against the grain of what we are normally presented. Otherwise we will get bogged down in hair-splitting differences among careerists who have built up their entire lives around a few good concepts and then feel obligated to defend these positions to the death.

Rather, this book is about opening up the interstitial spaces that exist in world-wide perceptions of political, social, cultural, and economic change. And using the theories that make sense to clarify rather than complicate matters. The section on American politics and political institutions above was raised as a reminder of what is expected of the intended reader, that she or he is aware of more than just the basics of upper level undergraduate knowledge of American government. The readers are expected to know the basics of real American governance, the practice of politics *in situ* in order to make most of the analyses in this book. It is also assumed that the readers are familiar with or have taken graduate courses on international political economy and or business fundamentals. The terms of reference, while generally "argon free," assume that readers come prepared with street level or academic backgrounds (or both) that provides the kind of depth that is required of the target readers.

Robert Gilpin's work on international political economy is a useful precursor to this text. While there are some problems with some areas of Gilpin's theoretical constructions, he certainly provides an intellectual survey of the kind of introductory landscape that we are still trying to navigate despite what all those wonderful articles in *World Politics, Political Theory, Political Philosophy and Public Affairs* argue, and in spite of the many divergent books serialized in terms of American government, American foreign policy, international relations (IR) theory, critical IR theory, normative political theory, modernity, and cultural studies.

Part of this book's intention is to generate sufficient evidence and intellectual provocations to challenge the theories that continue to dominate the intellectual scene without being neither boring nor benign. However, if you are a general reader and have already been thrown off course; suffice to know that there are two main debates that need to be known to make more sense of the impending chapters.

The first one is known as realism. While realism has a long and vaulted history across the European philosophical landscape, and has been deployed in many different ways, it also has a central binding argument. The argument begins with assumptions of a certain kind of human nature, and an anarchic world order where all nations are in competition for limited resources and for political, economic, and cultural survival. Realism involves the use of military force, combat power and other coercive elements of the state to support what used to be called the national interest and national interest objectives. Thucydides, Hobbes, Machiavelli, Clausewitz, Niebuhr, Morgenthau, Kennan (the "king of containment"), and their disciples would tend to support an argument that celebrates the centrality of the state as an actor that is sovereign above all other entities. Realism and its derivatives (such as neorealism and structural realism) are mainly concerned with the state as the basic unit of analysis, state actions, and relationships between nations such as foreign policy, and diplomacy. The egotism of realism and its central invocation of the word "power" in its classical and modern forms tend to obscure the finer details of life within the state itself and the prospects for safeguarding a stable future. As a result, neoliberalism was created. Neoliberalism shares many of the basic statist views of modern realism

14

but defines the use of power as a means of achieving relative gains rather than realists' and realism's absolute ones. Neorealism in political science has nothing to do with the Italian film industry, by the way. It has everything to do with analyzing the broad spectrum of international strategic studies. Neorealist experts also seem to be their harshest critics and include Kenneth Waltz, John Mearsheimer, Robert Gilpin, and Joanne Gowa. There is another residual consequence of realism called structural realism that focuses on civil society, deep structure and variations on a theme of what Joseph Nye has now re-claimed as "soft power." The great contributions of realism include classical balance of power theory, hegemonic stability theory, security dilemma, and game theory.

The second debate involves the neoliberal position. This is different from the kind of liberalism used in US domestic politics by scholars who wish to emphasize the importance of individual rights, Constitutionalism, and more, or less, government intervention in private life. Neoliberal discourse stresses the importance of MNCs and international organizations that support capitalism, non-protectionism, and "free trade." Proponents of neoliberalism tend to support the opening up of markets that are protected from or closed to capitalist intervention. Neoliberals also tend to support the WTO, IBRC, and the IMF. Neoliberals tend to marginalize the work of the UN although some weaker ones tend to accept it grudgingly. Neoliberal theory is idealistic in nature and purpose because it thinks that the world can be made a better place through openness and trade. At its best, neoliberalism is concerned with using capitalist machines to achieve worldwide freedoms for everyone. But as we will see, this is a political conceit. It is an elaborate metaphorical hoax because the neoliberals know that capitalism through MNCs and other business units have created widening and deepening divisions between the rich and the poor. In all countries. Neoliberals are everywhere as you can imagine. Many of us often expose our neoliberal sides when making big purchases of consumer products, but are classical liberal (limited government intervention) when showing our desire for more wealth. The primary academic philosophy of neoliberalism can be traced directly to Adam Smith, John Maynard Keynes and the Bretton Woods system.

If neoliberalism already seems naïve to you, then you are probably on my side. For many of the poor and the marginalized, neoliberalism is not the "giver-of-gifts" but the "extractor-of-surplus value" we now call "productivity." My work remains generally critical of both realist and neoliberal schools but I do concede that there are certain advantages and prospects in both schools. However, these two debates were very briefly introduced because I intend to use them as lenses to explain the politics of American globalization. Remember that there is a politics of American globalization because there is a problem with American democracy. It is too inveigled with historical romanticism that only a minority can see that one cannot really practice democracy through the direct election of 535 congresspersons and senators but not directly elect the most powerful office.

Therefore when we use the word realist we are referring to the assumptions made above and are concerned with the hawkish or dove-like actions of States as unitary actors in their bid for survival and their strategies for surviving modernity. When we use the word neoliberal, we are referring to the working of MNCs and other driving forces of globalization that want to open up and deepen the world. When I use the word "conservative," it usually refers to something that is not positive, and when I use the word "socialist" it is too far to the left for it to be practical.

THE LITERATURE

Speaking of which, there are approximately 16,755 books on globalization and global-related industries. Close to 80 per cent of these books refer to politics and, or political economy in some form or manner. 95 per cent of the literature on globalization involves money, finance, or economics. Less than five per cent are written by academics in Research Universities Class I (including this one plus two that have been written by former professors from my old graduate school). Approximately 55 to 80 new books will hit the retail market over the next calendar year. The retail market includes those in the public domain and those in the research environment. By this token, 99.67 per cent of the books on the topic of globalization are already outdated. For the average faculty member interested in globalization, it would take about two years of research for conceptualization and writing a manuscript, with limited research assistance, while teaching two undergraduate and three graduate courses a year. Another year and a half to two years can be devoted to the review process (which is not only getting more onerous, but also highly vindictive, given the comments of some "blind reviewers"). Therefore in total the data and resources that go into a book conceptualized three-and-a-half to four years ago would basically make it outdated the moment it goes to press. However, if you manage your time vigilantly, and are not otherwise committed to other projects, you could actually produce a book in 25 per cent less time. If you are an endowed professor whom no one knows but are in possession of many resources, you could give yourself another 15 to 20 per cent discount on time taken from start to finish (about 2.56 years). But if you are already a widely acclaimed and popular writer with a deep nexus of critics and supporters in addition to your endowed chair at an Ivy league university, you could churn out a couple of books a year at the very least. That is six months a piece. The quality of the literature on globalization so far in the books (that I have read in detail, those many more that I have looked for specific items, and the largest number that I have scanned through because the jacket or cover was catchy, or because it was written by a colleague, competitor or former teacher) is highly uneven to say the least. Some are merely produced for the mass market purely out of some editorial decision that something was needed here in order to make money. Well, this is not the case for academic books, as these editors always remind us, where there is a net loss for the publisher, or that academic publishing has traditionally never been about making money nor has it been a profit center. I am sure that money is being made. But we are sometimes too trusting as academics. Perhaps we are too willing to believe whatever the market experts tell us with only mild interrogatives and gentle questioning. Returning to our literature review on globalization, I would add that most of the books on this broad and general topic that have been written so far are either too full of technical jargon, or redundant and sloppy in making the arguments connect. The majority have simply been formatted for the mass market. I am sure that this book suffers from more than just these problems. Nevertheless, out of this amazing number of books on globalization I can only make two honest recommendations based on those that I have read or scanned within the disciplines of political theory, political science, international relations, and cultural studies. In other words there must be at least seven to eight hundred books on globalization that are completely different from my own research interests but are probably very worth reading by specialists in the field. By specialists I refer to those people who are familiar with the literature because they read widely and in depth, every day of their lives and not by academic rank or some aggrandized position somewhere. So out of the hundreds of excellent books that have been written on globalization, there are two that are fairly representative of the main stream arguments made in the literature. One book by Philippe Aghion and Jeffrey G. Williamson represents positive and lucid academic arguments within the literature. The book by James H. Mittelman on the other hand reflects what is commonly done in the literature.

The positively featured book comes in the form of Philippe Aghion and Jeffrey G. Williamson's *Growth, Inequality, and Globalization: Theory, History, and Policy* (Cambridge University Press, 1999). This book has been expertly written and leaves the reader with the impression of authors who are widely read and firmly acquainted with the economic literature on the subject. The reader quickly digests their arguments which are clear and lucid but may raise questions about globalization that occur in daily life, but are not present in their work. For example, how is it possible for Aghion and Williamson to consider inequality measures that converge on economic issues of the past without considering the political modalities that inform inequality of resource distribution on one hand with the inequality of political rights on the other? While their economic theory is certainly superior for its clarity and carefully worded sentences, they appear to have marginalized the most important cause of unequal human behavior in three distinct areas: political ideology, political structures, and thirdly, advances made in international political economy (IPE). If indeed, Aghion and Williamson's analysis seems a little "out-of-touch" with political life, then it leaves me as one of their readers purely convinced along the lines of an excellent academic argument.

This is not the case for the other book that I am unfairly using to represent the other stream of boring books on globalization. James H. Mittelman's work is conceived along more didactic and moralizing lines. Mittelman is conservative and prefers to remain satisfied with describing globalization's assets and liabilities. For example, he discusses the matter of time management as being central to "the structural changes in management" (*a la* the late great Susan Strange and the others from the European school) but fails to pursue the matter of the speeding up of time within space as seen in the work of William E. Connolly, Lash and Urry, Geiger and others. Does he not feel that there are important measures to be considered when his own notion of global dynamics is subjected to the compression of space precisely *because* of the speeding up of time, and the compression of time because of the collapse of space? The book is also somewhat pretentious in its desire to promote a causality of coherence that simply does not exist within its covers. Mittelman falls into the trap of trying to place an original starting point of globalization which of course leads to silly arguments about which civilization was the first to globalize (and therefore is superior or has been there and done that with all the value of a tourist's photograph). His book does not raise the greater question of understanding the implications of knowing more about the kinds of contributions that were made in anticipation of what we have received today by default or design. The book's co-authored chapters cannot lay claim to the larger voices they seem to want to represent and therefore sit most uncomfortably with the single-authored chapters. This gives the book an uneven style and 'feel'. But the most disconcerting point about the book is the misleading title: there is no clear, coherent or sustained argument about globalization's syndrome and by the time one discovers that there isn't any clearly demarcated "syndrome" the book is done being read. However, I am sure that there are clear reasons for all these sins that I myself am about to commit in this book, but hopefully with a little more style, pizzazz, arrogance, and wit. Let us now turn to the verses contained within the structure of this book and begin with three themes of that offer hope, progress and optimism. The three things that globalization is truly about. And perhaps a little bit more.

HOPE, PROGRESS AND OPTIMISM

While it remains one thing to say that the world will never come to an end, simplistically or otherwise, it seems equally probable that all human concepts of "hope," "progress," and "optimism" are deeply embedded within the psychological paradigm of social scientific analyses. Hidden within the artificial concepts of social science are probably linguistic-based explanations that constitute human fantasies of "hope," "optimism," and "progress." The macro-world is simultaneously a large container of billions of microcosmic individuals, of which a tiny percentage are interested in the philosophy of body and mind vis-à-vis the rest of the world. Today's globe is both reflector and reflection. The globe reflects human values and norms that bring celebration and tragedy. The globe is also a reflection of human minds in their quest towards developing the outermost fringes (or the innermost core) of human "hope," "optimism," and "progress."

Both animals and things that do not work are concealed from public view so as to hide us from the pain and suffering of nonhuman things and species gone wrong. These are only worthy of critical investigation for the sake of science. "Wild" animals are housed in zoos all around the world in a kind of freak show. The housing of "wild" animals and other fierce creatures in domestic quarters is both disabling and alarming. It involves the celebration of human control over other species, ironically, while thousands of homeless Americans (i.e., "domestically displaced persons") roam the *Streets of San Francisco* in spite of that great 1970s TV show, a Quinn Martin production starring Karl Malden and a young Michael Douglas in an American quest to beat the downtrodden crooks and social low life into the dark recesses from where they breed like waterbugs on a hot, mid-summer's afternoon all across the great prairie belt.

Like the leper colonies of the Middle Ages that were converted to public use in 17th- and 18th-century France that Michel Foucault described in *Madness and Civilization* (Vintage, [1965] 1988), the world seems to be moving towards increasing levels of institutionalization of the insane. The fear of being institutionalized results in many people turning to self-medication, if only to avoid being labeled with "madness." There is also a modern proclivity to simply ignore what goes on around us when we so choose, perhaps because modern human beings have developed an ability to remain callous and indifferent towards animals and things. There was a time when human civilization hid its "ugly side" from society. Then there came a time when these "freaks" were used for entertainment and for public spectacle. Later, as we see in Foucault, they were used both for entertainment and public forms of torture. As a precursor to the callous, human psyche, prison systems in the democratizing Western world wantonly used public hangings as a means of mass publicity. Public cruelty became a convenient mode of crowd control, like Roman public executions on crosses across the Mediterranean region not two hundred years after Christ was born. And apparently, long before the rise of militant, right-wing, fundamentalist Islam. The dovetailing of public executions and private fantasies was increasingly played out across the known Western world until the end of the Ancient Regime began cracking under the fat of its own weight. The emancipation of centuries of libidinal suppression across the globe would render itself justified in the increasing need to discover and punish new worlds and new peoples. But late modernity has in the 21st century thrown up a new kind of species of human being—one who has become so alienated, so nihilistic, and so exposed to human inflicted torture—that there is really little feeling left and it takes a big disaster for anyone to feel even the slightest tremor of remorse.

Later, such adversity and compunction disappears like yesterday's oily newspaper that was used to wrap fish and chips and disposed in London's Hyde Park. The public arena has therefore become part of a global marketplace of ideas where the wealthy can discover new and fascinating means of publicly exposing their power over worthless individuals who by means of hard work and continuous labor can only grab the attention of well-meaning but dull social workers striving for that place next to Mother Theresa in Calcutta, and St Bernadette in that famous epic movie, *The Song of Bernadette* (1943). But where there is hope there are always throngs of people who promote their optimism ever so seriously until it comes true.

That the work of young scholars such as Anne Y. Ilinitch, Richard A. D'Aveni and Arie Y. Lewin who continue in their optimistic quests for "performing economies" or the epistemic communities of equally young scholars like Susan E. Clarke and Gary L. Gaile[6] whose work represents ontological explanations within the framework of the economism of hope rather than political pessimism. However, we should neither be carried away nor misled by the suave but simplistic accounts of the Samuel Huntingtons and Thomas Friedmans of this world and their essentialist theories of absolutist outcomes about globalization and human civilization. There is no need for alarm, though when the alarm bell does go off it is indeed always too late.

There is almost no chance of planet earth colliding with a huge meteor shower going in the other direction. Or that the increase in industrial activity since 1945 at a geometric rate will result in global warming at a faster rate than even the most pessimistic of meteorologists can imagine. Yet, no one can say for sure that we will not go the way of the wooly mammoth in another 11,000 years. No one can say that these mammoths did not survive longer than the longest human civilizations. But we do know that the era of globalization contains so much information and so many attempts that are designed around improving the quality of life, changing it for the better.[7] Sometimes it seems that even in the 21st century, our notions of quality of life have not changed as much as much as they did a century ago within a pessimistic universe. Perhaps it is more attitudinal than we are willing to accept. It seems, though, that we haven't yet completely figured out the best means to achieve the best quality. In other words, Jean-Paul Sartre was wrong when he said that "everything in life has already been figured out," the question—for him—was "how to live life." Most human beings instinctively know "how" to live life, we just don't know the best way to improve the *living as a process* "aspect" of it, and the most telling logic is seen in the amount of time, money, and effort that is devoted to extending life. Or acquainting oneself with the causal factors that promote death as John Earman believes or the objectivistic arguments by Darwin O. Sawyer, and the intelligent interrogatives of Cornell West where identity is about desire and death. Even life after death.[8] Globalization features much in terms of death avoidance and life extension. A perennial favorite, the extension of life, features prominently in all human civilizations from the time of the Chinese and Indians, to the Babylonians, Egyptians, and especially the ancient Greeks. We all want to know how to live longer through religion. That is why many local synagogues, temples, mosques and churches seem recession proof. It's a big spiritual business—it is about ensuring an everlasting life after all that can be said and could possibly be done about globalization.

GLOBALIZATION AND THE
PROBLEM OF RELIGION

But the business of globalization is not so spiritual or mythical in the religious sense of the word. Religious globalization involves the commodification of the artifacts and rituals associated with the practice of Hinduism, Judaism, Christianity, and Islam (in the order of establishment) and other worldly religions.[9] Technology based religion is the watchword of modern religious survival. Even if one visits Roman Catholic churches across the globe today, one would discover Microsoft-based Powerpoint presentations of liturgical services alongside high resolution images of Christ (that make him even more lifelike than ever) are created by portable Japanese projectors with high density definition screens and super long-lasting filament bulbs made in India, and plastic casings made in China. But religious globalization is only one aspect of the entire process of globalization. But it is a big aspect that is sometimes very much in your face. Islam for example has been cited as being the fastest growing religion in America. According to the *New York Times*, there are currently between two to six million Muslims in America. Islamic leaders in America such as Sayid Syed, secretary-general of the Islamic Society of North America (ISNA), as reported in *The Washington Post*,

22

argue that there are about eight million Muslims in America. That represents about 2.6 per cent of the entire US population or 1.5 per cent for a politically conservative estimate of four million Muslims. There are also 2,000 mosques in the United States which is a reflection of the liberal values placed on the practice of freedom of religion. Interestingly enough, there are no churches or synagogues or Chinese temples in Jeddah or any other Saudi Arabian city. So much for the over-commoditized versions that Disney has created about the world of the Arabian Nights. And perhaps, Ali Baba and the Forty Thieves.

As I write this book near the city center of Singapore, my desk sits just miles away from 170 million followers of the Holy Prophet of Islam in the world's largest Muslim country.[10] In the aftermath of 9/11, Bali, Madrid, and Iraq, how does one react to this statement? Wonderful? Is it frightening? Awesome? A segue into one of the great global cultural feasts of Southeast Asia perhaps? A writer's geographical location seems acceptable as long as no one violates her right to freedom of opinion, freedom of disbelief, and freedom of movement.[11] But I must admit that the explosion in Bali was a bit of a scare. Like other aspects of globalization, religion is made in the service of some global vision. And religious globalization is dependent on and in service of the various holy lords: the Lord Krishna, the Lord Shiva, the Lord Jesus Christ, Lord Buddha or the Taoist Lord of War and whatever religious or secular icon that might predominate a given scene or context as in the aesthetics of meaning and value in the work of Witkin, Bacchetta, Franchot, Miller, Landsberg, Axelrod, Fuerch, Maynard, and Burks.[12] Religion provides hope for the masses in a limited, periodic, and temporal manner in the same way that other commodities provide instant but restricted satisfaction. It depends on how much time you spend on it. Some people don't need to spend too much time at a religious convention in order to get the message that they want to hear.

Some individuals need to punish themselves through the retrospective grievances of literary pilgrimages such as Brian May's "Memorials to Modernity: Postcolonialism and Pilgrimage in Naipaul and Rushdie" illustrates. Or send them wallowing within harsh literal pilgrimages of ordeal and torture often associated with the art of public (self-confessionalism).[13] There is every year, for example, a ritual in Mecca, called the "stoning of Satan." In that great city of Islamic culture where (that formerly non-Black rock called) the *Kabbah* is located, there exists another place that is reserved for the "stoning of Satan." The stones are thrown into a pit that represents Satan. In the rush to throw the stones into the pit, thousands are often squashed and pinned down often resulting in unnecessary deaths. No need to die for religion. Other people around the globe only seem to need to go to church on Easter and Christmas to feel that they have satisfied their religious duties. Others prefer to spend the highlights of their youth being totally irreverent and non-religious and then later spending the rest of their lives atoning for their sins in some way or form. There are also conservative Jews who spend their entire lives memorizing and repeating Holy Scripture and quotations from the Holy Torah while at the Wailing Wall. Sometimes, such devotion belies negative remonstrance from the State.[14] The State, as it were, appears to be fighting different kinds of wars inside and outside its walls. Consider for example Meron Benvenisti's *Intimate Enemies: Jews and Arabs in a Shared Land* (University of California Press, 2002), Joan Peters *From Time Immemorial: The Origins of the Arab-Jewish Conflict over Palestine* (JKA Publications, 2001), and John Loftus and Mark Aarons' *The Secret War Against the Jews: How Western Espionage Betrayed The Jewish People* (St Martin's Press, 1997). And one will eventually come to the same conclusion as Edward Said did, shortly before his death, when he mentioned that the levels of political violence and vengeance killings among Palestinians and Jews, Arabs and Israelis have reached such complex proportions that it has become virtually impossible to take any side of the conflict on intellectually meaningful grounds.

There is an order of Catholic nuns, the Carmelite Order, who keep a permanent vow of silence. As these nuns continue their daily prayer for hope, optimism and progress of human beings all over the world, I am frightened to run into my own epistemological quarter of social scientific training that tells me that without evidence, "God" never existed except in the mind's eye of a proud, arrogant, and selfish human being. I can always blame Nietzsche. He is certainly dead, no question about that. Nevertheless, I can't imagine anyone being able to keep vows of chastity, poverty, humility and silence given the gregarious nature of being human. So for all the global means of public entertainment and hedonistic displays of pleasure, I can only think of this minority group of speechless, voiceless nuns who nevertheless continue to believe in a globalized world that is coming to its kingdom's end. But not as quickly as Derrida, Habermas, Lyotard, or Rushdie might imagine.

Social scientists on the other hand, especially those brought up on a diet of rational methods and scientific proof, tend not to profess any religious conviction. Unless chained to a cross, they are unlikely to confess to anything. The *Enlightenment* theorists known as John Locke, George Berkeley and David Hume—almost a kind of essentialist joke about an Irishman, an Englishman and a Scotsman—were quick to disengage the value of such a Christian god who was of no real use to his followers it appears except to cause trouble. This was because the god of the Old Testament was the God of fire and brimstone, as well as plagues of locusts and frogs and snakes. By the time the New Testament God appeared, the authoritarianism inflicted on the world had increased as significantly as *His* power had waned.

But these holy books also never said anything about the dinosaurs and I could never explain to any of my students why. Religion and religious commodification continue to provide the kind of spiritual food for many who are depressed and in need of more than material wealth. Or in the place of material wealth. Sometimes, people justify their impoverished positions by condemning the rich and saying that they (the poor) could easily have had all that but chose not to because of some ethical consideration or because of another moral obligation or because of a lack of good fortune. Nevertheless, and, despite the presence of amoral, non-religious rationalistic social scientists, despite the absence of evidence of god, and despite the infinite number of academic articles and books published since the Enlightenment, *people still derive some strange spiritual sustenance from religion*. Marx was right about one thing at least. Religion is the opiate of the masses, a hallucinatory drug to elude a modern kind of Manichean skullduggery and drudgery of life in late modernity. What we need to know at this point is that while religion has its spiritual dimension, it is very much a big business that needs to consider the bottom line to survive. When there is something less than spiritual that is being fought over religion, such as revenge killings and the distant fight for constant oil supplies, than religion wears its evil face of pessimism. But at the point of death, when a Hamas fighter or Israeli trooper is at the point of dying, perhaps, religion does give some ultimate source of comfort. Who is to say who is more evil? Can even god solve the Palestinian and Jewish problem? Perhaps it is better if we don't ask. Religion in globalization provides a kind of eternal hope that Nintendo, X-box, or your new *Infiniti* or *Accura* can only hope to achieve in a materialistic kind of way and over a much shorter span of time. And at a much higher cost. So religion is a global good available locally for a moderate price of attendance. Free food and drinks are common at religious assemblies.

ABOUT THE GLOBE

When we think about the globe today, we realize that it is totally different from the globe at any other point in geological time. The globe of the gods has always been different from the globes possessed by man and the difference is what man pays in subservience and servitude. As that great self-taught Polish immigrant to England Joseph Conrad once said in *Blackwoods* (a 19th century English publication of some distinction) that remains a popular quote for many scholars elsewhere, "man creates gods in order to bow down and offer sacrifice to." There is a compelling disbelief in human (in)ability. And the one great disbelief that man, perhaps not all, but certainly many men have is that we could not possibly have created ourselves. It has to have been some other entity, some creature, some organism or some god.

Any activity that human beings have carried out over the past 85,000 years of their evolution would come to naught if the same cosmological instances that destroyed plant and animal life in the Pleistocene Age were to occur as it did sporadically (rather than in one big rush) between 1.8 million to 11,000 years ago. Yet there seems to be so much activity that is going round today that is seemingly ignorant of the fact that the universe is expanding at an expanding rate and that some stars within our own galaxy are traveling at over 300 km/h through space. There are always reasons for human ignorance.

Epistemologically, it is simply too difficult to ponder our entire ontological presence in our daily lives. We can't all be philosophers. Neither can we all be trench diggers or exotic dancers. But who is to say that any job is superior to another except for the presence of those things called responsibility and power? We study globalization today because of that thing called power. We have to ignore the fact that we are all probably hurtling through space to a point, say some three million light years away, where we will all crash and burn and there will be no semblance of our civilization for posterity. We focus on *globalization because it is a series of processes* that have come together, not always coherently, and not always completely rationally, to make our world today separate and distinct from any previous worlds or civilizations. Like what appears to be the scientific hypothesis about the ultimate end of our globe as we know it.

There is a politics of globalization because of the nature of man. It is in the nature of man to be curious, selfish and dissatisfied. It is more than mere Keynesian or Popperian views on life. It is more than the politics of blame on the histories of Masculine Western societies and the Feminized Eastern ones. We are not purely a cultural product of the things that were done in the past. Globalization is about the nature of man who loves to invent. We are alive in a world that has had a distinguishing characteristic beyond any other living species. It has promoted our dominance of the environment almost exclusively for over 2,500 years in the Western tradition, and even longer if we hark back to the Indian and Chinese versions of the story of our natural inclination to invent. We have more than merely invented images that represent our hopes and desires. If architecture is the celebration of physical and aesthetic values of successive and not successful periods of civilization, then it is also an invention. Man's ability to invent new things catalyzed the information and communications revolutions in the late 1980s and early 1990s. Anything that is invented today is now very quickly transmitted across the globe. Transportation costs are vastly different from the time of the fabled and romanticized journeys of Marco Polo or the classical inventory of Homer's Odyseus in *The Iliad and the Odyssey*. While invention is a keen factor in our nature, it seems reasonable, perhaps even logical, to assume that our inventions ought to lead us to things that serve us well, things that have function and purpose. Not quite. If we look at the economically most impoverished countries, we will discover that they seem to have the most fabulous aesthetic structures next to the slums that have housed their urban populations for decades since decolonization and national independence. It appears to be true that there is an inverse relationship between economic wealth and aesthetic structures in these countries. The relatively richer countries of the so-called Third World (a most unfortunate name that even the Communists rejected it) are cautious about constructing massively expensive buildings. However, their materially poorer cousins have such fantastic structures as to make the eye wonder where all the money came from.

This inverse relationship is a deliberate attempt to uplift the human spirit. It appears that man's creations are capable of uplifting the human spirit in ways that constant injections of food and medicines are unable to achieve. This is another invention of man. What relevance then do these structures have in relation to globalization? These uplifting structures—whether they are office blocks, government buildings, or functionless phallocentric structures representing national myths and legends—are important because they represent hope, progress, and optimism. These are the three buzzwords that keep man alive and motivated. Hope is needed whenever one feels dejected, and progress is the sounding board for moving on in life, while optimism allows us to understand why we are going where we appear to be going in the first place. The globalized world allows many more people to achieve in realistic terms what constitutes their versions of hope, progress and optimism. Perhaps it could be that we have never been able to live on bread alone.

When we began this chapter we started with the notion of how human beings and human civilizations have desired to extend life. This is not a defining characteristic of globalization. But what makes human life particularly different in a globalized world is that we now have advanced and complex technologies that are designed not only to extend life. We also use technology to extend the quality of life, improving the ways in which we live life through nutrition, healthcare, physical exercise, and lifestyle choices. The defining features of globalization as we know it today is about sustaining higher levels of quality of life, increasing our hope for a better future through optimism and progress. And human beings achieve this in three main ways: measurement, quantification, and creativity. Because we now have more accurate means of measuring our body of knowledge, we tend to resort to very precise mathematical measurements of our world with the hope that such precision builds on what we already know about ourselves and our environment.

There is a great desire among many social scientists to quantify and measure social changes in the same way that natural scientists endeavor to measure, quantify, and manufacture chemicals in laboratories. Yet once in a while there appears to be a breakthrough—using the scientific method—in paradigms that sustain our epistemological valuation of the world. Breakthroughs are often called thinking "outside-the-box." The scientific method and the methods used in the social sciences do not really allow for thinking creatively because there is a set of assumptions that have to be made before scientific inquiry can proceed. However, we do know that creative genius flows from challenging these assumptions and what has been taken for granted, despite how well that "good" may function and in spite of its use or value in society. So while there has not really been any significant or revolutionary change to the physics of the internal combustion engine, people continue to try to improve and modify it based on prevailing assumptions. This is why the shape and performance of automobiles are restricted and limited (with some exceptions, such as at *NASCAR*, *Daytona*, the international *F-1* [Formula One]) racing circuits. A creative genius will not be held back by the need, for example, to use fossil fuels to power the engine. Or even by having to use the old four/two-stroke engine as the power platform. Globalization helps in the sharing of technological knowledge about different ways of approaching problems.

Globalization is about speeding up the process of sharing knowledge and ironically, sometimes events such as the release of classified Cold War secrets often lead to new discoveries and new breakthroughs, such as the Internet. But the measurement, quantification, and creativity in globalization today is only a small aspect of what we are trying to control. Contrary to Heidegger's belief, technology is not only about the human ability to control the world and the immediate environment. So while the era of globalization may not last as long as the Pleistocene Age, human beings might still be in a position to intensify the value and meaning of life within a brief time span. Perhaps the answer is not to live any longer than we need to; or alternatively, live much longer than we possibly can, so that we have more time to figure things out.

Perhaps the answer is in limiting the amount of time that we devote to figuring things out, restricting the amount of time that we have devoted to measurement, quantification, and creative thinking. Katzenstein's criticism about the irreversibility of globalization is more profound than it appears. This is because the way forward or the way back may not necessarily constitute the optimal mode of achieving what we want in life. Globalization is indeed a mixed bag of competition and cooperation between individuals, communities, regions, states, NGOs, histories of difference, and languages of technology.

GLOBALIZATION AND AMERICANIZATION

Globalization is not Americanization but many people outside America and inside its walls often mistake the one for the other and not surprisingly. The reason for this is simple. American media networks. These networks not only provide all forms of entertainment but also reality TV, sports, prayer, religion, news, economic predictions, government positions, private sector analyses, and interactive "don't leave your couch" modes of home purchase through late night "infomercials." The secret is to broadcast everything and anything over a 24/7, 365-days-a-year period: it will certainly catch someone's interest.

As on *The Ship of Fools* we all seem to sail deep into the clutches of modernity while remaining blind to the other sailors and stewards. The central paradox of human beings is, as I have mentioned elsewhere in some obscure publication, no less, that we do not choose to be born and then have no choice about death. It seems that we are marked with the numbers *666* from the very start. This reminds me of what Henry S. Kariel used to say in a pleasant yet controlled voice, "This way to the gas chambers, ladies and gentlemen."

The American media is also marked by a homologous identity of dispersion and multiculturalism. By this I mean that there are so many different things, so many talking heads and so much information to simplify and convey that after awhile the news becomes real. The autonomy speaks for itself. The major networks are themselves models for foreign news networks who plug into its models of conveyance. This ensures that even old style films and outdated messages get re-spun for sale overseas. American media networks offer a plethora of American goods and services that are constantly being targeted at millions of Americans through syndication and copyrights. Their messages are often ones that encompass the American Dream of "hope," "progress," and "optimism."

The American media, in its attempt to remain objective and balanced and fair in its coverage (and search for profits), often includes and incorporates critiques of its own products and services. Many people continue to think that globalization is Americanization because of the colossal network interface that American media provides for the rest of the world. Otherwise most people who plug into the Internet and to sports and entertainment, efficiently translated into local and native languages of choice, would be unable to associate the kinds of values, mannerisms and norms that are depicted in American soap operas, in Hollywood movies, and serials that are made for cable television such as the *Band of Brothers*. And the most popular television programs called *Baywatch*, *Baywatch Hawaii*, and *Baywatch Nights* filmed "entirely" in Santa Monica, and exclusively on location in Hawaii, and Universal Studios in

Florida. America also has this idea that the world revolves around it. Many Americans for example know less about the world than the world knows about America. But chances are, you knew that already.

Not only are American audiences captivated and mimicking the characters in these programs, they also follow the spin-offs made available through magazines, tabloids, and souvenir items, while some even go to the extent of going to the ground armed with a hope of becoming an "extra" on these programs and movies themselves. The entire politics involves and revolves round cults of personality, media hype, individuated demagoguery, and the celebration of gods and stars who can not only be heard but can also be seen to have very specific human qualities. This rash of popular culture motivated by a sense of achievement and a search for status is part of the American Dream, and part of what has become the dream of many non-Americans who themselves desire to be part of that dream within their own linguistic idioms. The worldwide reach of Americanization as a product of spectacular production and instantaneous gratification creates a herd-like mentality among its clientele who themselves, once hooked on the experience of the kinds of stories that are told, cannot easily leave or completely disengage. And they have stories for everyone and for every occasion. The reasons then for mistaking American trees for the world's forests are because the audience often has no choice but to make comparisons. And when they see similarities being produced with a magical larger-than-life quality, it is in human nature to imitate. Imitation, the great philosopher said, is the highest form of flattery. But not all flattery stems from a desire to mimic the "original." Take the case of terrorism.

For many decades, "American" values were being promoted over American media and through its networks in the search for ideological dominance over the Soviet Union. With the increasing power of the English language as the lingua franca of science, technology and now the Internet, we can only guess why this did not happen earlier. In other words, while American television and radio were committed to their often patriotic messages during the Cold War (1955–1989), there were other people who were listening. And not all these people were in favor of the Americans. For many years, the guardians of the official French language, for example, have been combating the adoption of American English which to them must sound more hurtful than British English, which does not seem like the hegemonic threat that it was in the 18th and 19th centuries. However, the French resistance in this case with a small "r" did not result in violence and destruction. Rather, the mullahs and other Islamic religious leaders in many non-western countries were also listening and they were becoming increasingly perplexed as to the imitative behavior of their own followers. Somehow American popular culture appeared to be more interesting than deadweight repetitions of Holy Quranic verses. Suddenly, many of their followers seemed less interested in the pontifications in the mosques and more interested in the latest fashion statements and libertarian values that not only men but especially women could embrace and display. The turning points of course, and as we are aware, were the fall of the Shah of Iran and the ensuing Iran-Iraq war. While it ought to be said that most were probably less interested in the American entertainment scene, than they were probably unhappy with the way in which non-Islamic "values" were being "transmitted" across the world. The greater the energy used by these religious leaders to suppress information and entertainment from America, the worse the situation.

Then there is the duplicitous side of the American political economy. We can only truly appreciate this fact in hindsight because if someone told you that Saddam Hussein was America's number one enemy in 1977 you'd think that person was mad. Because he wasn't, he was working for America. If someone said that Osama bin Laden was working on our side in Afghanistan in the 1970s, you'd probably invite him into your own home to share a meal. And why not? He was on our side. The political economy of duplicity saw evidence of direct American involvement in the Iran-Iraq war in the "desert" diplomacy of former Secretary of State George Schultz:

> It was 20 years ago when Shultz dropped in on a State Department meeting between his top aide and a high-ranking Hussein emissary. Back then the Iraqis, who were fighting a war with Iran, were our new best friends in the Mid-East. Shultz wanted to make it crystal clear that U.S. criticism of the use of chemical weapons was just pabulum for public consumption, meant as a restatement of a "long-standing policy, and not as a pro-Iranian/anti-Iraqi gesture," as Lawrence S. Eagleburger told Hussein's emissary. "Our desire and our actions to prevent an Iranian victory and to continue the progress of our bilateral relations remain undiminished," Eagleburger continued, according to the then highly classified transcript of the meeting.[15]

32

The politics of American globalization began with an interest in developing its own agenda as a powerful alternative from that of the Soviets. America and its Allies in NATO believed that they had a worthy alternative that ought to be protected and preserved. This ran afoul of those who hated America because of religion, ideology, morals, cultural norms and the behavior of individual Americans overseas. Many Western tourists to Asia and the Middle East including those from America would often make clear their unhappiness with this ritual or with that local activity. But this was bearable. The problem really came from American military activity and malfeasance as seen in Hawai'i, South Korea, Japan, and Iraq. The problem begins with the kinds of military rituals that are steeped in the "traditions" of its military academies where little respect has been shown to women who naively sign up because they are led to believe that they can compete on physically equal terms. The pioneering work of Phyllis Turnbull and Kathy Ferguson on the state of military in Hawaii is only part of a larger politics of domination and abuse as documented in their chapter on "Oh, Say, Can You See?: The Semiotics of the Military in Hawaii" (*Borderlines 10*, University of Minnesota Press, 1998). These scholars predicted the inevitable events in Iraq six years ahead of schedule. Not even the CIA could do that.

The few bad apples in America's professional "band of brothers" have ridden roughshod over the cultural sensitivities of place and time. It was more than American G.I.s who visited local brothels, dance halls and tropical bars where women of easy virtue were to be found in Angeles City in the Philippines when the dictator Ferdinand Marcos was still around and before the big pullout from Subic Naval Base and Clarke Airbase. It was more than a top flight American commanding general making a flippant remark in a politically naïve and politically incorrect manner about a rape case involving an American serviceman and a local girl forced into prostitution on Okinawa. It was more than a few instances of American soldiers raping native women. It was because the entire political process appeared to represent an emasculation of the local male ability to defend what they would consider—after the work of writers like Said, Guha, McClintock, Homi Bhabha, Anne Allyson, and even Elspeth Probyn (to an extent)—their own possessions.

We are the wandering madmen riding the waves of modernity like that *Ship of Fools* that Foucault described so fervently in *Madness and Civilization* (1988: 7–9). Western modernity seems to challenge, question, and interrogate the traditional power bases of mullahs and their followers.

It seems to "distract" "Islamic women" from their "duties" as Muslims and provides (not even in the least sense of any feminist theory) alternative variations of identity; alternative modes of power relations; and different ways to decenter the single-minded authorship of Islamic masculinist control over women, or in the words of Hussaina J. Abdullah and Ibrahim Hamza, "rights independent of male ownership or control."[16] Also consider the position of earlier writers that predated the Iran–Iraq War such as Fernea and Bezirgan whose 1978-edited book begins with a quotation from a woman whom they describe as being a remarkably talented and beautiful poet whose only physical deformity was her up-turned nose but yet who was married three times and outlived all her husbands.

RESISTANCE AND COUNTER-RESISTANCE

Globalization is about opening up spaces that are closed and enclosing spaces that are open. It forces governments to liberalize commercial activities and weakens authoritarian structures of power through the Internet and political rhetoric surrounding international attempts at governance. Globalization is optimism at its best.

Man, as Aristotle believed, is by nature political. And as long as there continues to be an imbalance of power within communities based on tradition, modernization, culture, gender, primordialism, circumstantialism, racism, religion, and wide disparities in socio-economic classes premised on a domestic economy of fossil-fuels, there will be a politics of control, a politics of discord, a politics of resistance, and a politics of subversion that feed into the global reach of American globalization.

Why would any self-respecting, politically astute, religious Islamic leader allow his flock to be captivated by an alternative ideological presence while undermining his own? It was not because some Muslim leaders felt that Western discourse was a continuation of a historically imbalanced war between Muslims and Christians writ large in today's modernity. Rather, it was because the threat from America and things American was very real because it was political. It was political because it was believable and desirable. This is why you will find in any Asian city with a significant Islamic population several detractors from the religion. And these lapsed "followers" will be found doing very un-Islamic things such as indulging in premarital sex, alcohol consumption, being scantily

34

clad, dancing "lewdly" to the beat of loud Western-produced and locally-modified music.[17] These are kinds of things that "normal" American, European, and Asian teenagers and young adults seem to do in many Asian and Western cities all over the world. This is political. The situation confronts those who want to protect their traditional power bases that draw from the conservative control of teenagers and young adults. This is why in Malaysia for example, there are religious police whose job is to prevent these "things" from happening and to keep their flock on the "right" and "moral" track. One 1970s regulation in the Republic of Singapore stated that males with long hair would be served last by public officials. There were signboards everywhere that displayed what a male in long hair would look like. This was because males with long hair were seen to be mimicking the American Counter-Culture of the "hippie-loving," "communal-living," "easy-virtue," "drug-abusing" lifestyle of some members of its youth. What is often forgotten is that most Americans were not living on communes or consuming mind-altering hallucinogenic drugs. Many were indeed dying in the paddy fields of Vietnam. Yet America continues to stand out in the international news media because it has a very large image and its military has enforced that image consistently and with much brutality and terror.

The real images of American soldiers being brutally dragged through the streets of Mogadishu, Somalia after the killing of 18 American soldiers resulted in a total US pullout from that war-torn city. What on earth were Americans doing there? There isn't any oil or natural resources that could be conveniently tapped and plugged into the global economic network of trade. What was the DOD and the State Department thinking when they sunk innocent American lives in a place no ordinary American citizen would want to call home? Why plunge your fingers into a fire that is being constantly fed by a complex discourse of ethnic hatred, religious-motivated revenge killings, assassinations and gross xenophobia in the multiple proxy wars that are scourging central Africa as has been the case for centuries even before first contact with White colonialists (who no doubt gave them even more reason to settle their differences through public and personal political violence)? Africa is like a violent blood-spitting contest among innocent people who don't even know what they are fighting about any longer. Much like the Palestinian case in the Middle East. But at least interested parties in Washington, DC are willing to keep hope alive because of the strategic implications for the globalized economies of America and its Allies.

Somalia was a clear warning shot across the bow of the USS America. The caution was also seen in the kinds of responses that were reflected in the fortress architecture of US embassies overseas from Lebanon and Kuwait, to Singapore and the Philippines. While Americans thought they were sufficiently safe, there was at least from the end of the war in Afghanistan, a growing and widespread hatred of all things American. And the moderate Muslim leaders who must have known about the grumblings and rumblings and growing disaffection from among their flock must have turned a blind eye. They must have also turned a blind eye when the hat was being passed around for money and contributions towards "Islamic" causes. Whether or not these contributors knew how these funds were being funneled towards the planning, training, and execution for 9/11, Bali and Madrid is indeed a moot point. But to what extent is a Christian who donates to a cause an accomplice to violent IRA activity?

However, it does seem very clear that it is easier for the Islamic conservatives to collapse globalization into Americanization and vice-versa because it makes sense for them to blame the West for erosion of their traditional values. If America had not illegally and almost unilaterally invaded Iraq a second time to displace the brutality of Saddam Hussein (which was something they ought to have done in the first Gulf War but did not because American politicians never tell the *whole* truth) and his authoritarian empire, there would have been more terrorist activities. Many countries with large Muslim populations today are willing to (at least on the surface of ostentation) help the US in terms of intelligence gathering or arresting "the usual suspects" because they fear that they will become the next Iraq. The illegal US invasion created a moral dilemma for Republican Bush. He did not have the support of his usual foreign allies. He had to punish someone for 9/11. He needed to create a believable (and incredible rather than a credible) enemy. He must have thought that the American public needed another president with a strong Hawkish foreign policy. His dilemma was because if he did not strike, he feared a greater attack on the US. This was a president whose own legitimacy was questioned by the Democratic presidential nominee. Bush might not have made to the Oval Office if the final vote count had been marginally different. But the Americans and Bush's own enemies within the US are not satisfied with his foreign intervention in Iraq which itself is beginning to show promises of Vietnam *redux*. Condoleezza Rice herself was interrogated by a Congressional committee on the cautionary note and top secret messages that were part of the president's daily brief. Her performance was not stellar and the commissioners did not seem completely convinced by what she said. Arianna Huffington was right. Americans have been demoted from citizens to consumers, and had their Bill of Rights replaced with a Bill for Goods. After the Iraqi prisoners fiasco blew up, US Secretary of State Colin Powell expressed regret, US Secretary of Defense Rumsfeld was privately chided by Bush. Both apologized publicly on May 7, 2004. The same Republicans who supported Bush on the campaign trail; Democratic campaigners who can now be counted as political losers in the New Hampshire primaries; all patriotic Americans in the US and overseas; and those who planned and destroyed the World Trade Center on September 11, 2001 are all watching Bush on television as he undergoes the due process of the American political system. It is therefore the openness of the political system in all its liberal glory that has inefficiently and naively invited the terrorists into the US. And now the world is being gradually punished for their sins, not in the least, American citizens themselves. The reason why many people used to mistake globalization for Americanization has now been subsumed under the politics of xenophobia, ethnicity, racism, sexism, and ideology. There is no hope to recover these differences so it is better for us to understand that there will always be people who will think like this because it makes them feel righteous and morally upright like "so many signs that the expulsion of madmen had become one of number of ritual exiles" (Foucault [1965] 1988: 10).

Therefore it seems natural that human beings can only realize their full potential as political beings. As long as there continues to be large and wavering differentials in power across communities and within the globe based on ridiculous predispositions of wealth, poverty, tradition, modernization, culture, gender, primordialism, circumstantialism, racism, religion, fossil fuels, and socio-economic class— there will be a politics of control, a politics of discord, a politics of resistance, and a politics of subversion that feed into the global reach of American globalization.

If, as we saw at the beginning of this chapter, globalization is indeed not as irreversible as the economistic pundits would proffer, than we can rest assured even for a little while that there are significant and different kinds of global processes that are concurrent as they are reversible. Katzenstein was right in the sense that having more regional cooperation et cetera would lead to better outcomes, a kind of proto principle in the political science and international relations theory literature. But we must also look further. Hence we also examined the philosophical side of globalization, one that offer criticisms as well as promises of "hope," "progress," and "optimism." We have seen in this introduction that ancient religions cannot go untouched by the tremendous forces of globalization, but this does not mean that there will be no resistance. When resistance occurs, politics reaps the potential for democracy; but where resistance is absent, politics turns to autocracy.

This introduction covered a wide area of work that constitutes the meaning of globalization and the meaning of America's posture towards globalization. For many scholars globalization represents a compendium in modernity of different voices, different activities and different speeds that impact across neoliberal capitalist states and non-capitalist ones. Globalization is the vehicle on which modernity seeks out new sites to develop, change, alter and modify. Globalization is the new catchword for modernization into the 21st century. But unlike modernization which was concerned with the patterns of movement to and from and in between traditional societies and modern ones, globalization tends to unite diverse social, cultural, economic and political dimensions. While modernization was about exploiting local resources, globalization is about deepening the level of exploitation in global terms and across political boundaries. Under globalization, nothing is sacred, and nothing cannot be commodified or commoditized. Every thing created by man can be turned into a good or a service to be sold for profit.

THE CRISIS OF MODERNITY

The extent and depth of globalization's processes are mediated by two main components as we shall see in the subsequent chapters. The two main mediating conditions are speed and time. Globalization is about speeding up human activities at a pace that has never been previously thought possible. This is part of the reason why globalization is worth studying in all its different varieties. The neoliberal capitalist world order is likened to a Ship of Fools floating on a sea that is depthless and unexplored. Neoliberal capitalism flows across political and cultural boundaries with urgency and purpose. This is why there are different schools of thought when it comes to the meaning of globalization. It defies definition. Edward Said's view of the globe was articulated by the discursive pronouncements of Orientalists keen to make their mark on the exotic East. Said believed that there were pockets of known resistance all across the Orientalized world that sought to challenge modernity's tempo, demands and pressures that multiplied and conveyed through globalization of goods and services that are designed for the masses and the elites. More so, these products are designed for the masses to feel like elites and for the elites to feel that they are part of the masses. International terrorism and piracy are mere setbacks to the power of globalization. 9/11 has heightened the level of conservatism and the conservation of private values in public spaces. Terrorism will abate and modernity's military machines will seek out these pockets of disgruntled and disenfranchised terrorists with glee and zealousness. Is there a crisis of modernity embedded in the vehicle of globalization? Certainly, but the crisis is neither economic as Wallestein and Jameson believe, nor civilizational as Huntington has proclaimed. The crisis of modernity is no longer likely to emerge within Marxist class contradictions. Neither is this crisis looming for international trade unionism which no longer exists as a worldwide fellowship. The crisis of modernity will not come from religion or politicized society but rather from the loss of nerve among men. The crisis of modernity will come in the form of gender trouble. However, this is not the place for articulating this view. The crisis of modernity is worthy of a book-length argument but for now it seems that as long as the patriarchal neoliberal capitalist world system continues to function, this crisis will be averted to a point when the profit motif has exhausted itself. The speed and timing of the goods of globalization will force a greater disparity between the richest rich and the poorest poor. The middle classes will resolve along the lines of self-perception and continue to view themselves according to the upper or lower classes that they feel a part of. Lefebvre's view of globalization is contained in the physical architectural forms, between modernity and postmodernity, between function and form, substance and style. This kind of globalization will cure the tendency for middle class fractionalism. In other words, the sweet sauces of global goods will distract the largest working classes from fulfilling their Marxian heritage. And this might not necessarily be a bad thing.

The subsequent chapters identify and illustrate the themes and paradoxes in the politics of American globalization. But more importantly, globalization is not a phenomenon restricted to American politics, culture, and economics Globalization is a world phenomenon. Human beings experience globalization's processes through different rates of torque, dissimilar push and pull factors. The processes of globalization's many faces is an intractable mixture of ethnic and religious communities, political institutions, state actors, NGOs, politicians, journalists, financial analysts, economists, peasants, CEOs, consumers and producers, capitalists and socialists within the neoliberal world order of modernity. Globalization is unevenly mediated by technocrats, innovators, and IT specialists. Americans are a significant part of the processes, no less "prisoner[s] of the passage" (Foucault [1965] 1988:11) on the global *Ship of Fools*.

ENDNOTES

1   James S. Romm, *Herodotus* (New Haven, CT: Yale University Press, 1998).

2   J. Peter Euben, *The Tragedy of Political Theory: The Road Not Taken*, (Princeton, NJ: Princeton University Press, 1990).

3   Note the US Supreme Court case *Burroughs v. U.S.*, 290 U.S. No. 534, at 545. (1934). See also, *Anderson v. Celebrezze*, 460 U.S. 780, at 794–795 (1983).

4   Peter J. Katzenstein, "Regionalism in Comparative Perspective," *Arena Working Papers*, 96/1 (1996).

5   Guillermo A. Calvo, and Enrique G. Mendoza, "Capital-Markets Crises and Economic Collapse in Emerging Markets: An Informational-Frictions Approach," *American Economic Review* 90, no. 2 (2000): 59. See also D. Gale Johnson, "Population, Food, and Knowledge," *American Economic Review* 90, no. 1 (2000): 1–14; and Philippe Jorion, and William N. Goetzmann, "Global Stock Markets in the Twentieth Century," *Journal of Finance* 54, no. 3 (1999): 953–80.

6   See Anne Y. Ilinitch, Richard A. D'Aveni, and Arie Y. Lewin, "New Organizational Forms and Strategies for Managing in Hypercompetitive Environments," *Organization Science* 7, no. 3 (1996): 211–20; and Susan E. Clarke, and Gary L. Gaile, "Local Politics in a Global Era: Thinking Locally, Acting Globally," *Annals of the American Academy of Political and Social Science* 551, (1997): 28–43.

7   This is illustrated, for example, by Oded Stark, "Altruism and the Quality of Life," *American Economic Review* 79, no. 2 (1989): 86–90. See also, with an eye for comparison, N. F. R. Crafts, "Some Dimensions of the 'Quality of Life' during the British Industrial Revolution," *Economic History Review* 50, no. 4(1997): 617–39. There are alternative notions of the meaning of the "quality of life" social science and clinical surveys. However, most of the academic work revolves round the assumption that quality of life estimates usually make the assumption that the people involved are "normal" and not physically, emotionally or otherwise challenged. See for example, Sarah Rosenfield, "Factors Contributing to the Subjective Quality of Life of the Chronic Mentally Ill," *Journal of Health and Social Behavior* 33, no. 4 (1992): 299–315. This article raises further questions such as whether indeed such notions as "normal" and "quality" can ever be anything

but subjective and hence reconcilable within the idioms that are provided by the processes of globalization.

8   John Earman, "Causation: A Matter of Life and Death," *Journal of Philosophy* 73, no. 1 (1976): 5–25; Darwin O. Sawyer, "Public Attitudes Toward Life and Death," *Public Opinion Quarterly* 46, no. 4 (1982): 521–33; and, Cornel West, "A Matter of Life and Death," *October* 61, (1992): 20–3.

9   Bernard S. Jackson, "The Prophet and the Law in Early Judaism and the New Testament," *Cardozo Studies in Law and Literature* 4, no. 2 (1992): 123–66; Charles Liebman, and Bernard Susser, "Judaism and Jewishness in the Jewish State," *Annals of the American Academy of Political and Social Science* 555, (1998): 15–25; Gidon Levy, and Udi Adiv, The Jew The State Thinks is an Arab," *Journal of Palestine Studies* 13, no. 2 (1984): 176–78; Bernard Harrison, "Judaism," *Annals of the American Academy of Political and Social Science* 256, (1948): 25–35; Louis Bolce, and Gerald de Maio, "The Anti-Christian Fundamentalist Factor in Contemporary Politics," *Public Opinion Quarterly* 63, no. 4 (1999): 508–42; Mark Juergensmeyer, "Christian Violence in America," *Annals of the American Academy of Political and Social Science* 558, (1998): 88–100; J. M. Spieser, "The Representation of Christ in the Apses of Early Christian Churches," *Gesta* 37, no. 1 (1998): 63–73; Richard Werbner, "The Suffering Body: Passion and Ritual Allegory in Christian Encounters," *Journal of Southern African Studies* 23, no. 2 (1997): 311–24; Matthew C. Moen, "The Evolving Politics of the Christian Right," *PS: Political Science and Politics* 29, no. 3 (1996): 461–64; Mary-Jane Deeb, "Militant Islam and the Politics of Redemption," *Annals of the American Academy of Political and Social Science* 524, (1992): 52–65; Anita M. Weiss, "Women's Position in Pakistan: Socio-cultural Effects of Islamization," *Asian Survey* 25, no. 8 (1985): 863–80; or a less than complex and rather simple summation by Bernard Lewis, "Islam and Liberal Democracy: A Historical Overview," *Journal of Democracy* 7, (1996).

10   Unlike a Muslim state, an Islamic state is conceptually distinct and pragmatically difficult to implement in modernity. Indonesia is considered by political scientists as a Muslim-dominant country.

11   Salman Rushdie asserted something a little more intensely political, although only in literary terms, and was rewarded by a *Jihad* in his name, resulting in his retreat into the underground safety of the UK. See *The Moor's Last Sigh* (Vintage, 1997) or the one that got him in trouble, *The Satanic Verses* (Viking, 1989).

12   Robert W. Witkin, "Constructing a Sociology for an Icon of Aesthetic Modernity: Olympia Revisited," *Sociological Theory* 15, no. 2 (1997): 101–25; Paola Bacchetta, "When the (Hindu) Nation Exiles Its Queers," *Social Text* 61, (1999): 141–66; Jenny Franchot, "Unseemly Commemoration: Religion, Fragments, and the Icon," *American Literary History* 9, no. 3 (1997): 502–21; David B. Miller, "Legends of the Icon of Our Lady of Vladimir: A Study of the Development of Muscovite National Consciousness," *Speculum* 43, no. 4 (1968): 657–70; Marge E. Landsberg, "The Icon in Semiotic Theory," *Current Anthropology* 21, no. 1 (1980): 93–5; Paul Axelrod, and Michelle A. Fuerch, "Flight of the Deities: Hindu Resistance in Portuguese Goa," *Modern Asian Studies* 30, no. 2 (1996):

387–421; Patrick Maynard, "The Secular Icon: Photography and the Functions of Images," *Journal of Aesthetics and Art Criticism* 42, no. 2 (1983): 155–69; Arthur W. Burks, "Icon, Index, and Symbol," *Philosophy and Phenomenological Research* 9, no. 4 (1949): 673–89.

13   Brian May, "Memorials to Modernity: Postcolonialism and Pilgrimage in Naipaul and Rushdie," *ELH* 68, no. 1 (2001): 241–65; Parama Roy, "Oriental Exhibits: Englishmen and Natives in Burton's Personal Narrative of a Pilgrimage to Al Madinah & Meccah," *Boundary 2* 22, no. 1 (1995): 185–210; Indira V. Peterson, "Singing of a Place: Pilgrimage as Metaphor and Motif in the Tevaram Songs of the Tamil Saivite Saints," *Journal of the American Oriental Society* 102, no. 1 (1982): 69–90; and William LaFleur, "Points of Departure: Comments on Religious Pilgrimage in Sri Lanka and Japan," *Journal of Asian Studies* 38, no. 2 (1979): 271–81.

14   "A bill to criminalize women who hold group prayer sessions at the wall— also known as the Wailing Wall—which was passed in a preliminary reading on Wednesday, has horrified the Jewish majority, which is not Orthodox, not least because it seeks to circumvent a supreme court ruling 10 days ago to modernize the rules of worship at the shrine: 'If a man beats me up at the wall, he goes to prison for a year. If he rapes me at the wall, he gets three years. If I put on a prayer shawl, I go to prison for seven years. It's insane,' said a Jerusalem city councilor, Anat Hoffman." See Suzanne Goldenberg, "Women Face Jail for Wailing Wall Prayers," *Guardian*, June 2, 2000; see also, "Orthodox Prayer Bill Targets Women," *BBC Online*, June 1, 2000; and "Women at Jerusalem's Western Wall Meet Resistance to Equal Prayer Rights Won in Court," *CNN.com*, June 5, 2000.

15   Robert Scheer, "The U.S. Winked at Hussein's Evil," *Los Angeles Times*, December 30, 2003.

16   Hussaina J. Abdullah, and Ibrahim Hamza, "Women Need Independent Ownership Rights," paper presented at an international workshop on *Women and Land In Africa*, Emory University Law School, Atlanta, Georgia in collaboration with Associates for Change, Kampala, Uganda at the Entebbe Beach Hotel, April 24–25, 1998. See also, Elizabeth Warnock Fernea, and Basima Qattan Bezirgan, eds., *Middle Eastern Muslim Women Speak* (Austin, TX: University of Texas Press, 1978).

17   Such as the youthful, modern Indonesian dancer, Inul Daratista, whose current sexy forms of the "local" Dangdut dance from 2002–04 have antagonized Muslim (male) clerics who see her as a dancing she-devil.

CHAPTER 2

Fascinating America

The Business of Contradiction and Complementarity in the Political Economy

America is the modern face of Western Europe. American globalization is about surviving for the present and future benefit of its American stakeholders. In the 18th and 19th centuries, while the European colonial masters were entangled in different traditional diplomatic, cultural and religious differences, America was quietly expanding its power in terms of its physical geography. No one could possibly have forecasted the kind of future impact that the simple purchases modeled on the Louisiana Purchase from the French would have had in the 20th-century global economy. Consequently, the European product and manufacturing bases were too embroiled in nationalist tensions over a wide range of European made products that came under such powerful arrangements as the *European Coal and Steel Community*. European business concerns were continually torn by local demands for protection with overarching needs for creating an economic and political entity that would benefit all of Europe and not some parts of its developed Western states. The end of the World War II saw a torn and divided Europe with devastated cultural egos and emaciated economic structures. American military technology and economic power helped rebuild war-torn Europe and this process continued deep into the late 1950s as the world divided ideologically between the US and the USSR.

While Western Europe during the Cold War days was very much dependent on American military technology as R. D. Norton notes in his paper on "Industrial Policy and American Renewal"[1] and combat troop deployment in the face of the Soviet bear,[2] the European manufacturers and MNCs still had access to an entire continent of resources from the Low Countries, the Benelux economic confederation, the Seine, the Rhine, the Danube, and the Mediterranean coastal areas. However, Western Europe during the Cold War was neither a single nor a united entity, and it was militarily dependent on the North Atlantic Treaty

Organization (NATO). The US on the other hand, in pursuing its strategic defense policies abroad in Europe, the Mediterranean, Africa, the Middle East, and the Asia-Pacific, also had access to an entire continent of resources that belonged to a single political entity, i.e., the United States of America. Since 1945, America has increasingly established itself as the principle architect of neoliberal capitalism. This was in spite of the propagandistic politics of the Soviet regime, as illustrated by Vojtech Mastny's award-winning book, *The Cold War and Soviet Insecurity* (1998) and Martin Sicker's *The Bear and the Lion: Soviet Imperialism and Iran* (Praeger, 1988). Meanwhile, America helped rebuild Japanese and South Korean cities from their war-torn gloom until they ironically began competing with American consumer goods and services in less than 40 years' time as Hugh Patrick's influential work, *The Financial Development of Japan, Korea, and Taiwan Growth, Repression, and Liberalization* (Oxford, 1994) illustrates. This is similar to the mobilization of the military and civilian forces by Minos in *Thucydides' History of the Peloponnesian War* who built a great navy to master the Grecian Sea and to command Cyclades and enslave the Carians in the old customary ways of the Locraines and Acarnanians and the greatest parts of the Peloponnesus (Hobbes, 1959, "The First Book," sect 4-13, 3–9).

By the late 20th century, when the Cold War came to an end, American capitalist experiments overseas in Europe and the Far East culminated into a powerful US-centric nexus of advanced economic production. The American product manufacturing base that was highly advanced during the munitions factory era of the 1940s would serve it well in the post-War reconstruction era. The Americans made the shift from Fordist to post-Fordist and Just-in-Time production at an incredible rate. The range of American made goods and services ranged from experimental research to manufacturing and financial services, advertising, media services, and telecommunications infrastructure. America led the world in terms of its ownership of the World Wide Web, that 20th century invention by American scientists headquartered at RAND, Santa Monica, California, that was initially designed for American military communications during the Cold War. Despite these fantastic achievements, American capital brings with its process of neoliberalism some contradictory patterns.

America is the richest country in the world with some of the poorest people. America is one of the most peaceful countries on earth but with a modern history of sustained and bloody violence on American soil and overseas. The lighter side of American democracy appears to have an ugly side that is so much less appealing. The modern political history of American politics runs a parallel with a "sterile field of cares and ignorance, among the mirages of knowledge, amid the unreason of the world" (Foucault [1965] 1988: 12). Think about the fact that almost 35 million Americans live under the poverty line. Eight years after World War II ended, two in 10 Americans were living below the poverty line. When the Cold War began ostensibly in 1955, the poverty rate began declining as more Americans found jobs in the military-industrial complex and the politics of McCarthyism instilled fear and anxiety among bomb shelter-building Americans across the contiguous United States.

The level of manufacturing rose dramatically by the end of the 1960s in the face of Vietnam and as a groundswell against a backdrop of Free Love, Communal Living, Drugs, and Flower Power. Pro-socialist academics came under interrogation by FBI agents while those academics with socialist leanings continued to challenge America's hawkish moves in Southeast Asia, ostensibly to prevent the Domino Theory from being realized. The American war effort catalyzed the sluggish American economy by the early 1970s as the poverty rate was reduced to about one in 10 Americans. However, this did not take into account the population increases since 1958. By the time of the OPEC-induced oil crisis, about 23 million Americans were considered poor. What did the social sciences do with regard to the problem of poor Americans? It was only when Lyndon B. Johnson's administration raised the problem of poverty as part of its domestic presidential campaign did American social scientists in their behavioralist garb begin paying attention. Several pioneering institutes were established around poverty, such as the Institute for Research on Poverty in 1966 at the University of Wisconsin-Madison. Social science research helped document and analyze the problem of poverty and linked it with the larger problem of scarcity and unequal economic distribution within the United States. By the end of the 1970s and the beginning of the 1980s, more Americans went under the poverty line. Was there a link between American moves to globalize their domestic economy, with poverty malfeasance, homeless persons and mental illness? The rumor about increasing numbers of mentally-ill persons being left on the streets to fend for themselves was more likely attributable to the anti-American Soviet propaganda of the day rather than cuts in welfare.

The reality might have been that the over-burdened welfare state system was developing into an unmanageable Behemoth. Not surprisingly, a recent national survey by a conference of mayors indicated the following:

> Overall, requests for emergency food assistance jumped by 17 per cent this year and requests for shelter increased by 13 per cent, according to the 25-city survey by the US Conference of Mayors. On average, 14 per cent of requests for food aid and 30 per cent of requests for shelter went unmet. The annual survey pointed to unemployment and lack of affordable housing as the leading causes of hunger and homelessness. "The survey underscores the impact the economy has had on everyday Americans," said conference president, Mayor James A. Garner of Hempstead, N.Y.[3]

This means that while the American economy appears to be making an upward beat, the number of problems surrounding the concept of poverty and unemployment continue to dominate discussions within what can be called a welfare state mentality. The more handouts that are given, the more hands that will be reaching out to ask for more. The dilemma is similar to a Charles Dickens' novel like *Bleak House*, or *Oliver Twist*-ed and upsized onto the manifolds of America's great industrial cities and post-industrial culture. So while social science continues to gradually figure ways and means out of social problems, the nature of these problems thickens. Not by the decade or the year. Neither by the month nor the week. Not even the hour nor the minute. But by the second and millisecond. Not surprisingly, then, the malaise within behavioral social science continues to be echoed by such writers as Piven in the forward to one of the most influential and certainly the most important studies on welfare in America by Stanford Schram. In his book, *Words of Welfare: The Poverty of Social Science and the Social Science of Poverty* (1995), Piven introduces the main argument very coherently:

> Despite large amounts of federal funding to support social science research on the causes of poverty, little progress has been made in reducing poverty. In fact, it appears to have worsened dramatically in recent years. Part of the reason for this, argues Sanford Schram, is that policy analysis has come to serve the needs of the state at the expense of its citizens. In the case of welfare policy in particular, analysis is often geared

toward managing poverty rather than trying to lessen it, with a focus on controlling the behavior of "the poor." Moreover, research on poverty and welfare dependency is frequently based on questionable assumptions about the economic structures of late capitalist societies, thus neglecting the importance of perspective in social science research (Schram, 1995).

Schram's book went on to win the 1995 American Political Science Association's (APSA) Michael Harrington Award but the policymakers and politicians who should have read it, obviously did not, because the problems that the book raises continue to persist. Politicians and policymakers are themselves slaves to a system that keeps them on their toes. A large portion of their time is often involved with constructing a kind of "sustaining rhetoric" that helps keep them in office, ostensibly to pursue their national interest goals. But if they had read the book, their efforts do not seem to have contained the problems associated with poverty in America. Schram's book is only one of many intelligent responses by social scientists who are genuinely concerned with changing the system. But it is difficult to change a system that appears to deliver both good and evil goods and services, and where the pluses of globalization sometimes appear to outweigh the minuses. Where sometimes it appears that America needs to have a percentage of its population living under the poverty bracket as if to show that in a land of great opportunity, sometimes it takes more than a desire to raise yourself up by the bootstraps, especially when the prognostications of non-partisan research centers like the Washington-based Urban Institute makes arguments like "American Indian, Hispanic, and black students have little more than a 50-50 chance of finishing high school with a diploma. Graduation rates for whites and Asians are about 25 percentage points higher" (Urban Institute, 2000).

Clearly, the social sciences were doing something about the problem of poverty while simultaneously serving as a social voice of warning to America. But like most advice from social scientists, the warnings have been left unheeded. And all it seemed the federal government was doing was casting pearls after swine and throwing good money after poorly thought-out policies and misconceived ideas about poverty control and eradication, which were clearly not the answer. On hindsight, however, it always seems easier to challenge the past with the clarity of the present. Nevertheless, Americans became increasingly aware of the situation of poverty as the mass media took over the need to inform and perhaps educate the public about the problem of the poor, and the problem of the poorest poor which by the mid-1980s at the height of Reaganomics and the Star Wars Program rose to almost 30 million. How about the period just before 9/11? The US Census Bureau, for example, stated that the nation's official poverty rate rose from 11.7 per cent in 2001 to 12.1 per cent in 2002, while "median household money income declined 1.1 per cent in real terms from 2001 to US$42,409 in 2002." The Institute for Research on Poverty at the University of Wisconsin-Madison argues that in 2002, 34.6 million people or 12.1 per cent of the population were poor by the official measure of poverty. Social scientists are also aware that those living at and under the poverty line and are single parents or children are always the hardest hit because their levels of resistance against common social diseases is low, they often hold multiple menial jobs where they are likely to be exploited, and they are probably more prone to mental, physical, emotional and sexual abuse. Married families tend to be more able to withstand a loss of a breadwinner or the loss of a job better than single-parent families in the poverty trap. Some believe that by 9/11, approximately 1.5 American children out of ten lived in poverty. This is ironic because Osama Bin Laden and his terrorists attacked the World Trade Center (WTC) in New York because it represented the symbol of world capitalism. The terrorists attacked the WTC because it represented *successful* capitalism. It is ironic because it seems very clear that successful capitalism—that material success that Osama and his cronies are so envious of—comes at a very high price. American neoliberal globalization means that America's political leaders seem prepared to have an increasingly large proportion of America's youth and adult citizens live at or under the poverty line. If we look at the state of American globalization and its impact on the ethnic divide, the data is even more revealing about the kind of people that are willingly sacrificed, perhaps unknowingly to most tax-paying, God-fearing, law-abiding Americans. African Americans and Hispanic Americans are the biggest racial categories when it comes to impoverishment, while Asian Americans are the least likely to be impoverished. For example, Song argues that,

> Among the racial and ethnic groups, blacks and Hispanics suffered particularly high rate of poverty (24 per cent and 23 per cent, respectively), about three times higher than the rate for non-

Hispanic whites in 1999 (eight per cent). The poverty rate for Asians and Pacific Islanders was 11 per cent (Song, 2001).[4]

The differentiated social structure of poverty appears to have hit hardest those whose own generational and ethnic history was longest associated with American growth.

While Asian migrants might arguably be the latest members of the American Dream they do not seem to be carrying the same kind of political, cultural and emotional baggage that African Americans appear to be forced to carry. Music, dance tunes, songs, and sports are all areas where Black Americans have been chart toppers. Despite the phenomenal successes of these athletes and talented musicians, their success continues to be enslaved to memories of backwardness and deprivation. Rap musicians continue to lament the nihilistic world of fate. White spectators willingly cheer their favorite Black athlete on Monday night football or at the latest NBA, NHL, AL, and NL teams with great neutrality and genuine support. But are they equally willing to share their White neighborhoods with non-White people? And are Black people willing to share their neighborhoods with non-Black people? Many Americans seem to be substantively unwilling to accept non-White additions to their private lives. "White Flight" they used to call it. American can therefore be a very hypocritical place to live. No wonder political correctness has virtually assumed the lives of anyone who has to say anything in a public place. And it would also appear that as long as minority American citizens know their "place" in the public sphere and do not infringe on the suburban lifestyles of their majority co-citizens within a hypocritical milieu of politically correct words and phrases in the public space of schools, universities, and workplaces, there will be no backlash or return to the heady days of the Civil Rights movements of the 1960s. This is to say nothing about the interstitial political spaces between and among ethnic minorities in America or how Jews and Blacks, Chinese and Koreans, Muslims and Jews are able to get along, or perhaps, not get along within the American polity, "as the Athenians after they had erected their trophy, the place being an isthmus, prepared to take in the town with a wall, supposing if they got Miletus, the other cities would easily come in" (Hobbes, 1959, "The Eighth Book," sect 25, 517).

It appears that at least since 1945, two clear processes have increasingly emerged as supporting American globalization through its domestic economy: (1) the presence of an impoverished underclass of 8–12 per cent of the population; and (2) the presence of ethnic enclaves whose co-ethnics are at times represented through a politics of tokenism. We see a token minority representing all other minorities in children's television programming. We see the presence of an ethnic and cultural showcase that is part of America's secret recipe of success. This was clearly demonstrated by the cultural historian, Michael Kammen's work, *In the Past Lane Historical Perspectives on American Culture* (Oxford, 1998) or Cornel West's intellectually persuasive arguments.[5] We also see an America that is intolerant of public personalities who at one point are loved by millions but at another point are vilified by the same, such as O. J. Simpson, Martha Stewart, Michael Jackson, and George W. Bush. The US President was unable to explain his initial hesitance to disclose an incredibly timed sale of stock worth US$848, 560 in the Dallas-based Harken Energy Corporation while sitting on the Board of Directors "shortly before it was announced that Harken Corporation had very poor quarterly showing" (*US News and World Report*, 1992; Paul Krugman, *New York Times*, July 7, 2002; Arianna Huffington, *Pigs At the Trough*, 2003). Part of America's success route for individual stars is that when they rise, their rise is nothing less than meteoric. But when they fall, their fall is nothing less than a total crash and burn. The American public and the media that supports the spectatorialism that is America today have an insatiable thirst for entertainment as public distraction. Perhaps the distraction from the problems of their private lives, perhaps a need for the presence of public heroes and heroines, perhaps the desire for idols they can raise above their own lives as model icons for the future. Or perhaps idols and icons that represent what ordinary Americans really have no hope of ever attaining in several lifetimes. After all, one cannot legislate opportunity through affirmative action policies, nor through ethnic quotas and cultural-showcase realism. It is easy to see why the successes in America are always preferred than the failures.

America had won the Cold War. It had become the world's only military and economic superpower. It had the largest number of the genuinely richest people on earth, not as a per capita measure but by shear numbers. Yet, at the 21st century turnpike, America was looking at a worsening poverty situation among its own citizens. In 1997, three out of every 10 persons arrested nationwide—or 33.16 per cent of a total of 8,070,225 total arrests—were African Americans (US Department of Justice, 1997). Not surprisingly, the Justice Policy Institute based in

Washington discovered that there were "more black men in jail or prison (791,600) than enrolled in colleges or universities (603,032)." On March 8, 2000, the Honorable Representative Harold James, *Democratic Chairman, Subcommittee on Crime and Corrections* wrote a letter to the Pennsylvania House stating that "Blacks received at least 1.4 years more than whites for inflicting serious bodily injury in a robbery, and blacks received 1.3 years more than whites for attempting to inflict serious injury in an aggravated assault. African-Americans account for 56 per cent of Pennsylvania's prison population. By comparison, blacks account for only nine per cent of state residents, according to the 1990 census".

This startling report revealed statistics that had always been in the hypotheses' banks of American social scientists. The irony in the world's largest and oldest functioning liberal democracy with a history of wins in civil and legal rights since 1965 was that there was something wrong with the small picture. While the big picture showed that Americans at the turn of the 21st century were better off than their predecessor generations in the 20th century, the small picture revealed details of an ironic social stigma and apparent legal bias: while Blacks made up only nine percent of Americans state-wide in Pennsylvania, as an example, more than half of the inmates in prison were Black males. Blacks also tended to receive on average heavier prison sentences for the same crime that was committed by non-Blacks residing in the state. Was this a political phenomenon unique to Pennsylvania? Apparently not. For example, in 2002, the US Bureau of Justice Statistics reported a higher rate of incarceration among African Americans in the state of Wisconsin at a level that was 10 times more than Whites. In fact, the 2002 Report added that Wisconsin was leading the nation in this arena. In order to resolve state specific problems of growing crimes, the same federal government study discovered that Wisconsin also had the highest export of in-state prisoners (4,526 inmates) with the state of Hawaii (1,225 exported inmates) by the summer of 2001. This made Wisconsin one of four other states that had two out of every 10 in-state prisoners held elsewhere.

Earlier, we hinted at the presence of two secrets to America's success in globalization. Firstly, the presence of a constant underclass of poor persons, and secondly, an ethnic and cultural showcase of political tokens representing the liberal ideal of different images. However, there is a third secret to America's success. In 1945, US$100 could buy you property and furniture to furnish your newly acquired property. But most workers would take months to earn this amount. When we adjust this for inflation,

51

the US$100 in 1945 dollars is worth US$1034.44 today. Most Americans, based on current GDP per capita estimates, are able to earn this within a month. But it can hardly buy you a complete set of furniture let alone property in which such furniture can do its furnishing. The secret is in the fact that America must keep the dollar inflating at an increasing rate. It can never let it down. The moment that deflationary pressures appear is the moment the American Dream will disappear. This is why America, as the world's largest and most powerful neoliberal economy, needs to be propped up by as many capitalist countries and markets as possible. Otherwise it will begin an economic downturn from which it could never recover. And the top policymakers know this.

That is why Americans are indeed the world's largest debtors, because they manage to export their proprietary and ideological belief system overseas. It is about creating a complex web that shows about all a highly confident climate for investment, domestic spending, retail, manufacturing, construction, and financial services. And statistical social science has provided the means for calculating such confidence in terms of productivity, wealth acquisition, and related items such as the producer price index (PPI) and the consumer price index (CPI). We look at the CPI here since it is the index that reflects the cost of consumer choices for most Americans, and by extension, many non-Americans. According to the U.S. Bureau of Labor, the CPI "is a measure of the average change over time in the prices paid by urban consumers for a market basket of consumer goods and services. The CPI represents all goods and services purchased for consumption by the reference population (known as CPI-U or CPI-W). The Bureau of Labor Statistics has classified all expenditure items into more than 200 categories, arranged into eight major groups". The major consumer items according to the Bureau includes an entire range of what the average American consumer, from the US president to a US janitor is likely to consume: breakfast cereal, milk, coffee, chicken, wine, fuel oil, bedroom furniture; men's shirts and sweaters, women's dresses, jewelry; new vehicles, airline fares, gasoline, motor vehicle insurance; prescription drugs and medical supplies, physicians' services, eyeglasses and eye care, hospital services, televisions, cable television, pets and pet products, sports equipment, admissions; college tuition, postage, telephone services, computer software and accessories; tobacco and smoking products, haircuts and other personal services, and funeral expenses.

Does the CPI reflect reality? In a sense it does because it shows the relative changes in prices over time for a given place. However, the CPI cannot be used to illustrate differences in prices and the cost of living between points on the capitalist globe. There are other measures such as the Cost of Living Index and the "quality of life surveys" in the social sciences that try to provide measures of reality. Apart from its normal function of illustrating the costs that consumers are willing to bear based on their consumption patterns, the CPI is useful for illustrating another known but often not mentioned point. The CPI represents 87 per cent of the US population. This means that the poor are naturally left out of this representative statistic because they are indirect consumers. The poor are consumers in the sense of being insufficiently important to be included in the statistics. The data will therefore continue to reflect the needs and wants of those who can afford to spend, even on borrowed time (since all money has time value) and is a self-fulfilling prophecy. This is because the CPI is often used by federal, local and other regulatory bodies in their profiling of costs. The CPI is also considered an important variable by market analysts in their predictions of economic health. Also, it reflects what Madisonian democratic theory has been warning us of all along: that the tyranny of the majority will enslave those who are in the "minors."

Does the wide variety and range of goods that are generated for consumers mean that Americans are spoiled for choice? In a very grave sense, the answer is yes, because consumer choices provide a sense of the kind of globalization that is being exported to the rest of the world. The Bureau of Labor's range of goods and services also illustrates what kinds of goods are consumed elsewhere in modernity. It is a reflection of the kinds of goods and services that are in fact necessarily consumed elsewhere in the capitalist world from Athens (Ohio) to Athens (Greece), Tokyo to Trinidad, Boston to the Bahamas, and Paris (Texas) to Paris (France). While most Americans are living lives in which they are spoiled for choice for food, medicines, consumer durables, and automobiles, most people on the planet are living below the poverty line. All this talk of poverty is depressing. Yet America needs to keep hope alive, and to maintain cultural icons who represent the American way. It comes to no one's surprise that the 2004 Miss America, the global ambassador of American culture and values, has a graduate degree from an American university. It is even less surprising that her favorite food is McDonald's extra-value meal. In 2001, the author of *Reefer Madness*, Eric Schlosser, introduced *Fast Food Nation* where among other things, he claims that Americans "spent about $6 billion on fast food" in 1970 and this amount rose to "more than $110 billion" in three decades and hence more than the amount of money that is spent on "higher education, personal computers, computer software, or new cars."[6] This is indeed important because American fast food has been a major force of its globalization strategy. While Schlosser's book may make its reader want to rethink eating fast food, we are concerned in this one with rethinking the course of American globalization and how such powerful MNCs such as KFC, Coke, McDonalds and MTV are in the game of global domination as much media pictures from American TV portray them. And now we turn from the politics of fast food to the politics of pet food.

The American pet food industry was worth US$11 billion in 2001 (Animal Protection Institute, January 29, 2002). This is almost the amount of funds that have been devoted under the Stewart B. McKinney Homeless Assistance Act of 1987, in which the US Congress "recognized the need to supplement 'mainstream' federally funded housing and human services programs with funding that was specifically targeted to assist homeless people. Over US$11 billion in McKinney funds have been appropriated since then, and billions more have been provided through other federal, state, and local programs and benefits" (*Homelessness: Programs and the People They Serve*, December, 1999). Homeless persons are likely to be non-Hispanic Whites (41 per cent) and African Americans (40 per cent), 11 per cent Hispanics, eight per cent Native Americans (*Homelessness: Programs and the People They Serve*, December, 1999). It is interesting to note that about half of all homeless persons have never been married and the other half have been married at least once but the marriage has ended in separation or divorce, with at least 56 per cent remaining in the same communities where they were first domiciled, or had friends or relatives.

Interestingly, the GDP per capita for Latin America was US$3,385 in 2002. There are approximately 454.7 million Latin Americans. The amount of money spent by Americans on the pet food industry in a single year is about 75 per cent of the combined GNP of Argentina, Brazil, Chile, Colombia, Ecuador, Mexico, Peru, Uruguay, and Venezuela. That is to say that US$11 billion pet food industry draws a startling comparison when compared to the combined populations of nine other sovereign countries, people who live just South of the United States. The US$11 billion industry supported 60 million pet dogs and 75 million pet cats in 2003 (Pet Food Institute, April 14, 2004). This means that most American households have at least one pet. The pet food industry is nothing when compared to the other spin-offs from pet ownership in America. For example, the 1998–2001 American Pet Association Polls of 17,121 pet owners in February 2003 revealed several interesting facts about consumer behavior that could only happen in such an advanced, post-industrial country as the United States. Most pet owners bought Christmas gifts for their pets and celebrated their pets' birthdays by way of the purchase of a gift, a special meal or a new toy. At least half of the American pet owners surveyed believed that they were more attached to their pets than other human beings. This included the 67 per cent of pet owners who allowed their cats to sleep anywhere they want including their master/mistress' beds. This may not seem consequential to you except when you realize that there are also 3.5 million homeless people in America with almost 1.35 million of the homeless being children (Urban Institute 2000).

If a 40-pound bag of the cheapest generic dog food costs US$10 with approximately 68 million dogs in the United States, and if American pet dogs consume on average one bag a month, we are looking at US$680 million spent on dog food alone. Don't even consider the costs of getting rid of dog waste in public places and private homes, and forget about the fact that on average each dog owner is likely to spend US$196 on veterinary medicine and pet clinics in a single year. There are more cat owners than dog owners in America, and although cats are self-cleaning, they do consume food and need veterinary attention which itself costs the average cat owner US$104 per year (*The Humane Society of the United States*, 2004). While most Americans were surfing hundreds of channels through pay-per-view and satellite TV, most Africans were trying to make ends meet, and the highest-paid Indonesian civil servant in the heady days of former dictator President Suharto made US$400 per month in the late 1980s. The lowest-paid Indonesian was paid about US$13 per month as a volcano-watcher. This means that Americans spent more at the vet than the poorest Indonesian civil servant earns in a year.

Now, in contrast, imagine a country where there are 16 million sport utility vehicles (SUVs) that are designed for off-road use but only five per cent of that total is actually used for off-road functions. For example, Ford Motors reports that over 80 per cent of its SUVs have never even been taken off-road. This means that this country, where urban density has reached enormous proportions and has resulted in cramped spaces for everyone, drivers compete with huge, gasoline-guzzling, fuel-inefficient and over-sized sport utility vehicles that are really not designed for use in the city most of the time. Thousands die each year from car crashes but if the crash involves an SUV and a non-SUV, the chances of the non-SUV driver surviving that crash is reduced further. The imaginary country is, of course, very real and there are rather morbid statistics to prove the dangers involved because of the SUV overpopulation. The Detroit Project, which is an anti-SUV lobby, argues that massive SUVs such as the Chevrolet Tahoe "kill 122 people for every million models on the road" while a Japanese car such as the Honda Accord "kills 21 for every million on the road" and that "injuries in SUV-related accidents are more severe." Even if these statistics were only 50 per cent true we would have a very severe situation on hand in American city streets. So why are there so many SUVs on the road despite the strong lobby against this and despite the many problems that are associated with SUVs in accident situations? Part of the reason is in the desire among SUV consumers for upsizing consumer products. Americans think big. Size apparently is a factor in image building. If you win a lottery or inherit a windfall, or suddenly turn into a professional athlete or a popular MTV singer then you are not the average consumer. And if you did make it big you would not want to buy the cheapest most fuel-efficient car or the lowest cost foreign import. As a trendsetter, your public would expect you to represent the larger-than-life image presented over media broadcasts into everyday life. Hence, you would probably buy the biggest SUV available on the market such as the three-ton fully-loaded Ford Excursion. This is nothing to say about the kinds of fun that Freudian psychologists would have with such a concept of size. But most people in the US are not professional athletes, nor come from wealthy WASP families, don't have connections with the mob, nor possess some stunning ability to outlast, outlive and outsmart everyone else in their chosen industry.

The average American consumer is unable to make all the big purchases that movie stars, Harvard MBAs, and wealthy Wall Street types can make. However, the average consumer—who feeds into that giant machine called globalization—may have the same aspirations as these wealthy icons of consumerism. Therefore, if we cant all be like Arnold we can at least own a Hummer and pretend to be like him. Also, whether you are wealthy or poor in the US, advertising is going to hit you sooner or later. Upper class (old money), upper-middle class (the newly rich) and middle class Americans (the majority class) and lower class Americans all watch the same advertisements on television. And while their pocketbooks might not be able to manage a new car or a second home at a fancy address, their hopes and aspirations are limitless. It is part of the American Dream. It does not matter that for every successful millionaire there are over a million failures. It does not matter that some of these images that are broadcast over television are mind-bending constructions of reality which no one can truly afford and those who can, can't afford the time. The American Dream is quite different from the passions of the Corcyraeans who desired to rob other people of their dreams by blocking out the light for any other dream to occur through their ambassadors and auxiliaries in that Athenian summer (Hobbes, 1959, "The Third Book," sect 85, 207). People often forget that the reason it is called the American Dream is because of the second part of the phrase, and not the optimistic adverbial that can somehow magically modify a dream into a reality. So back to the advertisements. In terms of SUV advertising, the budget in 1990, again according to the Detroit Project, was US$172.5 million. A decade later, this amount rose to a whopping US$1.51 billion. And you thought that the US$11 billion that was slated to help the poor was meaningful. The power behind American-made products is in national identity. In the post 9/11 era, it has become even more important to outwardly display the national colors. This means that one's patriotism cannot be in question when the nation is under attack. And what better way to reflect that patriotic cause than by buying American? Combined with the aggressive marketing strategies of GM, Ford, and Chrysler, buying big is a win-win situation in the face of any war overseas. And the profits are enormous. For example:

> In 1998, GM, Ford and DaimlerChrysler earned US$2.8 billion, US$6.7 billion and US$6.47 billion respectively, for a total of US$15.97 billion. On February 25, 1999, Ford Motor Company unveiled its newest and biggest SUV yet: the Ford Excursion. The Excursion, which is not classified as a light truck, is intended to compete with the Chevy Suburban, which has long been the "King Kong" of the passenger vehicle market. Each Excursion is expected to sell for US$45,000 to US$50,000, and earn a profit of US$12,000 to US$20,000. The technology exists to make SUVs and other light trucks more efficient, but automakers have failed to prioritize fuel efficiency in the design of their vehicles. Passenger trucks have been getting bigger and heavier culminating in the 19-foot three-ton Ford Excursion that was

released this year. The result of investing in body building and not in efficiency technology is that light truck fuel efficiency has actually declined in recent years (Public Interest Research Groups, 2004).

Despite the fact that most American-made automobiles have parts made all over the world and despite the fact that most of the workers of these parts don't even speak American English does not seem to matter. Because if you are American, you need to show that you are American by buying American. And America is always associated with the word "big." But if you ever get a chance to drive that Ford Excursion, and feel the power behind the wheel of the largest most powerful SUV in the world, you might be tempted to show how American you can be.

In 2000–2001, Americans spent about US$120 billion on improvements and repairs to their homes (*Austrade*, Australian Government, April 13, 2004). Americans also drank more beer, more wine, and smoked more cigarettes than all of Southeast Asia combined. American fruits and vegetables that are disposed off in bumper harvests could feed millions of starvation-level people in Africa. The total combined disposable wealth that Americans spent on SUVs alone would be sufficient to keep a small African country like Namibia and larger ones like the Sudan and Congo "in the black" and afloat for an entire fiscal year.

American pharmaceuticals produce enough legal drugs to keep entire South Asian nations like Nepal and Bangladesh sedated for months. The number of illegal immigrants that the US supports in the underground economy is sufficient to run small banana republics out of business. Speaking of another kind of business within the great state of California, it appears that:

> Americans spend more money at strip clubs than at Broadway, regional theatres and orchestra performances combined. The industry has mushroomed since the 70s, when a federal study found that it was worth little more than US$10 million. Now the US leads the world in pornography; about 211 new films are produced every week. [The City and Country of] Los Angeles is the centre of the film boom and many of those in the trade are otherwise respectable citizens. Nina Hartley, a porn star, told Schlosser: "You'd be surprised how many producers and manufacturers are Republicans." The majority

of women in the films earn about $400 a scene. At the moment, there is a surplus of women in California hoping to enter the industry. The internet has provided a fresh and profitable outlet. In 1997 about 22,000 porn websites existed; the number is now closer to 300,000 and growing (*Guardian Unlimited*, 2003).

In 1999, the US pornographic industry was worth a ballpark figure of between US$1–3 billion dollars. This is a very conservative estimate. For example, Eric Schlosser thinks that Americans spend at least US$8 billion in porn, but in 2001 Schlosser said that Frank Rich of the *New York Times Magazine* estimated that revenues from porn were much higher and amounted to at least US$10 billion.[7] In 1999, the porn industry hit a slump when Tony Montana contracted AIDS and was alleged (according to some industry insiders) to have also infected 65 other actors. Porn stars are tested regularly for AIDS because about 83 per cent of them prefer to take the high-risk, high-satisfaction route of having on/off screen sex without condoms. Again, in April 2004 the underground porn industry in the Untied States estimated to be worth at least US$3–5 billion grounded to another halt because three cases where porn stars tested positive for AIDS. The Adult Industry Medical Care Foundation (AIM) suspects that 45 other actors may be infected and stated that only 17 per cent of the actors wear some form of protection such as condoms. Public information is readily available on the medical health of these actors who risk their lives in the sex work industry that continues to play a hide and seek game with the IRS and use different underground modes of marketing its products while seeking shelter in between legal jurisprudence that provides sufficient gray areas for this burgeoning industry. While AIM and AFP reports that the porn industry has grounded to a halt because of the ill-fortune of the three sex stars, no American can honestly believe that no one else is making porn. It simply cannot be believed. The US porn industry is what I call a recession-proof industry which is turned on 24/7, 365 days a year. It is always on tap because there will always be a demand for all kinds of pornographic paraphernalia.

While it is virtually impossible to gauge the net worth of all ordinary tax-paying citizens, it is virtually impossible to gauge the specific value of the underground porn industry which many ordinary citizens condone or support, directly or indirectly, at some point in their lives. US pornography—as the sale and purchase of human sexuality and the gross exploitation of men, women, and children—continues to play an important part of the American global economy. American porn represents different things to different people. For the moral majority proponents, American porn is Satan on earth. For the American Muslims and Jews, porn is the evil of man expressed on human kind. But for many people, porn is the solace by which they can overtly or if necessarily, secretly, derive some degree of escapism and satisfaction from consumption. For the politician who is about to be elected, pornography is sinful and is the gross exploitation of sex workers and many who stand for re-election know the value of keeping silent on such matters, as long as porn remains restricted to certain districts of the city, away from influencing the urban youth, and within control of the city's urban cops.

There are different explanations in the reports of crime, prostitution, and pornography in American cities. Some believe that the workers are to be blamed for their individual choices as much as the johns and the pimps. But some social scientists believe that the reason for this underclass of people remaining trapped in this vicious cycle of poverty and pornography is a result of a larger, highly complex social problem of crime, underworld bosses, gangsters, illegal drug trafficking and drug abuse that continues to embed itself within each successive generation of people. And there is no way out. All exists are sealed. And if you tried to get out, you'd be coerced by peer pressure or threats of personal violence to yourself or your family. Some have even gone so far as to blame it on the White suppression of Black people, on police brutality and corruption, and on the human flesh trade.

For the social scientist, much depends on how you look at the *problematique* and at which point you enter into the fray. One thing is sure: you will never come out with the same assumptions or premises you went in with. The US$3–5 billion pornographic industry has effectively and very efficiently used technology to its fullest advantage. It would seem that any American parent or any other parent in modernity would be hard pressed to control the movement of pornography over the Internet, despite raids, stings, and arrests by Interpol, the UK constabulary, the FBI, and the various branches of US police enforcement units in the US and (primarily Western) Europe, "where madmen and madness become major figures in their ambiguity: menace and mockery, the dizzying unreason of the world, and the feeble ridicule of men" (Foucault [1965] 1988: 13). The porn industry is also highly sensitive to market demand, secretive where it has to be, and open where it can be.

US porn is highly adaptive to other world societies too. While the pornographic empires of Hugh Hefner and Larry Flynt may be on the decline in terms of *Playboy*, *Penthouse*, and *Hustler*, many other modes of exporting American pornography continue to emerge. There is even a sub-black market for the black market that imitates and copies ironically, the already illegal copies of porn on video, DVDs and VCDs in Asia (for example). Is there any rationale in legalizing porn? Would there be a sharp fall in demand if the forbidden fruit was suddenly made as easily available as fast food? It appears that the Christian right continues to be too strongly committed against such moves and has lobbied for decades using all kind of strategies from attacking porn at the source, increasing policemen on the beat, fire and brimstone sermons on the Sabbath, anti-pornography bonfires and the like. But it seems that the roots of US porn as a virtually non-taxable good run deep into organized crime syndicates, some members of the political class, corporate big wigs, members of the clergy themselves, and the people who chose to live on the dark side of Gotham City.

The estimate for the US market was already more than enough to run the government of three to four medium-sized Asian countries like Malaysia, the Philippines, Thailand, and Vietnam while materializing policies on the nutritional requirements and healthcare benefits for these countries for two to three years. The US porn industry is a crucial sector in the politics of American globalization. And it is being used for increasing the non-taxable revenue of millions of Americans and illegal immigrants who benefit in cash or in kind. The economy gets lubricated by the porn industry. If it were eradicated, completely obliterated from the face of urban America, there would probably a higher level of violence, abuse and other forms of domestic violence across the country. As long as there is demand for smut, there will always be a global market for it. Despite what decent ordinary White, Black, Hispanic, Chinese, Korean, Eskimo, Native, and Other Americans are trying to do across the country, they have themselves taken some part in this burgeoning industry that seems so central to the nature of the beast. And to the nature of man.

The nature of being human is political. Man, as Aristotle believed, is by nature political. And as long as there continues to be an imbalance of power within communities based on tradition, modernization, culture, gender, primordialism, circumstantialism, racism, religion, fossil fuels, and socio-economic class there will be a politics of control, a politics of discord, a politics of resistance, and a politics of subversion that feed into the global reach of American globalization. The order of succession is noble. And there remain limits to what the American public as a whole can tolerate politically. It seems to be able to tolerate the extremes of free speech and the right to bear arms. At some level, many foolish citizens even continue to tolerate the presence of the National Rifle Association (NRA).

Yet America seems willing to provide simultaneous support for the intrepid criticism of a new breed of social and political critic in the names of Michael Moore, Eric Schlosser, and even former Republican columnist, Arianna Huffington. American politics seem to accept the extent to which the relatively porous boundaries between conservative politics and liberal ones sometimes overlap, cross-over or even get mixed up. It would seem that the only thing that American globalization and its economic, political, social and cultural processes fear is death. Though not completely. America cannot simply legislate between the fine lines that are drawn between satire, freedom of speech, freedom of expression, the right to publish, the right to voice opinion, and the right to bear arms without consequences. Up till now for example, the academic jury is disunited in its analyses of the impact of the "Brady Bill":

> On November 30, 1993, the *Brady Handgun Violence Prevention Act* was enacted, amending the Gun Control Act of 1968. The Brady Law imposed as an interim measure a waiting period of five days before a licensed importer, manufacturer, or dealer may sell, deliver, or transfer a handgun to an unlicensed individual. The waiting period applies only in states without an acceptable alternate system of conducting background checks on handgun purchasers. The interim provisions of the Brady law became effective on February 28, 1994, and ceased to apply on November 30, 1998. While the interim provisions of the Brady law apply only to handguns, the permanent provisions of the Brady law apply to all firearms.[8]

All US presidents so far have disagreed among themselves over the interpretation of the Brady Act. The *Right to Bear Arms* is for all intents and purposes an anachronistic law in American modernity. The *Brady Act* (1993) clearly helped reveal that the NRA's vested interests and activities over the "gun and ammunition" political economy it supports and advocates was vulnerable and not as politically invincible as once believed. Who wouldn't? These people are directly responsible for promoting an environment of weapons' ownership among citizens, aliens, felons, and psychotics. Despite the informative work of satirist Michael Moore in his well-researched documentary, *Bowling for Columbine* (2003), the politically-charged gun debate has ironically been supported by people like Charlton Heston who seem immune to the urgency of an issue that has resulted in the deaths of thousands of Americans from gun-violence, gun-related crime, and gun-related accidents. How can the NRA not think that it is perpetrating a business that can only be made worthwhile by dismantling?

This chapter has illustrated the complexities of America's rise to the top of the capitalist heap; in a sense it is in praise of the folly of capitalism. It has demonstrated the startling contradictions and complementarity of economic, social and political norms that have emerged over the last 60 years of the American century. America refuses to allow the rise of alternative hegemonic powers that might challenge its privileged status. And while Americans want true and genuine peace in the Middle East, the political system does not allow a sufficient continuity of policies between Republican and Democratic Presidents, despite the presence of a perennially powerful Jewish lobby to boot. Also, it is common knowledge that the US imports 2.5 million barrels of oil a day from the Middle East, but what is not often known is that the US spends US$60 billion a year to maintain its military presence in the Middle East (The Detroit Project, 2004). The new Department of Homeland Security (DHS) will take at least another two years for its staffers to settle in and discover their actual jobs. This is the latest cabinet-level department to be created in the wake of 9/11. There are many bureaus in the DHS and one such example is the National Incident Management System (NIMS). Other examples of bureaus within DHS are the Science and Technology Directorate, the Analytic Services Incorporated (ANSER), and the Homeland Security Institute (HSI), a Federally Funded Research and Development Center (FFRDC). The NIMS bureau performs the function of standardizing reporting procedures and the management of incident protocols for all levels of state and society (*DHS Website*, 2004). Max Weber introduced the concept of the "bureaucratic iron cage" in the early 1900s. The "iron cage" syndrome work this way: for every bureau that is collapsed in the drive towards administrative efficiency, there are other bureaus that will have to be created in its place. When one bureau is dissolved, others will have to be created to take over the function it plays. This trend continues till there is a complex mass of bureaus that exist to map out and control every aspect and dimension of human society in modernity. The growth of the bureaucratic machine will continue until every possibly eventuality stemming from the nature of man can be anticipated and prevented, circumvented or re-invented. It would appear at some level that technology is the key, and the solution, to these problems. But technology as it stands in late modernity today is still far behind human intelligence and the human capacity for civilized behavior and uncivilized destruction. In addition, uneven levels and pockets of economic development across the globe mean that there will always be a ready and willing market where problems are resolved through the creation of such administrative structures. Ironically, this is because for all we know about previous and current civilizations, we still know very little about ourselves and the nature of man. Perhaps philosophy and political theory have the answer. But then again, perhaps not. This is because the nature of man is unpredictable.

The unpredictability of man in modernity gives rise to the concept of a series of administrative structures that serve to function as ways and means of controlling man and his actions in modernity. The *Ship of Fools* that Foucault mentions needs such iron cages. These cages act as centers for structuring society and for controlling behavior. In the case of the DHS and its bureaus, the iron cage grows because there are simply too many abnormal fools running around the vessel, our metaphorical *Ship of Fools* in modernity, and trying to destroy it by running it aground. Ostensibly, these abnormal people are considered insane, mad, and criminally incorrigible because they do not share the norms and values of the larger majority who wish and desire a stable and peaceful life.

Life for these terrorists on the *Ship of Fools* revolves round personal sacrifice of innocent men, women, and children. It is ostensibly about the difference in norms but in reality, it is also about self-hate and a desire for destruction. The desire for destroying the world as they know it stems from the evil side of nature that rises from the heart of the terrorist. No one really knows whether it is purely ideological, religious or political. We know that it is substantively all these components that are mixed in a potent and explosive cocktail. Therefore, the resources that could otherwise be used to manage poverty or increase welfare benefits are now necessarily diverted towards the iron cage of counter-terrorism. Encountering the terrorism of modernity demands deeper and greater administrative measures for anticipating, out-thinking, and out-strategizing the intelligence and operational networks of Al-Qaeda and the Jemaah Islamiah. But there will be more groups as we proceed. This is only a slice of what appears to be a pattern of terror that traces its roots to the barbarians at the gate. This means that funds that would otherwise be spent on education and poverty will now be transferred towards national security, which in terms of military defense spending was already a multi-trillion US dollar economy on its own. Al-Qaeda and the Jemaah Islamiah are destroying the name of Islam to a point to which it may never recover as a legitimate religion in the United States of America, if the rampant killing and beheading by these extremists continues. The recent attacks o Najaf in Iraq in the fall of 2004, and the reports by CNN and the BBC World News on August 21, 2004, reveals the kinds of political socialization that continues in Islamic schools across Washington DC. The Ambassador of Saudi Arabia claimed that the textbooks claiming other religions as false by state-approved texts for very young school-going children were under review. In a strange historical predilection, a similar and contrasting war had occurred just two hours north of Najaf by slow plane over 2500 years before: "In the meantime after Potidaea, was revolted and whilst the Athenian fleet lay on the coast of Macedonia, the Corinthians, fearing what might become of the city and making the danger their own, sent unto it, both of their own city and those of the other Peloponnesians which they hired to the number of sixteen hundred men of arms and four hundred light armed" (Hobbes, 1959, "The First Book," sect 60, 34).

The existing contradictions of the extremes of wealth and poverty within a world class capitalist system are the secret of America's success when complemented by political structures and social norms that help steer greater confidence among people who believe in themselves and continue to be fascinated by America and the politics of American globalization. The Nathaniel Ropes Professor of Political Economy at Harvard University's Department of Economics, Alberto Alesina, and his colleague, Edward Glaeser, the former Paul Sack Associate Professor of Political Economy, quote the *World Values Survey* where one of the many interesting findings is that "60 per cent of Americans believe that the poor are 'lazy' [while] only 26 per cent of Europeans hold this belief … It seems easier for White middle class Americans to consider the poor less worthy of government support if they think of them as different. To put it crudely, but candidly, indifference comes easily if the poor are assumed to be mostly Black. This is more difficult in Norway where rich and poor are White, often blond and tall."[9] Of course the co-authors offer more empirical support for their claims than what can be presented here, but one cannot be easily convinced of their essentialist and reductionist approach in their "social scientific method." We are not sure how they figure the jump from the 'perception of values over poverty' and correlate this with racism and "Blackness." Therefore, it seems that for these co-authors to suggest such a correlation might require much more empirical work than merely economistic hypothesizing.

However (and this is where their main concern lies), I can believe scholars who argue that the US welfare state is much less generous than the ones used in Europe, and that the reason for such generosity in Europe is because of the culture of pluralistic politics as we will visit towards the end of *Chapter Five* on *'War'* in this book. Pluralism involves the creation of a polity over time that engulfs the entry and exit of different and competing interest groups, activist groups, specialist and expert groups with a view to enhancing creativity through over-lapping layers of interest within society. Pluralism American style demands that each group and each member respects the presence and the existence of other groups. Therefore there is a *rights'* argument to be made about the nature of pluralism because it is only through a shared belief in the respect for the individual and the community to be different can such pluralism work. Yet there are many problems with such an idealistic political persuasion as seen in the existence of racist and sexist groups that resort to political violence to achieve their ends.

Nevertheless, the pluralistic political culture is made possible by the process of proportional representation where minorities will have a greater chance of being represented in the political process. On the other hand, the plural American political culture built on neoliberal capitalism is not as fermented as the older European version of pluralism. This is not to say that the Europeans have a superior welfare system, and like the *Narrenschiff* that their colonial policies were only about "carrying their insane cargo from town to town" (Foucault [1965] 1988: 8). Or that there are significant political gains to be made from adopting a more European-type pluralistic political culture. The problems are different for both cases. It seems that neither the European pluralistic political culture nor the less fermented American plural political culture present real alternatives to the liberal, libertarian, or communitarian citizen.

Also, we can now understand why the problem of racism within the pluralistic culture of America is naturally reflected in its legal history since the forced migration and sale of the first African-American slaves in the early 17th century to the establishment of what came to be called the Jim Crow laws, and eventually, the prevalence of public common sense that culminated in formal Civil Rights legislation of the mid-1960s. But by no means is the story of primordialism and the essentialist attachment to race over. Indeed, the Rodney King riots and the daring pronouncements of Klu Klux Klan dragons on older episodes of 1990 talk shows have done little to reduce the level of embedded racism in the United States. Neither have the words of anti-Semitic clergymen and preachers abated the issue. If racism continues to exist in such countries as the United States, despite its long history of liberal democracy, what chance do developing countries the world over have in combating and winning this war? Just because people don't talk about it means that it is over. Racism continues to present itself in employment, education, housing, property acquisition, and civil society structures.

The fear is that if the ISR *World Values Survey* is indeed reflective of current trends, then we can say that racism and the welfare state is here to stay for a longer time than socialists, communists, and liberals would care to admit. This leads us to believe that perhaps a clearer and more lucid distinction might be made between those who support the idea of precision and accuracy in the social sciences, and (as distinct from) those who support the normative challenges that make some sense (but not much) of the public's hallucinations "in Thierry Bouts's *Hell*, with the nakedness of the damned" (Foucault [1965] 1988: 21). What we desire in this book is a greater understanding of globalization through an examination of the American model simply because America *is* a global power with many humanitarian and sympathetic dimensions. The American oeuvre is not overly limited or shackled by the mistakes and problems created by the military and the CIA as we shall visit in the subsequent chapters of this book.

It is very important that we do not consider America to be as ominous and damned as Thierry Bouts's Hell. Neither can Nietzsche's view of a super powerful being be adequately applied to American politics. Foucault was describing modernity writ large, and Nietzsche was interested in restoring the faith to a people that had been misplaced by medieval Christianity. Foucault was warning us about the hallucinatory effects of engaging in potentially dangerous exercises that can stem from an immoral view of being human and living in humanity. Nietzsche was warning us about the death of a god that was no longer useful. The death of a god that had passed on and died despite the rise and continuity of the global marketplace. This is why it is possible today to continue to be materially successful without advocating any one religious view, or espousing any single religious doctrine no matter how ancient, no matter how proven, no matter how convincing.

Americanization is a thing of the past. It is a thing of the past because there is no single Board Room in which all the CEOs of American MNCs sit together to plan and strategize the domination of the world. Militarily, America knows that it cannot ride roughshod over competing cultural and economic paradigms. American cannot convert the world by force even it wanted to do so. Those skeptics who believe that American militarism is an uncontainable indication of its desire for global supremacy fail to remember that much of the American military motif has been done in response to potential dangers. And here lies the problem. Because American governments have tended to be reactive rather than proactive up till 1945, it can no longer allow for another Pearl Harbor to occur before something is done about it. It can no longer allow for another 9/11 before congressional hearings discover that the intelligence services were correct and had played their part. The problem for the rest of the world is that American foreign policy in its proactive mode is becoming increasingly paranoid and when strategy is modeled on paranoia, mistakes are made. This is why even though America had illegally invaded the autocracy of Saddam Hussein, they were right to put a stop to his inhuman torture of Muslims and political opponents. America was right in ceasing the ethnic pogroms of Saddam in the Middle East. But America was wrong in misleading its people, and its allies in the UK and the Asia-Pacific with the search for weapons of mass destruction. Until today, there are no signs of WMD. This is why America seems provocative and evocative. It provokes those who do not share its ideological values and evokes others to embrace them. Does America use the threat of power to convince? Yes it does, but not in the way that the old colonial masters used to employ. America is not a colonizer and the world, led by the American people, and guided by the philosophy of John Locke, should ensure that it does not become one. This is the new order of things.

America cannot invade Cuba despite its being a huge thorn on its front yard. America continues to retain the title of Heavy Weight Champion of the world not because it is the best at everything but because Americans believe that they can do everything to the best of their ability. There is a tremendous level of self-confidence among American business leaders and political leaders. Their confidence seems to cover as many bases of the global neoliberal world order as is humanly possible. Many who convert to the American Dream of hope, progress and optimism cannot and do not want to leave.

What fascinates many views of America from the outside is that despite the complexity of American bureaucratic apparatuses, despite the widening gap between American politicians and American voters, despite the differences within American cultural communities, America continues to function as a powerful and united entity. It moves onwards and forwards. Americanization may be dead, but American leadership on the global stage is very much alive. And it is the job of every scholar interested in modernity and globalization to criticize such dominance.

American modernity is fascinating because it seems to be able to drive the world economy at a speed and pace that no other civilization or community or nation has ever done previously. The British experiment with colonialism attempted to achieve this global dominance but failed because the strategy was unilateral. The resources and profits that were gleaned from its colonies were directed inwards to reward the crown. The rest of the surplus value extracted from the British colonies across the world was redirected towards stabilizing the Empire and controlling its dissidents. America has surpassed British history of global control because it provides in-built opportunities in ways that no other benign hegemon, least of all the former Soviet Union, could provide. America is a fascinating phantasm of hope, optimism and progress because its political ideology of neoliberal democracy seduces and subsumes American citizens and non-American foreigners. It is the seductive effect of American neoliberalism that is paving the way forward as a model for other powerful states in the making such as China and India. Will America give up without a fight if its place at the top of the economic pyramid is challenged? Well, according to neoliberal theory, it should not give up at all. And in fact, the America that supports the importance of free trade would certainly welcome competition, isn't it?

We live in a world where most people born after 1965 have heard of America and Americans, though this is not true the other way round. Isn't this the litmus test of a true and genuine global hegemon where other people and societies have to study your country, and not the other way round? The political and economic models that America has proposed to the world however have not been returned without criticism as we see in the World Trade Organization or the International Monetary Fund, or even the World Bank. The US is however able and willing to support causes that further the American ideals of life and liberty as long as its national interests are not violated. Friend can turn into foe overnight. The loyal are rewarded with economic investments, the disloyal left out to suffer in the desert till they have learnt their lessons. Is America all about brute force? Not quite. This is because America seems to respect the rights of American citizens to challenge the very fundamentals of its own philosophy of being in modernity. But not that of foreigners. America continues to grow because it is the land of incredible opportunity. For every terrorist that wants to bring America down, there are hundreds of thousands who want to make America their own home.

For every terrorist who thinks that America is an evil satanic dictatorship, there are millions who perceive it as a haven for political refugees and those prophets who are not welcome in their own lands. It would seem that most people would like a slice of American pie. The world was watching when the British handed over their oldest colony of Hong Kong to China under its last governor Chris Patten. The world also saw how many Chinese Hongkongers who had served faithfully in the name of Great Britain had their passports had returned to them without possible entry into the UK as full-fledged citizens because of an immigration decision. The old adage about one's word has taken on a new and different meaning simply because there are insufficient resources to maintain the ideals of a socialist past.

BBC World reported in late August 2004 that Scotland Yard (otherwise known as The Metropolitan Police Service) was trying to resolve the problem of crime in Greater London. The report stated that persons of Indian origin made up four per cent of the population but were involved in 16 per cent of the crimes. The report also mentioned the street along which there were many famous "curry houses." How is America different in this respect? What measures have American local government implemented to prevent such racial profiling? Does America have an equivalent story of the inability of police to curb crime in the cities? How many of us must fall victim to these facts of urban life before something is done permanently about it? The perversity of crime and the pervasiveness of ethnic hatred is a phenomenon that has come to engulf the modern world. It is up to individual communities to police themselves and to maintain vigilant over the possibility of disruptive actions against their cultural and social norms and values. It is too late already if one is going to wait for scholars to create models of articulating public cooperation. It is too late already if communities and individuals wait for the state to create corridors of trust and self-confidence. The problem of poverty is something that is globally shared. China hopes to reduce its problem of poverty by 2015. But it will fail without economic investments. These investments will not flow smoothly if China continues its ideological diatribe against democracy and positive democratic values. China, India, and any other trading partner of the United States must work in closer cooperation with the states that support freedom. The freedom of the individual and the freedom for creativity is no one's copyright. America is fascinating because there are pockets of success at the community level that become model communities to be emulated across America. Some do not even have a distinctly physical base such as "The March of Dimes: Walk America" that tries to save the lives of young babies and children. There are similar instances and examples in the UK too and I am sure that readers will be able to make connections with these realities. The important point that is being made here is that America is a globally exciting place because it happens to be one of the best places for energetic growth in the world today. In spite of the problems associated with hate crime, mercy killing, police abuse, and the military, there is still ample space and time for any individual or community to develop. The UK unfortunately lost this chance when it could not protect its colonial possessions in 1939. The age of Great Britain has long gone and is very unlikely to return. America is in a favorable position to positively create spaces and sites of increasing prosperity without brute force. America is today's model for the future.

ENDNOTES

1   R. D. Norton, "Industrial Policy and American Renewal," *Journal of Economic Literature* 24, no. 1 (1986): 1–40.

2   Read for example, Uri Ra'Anan, "Soviet Strategic Doctrine and the Soviet-American Global Contest," *Annals of the American Academy of Political and Social Science* 457, (1981): 8–17; Ali Farazmand, "Globalization and Public Administration," *Public Administration Review* 59, no. 6 (1999): 509–22.; Robert L. Pfaltzgraff, Jr., "The Emerging Global Security Environment," *Annals of the American Academy of Political and Social Science* 517, (1991): 10–24.

3   Sewell Chan, "Survey Indicates More Go Hungry, Homeless Aid Lacking as Greater Demands Conflict With Improving Economy," *Washington Post*, December 19, 2003, A11.

4   Xue Song, "American Poverty and Welfare Reform," *Perspectives* 2, no. 6 (June 30, 2001).

5   Readers may wish, as an interesting alternative to the cultural history of Kammen, a more philosophical approach as suggested by R. Fred Wacker, "Assimilation and Cultural Pluralism in American Social Thought," *Phylon* 40, no. 4 (1979): 325–33. See also, the cultural politics of difference in Cornel West, *Keeping Faith: Philosophy and Race in America* (NY: Routledge, 1993).

6   Kathryn Eastburn, "American McHistory—Eric Schlosser's *Fast Food Nation* is About More than Just Burgers and Fries," *Baltimore City Paper Online*, February 28–March 6, 2001; and CBS News, "Americans are Obsessed with Fast Food: The Dark Side of the All-American Meal," January 31, 2002.

7   See also Eric Schlosser, *Reefer Madness and Other Tales from the American Underground* (London: Penguin Books, 2003), p. 269, fn. 112; Duncan Campbell, "With Pot and Porn Outstripping Corn, America's Black Economy is Flying High—Illegal Migrants Provide the Muscle for US Black Market," *Guardian Unlimited*, May 2, 2003.

8   "Implementation of Permanent Provisions of the Brady Handgun Violence Prevention Act," Department of Treasury, Bureau of Alcohol, Tobacco, and Fire Arms, *ATF News*, October 29, 1998.

9   The distribution and management of the survey data is directed by Ronald Inglehart at the Institute for Social Research of the University of Michigan; Alberto Alesina, and Edward Glaeser, *Fighting Poverty in the US and Europe: A World of Difference* (Oxford University Press, 2004).

CHAPTER 3

American Globalization and Asia

What Can Asia Learn From the Business and Politics of American Modernity?

Imagine an underground passageway that is five feet wide with windows full of goods stacked up to the top of the corridor that the back walls are totally hidden. A bustling two-way movement of buyers, sellers, investors, tourists, terrorists, gun runners, ordinary decent families, police, military personnel, diplomats, government bureaucrats, politicians, peasants living under the poverty line, slum dwellers, and homeless persons serves as a channel for the exchange of trade, commerce, ideas, sorrow, emotion, and technology: this is the connection between the politics of globalization between America and Asia. It is about a fantastic journey, full of life and death, and surrounding a definitively impervious lantern that gives off the light of hope, optimism and progress—like the fantasy getaways of SoCal's burning porn industry, "another symbol of knowledge, the tree (the forbidden tree with the fruit of immorality and of sin) once planted in the heart of the earthly paradise, has been uprooted and now forms the central mast of the *Ship of Fools*" as adapted from Foucault's work on *Madness and Civilization* (Foucault [1965] 1988: 22).

This situation is well illustrated in particular by J. Lodge Gillespie's romantic tropes in the "rhetoric and reality" of America in Southeast Asia after the Pacific War. His work helps connect readers with the re-discovery of the fact that the complexities of domestic US economic influence have increased tremendously since the 1960s.[1] One such area is in technological hardware and software. Communications' hardware keeps changing with urban planning strategies to improve and develop connections, for example, between airports and their delivery sites.

THE AIRLINE BUSINESS

The power of the American and European airline industries are so apparently seamless that there have been no other major competitors to their virtual monopoly since the end of the Soviet empire in 1989. Even during the Cold War, Soviet-built airliners did not perform as well nor were as serviceable as those built by American and European consortiums. Until today, the powerful American and European airliners that criss-cross the world as they speed up the processes of globalization continue to dominate. There are no real competitors from Japan, Africa, the Middle East, Asia, or Latin America.

Within the United States, the physical limitations of the hub and spoke systems that form the basic infrastructure of the American airline industry today had its fundamentals in airport planning and design in the 1950s. A decade after World War II, American airfields began demilitarizing their war-time functions and were converted from short grass-patch airfields into long, multiple runways, high-grade gravel tarmacs, and new airport lounges that included amenities one found in the city-centers. Additionally, these new runways could take on the weight and intensity of jet-propelled aircraft that became particularly popular from 1959. The hub and spoke system illustrated its usefulness in the mid-1970s. This system was designed to meet the demands of higher passenger volumes and set in place a stable yet competitive environment that also saw the lowering of costs of passenger tickets across the US relative to the time and place of departure and arrival. The hub and spoke system subsequently demanded that shorter haul aircraft were needed to transport their passengers from the spoke cities to the hub airports across hundreds of miles which saw the realization of authentic non-stop travel as we expect and demand as air travelers today. Americans, Europeans, Asians and virtually any other air traveler across the globe are in a position to enjoy the utility of non-stop air travel today because of these innovations in communications technology. Here, we recall Heidegger's definition of technology as involving the ability of man to control his environment through artificial means, and therefore does not have to merely be limited to the stereotypical metaphor of technology as necessarily computer-based innovations but entire strategies of change.

However, the technology applied in the American airline technology in the mid-1970s compared to today's technology makes it somewhat of a misnomer to define today's short-haul airplanes in terms of the planes of yesteryear. This is because short-haul aircraft today are more powerful, fuel efficient, much faster, more comfortable, safer, and can carry a higher passenger load than their predecessors. While the basic design of the Boeings, McDonald-Douglas, and Lockheed (and their European competitors such as Airbus Industries) aircraft have not changed dramatically since 1971, the absolute volume of passenger traffic demanded the rise of a new kind of air travel within the contiguous United States and Hawaii. This demand was met by the use of low-cost, frill-free, carriers that could fly directly from city to city rather than through the hub and spoke system. Thus, it was only communications technology that has enabled an apparently anachronistic practice from the 1970s to reappear as a solution in the 1990s.

The globalization of communications technology and the theoretical dynamics behind new systems have served as a model for European and Asian modes of travel. The American hub and spoke system has therefore been circumvented by the use of more powerful and efficient lower cost, multiple short-haul airline flights on small to medium sized aircraft. The demand for such aircraft continues to add to the employment possibilities for American job seekers. By the early 2000s, such Asian countries as Singapore, Malaysia, Thailand, and Indonesia have also begun their push towards the use of these shorter, low-cost high-turn-around domestic airlines. The long learning curve used in America and Europe has enabled a much shorter learning curve to be applied in Asia with the basic tenet being the Concept of Open Skies. The strategy of low-cost carriers requires faster turn-around and keeping the planes in the air as much as possible over shorter distances across the densely populated Asian cities. Airlines are only one source of multiple passage ways in modernity.

There are many other forms of multiplying the effect of these passageways crisscrossing American and Asian cities. For example, the airline flights from New York to Singapore in Southeast Asia, and from Chicago to Chengdu in China, are increasingly mediated by cheap airfares, better service, more value-added quality, low-cost bus fares, and inter-city train systems. Competition is a killer. These multiple passageways are also catalyzed by information and communications exchanges. Singapore Airlines (SQ) for example has a 49 per cent stake in Tiger Air, a low-cost carrier, which is in partnership with the European-based Ryan Air. The decisions made usually come from the very top of the business structure in Singapore and often involve the politicians themselves. Many SQ pilots left after wage negotiations broke down in early 2004 and the former Senior Minister (SM) Lee Kuan Yew had to resolve the issue. We must remember that Lee was in power ever since the days of the old Malaysia-Singapore Airways (MSA), TWA, Pan-American, and the British Overseas Airline Corporation (BOAC) existed.

The newly-appointed 2004 Minister Mentor in the Singapore cabinet, Lee Kuan Yew is known for his authoritarianism. Not a model of American liberal democratic leadership, Lee proved himself a tough-talking, single-minded, and impatient political father. He demonstrated a remarkable in-depth knowledge of societies and cultures from routinely reading several books at one go and from surrounding himself with up to the date details of matters on world and regional politics. He taught himself Chinese when he was in his fifties because he thought that it would help Singapore's understanding of the bourgeoning Chinese economy. He has made some important insights into world events and even received a standing ovation from having addressed a combined session of the US Houses of Congress during his term as the longest-serving prime minister in the British Commonwealth. Lee was head of government from 1959 to 1990 when at the height of his legal power, he transferred his post to Goh Chok Tong.

On August 12, 2004 after 14 years as prime minister, Goh himself transferred power to Lee's eldest son, Lee Hsien Loong. Despite continuing foreign criticism and Internet allegations of dynastic politics and nepotism, Singaporeans from all walks of life appear to have become endeared to the younger Lee's charismatic style. Loong, as he is affectionately known, has the support of the third generation leaders that he had himself hand-picked and the support of the powerful People's Action Party (PAP) and its members of parliament. The new Prime Minister Lee holds a graduate degree from Harvard University and is a pragmatic realist. He supports his father's belief in the importance of the US military presence as a countervailing force in Asia. This is not surprising given the much larger, periodically aggressive, Muslim-dominant countries that surround the secular island state of Singapore.

Singapore began with a stormy birth. The country's first Chief Minister was an experienced labor party politician named David Marshall a son of one of the Diasporic Jewish families in Singapore. Marshall was a popular lawyer and his story is told by Chan Heng Chee's *A Sensation of Independence: A Political Biography of David Marshall* (Oxford, 1984). Chan is currently Singapore's ambassador to the United States and was co-opted into the local establishment in the early '80s. Apart from Oxford and Cambridge universities, the Singapore government regularly sends its top civil servants to Harvard, Stanford, Princeton, and MIT to pursue graduate work. Singapore also sends it top fighter pilots to the US Air Force Academy and has regular exchanges with the United States Air Force (USAF), US Special Forces, and US Army units. Not surprisingly, many scholars who have returned from the US have keen insights and at times, a proclivity for American public policy, although this is always tempered by localization needs.

ABANG-ADIK? SINGAPORE AND MALAYSIA

The word "abang" in Malay refers to the older brother and "adik" as the younger one. For many years Malaysia assumed the role of the "abang" but Singapore has never really accepted the title of "adik." It is possible that these metaphorical familial labels could be reversed if we use different yardsticks of performance, such as GDP per capita. Nevertheless, there are many reasons why Singapore and Malaysia are successful capitalist countries and each competes against the other for US and other world investments—like two brothers tied together by blood ties, but quarrelling periodically—and sometimes the competition spills over onto the political realm.

Singapore's efficiency and international success is attributable to a tightly-run, carefully controlled society, depoliticized polity from 1959 to the middle of 2004. Singapore is known for periodically implementing controversial domestic policies. For example, the island state manages its traffic situation with an iron hand calculated to reap a big profit at the same time. Singapore is the most expensive place to buy a motorcar in the world, and Malaysia is not very much cheaper. The Singapore government collects billions of dollars in several main ways: (1) income and business taxes; (2) from Certificates of Entitlement (COE) that allow a person to legally purchase a car; (3) from the collection of a 150 per cent tax on imported cars (none are manufactured in Singapore), and from the 10-year age limit that is placed on the lifespan of each COE. The lifespan of cars can be extended but at cost. So if you need a car for more than 10 years, you have got to keep buying one at least once every decade. The reason given for implementing the 10-year limit for each COE was because it was supposed to keep the car population young and therefore reduce the possibility of mechanical failure and the problems associated with older cars. However, this policy has not shifted with the changes and improvements in vehicle technology. Singapore also has a three-quarters-full-tank rule, the world's first Electronic Road Pricing (ERP) system, a world class international airport, a meticulously clean and artificially green city, and a highly-efficient mass mover of people called the Mass Rapid Transit (MRT) system which is a cross between the San Francisco-Oakland Bay Area Rapid Transit (BART) and Hong Kong's Mass Transit Railway (MTR). But the MRT is much cleaner, more efficient, and many times more secure than the BART or the MTR. Singapore has a compulsory national service law for male Singaporeans, and Malaysia recently implemented its own form of national service.

The three-quarters-full-tank rule requires Singapore cars to have at least that much gasoline in their tanks before entering Malaysia by the two causeways that connect the two countries. This was ostensibly implemented at the request of Malaysians living in the state of Johor that borders the country. Singaporeans who filled up their gasoline tanks on the Malaysian (Johor State) side were accused by Malaysian groups in Johor of pushing up the cost of living in that state. However, the three-quarters-full-tank rule also protects Singapore's monopoly over the retail gasoline market made up of Esso-Mobil (Exxon-Mobil), Shell, British Petroleum (BP), and Singapore Petroleum Company (SPC). The companies often seem to raise and lower their prices at distinctly similar times. But whether the prices are higher or lower, the Singaporean car owner and driver ends up paying. For all its control over Singaporean public policy, the government has said that it does not want to interfere with the price mechanism despite allegations of cartel-like pricing (by these oil companies) over the Internet, in the local coffeeshops, and other sites of resistance for disgruntled Singaporeans. BP announced its withdrawal from the retail oil sector in early 2004, and will have its outlets bought over by SPC.

The relationship between Singapore and Malaysia has been undulating. There are territorial disputes and differences that date to the time when both were colonies of Great Britain. Malaysia has complained about Singapore's close links with Israel. Singapore was unhappy with the backtracking of the Malaysian political leadership over issues confronting the two countries. When Deputy Prime Minister Lee Hsien Loong visited Taipei before becoming prime minister, he received a stern warning from the People's Republic of China. Malaysia's Deputy Prime Minister took advantage of the situation to advise Malaysians not to antagonize China's sovereign policy. Interestingly enough, the land that houses the temporary site of the Malaysian Embassy in Singapore used to be the site of the old US Embassy. Singapore is the only country in the world that has another country's railway near the middle of its city-center at Tanjong Pagar and it appears that the Malaysians don't want to leave.

Singapore politicians believe that Malaysia tends to use island-state as a "whipping boy" whenever the Malaysian General Election draws near. Malaysia and Indonesia held mass military exercises close to the Singapore border on August 9th, which is Singapore's national day. Malaysia has consistently been an outspoken member of the Organization of Islamic States and is a strong believer in ummah or universal Islamic brotherhood. Before 9/11, Bali, and Madrid, Malaysia's foreign policy output was highly inflammatory against the US and highly anti-Semitic. However, since Prime Minister Abdullah Badawi took over in October 2003, there has been a significant reduction of the political rhetoric against Americans and against Jews. Singapore drew the indignation of Malaysian political leaders when it invited Israeli President Chaim Hertzog for an official visit in 1984, and much earlier when it deployed Israeli Defence Force (IDF) consultants disguised as Mexicans in the early days of its fledgling army. Current Prime Minister Lee believes that Singapore is a steadfast ally of the United States and will remain as such as long as America does not interfere with Singapore's domestic politics. Singapore and the US share many similar views on the global balance of power, and in the aftermath of 9/11. Singapore also supported the US invasion of Iraq when most other Southeast Asian countries considered the event both illegal and a precursor to further American global interventionism. One clear model of "intervention the other way" into the global arena is the case of the global company Singapore Airlines (SQ).

SINGAPORE AIRLINES AS A GLOBAL COMPANY

Singapore is a small island state with a global name, where the government would have the people believe that there are many places to fill and little talent to go round. At least this has been the reason behind former Prime Minister Goh Chok Tong's policy on foreign talent and global talent. But the number of home-grown talented Singaporeans will continue to deplete nevertheless because most ethnic Chinese Singaporeans, who make up about seven to eight persons out of every 10 citizens, are not replacing themselves. The issue of low fertility levels and replacement levels not going up but hovering precariously below national benchmarks can also be seen in the case of Singapore Airlines (SIA) that has had to depend on many foreign pilots for its worldwide success.

Ever since its inception, Singapore Airlines had been a major purchaser of Boeing aircraft, especially the very popular 747-series "Jumbo Jet," the 737-series, and the new 777-series at the cost of billions of American dollars. SIA will also take delivery of the world's first Superjumbo the European-built Airbus A380. Nevertheless, SIA continues to remain a big investor in the former Seattle-based company. Singapore also remains one of Boeing's largest and most credit-worthy customers. SIA had become the "best airline" in the world with the right blend of local administrative expertise and primarily American technology. This meant that Singaporeans and foreigners had big stakes in SIA as the national carrier reaped hundreds of millions of dollars worth in profits in the best global success story of airline management in modernity. This also meant that SIA was a national resource and was being carefully watched by its competitors and the government that had created it. In the winter of 1980, the Singapore Airlines Pilots' Association (SIAPA) began a "work-to-rule," non-violent, peaceful, "strike action" after being unable to agree with their newly-minted collective agreement. SIA was considered a national resource in the local economy, and SIAPA was eventually de-registered in 1981. The local papers reported that 15 leaders were charged with commencing illegal industrial action and convicted. It continues to be illegal to initiate industrial strike action in Singapore today.

Some 24 years later, in 2004, there appeared a replay of the events of 1980 but with different pilots. Lee Kuan Yew had warned the pilots previously that "he did not want to do them in, but won't allow them to do Singapore in." The implication in 2004 was that someone in ALPA-S, the local pilots' union, had been covertly muddying-up the waters through illegal backdoor negotiations and was about "to do Singapore in," to destroy the nation. This person was singled out by (former Senior Minister) Minister Mentor Lee Kuan Yew for instigating trouble between ALPA-S and the old SIA management. After several months of public and private negotiations the matter was resolved between the new ALPA-S union leadership led by less truculent man, an SQ pilot called Mok, who was only very willing to work closely and with full cooperation with the new management team. At the end of the strained relations between the pilots' union and their senior management, the local newspaper, *Straits*

Times, proclaimed wage increases for SIA staff, while some of their top flight senior managers ended up working for the other Singapore airline, Tiger Air.

The "mud-raker" or instigator singled out by Lee Kuan Yew was a former SIA pilot called Ryan Goh, a Malaysian citizen with permanent residency (PR) in Singapore and PR status in Australia. Because of the incident, Goh was considered an undesirable resident by Home Affairs' Minister Wong Kan Seng (a minister is of the same rank as a US department secretary and a Singapore ministry is generally equivalent to a US government department). Goh's appeal to have his Singapore PR status reactivated after it was revoked so that he could continue working for SIA was turned down. He moved to Australia. However, there was no move on the part of ALPA-S or other SIA pilots to defend Goh in any public manner. Perhaps this might have indicated that Goh himself did not have any support from the pilots themselves or the pilots who supported Goh withdrew when they sensed danger. It seems plausible that when Goh's pilot friends sensed that something was wrong, they immediately did not want to "get involved" in the matter. This also tells us that the camaraderie and brotherhood among SIA pilots are not as seamless and unproblematic as some observers might have thought. This raises the question of how Lee Kuan Yew (who is usually preoccupied with national and international matters as the senior minister in the Goh Chok Tong cabinet) was able to quickly pin-point that one man was behind it all. Clearly, Lee's intelligence was very accurate. Goh's fellow pilots and, or, the people who worked with him in SIA must have let the cat out of the bag reminding us of an intriguing modern narrative involving "an Uncle Tom" or perhaps even Michael Caine's reprise in *The Whistle Blower* (1986).

There are different classes of pilots within SIA such as younger Malaysian pilots (entry-level), older Singaporean pilots (entry-level), and foreign-based pilots. Apart from the differences in training because of the different fleets of aircraft, these different classes of pilots might lead to divergent views and opinions among the pilots if each class enjoys different remuneration packages in this global company. The incident with ALSPA-S also reveals something about the kind of pilots SIA hires, the nature of trade unionism in Singapore, and the ability of unionized workers to articulate their views. We also see that the state in Singapore continues to be illiberal towards illegal back-room deals or strike action particularly when such national resources such as SIA are involved. This

81

is because large amounts of tax-payers money went into the building and success of the global company. The pilots however appear to get the lime-light because of the nature of their job and the reputation that goes with being and becoming a pilot, whatever that might entail.

But there were many significant players in the creation of SIA as a global company such as J. Y. M. Pillay and his team who were some of the primary architects of SIA's surging global success story. While it is unlikely that 1,600 airline pilots can "do Singapore in," it seems illogical for individual pilots who represent a disenfranchised minority of workers on the Singapore payroll to be able to hold the company (and Singaporeans in general) "ransom" or to "blackmail them" for better pay or working conditions et cetera. On the other hand, SIA has a very good reputation to uphold. And the treatment of its entire staff must continue to reflect the global standards that it has set for the airline industry worldwide. For example, SIA pilots should be paid what is fair to them. Their salaries should be pegged to a percentage of a list of top global carriers, and not the medium sized carriers or a mixed bag of carriers. In any global industry, if you do not want people to leave, you should pay them what is fair. The operating theory for global success is that one should not under-pay some people in order to over-pay others. Because when people discover that you are cheating them of the wages that their contemporaries are receiving, you get bad press. There is a gulf of difference between labor union management in the US and the ones in Singapore. The global position of Singapore Airlines continues to signify its importance as an employer of thousands of Singaporeans and foreigners locally and overseas and the state is unlikely to fudge issues with any union within the Singapore Airlines Group that infringes or tests the limits of its state-determined boundaries of labor action.

Despite the lack of fanfare and a legal tussle over the brand-name, Tiger Air was eventually launched in August 2004 after receiving its airline operator's license from the Civil Aviation Authority of Singapore (CAAS). Tiger Air is confident of attaining close to 200,000 passengers by the end of 2004 and predicts that it can turn a profit by 2005 in its first year of operation from 23 August 2004. In order for low-cost carriers or airlines to turn a profit, they need to keep the planes in the air. Yet some pilots who prefer not to be named have observed that most of these planes are in fact parked empty on the ground and overnight. This means that they are incurring parking bay charges while simultaneously incurring costs to staff on the payroll such as engineers, cabin crew and technical crew.

If there are no multilateral sector agreements between and among Southeast Asian nations over the use of airspace and airports, then there will not be any passenger volume and no profit, only losses from day one. Nevertheless, Singapore Airlines, Value-Air, Tiger Air and other smaller companies in Southeast Asia seem adamant and willing to spend an estimated amount of over US$1,000,000 by the end of 2015. This is a large amount when compared to some experts in the global airline industry that claims that recurrent costs of international operators are likely to hit US$10 billion in the short term.

Why would such companies go into such an early stage of competition when their own national carriers could easily purchase more small planes for this sub-corporate function? Some pilots working with SIA believe that it is about product-branding and prestige. SIA has won many awards. It has taken many years to develop its reputation for world class travel. It has learnt from the American experience, Western European lessons, and Asian know-how within and without the airline industry. Therefore it would be foolhardy to squander SIA's reputation on a low-cost airline like Tiger Air. Hence the stake that it has in Tiger Air. A more detailed and technical book on the matter of the international airline industry is one by Rigas Doganis, *Flying Off Course: The Economics of International Airlines* (Routledge, 2002). This book is worth paying attention to if readers are more interested in the opportunity costs of running an international airline.

SIA is such a global communications and hospitality industry that is has American airliners, European airplanes, serves French champagne, Asian cuisine, uses foreign-based pilots, and has made headlines by the "Singapore Girl" concept. The exotification of Asian women has been a useful mode of wealth-creation. Ironically, the Singapore Girl image is one that now includes women who are not from Singapore but instead from Japan, Korea, Malaysia, and India. Can the global traveler really tell the difference? Therefore, a prestigious company like SIA could not possibly join the fray of the low-cost, frills-free airline industry because it would eradicate its hard-won premium for world class travel.

But there is an alternative assessment. One hypothesis could be that a cash-rich corporation could merely pump money into such low-cost carriers to bankrupt their competition in terms of a "beggar they neighbor" strategy. It is commonplace to have many different major stockholders in any one company. These companies are not autonomous entities because of the sheer amount of capital that needs to go into their establishment and maintenance. However, it seems plausible in the cut-throat world of modernity that a cash-rich super-holding company could hypothetically strategize to bankrupt the competition by creating a false scenario in which good money begins chasing bad money, like throwing pearls at swine. Eventually, the competitor companies would bankrupt themselves not because they were inefficient, but because they were chasing after the mythical dragon of demand that was not there. There is currently, however, no evidence to support this hypothesis, and low-cost carriers might eventually pave the way of the future if the Open Skies agreements are signed. Whether or not the use of the low-cost carriers in Southeast Asia, Korea, China, and Japan takes off based on the American experience remains to be seen. There are many reasons for these countries—like most other countries in late modernity—to resist foreign takeover of traditionally protected local industries. The survival of these local industries is tied to a larger political complex of periodically elected politicians whose own fortunes are tied to their voting public.

THE GLOBAL EDUCATION BUSINESS

Asia has learnt much from America by creating opportunities for its young and old people to take advantage of American educational opportunities. There are many instances and examples of how Asians and Southeast Asians have learnt from American educational modernity and benefited from these experiences. American educational systems have been emulated and modified all over the world and have even had a tremendous impact on the conservative Western European educational systems. Asian elites are often trained at American universities and work in American business enterprises regardless of historical affiliation, economic ideology or political ideology. This phenomenon is illustrated in South Korea, Thailand, and the Philippines, economic allies such as Singapore and Japan, critics of America like Malaysia and Indonesia, the authoritarian military junta in Myanmar, Communist China, former adversaries such as Vietnam, and former British colonies such as New Zealand and Australia. These elite graduates from nominal American universities and those who graduate from American military colleges and universities return with some knowledge about America and with some idea about the American way of life, perhaps even the American Dream. Their influence eventually trickles down and percolates into their own indigenous or national communities. Asia has therefore is a blend of historical educational systems introduced indigenously and from first contact with Portuguese, Spanish, Dutch, and British colonialism. The massive changes to Asian education systems and their inherited biases from the colonial period were interrupted by the outbreak of World War II. This was the major turning point for the region. It saw the rise of postcolonial nationalism all across the region and the world that would persist through the Korean War, the Vietnam War, the Cold War, the Gulf Wars, and 9/11. The synchronous adjustments made within the national Asian systems of education over two hundred years of modernization have had an uneven effect on the relationship between these countries and the western world. The unevenness of the educational experience with English as the language of science and technology, and of communications and information, would mean that those countries with scholars trained in the English-speaking world would potentially possess the advantage over other nations in Asia with regards to the pressures to globalize. However, the case of the Philippines is a clear exception as analysed in Rappa and Wee in *Language Policy and Modernity in Southeast Asia*. There are other factors that have helped or hindered Asian responses to modernity and towards globalization. A significant factor is the presence of the US military in the region as a countervailing force against major forms of aggression. While the US presence is a clear deterrent in the post-9/11 era, it was not always a welcomed presence in the Indian Ocean or the Pacific Rim. And while the US presence in Southeast Asia itself has had a tremendous but silent effect on curtailing potential flashpoints and tensions within the region as seen in Korea and the Taiwan Straits. Naturally, there are also other languages that have had a significant impact on the region through foreign education systems such as French and Dutch but these languages are themselves not as widely accepted across the world as English. The business of education in Asia is highly political because it involves factors of national policy, local community, cultural norms, and rising expectations of the voting public. The tension will continue to exist between foreign talented skills and local talented skills.

Education is a serious business in Singapore and this issue ranks high on the national agenda, alongside economic performance, defence and security. Singapore is a clear beneficiary of the American military presence in the Pacific and its benign hegemonic role in the region. The likelihood of war breaking out between China and the island of Taiwan for example is dependent on the ability of Washington, Beijing and

Taipei's diplomatic conferencing abilities. Southeast Asian economic stability will suffer from an East Asia that is turned into another Middle East. There are many problems with American society that become only too real and almost unbelievable unless you visit the actual places themselves such as Los Angeles' South Central. However, America possesses many positive qualities that can easily be emulated by Asia and one of these models is that of the cultural melting pot of people. In the Singapore case, the ethnic management strategy designed by Lee Kuan Yew and the first generation leaders have outlived it purpose. There is no longer a need to continue with the cultural showcasing of Chinese, Malay, Indian, Eurasian, and Others. This ethnic management strategy has served Singapore well but now it the time has come for it to go. The real solution to Singapore's very real fertility problem lies in the deconstruction and ending of the island state's current ethnic management strategy. In 2004 for example, the total fertility rate (TFR) was 1.26, thereby forcing the new prime minister, Lee Hsien Loong, a former military general, to announce what for Singaporeans were radical and new policies to jump-start the fertility problems of this tiny Southeast Asian dynamo. Naturally, the real solution to Singapore's fertility issues is a change in cultural value systems among Singaporeans. Singaporeans should not discourage inter-ethnic marriages. Goh Chok Tong certainly did not stop his daughter from marrying an English businessman.

SPECIAL ASSISTANCE PLAN (SAP): TOO CLOSE TO NIETZSCHE

Singapore has a world class education system that has resulted in many of its students performing very well across university campuses at the best educational institutions the world has produced. Singaporeans have won mathematics and science Olympiads, and Law Moot court debates as well as English Plain-Speaking contests. Recently a Singaporean on a military scholarship to MIT earned his Master and Bachelor degrees in record time. Why does Singapore need Chinese SAP schools? How about Tamil or Malay SAP schools? What are the global benchmarks for SAP schools? Are there such schools in the US or Europe? The SAP schools are part of the elitist nature of the education system. They would not be problematic if there were similar schools for Malay, Tamil, and Eurasian students. Alternatively, these Chinese SAP schools would not be problematic if they *also* allowed the study of Chinese, Malay, various

East Asian languages, various Indian languages, and the more popular European and American languages such as Dutch, French, German, Portuguese, and Spanish.

However, rather than being part of the meritocratic educational system, the Chinese SAP schools go against the grain of meritocracy since students from the "minority" ethnic communities do not have the same degree of motivation to study Chinese at the first language level. Neither do these students have the same cultural ballast to support studying in such an environment even if they chose it in the first place. And if a Malay or Tamil or Eurasian wanted to study at a SAP school, they would have to study Chinese at first language level (which is perfectly acceptable if there were only Chinese people living in Singapore) and not their own chosen mother tongue. To make matters more complicated, there are also no Tamil, Malay or English SAP schools. And there don't seem to be any plans for such schools either. There are also only a token few non-Chinese Singaporeans in SAP schools. Does this mean that there is no demand from non-Chinese Singaporean students to attend SAP schools? Of course, but how does the government explain such a lack of demand among non-Chinese Singaporean students? While PRC Chinese students are scrambling to meet people from other places and of other cultural backgrounds, why is the Singapore government trying to move in the opposite direction? Is it purely economic or is it highly Nietzschean? On the other hand, Prime Minister Lee Hsien Loong has announced that there will be similar schools constructed for non-Chinese Singaporeans, but when and how long this might take is anyone's guess. The Prime Minister is known for working much faster than the rest of his staff and now that he is the head of government, the government ministers and civil servants need to have to work as fast as he does in order to keep up with him.

The reality is that the Chinese-emphasized Special Assistance Plan scholarships and "SAP scholarships" have been implemented in Singapore for a long time and this long gestation period gives Chinese Singaporean students an extra edge. Most Singaporean parents would probably not mind this except for the fact that there are no SAP schools designed specifically for non-Chinese language. This seems to suggest that Singapore's strategy for surviving modernity is not too far different from some aspects of Malaysia's global search. Malaysia believes in proactively helping the indigenous people and the indigenous Malays in particular. Singapore seems to assert an idea of meritocracy, but with an edge for

Chinese Singaporeans. This can also be seen in the number of Chinese Singaporeans who become President Scholars (highest and most prestigious scholarship), Singapore Armed Forces Scholars (SAF) Scholars, and Overseas Merit Scholarship (OMS) scholars and the number of non-Chinese Singaporeans. What exactly is the message in this educational medium?

THE SOLUTION FOR THE SAP

This also means that for much of their precious, early, school-going life, the elite Chinese Singaporean students at SAP schools will hardly get to mix with non-Chinese Singaporean children. By the time the school day is over there will hardly be time for mixing with other children if their parents are driven to send them to other co-curricular activities such as ballet, piano lessons, or golf lessons. What kind of policy is truly being promoted here? Simply because these SAP schools have worked previously without public protest does not mean that they are widely accepted. This brings Singapore close to the kind of affirmative action *bumiputera* (son of the soil) policies for Malays that are used in Malaysia's education system. No Singapore citizen begrudges Chinese Singaporeans and their ancestors for the hardwork that they have put into building Singapore. But there were also many Indians, Malays and Eurasians who played significant parts in the building of modern Singapore. There continues to be is a serious need for proper and neutral research on educational policy on the SAP and the Malay-Muslim Madrasah or religious schools in Singapore.

Resources for Chinese-language acquisition could be channeled away from the SAP schools and towards making Chinese-language more readily available as an option for *all* native and non-native speakers of Chinese since the government is convinced that China is the next big thing for the youth of Singapore. This would mean that any Singaporean could work in China in the future, not only just 200 Chinese Singaporeans. Perhaps one reason why American's own talent does not seem to be dwindling is because of its immigration policies and also because of its belief in the idea of citizenship that is not based along ethnic lines. There is elitism in the American model, but Americans are very careful about trying to resolve the problem of race in education, and Singapore's education policy makers could take a leaf out of the book on American educational meritocracy.

THE BIG FOREIGN INVESTOR

America is Asia's biggest foreign investor outside the region. America has had its hand in the political and economic pies of Japan, South Korea, Vietnam, the Philippines, Thailand, Malaysia, Singapore, Brunei, Indonesia, Australia, New Zealand, China, Taiwan, India, Nepal, Bangladesh, Pakistan, Sri Lanka, and virtually the entire Pacific Rim which the US Seventh Fleet seems to claim like its own backyard swimming pool. America, when compared to the rest of the world, has another comparative advantage. The US has "a relative abundance of educated, skilled workers, and a relative scarcity of educated, unskilled workers. This is suggested by the fact that US exports embody a much higher ratio of skilled labor to unskilled labor than its imports or manufacturing production for domestic consumption" (Pryor, 1999: 478–9).[2] On the whole one can say that Americans are better treated and more welcome in Asia than in Africa, the Middle East, perhaps even Europe. The richer America gets, the more people want to get something out of it. Take the case of the Organization of Petroleum Exporting Countries (OPEC) for example. When OPEC decided to command a higher premium on its barrels of "black gold," it restricted supply to create an artificial rise in prices in 1973. The oligopolistic nature of the oil industry through its corporatist cartels controlled the global oil industry and the nations that were most dependent on them, namely Japan, South Korea, Singapore, and all the Western European countries. This was indeed a bad time since it was at the height of the Cold War with the Soviet Union. America did not need the additional pressure from the oil states. After World War I, the US was the world's largest producer of oil with close to 70 percent of the world market share. When faced with the pending shortage of oil reserves the CIA staged a coup in 1953 in Iran and returned the Shah of Iran to power. During the Cold War, the US also produced sufficient quantities of oil and natural gas from the Gulf of Mexico and its other oil fields in Oklahoma, Texas, and Southern Florida to run most of its economy modestly with fewer cars and more efficient use of fossil fuels. However, a drastic supply cut would have crippled the growth of America's urban population and limited the completion of its complex system of interstate highways, and most importantly, the Military Industrial Complex.

If we read Edward Said's seminal work, *Orientalism* (1979) correctly, we would consider the Middle Eastern states back then as being part of the Near East, at least historically. Despite such historical knowledge and cultural critique, there continues to be much ignorance about the complexities of the Middle East, such that America is not capable of full comprehension. The neoliberal capitalist world order has been supported by the reasoning and rationale of the *Federal Power Act* (1920), the functions of the Federal Energy Regulatory Commission (FFRC), the US Department of Energy, and the US Nuclear Regulatory Commission (NRC).

The complexity of political and economic consequences on businesses never fails to surprise. Although it was a fact that American MNCs were hardest hit by the OPEC-induced recession, all these MNCs had to do was to dispose of their least profitable overseas assets. The MNCs would then concentrate on the diversification of the local product base. "Clearly, for OPEC as a whole, the quota system offers higher collective revenue, but the gains among members are quite disparate. For the most part, the small producers such as Gabon, Algeria, Qatar, Indonesia, and Nigeria benefit significantly" (Griffin and Xiong, 1997:299) "because of the enormousness of the Saudi reserve base, when Saudi Arabia matches cheating, it is producing reserves it would otherwise produce in the distant future" (Griffin and Xiong, 1997:308).[3]

American politics appears to forgive those who have confessed their crimes, served their time of shame, and tried to make good. America is especially forgiving of those who achieve the American Dream of material success and grandiose public displays of wealth. This is why there will never be a shortage of new contestants for Hollywood's raucous movie production centers or new entries for the Miss America contest or try-outs for the professional sporting leagues. People want to become famous and then want to receive as much public adulation and media glamour as possible. Like madness, it involves the

> "values of another age, another art, another morality are called into question, but which also reflects—blurred and disturbed, strangely compromised by one another in a common chimera— all the forms, even the most remote, of the human imagination"(Foucault [1965] 1988: 29).

It is not in the least an open "secret" in America to say the least about the chimera of human imagination.

Singapore was particularly hard hit by the OPEC oil crisis in 1973. As a struggling Southeast Asian economy that was seeing the vestiges of American defeat as total and a complete rout in Vietnam, the genuine economic and financial architects of Singapore namely Goh Keng Swee and Hon Sui Sen were particularly interested in making the Singapore economy work. As a result there was a shift in emphasis towards diversifying the kind of MNCs from Western European and America such as Rollei, Texas Instruments, DuPont, Hewlett-Packard, Phillips, and expanding the capacity of Mobil. But Singapore was alone in this quest. While many Malaysian politicians of the period hoped for Singapore to fail after it was forced out of the Federation of Malaysia in 1965, the converse became history. But the magnitude of Singapore's success was attributed to an alignment with Western countries, especially the United States, and it was perceived negatively especially by Muslim dominant countries such as Malaysia and Indonesia with its masses of poverty stricken citizens at that point in time. Singapore's success was in its ability to attract MNCs when the other countries in the region were debating the advantages and disadvantages of Import Substituted Investments (ISI). In addition, Singapore's secret use of Israeli consultants for its fledgling army worsened the relationship with its Southeast Asian neighbors and increased the level of suspicion of the Muslim-dominant states. While Singapore adopted a policy of trading with any country regardless of political ideology, Malaysia and Indonesia did not think that the use of American economic know-how and Israeli military tactics was a step towards building ASEAN brotherhood. This also made life less easy for Americans who were working in these countries.

There are some compelling reasons to think that Americans are indeed not welcome in Asia. This chapter examines, in some detail, why America is important to Asia in terms of the historical complications that have arisen over the deep American military and economic interests in Asia. America has a special and close relationship with many Asian nations, especially now in the post-Cold War, post-9/11 era where its dominance as the international military hegemon and to a certain extent, economic hegemon, continues to be visited on different Asian constituencies for different reasons.

WHAT HAUNTS AMERICA IN ASIA

America has a long and complex modern history with Asia. Much blood has been spilled on both sides. Unnecessary blood spilled mainly over ideological differences, administrative inaptitude, and media falsification. Take the Vietnam War for example. When a country's soldiers go to war, they have to be professionally and psychologically prepared. American soldiers were not. Some were conscientious objectors. Most were draftees. Others like William Jefferson Clinton dodged the draft by going overseas to study at Oxford. If you didn't have money or smarts, or if you came from a low-income neighborhood in the inner cities or from somewhere in the south and had never even seen an ocean, you'd probably end up in Vietnam. Apart from the ideological ill-preparedness, once the President committed American citizen-solders to the fight, there should have been complete moral and social support. There was not. American liberalism, with its great respect for differences of opinion and democratic divergence, threw up a range of conflicting ideals which ended in widespread protests at Bowling Green University, the University of California and the University of Hawaii at Manoa. Look at successful wars that ended quickly. They all had the complete support of the public. This was not the case in Vietnam. When the stories of the cover-ups of the war's stagnation leaked out, the media naturally came in and made it worse through sensational reporting. The army itself was not completely blameless. For example, the war was used, as usual, to deploy new and different kinds of weapons. But the war was also used as an excuse to try out different kinds of drugs on its soldiers in combat, and when one watches such movies as the psychological thriller about the Vietnam War called *Jacob's Ladder* one might not be able to tell the difference between fact and fiction. What kinds of fact dominated the discourse of Vietnam and post-Vietnam War America? To what extent were the 50,000 lives lost a worthy statement of Duty, Honor, and Country? How many more millions will have to sacrifice their lives, knowingly and unknowingly, under the "Call to Arms" and the political rhetoric of the "Defense of the Nation"? The trumpet call to war is a testament of the preparedness of a country to sacrifice its men and women for the defense of the larger good. Yet if we were to invert this situation from a non-Western point of view, how easy would it be able to be understood? How many of us can really understand the true meaning of why the Vietnamese fought so tenaciously for what must have appeared to be a hot, humid, malaria-infested intertwining set of swamps and rugged tropical terrain that eventually began to be filled with the corpses of the millions who died without a lasting social or ritual memory, or a testament to their names, families and villages?

Vietnam was a sullen war that continues to be fought by the ghosts of idealistic patriots whose own people did not support them. When they returned to their homes in the inner cities, middle class suburbia, the American West, and the Deep South, there were no parades or celebrations. People looked at them with suspicion and disgust. Their fellow Americans. This again was aptly captured in *The Deer Hunter*, *Hamburger Hill*, *The Long Road Home: Vietnam Revisited, 1969, Regret to Inform*, and *Some Kind of Hero*. There were others that seemed realistic and sufficiently gory but were somewhat less convincing such as *Born on the Fourth of July*, *Full Metal Jacket*, *Good Morning, Vietnam*, and *Missing in Action* because they were more concerned with their performance at the box office which was uneven in the end.

By way of comparison, there were thousands of American soldiers killed in action against the Japanese forces during World War II many of whom continue to be unaccounted for till today. Some of their own sons, those who were old enough to have children, went on to die in Korea and in Vietnam. There have been at least 5,000 to 8,000 American soldiers who have gone missing since the end of the Vietnam War. Close to 60,000 Americans are now dead or missing in Asia in the ideological cause of democracy. During the Vietnam War alone, America had devoted over 2.5 million soldiers and civilians. This may be seen in the history of US warfare in Asia described for example by Michael Maclear, *The Ten Thousand Day War: Vietnam, 1945–1975* (St. Martin's Press, 1981), and more recently by Peter S. Kindsvatter in *American Soldiers: Ground Combat in the World Wars, Korea, and Vietnam* (University Press of Kansas, 2003).

There are also signs that Asia is turning increasingly towards American and Western ideals of freedom and democracy as seen in Kazuo Kawai's *Japan's American Interlude* (University of Chicago Press, 1960), Elizabeth J. Perry's *Challenging The Mandate Of Heaven: Social Protest And State Power In China* (M. E. Sharpe, 2001) and Bill Robinson's objective analysis in *Promoting Polyarchy: Globalization, US Intervention, and Hegemony* (Cambridge University Press, 1996). One could extend these powerful discussions by asking why military tacticians in Vietnam did not learn from the lessons from America's own civil war experience, for example, at Appomattox.

Asia's discomfort was most clearly demonstrated by the North Vietnamese during the Vietnam War. However, since the end of the Vietnam fiasco where Americans at home received mixed signals about Americans overseas in the rice paddies, American foreign policy towards the region (known by the Department of State as part of "East Asia") has been mixed, if only lukewarm. By this I mean that American foreign policy was dominated by ideological interests and the need to stem the influence of two kinds of communisms. One was the Soviet-supported motif adopted by Uncle Ho and the North Vietnamese, and the other kind derived from Mao Tze-tung Thought that led the way to the punishment "of both good and evil" supporters of their respective regimes.

The ideological subdivisions in the World War II were politically overt and caused severe tension between the Soviets and the Chinese across their Eurasian borders with limited skirmishes and exchanges of small arms fire. However, these subdivisions did not mean that it would make the ideological problem any less simple for the US. At some level, the DOD and the DOS were—as institutional competitors—unable to take advantage of the Sino-Soviet divide and manipulate it for their own benefit. One clear dividend was the new level of rapprochement that was achieved when Richard Nixon made his historic visit to China. This forestalled China's own interests in reclaiming Taiwan by force which itself was being indirectly supported by the United States and some of its allies. When Mao Tze-tung died on September 9, 1976, a new era of modernization was gradually unleashed and raised the stakes between the US and China, again in terms of committing to its role as a dominant land power in the East while trying to break through the rudimentary and inchoate policies and politics of Mao's widow and the other members of the Gang of Four. The two-year window known as the era of deMaoization[4] that began ostensibly after 1978, saw the PRC endeavor adjusting to the problem of political succession, while strongman Deng Xiaopeng continued to solidify his position and quash his enemies within the Party, the grassroots cadres, and the PLA. This was anticipated in Peter R. Moody Jr.'s *Opposition and Dissent in Contemporary China* (Hoover Institution, 1977). The internal crisis in China in the 1980s saw greater American predominance in militarily establishing itself in a more entrenched manner than ever before. American warships and entire fleets roam international ports of call with limited local resistance. Its nuclear-powered aircraft carriers that are designed to theoretically travel without stopping for two decades. These Behemoths of the Ocean are only restricted by the need to re-stock and re-store the basic necessities for human consumption and the mental well-being of the crew. For these reasons, the globalized world of consumption would expect a significantly different variety of goods and services such as DVDs, PC CD-ROM games, and other technologically-based products that would never have been thought of by sailors in the 19th century. This makes one wonder about the sort of goods and services might be provided over the next half century.

The rise of Reaganomics would also result in the depletion and bankrupting of the Soviet military budget through the Star Wars program. No one even knew that Star Wars might not work. The important point in the chase to end the Cold War came suddenly. Gorbachev's unfortunate twinning policies of *glasnost* and *perestroika* resulted in the internal exposure of a deeply corrupt and inefficient system within the Soviet Union and its Soviet satellite republics across Europe and Asia. Therefore, the politics of American globalization was achieved in a hurry, very much by non-Americans themselves who in their own attempts to compete with the superpower failed to live up to the ideological and practical extent of their economics. The end of the Cold War and Bush Sr.'s announcement of the New World Order in 1990 unleashed the hope of having freer trade now that the command economy had proven itself unproductive and irrelevant for the progressive economics of the 20th century.

However, Bush's New World Order did not see any dramatic increase in free-trade in Asia even by 1999, a decade after the Cold War had ended. The Asian Free Trade Agreement (AFTA) is still standing as a possible ideal goal for the future but the responses from Southeast Asian countries for example have been mixed. At a more dangerous level, the North Koreans continue to expect special treatment from the United States. The communist North is also vilified by the continuing American military presence in the South. There was a great possibility for a limited but destructive war emerging in the Korean peninsular as the North Korean harvest failed and its aging political leadership went through a difficult period covering up the death of Kim Il Sung in 1994. Policy analysts at RAND were concerned as far back as 1989 about Kim's preparation for nuclear war with the South. There is a continuing need for American executive intervention in North Korea as seen in June 1994 and August 2003 when North Korea felt that it was under threat from Western imperialist powers, notably the United States, because of its ideological beliefs that must appear problematic if not totally anachronistic to some of its left wing critics within the controlling political party. The Chinese themselves desire American wealth and support for the old Most Favored Nation (MFN) status. The Chinese Communist (CCP) Party wants the wealth without the responsibilities that are attached to democratization. The CCP and the top leadership's actions during the Tiananmen Square episode is a case in point. Depending on your point of view and your perspective, it might have been a massacre, a pro-democracy movement, a class-struggle, a counter-revolutionary struggle, an act of sabotage, or the work of terrorists. Again depending on where you stake your political values and ideological vantage point, it would appear at least ostensibly that Tiananmen in 1989 was an overt act of state control and intimidation against a political movement designed to weaken the CCP. Naturally, the next big place to democratize is Communist China, and despite the academic and political rhetoric about the One China Policy, it seems very clear that Taiwan is a sovereign and independent country on its own with a visibly different set of values and principals since it thwarted Mao's intention to complete the People's War in 1955. However, whether or not the US will interfere with Taiwanese or Chinese sovereignty seems moot now. On one hand the US officially only recognizes China. On the other hand, the US has sent its fleet into the Straits again. There appear to be mixed signals coming from the US and this is where Americans might become embroiled in another hot war if it does indeed break out. A third perspective presents itself in terms of the literature on brinkmanship and the extent to which each side might be bluffing through the mobilization of military and paramilitary units along their coastlines. The view from Asia is one of a political balancing act between and among three capital cities, two in Asia, one in North America. The Chinese have believed for a long time that Taiwan, the last frontier and renegade since the People's War of Liberation in 1949 will eventually be reunited. Beijing fears that if it backs down on the Taiwan issue, the island will become an entrenched bastion of democracy for overseas and local Chinese democrats who have now tasted the fresh and variegated fruit of western neoliberal capitalism. Should ASEAN intervene? Are economic sanctions from the US signposted along the road to Chinese democratization and capitalism? Time will prove that the eventual break-up and breakdown of Communist China will doubtlessly see a supreme costs of lives sacrificed in the name of ideology. Lee Kuan Yew, the Minister Mentor and octogenarian leader of Singapore has argued forcibly for the inevitability of China's rise to power through its manufacturing base. He has argued that the 21st century is the Pacific Century and that the motor behind Asian resurgence is China. He might be correct. Let us hope that he is correct. Because if he is wrong, then we will see China break-up and break-down in less than a decade because of corruption, nepotism, Party disunity, and the disenfranchisement of the People's Liberation Army from the benefits of capitalism. It would be more prudent for China and Taiwan to develop their economic relations and to keep their diplomatic channels open. The avoidance of war over the Straits and the Island of Taiwan is to every one else's benefit. No one wants to see dead Americans on the streets of Taipei, least of all the American public.

DISCOMFITURE WITH AMERICA

Despite the widespread discomfort with American presence throughout Asia and in spite of its winning the Cold War without firing a single shot, there continue to be deeply-held anti-American sentiments in Asia. On a lighter note, its allies, such as Singapore—a Republic without republican values—would periodically lay down the law against American interference. For example, an American diplomat was thrown out of Singapore in retaliation for what is considered foreign involvement in local politics in the "Hendrickson Affair." E. Macon Hendrickson was the first secretary at the US embassy in Singapore and was expelled for "meddling in Singapore politics" in 1988.[5] Singapore under Prime Minister Lee Hsien Loong will be no less tough, despite the third prime minister's jocular demeanor and diplomacy. In Malaysia, the federal government in Kuala Lumpur vehemently rejected American claims in 2003 about a clandestine meeting of Al-Qaeda related operatives in its capital Kuala Lumpur that was alleged to have occurred before the 9/11 terrorist attacks. The US later agreed that the meeting did not take place. Social scientists from top-notch universities in America have found difficulties penetrating and understanding Malaysian politics and culture. There is bureaucratic resistance and foot-dragging because the political masters, especially when Mahathir was in charge, were anti-American in many ways. For example, when he was in power, Mahathir launched his "Look East Policy" which was designed to emulate Japanese methods of teamwork and values as opposed to Western and American norms of trade unionist activism. While visiting the leader of the *National Justice*

97

Party (now a fledgling opposition party in Malaysia) the former US vice-president Al Gore antagonized Malaysia's incumbent leaders. Al Gore is neither known for a John F. Kennedy-like charisma or as possessing the wit and stature of the now deceased Ronald Reagan, however, he certainly was able to ruffle Malaysian cabinet ministers' feathers:

> Among nations suffering economic crisis, we continue to hear calls for democracy in many languages, "People Power," "Doi Moi," "Reformasi," Mr. Gore said at a dinner that included Malaysia's top leadership. "We hear them today—right here, right now—among the brave people of Malaysia." The speech stunned and infuriated Malaysian government officials. So tense has the political situation been in Kuala Lumpur over the last few months that using the word "reformasi" in public has landed many protesters in prison. "It's the most disgusting speech I have ever heard in my life," said the trade minister, Rafidah Aziz, a close ally of Prime Minister Mahathir bin Mohamad. "I hope I never live to hear another one from anyone like that." "There are narrow-minded people in this world," she said, "but certainly that reflects an unabashed intervention into local affairs" (*International Herald Tribune*, 1998).

Much to the chagrin of the dominant local political climate, Gore praised the *Reformasi* supporters of the (imprisoned and former) Malaysian Deputy Prime Minister Anwar Ibrahim.[6] In Malaysia, it is not considered appropriate behavior when you are a visitor in someone's home to criticize that person's home from within his house. This is considered taboo in Malaysia, as it was in Singapore's "Hendrickson Affair." Whether or not Gore's speech in Malaysia was part of his campaign to get media attention for his presidential candidacy is unknown except to his personal advisors. However, what is interesting is that no other American leader who was actually in Malaysia has criticized it openly.[7]

Gore's comments unleashed a torrent of outrage from indignant politicians and newspapers amid charges that he was interfering in Malaysian affairs. Prime Minister Mahathir Mohamad described Gore's remarks as "disrespectful" and "offensive." Foreign Minister Abdullah Ahmad Badawai branded the remarks "unwarranted," "provocative," and "abhorrent." Saying that the United States would be responsible for any "rupture" in Malaysia's multiracial harmony, he accused Gore of supporting a "*form of terrorism*".

...Ambassador John Malott defended Gore on Friday, saying he only called for democracy and was not inciting people to violence ... Malaysia could not be called a democracy just because it held elections. "Democracy is not simply having elections," he said. "Stalin held elections. Even Hitler held elections."[8]

Gore drew attention from the local and regional media because of the Anwar case. Anwar was a young, highly capable and rational political leader and former Deputy President of the largest race-based political party in Malaysia called UMNO. The United Malays National Organization (UMNO) is *primus inter pares* dominant in the National Front (NF). The NF, also known as the Barisan Nasional (BN), in Malaysia is the political umbrella for all the other dominant political parties that have ruled the Federation since 1971. The BN was the creation of ethnic riots in May 13, 1969 after a state of emergency had been declared because of fighting between Malays and Chinese. Malaysia has not seen such massive and widespread riots since those heady days of ethnic chauvinism and communist insurgents. Anwar was spotted by Mahathir when he was a student activist. Because of Anwar's background in Islamic studies he was very capable of swinging the right wing Malay ground towards the moderate center UMNO party. Anwar was also marginalized from UMNO at the onset because of his radical views and hence reminded Mahathir very much of himself when he first started his political career in the 1960s.

Unlike Mahathir, who was professionally trained as a medical doctor at the University of Malaya in Singapore, Anwar Ibrahim had a humanities background with a specialization in Islamic studies that made him more in touch with the people, the *ummah*, or the universal brotherhood of Muslims. He became like the hero in one of Chinua Achebe's novels, *A Man of the People*. Or perhaps one of the anti-heroes that one can possibly imagine in *A Hundred Years of Solitude* or Arianna Huffington's delightful *Pigs at the Trough* (2003). However, critics (and ordinary people alike and who are) on the street are divided over what really happened in terms of his sacking. Some say that he was sacked because he was planning to unseat Mahathir. This would have been considered an act of gross ungratefulness in Malaysian politics. Another argument involves a counterfactual suggestion that it was about political revenge by powerful politicians, much more senior in age and experience than Anwar, but who were passed over during Anwar's meteoric rise to power. The official reason for Anwar being sentenced to six years imprisonment was because he had sodomized someone and that any homosexual act is considered a crime in Malaysia. Around the time of Anwar's arrest, a mysterious book was rapidly circulating. It was called, "50 reasons why Anwar should not be prime minister."

In 2003, Prime Minister Mahathir Mohamad made more anti-Semitic remarks. Note that the Malaysian prime minister is the head of government in the way that the US president is the head of government too. Mahathir said that the Jews were behind 9/11, however, he defended his remarks by saying that they were taken out of context and said that he meant no offence by saying that Jews ruled the world. In his speech at the 56-member *Organization of the Islamic Conference* (OIC), Mahathir said, "Jews rule the world by proxy. They get others to fight and die for them" (*CNN*, 2003; *BBC*, 2003; *IHT*, 2003). Mahathir said that Muslims had achieved "nothing" in their 50 years of struggle against Israel citing the fact that Jews had invented powerful ideological arguments like socialism, communism, human rights and democracy. This means that everyone, including Jews, could no longer be persecuted over of equal rights. As a result, Mahathir said Jews, "gained control of the most powerful countries and they, this tiny community, have become a world power." He admitted surprise that over a billion Muslims could be held at bay by only "a few million Jews." Naturally, the speech drew a mixed bag of responses. The OIC members gave him a standing ovation. But the United States, Europe, Israel and Australia regretted his statement. A senior White House official said:

> Prime Minister Mahathir's bluster and polarizing rhetoric are not new. But his most recent hate-filled remarks further cement his legacy of outrageous and misguided public statements. We urge leaders of all faiths to publicly condemn these vile statements (*CNN*, 2003).

The UK's Foreign Office, the equivalent of America's State Department, contacted Malaysia's High Commissioner, Mohammed Dato Abdul Aziz, and "expressed concern" about Prime Minister Mahathir's comments in his speech:

It's unfortunate that Mahathir chose to make these remarks which we regard as unacceptable. It's particularly regrettable that some of his positive and welcome messages, such as negotiation being the right path to peace and the futility of terrorism, have been obscured and overshadowed by racist remarks (CNN, 2003).

Known for his powerful rhetoric, confrontational remarks and provocative leadership, Mahathir has shown himself to be a wily politician who has wrested power for over 22 years. This means that up till he transferred power to his deputy, Abdullah Badawi[9] in October 2003, Mahathir was Asia's second longest-serving prime minister. In the course of those two decades, Mahathir has antagonized many other heads of government including Australia's. Mahathir's comments are often not taken lightly. He is not known to be a man who minces his words. His words were indeed not taken superficially because of his own experience in politics. Because there are no terms limits to Malaysia's form of democratic governance, Mahathir has served continuously as Prime Minister over five US presidential administrations from the time of (the indecisive power of) Jimmy Carter, (the old Californian movie premiers of) Ronald Reagan, (the creative genius and innovative antics of) William Jefferson Clinton, (the "new taxes" that did not come from his lips but from the hands of) George Bush, and (the important consequences of the ineptitude of the bush-whacking) George W. Bush. Mahathir had to tolerate all these different and divergent personalities. If one were to include the time that Mahathir had spent in politics, including the amount of time that he served in the *Dewan* (Malaysian federal parliament), one would have to include three more US presidential administrations: those of Lyndon B. Johnson, Richard M. Nixon and Gerald R. Ford administration. Mahathir is known for his "rationalistic" economic policies. And some wild remarks about foreigners.

As long as the issue of Jews and Israel does not arise, Mahathir is known for making very persuasive arguments. For example, when most democratic-preferring Asian countries were looking toward the United States economy and Western MNCs for economic development, Mahathir told his public to look Eastwards towards Japan (and then later, China but in a limited sense). Mahathir's "kampung economics" or village economics resulted in his personal rejection of the IMF aid package that was offered with several strings attached during the 1997–98 Asian currency crisis. If he had not pegged the Malaysian Ringgit and had followed IMF suggestions, the Malaysian economy would have been in turmoil and started a deep downward spiral towards economic depression. But whether or not Mahathir's "kampung economics" was a result of his wariness of the IMF as being controlled by the US is another matter. Mahathir was not alone. For example, in late April 2004, the acting managing director of the IMF Anne Krueger herself mentioned before a joint IMF-World Bank meeting that the IMF "may have contributed in some instances to insufficient spending on infrastructure, at least in the short run."[10]

"Asia's discomfort with America" can be summed up in terms of what is perceived as the politics of interference by a global hegemonic power. If you don't understand what this means, imagine if any Asian country were to send its soldiers, statesmen, economists, social scientists, teachers, educationists, and diplomats into your cities and told you all what to do in public. Imagine a world in which Asians from Asia, not Asian Americans, were making decisions about the way your country ought to work. Imagine a world in which your human rights records, your labor laws, and your social security system were continuously being analyzed and questioned by non-citizen, non-domiciled foreigners. A world where you had to depend on Asian investments in order to achieve a certain standard of living, to feed your children, to educate them, and to try and create a better world for them. If you can imagine all this and accept it as good and well-meaning advice that may go against your own cultural practices, then you might be able to understand what it feels like to be told what to do by foreigners. Perhaps some Americans wouldn't mind being told what to do as long as the system works.

And as long as the World Series, french fries, Budweiser, Coors, Miller Light, Mass' Bass, the Rose Bowl, and the Superbowl remain untouched. But what if you thought that the system was, by and large, working and you had these Asian leaders in your face anyway? Or Asian military hardware on the tarmac at SFO, Honolulu International, Dulles, JFK, LAX, and Chicago-O'Hare? How would you feel if Asian soldiers raped young American girls like the ones that were raped by American GIs in Okinawa? How would you like it if your teenage daughters and sons were dancing in droves to Asian music you could not understand or if your sons and daughters were wearing Asian clothes (whatever that might be) and mimicking Asian mannerisms (or whatever might be the equivalent in US cultural currency)? If you can imagine this kind of world—whether you accept it or reject it—then you are beginning to understand the politics of American globalization.

THE OTHER WAY ROUND

If in one's heart of hearts one is fearful of Asians or if in your heart of hearts you don't mind them being around as long as they leave your [ethnic] family alone, then you can imagine, in what might be called a bizarre world of opposites, how the politics of interference and the politics of foreign intervention works in Asia: not so much Rudyard Kipling's *White Man's Burden* (1899) but the film by Desmond Nakano called *White Man's Burden* (1995) in which the Black-White world that you might be familiar with is turned upside down and suddenly African Americans are part of the social elite *et cetera*. There are other more compelling reasons to suggest a politics of American globalization in Asia. If we think specifically in the terms of universal human rights, then there are too many lives that have been changed because of America's presence. There are too many reasons to list them all. If we can forget the hatred that the Moro rebels have for American soldiers and American money since the heady days of the Marcos dictatorship while American presidents Nixon, Ford, Carter and Reagan conveniently turned a blind eye.

When we talk about American globalization in Asia we are really referring to a political paradox. This political paradox allows for a minority of people, having bothered to vote consecutive governments in charge while most of the silent majority (might have) made it to limited protests, remained apathetic, or were consumed by their own struggle or commitment to the bottom line, profit margins, monthly quotas, stock options, the Knicks, depression, legal drugs, illegal drugs[11], nicotine patches, Zoloft, weed, Marlboro Lights, Ecstasy, Viagra, Lipitor, Aricpet, or other products of powerful American pharmaceutical corporations like Pfizer Inc. Let us now ask again what this has to do with the politics of American globalization. For the answer we need to turn to an interesting political phenomenon raised in the previous paragraph.

THE POLITICAL PARADOX

…the US is basically a one-party state—the business party with two factions, Democrats and Republicans. Most of the population seems to agree. A very high percentage, sometimes passing 80 per cent believe that the government serves "the few and the special interests," not "the people." In the contested 2000 election, about 75 per cent regarded it as mostly a farce having nothing to do with them, a game played by rich contributors, party bosses, and the public relations industry, which trained candidates to say mostly meaningless things that might pick up some votes. This was BEFORE the actual election, with the accusations of fraud and selection of Bush with a minority of the popular vote.[12]

While many do not agree with the socialist politics of Noam Chomsky, he does make an interesting point about the support that the American people really have for their government. The 2000 presidential election was clearly a result of institutional lethargy backed by a conservative Republican Supreme Court. That is why Bush is in charge today. While Chomsky's influence is a direct result of his work at MIT in linguistics, his politics is not entirely convincing because it does not appear to answer many of the questions that are raised by American liberals. However, he does have a point with regard to representative politics and reality. It seems that the American people's lethargic attitude towards the government has resulted in the government doing whatever it thinks best anyway. And this affects the nature of its global presence everywhere in the world.

America cannot help but interfere in politics overseas and in this case in the politics of Asia. It appears that the kind of liberalism exported by American government is the kind that needs to engage with the people and their communities. It is the kind of ideological politics that is universalistic in nature, where the standards of value and morality are clearly defined by those in power. It is particularly distressing for Asian countries that have their own traditions, rights and wrongs, moral belief systems and customary practices. American government overseas is often, though not always, insensitive to the practices of foreigners in their own land. It is also about punishment. It is about punishing the guilty until they are converted. It could be a more subtle form of Spanish Inquisition with the light touch of a Mel Brook's musical from *History of the World Part II* (the one with the "Jews in Space" trailer). American government is often unable to accept the fact that there are people whose ideas and value systems are different from that of the Western democratic tradition. This is ironic. In fact it is more than ironic. It is a political paradox.

The first part of the paradox is the fact that American government overseas is aggressive to the point of bullying smaller nations. The US has conducted wide scale offensive, defensive, retrograde and covert military operations throughout Asia and the Pacific. The USAF is capable of attacking any point in the world, let alone Asia, at the behest of the Commander-in-Chief. The US Army has more continuous combat military experience in Southeast Asia than any other land or amphibious army in the world and any other time in history. The US Navy has virtual control of all international waters (let alone Asia and the Pacific) and continues to move freely to dominate and control without hindrance or challenge since 1989. America dominates most of the world without necessarily controlling all of it all of the time. The American government is therefore for all intents and purposes hegemonic and supreme. Such military dominance cannot find a conventional adversary. This is why the terrorists are so successful. Conventional warfare is unable to fight terrorism. Nuclear warfare is way out of the ball park. Such military dominance also finds that many smaller nations react with fear, hatred and suspicion. Many nations with large Islamic populations, such as Malaysia, Indonesia, and China, pose potential problems for anti-terrorist organizations. Such military power is often reciprocated with political platitudes and rhetoric that arise out of feelings of fear for the safety of their own country. No country in Asia wants to be branded another Iraq because no one can stop the invading power of an American military attack. And as America has done it illegally before, it can do it again.

The second part of the paradox is that Americans have elected successive American presidents who all share some common ground when it comes to foreign policy. In effect, the old adage about democratic presidents being doves and republicans being more hawkish is completely untrue. There is very little evidence to support ideological differences between democratic or republic presidents. This leaves us with over 200 years of data that, I hypothesize, will prove beyond reasonable doubt that US presidents are generally hawkish on foreign policy and doves on domestic policy. This might be why they score well on foreign policy initiatives that are relatively more removed from the average Joe Smith and Jane Doe than are domestic ones which directly affect these citizens. So far we have a situation where America dominates militarily through fear of inflicting political violence. We also have a situation where political party ideologies are generally irrelevant to the formulation of foreign policy and where US presidents are fairly consistent in pursuing their foreign policies regardless of party differences.

Now we come to the interesting part of the paradox. *The People.* They are the ones who have elected these presidents and these governments which have generated these politics of fear and control: it seems to be common knowledge to everyone but Americans, America defends the liberty, life and the pursuit of happiness of 300 million Americans even if it means impoverishing the rest of the world. The American people however, often do not support the kinds of policies that have emitted from successive US presidencies. The American people are often against the kinds of atrocities committed by Americans on locals overseas and committed on Americans by locals overseas. In fact, voter turnout for most American elections is low. This means that most Americans, in my estimate, a majority of about 35–43 per cent do not support what the American government is doing overseas. Naturally, right-wing Americans might tend to believe that whatever the government does is best for the country. But they are in a minority of about 8–13 per cent. On the other hand are Americans who actively oppose American intervention wherever and however it might be executed throughout the world. Therefore the political paradox arises because most Americans do not support most of the different kinds of US government policies overseas and in Asia because most Americans do not go to the polls. There are, of course, various reasons for this though a discussion of this issue is not the scope of this book. The political paradox arises because most Americans do not support the kinds of policies that are implemented overseas but have to pay the price for being American. Ordinary American citizens continue to be targets for kidnappers, terrorists, blackmailers, and fundamentalists because of the kinds of foreign policies that are promulgated by American governments supported by a minority of Americans. Do you really think that all those Hispanic-Americans, African-Americans, Chinese-Americans, Korean-Americans, Irish-Americans, Italian-Americans, German-Americans, Russian-Americans, Jewish-Americans, Polish-Americans, Native-Americans and Armenian-Americans you know or see every other day actually voted for all those congressional talking heads on CNN and locally syndicated television news broadcasts? I think not. The political paradox works like this. Most Americans since 1945 have not voted for the kinds of politicians and the kind of policies that have come out of American government but still pay the price for being American anyway. This is why Americans seem to believe in one thing but their government appears to do something else.

American foreign policy is shaped and influenced by think tanks such as RAND, independent social scientists, military advisors, the American media and covert operations by the CIA. This does not mean that there has always been a coordinated and singular mission for all Asian countries and the rest of the world. The US system of government and politics is built on checks and balances of power and interlocking institutional validation. The Framers of the Constitution had intended this system of checks and balances to prevent the kind of absolutist abuse that was featured in King George's England. They wanted to circumvent the authority of dynasties with monarchs who had ruled by fear and complete subjectivity. This is why American political institutions tend to compete for influence over the public domain rather than complement each other. In competing for power, there is a clear and added advantage of showing independently how objective and productive one can be with limited resources in a given time frame. This is very unlike the British system where senior administrative servants with years of cumulative experience slowly percolate ideas downwards from their political masters and upwards towards them; they do not compete for influence over one another. Rather, the British system involves behind the scenes discussions and agreements among the top civil service heads who often have the same Oxonian educational background and whose families have met at the same clubs for generations. The American system, in trying to be meritorious, has created disorder in a world of order. And the system desires creativity out of competition while the British system tries to instill discipline and creativity through what that famous English philosopher Edmund Burke called the *wisdom of the ages*. In an attempt to avoid stupidity for all time, the wisdom of the ages involves incremental and gradual decision-making that is based on careful and logical deduction from as many possible views sharing their knowledge at the same time. The American system involves independently creating different subsystems that have to discover their own means of achieving the mission. This is why American policy in Asia and the rest of the world sometimes appears inchoate or contradictory. This is why there appear to be different systems of management handling different situations rather than a singular whole. The problem for American was that after 9/11, this old method of institutional independence was seen to be theoretically weak, especially in terms of intelligence-gathering and analysis. Although in theory such a system ought to be superior, and produce different and creative points of view, when push came to shove, the American method did not produce the kinds of results that were intended. Hence, the creation of the DHS and its various integrative bureaus that connect intelligence, security, political, legal, research, and civil society groups. Critics of the new political institutionalism and supporters of the philosophy of the Founding Fathers (who may not necessarily be the same bedfellows) believe that it is the executive malfeasance that has led to the inability to react rather than the institutions themselves. For example, through the congressional deliberations and meetings on the matter of 9/11, many feel that sufficient intelligence and early warning was presented to Bush for him to act but he failed. If you listened to the testimony of Condoleezza Rice, Bush's national security advisor, you may leave wondering what exactly was done and why was it done in such a manner. Watching CSPAN often leaves American viewers with more questions than receiving clear answers. Perhaps it was the nature of the questions being asked by the congressional committee members. But in the case of Rice, the questioning did not produce clear answers to the what, why or where about the issue of 9/11 and the president's inability to respond.

The President defended his position by stating that the intelligence reports were not specific enough to act on. Perhaps for the president, the secret reports were so vague and broadly worded that the message sounded like a passage from Nostradamus predicting the present from over 600 years ago. They could have meant anything. The writing on the wall was so vague that America (and Americans) could have been attacked from any single direction and at any point in time and no military or paramilitary force would have been able to have come prepared. No, the problem of political institutionalism or executive disorder and the creation of new departments are not of particular concern here. Rather, what seems to be the key is for Americans to realize that their overseas identities are being determined by a minority of people who bother to vote and participate fully in the American political process. Americans are also politically apathetic and while one set of demonstrations are raised over one issue; the matter soon fizzles out of social memory except for social scientists to analyze years later.

Another key to resolving American problems in Asia and the rest of the world is in changing the kinds of things that the DOD and the State

Department are doing overseas. It is about resisting the kind of impression that the state is giving about the individual. If this attitudinal change is not effected soon, there will be more innocent American blood spilled in Asia and the Middle East because of the political egos of a few men in power. And the kinds of punishment that they sought to distribute that "multiplies by nature insofar as by punishing itself, it unveils the truth" (Foucault [1965] 1988: 30).

OIL

I really can't understand why some people earnestly believe that the US is interested in the Middle East for altruistic reasons such as human rights, non-oil trade, or Mediterranean tourism. American troops were not trying to keep the peace in the Sudan, the Republic of Congo, East Timor, or Kashmir. The reason is because these places do not produce sufficient quantities of oil for export to make them sufficiently attractive and worth the trouble of establishing diplomatic relations, economic, social and cultural exchanges, and military assistance. Inasmuch as the US is interested in preventing war from breaking out between China and Taiwan because of the gross amount of investments that it has in both countries, there is a similar reason why the Middle East Peace process appears to be a never-ending story. American foreign policy is always dictated by its national interest. And the national interest of the MNCs and Military Industrial Complex that control much of American life is "oil." We should recall at this point that the *Ship of Fools* metaphor suggests that the only reason why the US is so interested in the Middle East is oil. Oil sustains American neoliberal globalization. Let's not pretend it is because of democracy, to protect Israel, to ensure the safety of Americans, or to promote free-trade or world peace. These are only secondary objectives. The US State Department knows full well that without oil, the entire US economy will collapse, and the American Dream will implode. This is a fact. The two Gulf Wars were ostensibly about removing dictators like Saddam Hussein. The Shah of Iran and his troops committed similar atrocities when they were in power (similar to the Russians before *glasnost* and *perestroika*; and now that the "Russian mafia" seems to be in charge of many areas, rather than state or the KGB). The real reasons are the oil fields beneath Basra in Southern Iraq. There are three types of crude oil that Saddam and his henchmen hid under the desert. Some analysts say it is between 5–7 per cent of total world production per day. Others say the figures are much higher, perhaps high enough to solve American oil problems for the next quarter of a century. There are also sufficient oil and natural gas reserves in that region to make anyone want to invest in a stable and democratic-loving Iraq. For example, in his story that begins with the death of a *Ship of the Desert*, John Cassidy argues that:

> With the exception of its Southern neighbor, Saudi Arabia, Iraq has more oil buried underneath it than any country in the world: a hundred and twelve billion barrels in confirmed reserves ... more than 600 wells, which produce three streams of crude: Basra Regular, Basra Medium, and Basra Heavy. The oil is trapped at such high pressure that when a well is drilled it gushes out by itself, so there is no need for the "nodding donkeys."[13]

An American national interest in the Middle East or in the Straits of Malacca or in China and Taiwan is really about protecting America and Americans. These and many other places serve as important and strategic locations for the ensuring the smooth flow of American goods and services. Let's call a spade a spade. The main reason why America seems to be here, there and everywhere is because it is safeguarding the American way of life, perhaps the American Dream, and certainly not merely for human rights assistance or aid for natural disasters. Is there anything wrong with possessing such overt and Machiavellian stratagems? Not if America remains a benign hegemon that truly believes in free trade and not the new protectionism disguised as free trade.

THE FIGHT AGAINST TERROR

There are compelling reasons to believe that there are significant terrorist networks in the Southeast Asian region, South Asia and the Middle East where the hatred of Americans and Jews appears to be most severe. However, the US Department of State in February 2004 also believes that there are strong indications of a fundamentalist Islamic presence in China. While Chinese Muslims are a minority, the numbers are not insignificant. It is not inconceivable to consider that out of the 20 million Chinese Muslims, a handful of fundamentalists may be easily linked to acts of terror and terrorist training. Twenty million is about the population of Malaysia which in turn about the size of New Mexico. For example, even as far removed as China was from the Middle East, "Islam advocates peace and more than 20 million Chinese Muslims love peace and oppose war" voiced by the Islamic Association of China (*Times of India*, Saturday March 22, 2003). Clearly this was not only a kind of resistance against the wrongful American invasion that went against UN resolutions and the UN Security Council, the resistance also reflected a move by the Islamic Association of China to establish a political connection with other Muslims across the globe who shared the same sentiment. Not surprisingly, the US State Department also fears that from among the 20 million members that the Islamic Association of China claims to represent are a minority group of right wing fundamentalists who are likely to support aggressive action against the US and its Allies. Otherwise why would they have to identify themselves as Chinese Muslims and not just Chinese? Otherwise, why did this association not vehemently oppose the 9/11 terrorist attacks in New York?

China has undergone rapid changes in state and society since deMaoization and the implementation of the four modernizations. The end of the Cold War left China without its sometime ally the USSR. The end of the Cold War weakened international socialism. Chinese communism has succeeded because it is socialism with Chinese characteristics. The adaptive Chinese strategy of having pockets of capitalist development was not a clever reconstitution of its political ideology to suit global capitalist pressures, but a realist reaction from having no choice at all. China was thus forced to recognize that the United States was now the clear ideological victor. China, as the world's most populous nation and the ideological adversary of the United States would now be expected to make concessions at some level. As a result, China has indeed become a little less inscrutable and has made moves to impress upon the United States, that it is more of a friend, and at the worst, not an enemy. As a result, the United States has rewarded China several times with Most Favored Nation status and with millions of dollars, worth of investments. There are many Chinese of the younger generation in the larger cities, such as Shanghai, Guangzhou, Nanjing, and Jinan, who have begun to mimic American popular culture. American globalization in China is therefore looming on the horizon as a kind of counter-culture that the state authorities are keeping an eye on. At the same time, the strength and value of the greenback as an international currency benchmark in the post-Bretton Woods era has grown from strength to strength in China since the end of Mao. Chinese authorities are beginning to realize the value of American English and an American university education. Many Chinese see the value of the green card as a ticket out of poverty and there are many Chinese who would love to marry American to enhance their social and occupational mobility. Despite the severe setbacks of 9/11 and the anxieties with global terrorism, America is still attractive to foreign migrants. This is part of the power of American global politics. The day that America no longer is attractive enough for people to want to migrate to is the day that marks the end of the American era. This happened to Italy in the 15th century. It began in France and the United Kingdom in the 20th century. It might happen to American in the 21st century. There are 666 cities in China and one can imagine if each of those cities with millions of people are now, as you read this book, being targeted for some kind of international fast food chain in the classic style of McDonalds Corporation.

Furthermore, perhaps as a testament of good faith in the 9/11 era, the Chinese authorities have cracked down on Chinese Muslims. Whether or not this was politically motivated is not the question; it was definitely politically motivated. The question remains as to what kind of dirty politics were involved in motivating the police attacks and the state intervention. The issue of Islamic terrorism takes on different avenues of interpretation. Often, innocent Muslims might be victimized and the point remains about the *quid pro quo* of it all:

> ... a group of young men kneel together for evening prayers ... from the Koran ... The men, all Turkic-speaking Uighurs, cannot worship at any of Shanghai's half-dozen mosques, as they would risk being spotted by undercover police informants searching for suspected Islamic militants (*UPI*, 2002).

Only the men are allowed to pray. In modern urban cultures across cities in the Czech Republic, Canada, Mexico, Latin America, in most Western European cities, and in cities that stretch across the United States from Orange County to the New Jersey turnpike, such an act is considered sexist and unfair. It reminds us of the time when American white persons and American black persons were separately bussed in the heady 1960s. In the much earlier African-American rights, legislation in Justice Brown's decision in *Plessy v. Ferguson* (1896), and the segregationist issue in *Brown v. Board of Education of Topeka* (1954), or in the abortion rights case, *Roe v. Wade* (1973).[14] But the terrorist attacks tended to cloud such segregationist issues which would be left by the wayside if not raised at a point where an intelligent reader is looking out for matters pertaining to terrorism. In this case it is a different kind of terror, the kind of terror that reveals the placidity of Don Quixote's death "which at the last moment has rejoined reason and truth. Suddenly the Knight's madness has grown conscious of itself and in his own eyes trickles out in nonsense" (Foucault [1965] 1988: 31).

Nevertheless, returning to the matter of the politics of terrorism in China and the role of the United States in trying to abate the matter, we see that the US is indeed considered an important nation for China. And the Chinese authorities have gone out of their way to display resolve. But the question remains as to what kind of dirty politics is being played out and whether the state authorities can see the forest of innocence for the trees of the guilty in the case of the Uighur, pronounced /wee:gur/:

> ... Following the Sep. 11 attacks in the United States, China launched a major offensive in Xinjiang, sending soldiers into the region's cities and towns to close mosques and arrest scores of suspected separatists ... "Uighurs ... have been the main target—mosques have been closed down, Islamic clergy have been detained, and Uighur books have been burnt ... Thousands of young Muslim men fled to other regions ... such as Tajikistan and Kyrgyzstan, slipping out through China's porous mountain borders. In January, China published a lengthy report alleging the East Turkestan Islamic Movement [ETIM] ... had received money, weapons and training from Osama bin Laden's al-Qaeda ... Jailing community leaders and intellectuals on trumped up 'state secrets' charges and repressing Uighur culture has nothing to do with combating 'terrorism,'" Amnesty said. "It is a systematic denial of basic human rights ... the US State Department said it had added the ETIM to its list of terrorist organizations and agreed to freeze the group's assets (*UPI*, 2002).

Here again we see the power of American liberalism in the argument being made by Amnesty International. While the Chinese state is eager to display a strong anti-terrorist stand, the way it has gone about making such a stand has made it appear rather duplicitous. Amnesty International saw the human rights violations coming, as it is indeed a very thin and perhaps even vague line between what these militant Chinese groups do and what they are perceived to be doing. China takes its sovereignty very seriously, as do all other states in the globalized world. Subversion is a very serious threat to state security and it becomes very difficult for any state authority to prove the extent and depth of subversion since the normal laws of evidence do not seem to apply to those hoping to overthrow legitimate governments. However, it wasn't just the Chinese authorities who were working on the anti-terrorist aspect. Apart from the Chinese intelligence reports and police reports about these activities, the Americans had their hand in this pie too:

> Less than a week later, the US embassy in Beijing said for the first time it had evidence that the group was planning terrorist attacks on foreign embassies and interests in Bishkek, the capital of Kyrgyzstan. "We have evidence that the ETIM have been planning attacks against US interests abroad," a US embassy spokeswoman told UPI, refusing to comment on the apparent shift in policy. China's foreign ministry in Beijing refused a request to answer specific questions from *UPI* about the US allegations against the ETIM, but instead issued a brief statement welcoming last week's decision (*UPI*, 2002).

The changes and twists and turns in American policy indicate that the top people don't always know what they are doing and hence the answer, like China, is to hide behind the iron curtain of bureaucratic secrecy. This means that the information will eventually be leaked in some other way. And so the next step for the state is naturally, to offer even more rhetoric about how two ideological enemies are actually capable of cooperation, one out of fear, the other out of blood lust:

> China is prepared to make joint efforts, enhance mutual consultations and deepen bilateral co-operation with the US in the fight against terrorism," the foreign ministry statement said ... the U.S. State Department's listing of the ETIM as a terrorist group means Xinjiang's struggling liberation movement is now fighting a war on two fronts: one at home, against the Chinese government's repressive policies, and the other overseas, to win back the support of the international community. "We are completely shocked by the US allegations," he said ... To date, neither government has provided verifiable proof of a link between bin Laden and the separatists in Xinjiang, though US-led forces in Afghanistan

114

did capture Chinese Muslims fighting with the Taliban ...
Hasan Mahsum, the ETIM's leader and China's most-wanted
fugitive, denied allegations that his group had ties with bin
Laden and al-Qaeda during an interview with Radio Free Asia
in January. But the existence of such a group has apparently
been enough to convince the Bush administration, and Uighurs
say they fear the US move will further sanction China to crush
any remaining peaceful dissent. "We are fighting for our
freedom, not for the overthrow of Western governments," said
Tusin. "Our anger is not directed against the US and the
international community, but against the Chinese government
(*United Press International*, 2002).

It should also be noted that with the loss of over US$8 billion worth
of oil reserves when the Shah of Iran fell to Islamic "revolutionaries" in
1979, while the media naively overplayed the problem of the American
hostages, the US decided that an alternative pipeline to the Russian
oilfields would be the most viable alternative. Therefore the war in
Afghanistan is also about oil and not merely about the search for Osama
and his terrorist henchmen. Perhaps the Uighurs were too politically
embattled or naïve to understand the connection with oil. The Chinese
authorities are not as duplicitous as their war on their "own citizens"
appears. After all, since the ETIM has openly declared a war against the
Chinese government it has given the state no other choice but to do
whatever it can, however it can, to prevent the overthrow. No other
secessionist movement in China has worked for so many dynasties. It
seems unlikely that the ETIM, even with Amnesty's soft power help, is
likely to succeed. Amnesty officials are themselves considered suspects
within the intelligence game because they are clearly not asking the rebels/
freedom fighters to lay down their weapons. Despite the expression of
American diplomatic concerns, the ETIM rebels appear to have done
what Osama had done many years before when, ironically, he was trained
by Americans themselves. They have gone underground. Going
underground in a globalized world means that they can surface almost
anywhere in the world and at any time through almost any one. The
amount of resources that would be needed by China and America to
stage a specific war would erode the value of economic investments in
China from American sources. It would be a wasted effort. This is because
Osama was trained by the Americans, unlike Saddam who was discovered
soon after the invasion of Iraq in 2003. It was after all, just another war

115

for the Bushes. But whether it was really a just war is currently being dramatized by the American and international media networks.

Writers like Lowell Dittmer may claim that the biggest problem of globalization in East Asia is the problem of regionalism and while internationally influential scholars like Katzenstein might tend to agree with the importance of the regionalization thesis, the question for America in particular remains to be one of commitment and cultural sensitivity to the local labor and social practices. Just treat people like you would in the States. That is how the US government and its employees overseas and in Asia ought to treat other human beings. However, this is increasingly problematic because in the post-9/11 era, everyone, even Americans come under suspicion for possible terrorism. While Lowell may have argued in the journal, *World Politics*, and elsewhere, that terrorism has not made a big impression (Lowell, *World Politics*, 55, 1, 38–65) he is indeed totally wrong. This is because East Asia and the rest of Asia have been terrorized by different schemes and invasions over the millennia. Does merely a more modern definition of illiberal terrorist acts make former Portuguese, Dutch, French or British colonialism any less a form of institutional terror just because these are now established democracies with democratic practices built deep within their polities and political culture? Perhaps not in this era of late modernity.

AMERICA AND THE ASIAN CURRENCY CRISIS

Most Asians would not link America to the 1997 Asian currency crisis except for what is perceived as a controlling role that America has over the IMF. But there was much more involved. For almost a decade before the currency crisis (sometimes called the financial crisis) the Thai economy was experiencing high single-digit economic growth. Unethical and greedy currency speculators, noticing the structural weaknesses in the Thai system, began making deep speculative attacks on the Thai Bhat that forced the military-led government to float the currency on the international market. This further exposed the softness of the currency. The speculative attacks reaped huge profits for the American based speculators who left the Thai government vulnerable except for a quickly put together IMF aid package that helped stem the currency's free fall in value. The crisis in Thailand revealed that the construction industry had been financially overextended and currency speculators,

116

attempts to make a fast buck resulted in catalyzing what could have been contained at the national level. However, the level of corruption prevented an earlier diagnosis of the problem that could have thwarted the problem. The crisis in Thailand reached such dramatic proportions because of the speculative attacks from the outside and because of the unbridled greed and corruption on the inside. Speculative attacks were not limited to the Baht but were also aimed at the Hong Kong Dollar, the Indonesian Rupiah, the Malaysian Ringgit and even the Philippine Peso. While the South Korean Won and the Singapore Dollar remained relatively unscathed because of their sound economic fundamentals when compared to the other Asian countries, the currency crisis spearheaded by the currency speculators also put strong pressure on these two countries, economies.

Also, the close connection between Asian currencies and the US dollar meant that any changes in financial movements in any of the Asian stock exchanges would bear an impact on other bourses in the region. The crisis exposed the weak structural defects in the local banking and financial structures that were themselves caught in a heated race to develop faster growth with limited financial liberalization. More importantly, the financial crisis caused panic and shrunk foreign investments costing billions of US dollars which undermined investor confidence in the region. The result was obvious. Southeast Asian share markets went into a recessionary spiral that lasted for almost six months as hundreds of thousands lost their jobs. The economic disparities between the richest rich and the poorest poor also deteriorated in Indonesia, South Korea, Malaysia, Thailand, and the Philippines reflecting the kinds of income differentials experienced by so-called "First World" nations under a recessionary climate. However, the remarkable economic growth of the fastest growing region in the world—East Asia and Southeast Asia—meant that these countries had achieved in 10 years what it took the West decades to achieve. The financial crisis had severe political implications. Thai Prime Minister Chavalit Yongchaiyudh was forced to step down and dissolve his cabinet because of his inability, *inter alia*, to steer the country out of the recession in sufficient time. Most evidently, the crisis saw the end of the authoritarian rule of Indonesian president Suharto who had governed since the mid-1960s and who had personally overseen the rapid modernization of Indonesia, especially Java, the annexation of Timor in 1975, and the forced migration of ethnic communities across its 17,000 islands.

117

Timor, for example, was a former colony of the mercantilist colonial Power of the Portuguese and made a self-declaration of independence from Lisbon on November 28, 1975. The Portuguese were unable to do a thing. However, Suharto's troops—some of whom were allegedly involved in the "false" declaration of independence—illegally invaded and occupied the island. The UN, the United States, and Portugal were unable to do a thing about the atrocities that were to develop. Over the next two years from 1976 to 1996, over a quarter of a million individuals were tortured and killed by Indonesian armed forces. On August 30, 1999, UN-sponsored referendum unseated the dictatorial stranglehold of Suharto as the people who were still alive voted unanimously for independence, and this time from the Indonesian colonizers. However, Indonesia, under successor-elected presidents since Suharto fell from power in 1998, continued a pogram of violence to prevent political independence from Jakarta. Despite the atrocities committed by the soldiers of recent presidential contender Indonesian General Wiranto, the former Indonesian colony of "East Timor" was finally recognized worldwide as an independent and sovereign state on May 20, 2002.

It is interesting how the United States showed an exceptional level of disinterest in this situation. Perhaps the main reason is that Timor does not pose a direct threat to the US, nor perhaps ever will. Neither does it interest the US in economic terms. Or perhaps it is the State Department's tacit recognition of what might have been considered to fall under the Portuguese sphere of influence up till 1975. Wiranto had been commander of the troops in the final days of Suharto's regime and also served under B. J. Habibie and Abdulrahman Wahid.[15] As the former military chief of Indonesia, Wiranto has said that he would not accept personal or legal responsibility for any crimes committed by his troops in East Timor. General Wiranto,

> ... was proud of his record, and would not resign his cabinet post because that might be interpreted as an admission of guilt. *Straits Times* said, however, that the general had left open the possibility that he might resign if the Indonesian president demanded it on his return from overseas. Last week President Abdurrahman Wahid called for Wiranto's resignation after a government report blaming him for atrocities in East Timor. Indonesia's human rights commission recommended that he and five other senior generals be prosecuted for their involvement in the violence that followed last year's

referendum on independence, in which at least 250 people died
... The president has said that he intends to pardon Wiranto
even if he is found guilty of human rights abuses ... The
president also confirmed that he had no intention of seeing
the general imprisoned. He said, "I will pardon him. For the
past several years we have been good friends, despite whatever
he has done in the past" (*BBC News*, January 8, 2000).

Wiranto won Golkar's initial nomination for president easily even
though he was:

indicted for crimes against humanity in neighboring East
Timor ... Wiranto's victory is expected to cause concern in
the United States and other Western nations. *Washington Post*
reported in January that the US has put Wiranto and others
accused of crimes in East Timor on a visa watch list that could
bar them from entering the country. United Nations-funded
prosecutors in East Timor indicted Wiranto last year over the
Indonesian army-backed militia bloodshed during the
territory's bloody breakaway from Jakarta in 1999 ... "Monas
Square did not become a second Tiananmen Square ... and for
that the people have to thank him." The general's last public
office was as security minister under [former] president
Abdurrahman Wahid ... [who] sacked him in 2000 in what was
seen at the time as a successful attempt to reduce the influence
of the powerful military over the government. Wiranto
launched a high-profile campaign for the Golkar nomination,
flying to numerous speaking engagements across the
archipelago and sometimes crooning to the crowds. He has
issued a CD of his love songs. With 91.8 million votes counted
so far from the general election, Golkar is set to replace
President Megawati Sukarnoputri's Indonesian Democratic
Party of Struggle (PDI-P) as the largest parliamentary party.[16]

The impact of Wiranto on the US was one that most Americans
probably did not even realize. It was something like an ordinary citizen—
paying taxes, sending the kids through college, and saving for a rainy
day—who was hit by an influenza bug and recovered from it without
even knowing that he or she was sick in the first place. Following the
other Asian bourses like the Hang Seng, the SES, the KLSE, and the
Nikkei, the Dow (in America) plunged about 8 per cent while the NYSE
was forced to suspend trading based on biased consumer sentiment and

fears that the Asian economies might go into remission and collapse. This would mean that the over-extended banking loans by Japanese investors would cause the collapse of many companies in Japan that were trying to ride the East Asian and Southeast Asian economic wave to get out of their own economic doldrums. It was as if the wave collapsed right under them before even reaching its peak.

During the Asian currency crisis, Alan Greenspan argued for the important role that the IMF had to play in the face of stiff resistance from members of Congress from Republicans and Democrats alike. Greenspan said that "the IMF's role is to create 'platform' for the reconstruction of market confidence in Asia."[17] Despite the work of pro-IMF supporters such as Greenspan, IMF apologists, and academic neoliberals who preferred to defend the IMF's so-called "market liberalization" policies, the failure of the IMF as an international organization speaks for itself.[18] The IMF almost, as Stiglitz argued, brought the world economy into a global meltdown. The IMF clearly displayed its inadequacy as an international organization or as any kind of lender of the last resort. A compelling loss of the IMF's reputation was a result of its own agenda to impose its own brand of liberal economic "theory". The IMF may have been designed to play a specific role but when crunch came to crisis, it could not deliver sound financial advice. For example, if Malaysia had accepted the IMF's financial aid package and illogical financial changes to its national financial system, it would have been a disaster for Malaysia and many other Southeast Asian countries. The paper by Makin, for example, suggested that "the recent financial crises of East Asia and other emerging financial economies have exposed major structural weaknesses in their banking sectors and financial systems, which have acted as the major conduits of foreign savings" (Makin, 1999: 678). He goes on to suggest with naiveté that there is a need for such countries to follow rigorous international banking standards. If this had indeed been the case, the IMF's 'aid package' and 'political agenda' would have worsened the Asian financial crisis and made the recovery process last even longer. Doubts about the validity of the IMF in Asia also fueled anti-American sentiment to a certain extent since the IMF is seen to be largely controlled by the US (Scalapino, 1999, 1). A more convincing argument was made about the crisis by Henry Laurence, in his paper on "Financial System Reform and the Currency Crisis in East Asia" (1999).[19] One of his main conclusions, given the time that the paper was published, is understandable and makes sense.

The ongoing experience of Japan illustrates the political difficulties of reforming a financial system. Finance, more than any other sector, is liable to be closely interwoven with political control and therefore may be the hardest sector of all to liberalize. An absence of external pressures—for example, as can be inflicted either by speculative currency attack or the IMF—has meant that both Japan and China have been slower to undertake real reform than they should have been (Laurence, 1999: 371).

What domestic bank in the West does not have structural problems? It is clear that in the Asian case, financial speculators like George Soros manipulated the weaknesses in the system to their advantage without considering the ethical impact on the entire economy. Rather than solve the problems as Makin and others in the minority have suggested, it would have made the recovery from the financial crisis a much longer and more difficult process. During the Clinton administration, US "bargain hunters" who were "purchasing Asian enterprises fed sentiments hostile to Washington" (Scalapino, 1999:2).[20] Do we really have to invoke Joseph Stiglitz's analysis of the Asian financial crisis to explain the level of idealism and ignorance in Makin's defence of the IMF? No matter how sound the financial structure might be, as often is the case, all it takes is for one person to demolish the entire structure.

Take the case of the oldest merchant bank in the United Kingdom. In 1995, the unethical and deceitful activities of a relatively unknown trader named Nicholas Leeson led to the demise of a world-renown bank. Leeson was a 25-year old Londoner with no real trading experience in Asia. He worked in Singapore at (what is known as an unseated company called) Baring Futures (Singapore) Pte Ltd. According to the *Final Report of the Bank of England* on this matter, the collapse of the oldest British merchant bank was a result of unauthorized work performed by Leeson in Singapore. Like other rogue traders, Leeson covered up his massive debts by creating the impression of confidence through false accounts, in a way that was similar to "the politics of the unethical" that led to the filing for Chapter 11 in the Enron case. Leeson also took advantage of an organizational restructuring of the parent company with the establishment of the Baring Investment Group. The reason for the collapse of the oldest British merchant bank was a simple one: the absence of supervision.

The bank should not have allowed Leeson to manage the whole operation unsupervised. Leeson was both the chief trader and head of settlements. It is the story of financial risk gone awry. The case shows a special kind of risk that speculators are willing to take regardless of the possibility of failure and the impact of such failure on the larger economy. Barings Bank had a very "sound" system that had worked for centuries. Barings Bank, formerly known as Baring Brothers and Company, was founded in 1762 during the time of the philosophical Enlightenment in England. The bank collapsed on February 26, 1995. This is represented in "the false punishment of a false solution, but by its own virtue it brings to light the real problems which can then be truly resolved. It conceals beneath error the secret enterprise of truth" (Foucault [1965] 1988: 32).

The next section looks at the enterprising relations between America and some Asian countries. While all Asian countries deserve attention in this globalized world, these countries in particular seem to be of political and economic importance to the US: China, Japan, Malaysia, and Thailand.

CHINA AND US

There is much melodrama, tragedy, and mimicry in Chinese movies. Some such examples may be seen in the work of Chinese movie directors Zhang Yimou and John Woo. Yet their influence in action and drama packed films from Hollywood have significantly changed the ways in which action movies are now produced and directed. This is indeed a far cry from the time of Bruce Lee. He was the most impressive and influential martial arts exponent of his era. He continues to remain a legend not only in Asia but across the world. Even people in Middle America have at least heard of the legend of Bruce Lee. But the diffident Lee (also known in Cantonese as *Lee Yuen Kam*) could not even make a small impact on Hollywood because of its racism against Chinese. All he could secure for his prowess was a minor, supporting, and voiceless role as the henchman to the Green Hornet. He was passed over for the role of Kwai Chang Caine in *Kung Fu*, ultimately played by the American actor David Caradine. In an ironic twist of fate, Bruce Lee's own son, Brandon Lee, died in a freak accident while on the set of *The Crow* in 1993.

Because China has about the same geographical land size as the contiguous United States, it produces the potential for a similar if not greater amount of current and potential natural resources as Vaclav Smil argues in "China's Energy and Resource Uses: Continuity and Change" (1998: 935).[21] China emits more greenhouse gases than the Russian

122

Federation or the United States (Pryor, 1998: 949), making it the world's largest polluter. Of course, the Chinese government's position is not surprising, and according to Pryor, it blames the rich countries "for the rise in greenhouse gases both for current emissions, and in a cumulative sense, and hence it concludes that the developing countries need not do anything to limit their emissions until they reach the developed world's level of per capita emissions as well as its historical cumulative emissions" (Pryor, 1998: 949).

China remained relatively unscathed during the 1997–98 currency crisis because it lagged behind the Tiger Economies in the capitalist rat-race for wealth. This had two main implications. Firstly, Chinese leaders could sit back and observe how the other Asian countries and the IMF scrambled to resolve the problems created by George Soros and other currency speculators, and secondly, it created a context in which investors, now wary of the Tiger Economies, were willing to look elsewhere in Asia where, for example, land and labor costs were so minimal it would be inconceivable not to think about investing in China.

But China has political problems and foreigners are not always aware of the economic and cultural norms that govern Chinese business practices there as seen in the Singapore case in Suzhou.[22] The transfer of software and economic modeling based on the Singapore experience was a US$13 billion bet that remains unpublished for public inspection. Despite the lessons from this debacle, Singapore continues to be the sixth major investor in the Chinese mainland's city of Liaoning with over US$818 million invested (*Straits Times*, April 21, 2004). And the US continues to be the single largest investor in China.

The most interesting about China is that it has been pursuing a very interesting course of propping up its foreign currency reserves by bulk-purchasing long-term US government bonds. After Japan, China is the second largest purchaser of US Treasury bonds, which has become a major reason for the inflating US deficit. Some financial analysts argue that a sudden stoppage of Chinese bond-buying would force US interest rates upwards, although Alan Greenspan, the Chairman of the Federal Reserve has not verbalized this as yet. Greenspan is known for his very careful selection of words when speaking in his capacity as the world's most powerful and longest-serving central banker.

The Chinese are making a lot of sense by buying into stronger currencies through bond issues in Europe, Asia, and the US with a threefold intention. Firstly, it gives the Chinese Renminbi an external form of validation since it is currently not convertible in the ordinary sense of the word. Such validation results in strengthening the potential power of the Renminbi or Yuan and increases investor confidence that its currency is potentially worth "that much" or "that little" in terms of its present exchange rate of about 8.28 *Yuan* to the *US dollar*. The second advantage of the Chinese bond-buying spree is that it prepares the currency for a strong beginning when officials finally decide that it can be floated internationally. However, it is unlikely that the State Administration of Foreign Exchange will press for floating it internationally in the near future since China continues to benefit from pegging the *Yuan* at its current rate which gives it complete control over its future rather than being left to the global pressures of currency movements in, for example, a given basket of currencies. The third advantage of the Chinese strategy is that China now has massive forex reserves of the greenback totaling close to US$450 billion in the second quarter of 2004. This means that American taxpayers will continue to bear the risk of being overextended to Chinese purchases and overexposed to the possibility of China's sudden stoppage of its buying spree—which would cause great inflationary pressures on the US domestic economy.

The authoritarian structure of the Chinese economy—with its pocket full of capitalist enclaves along the coast and in Shenzhen, Suzhou, Hong Kong, and Shanghai—will allow it to use political coercion, military force, and economic instruments to keep the cost of labor low. This means that rather than China becoming a huge market for foreign countries, the country will use its position as a late economic developer to make the world a place for Chinese goods. This situation will improve as investment, technology and capital continues to flow into the country. The Chinese Communist Party (CCP) is also observing very closely Hong Kong's constitutional development in terms of this pocket of capitalism under Chinese communism (*Straits Times*, April 26, 2004). Recall that China remained virtually unscathed during the 1997–98 Asian currency crisis because it was simply not sufficiently plugged into the system. But not everything in the Chinese economy is completely in the hands of its financial controllers. Increasing globalization and higher levels of investments from the US and Europe will force its local workers to demand better wages for higher productivity. One cannot join the global capitalist economy and not suffer the negative effects of getting a hangover once in while. China's high single-digit growth rates are a typical reflection of a rapidly industrializing economy and do not necessarily project the potential for economic growth in the long run.

There are also the negative effects of capitalist development in a country that is already so demographically large that 'corruption' is a normal way of life. It isn't only in China, it's all over the world wherever people gather to live and work in communities. Call it "business networks," "guanxi," or "interpersonal relationships," or "economic culture" as detailed, for instance, by Yadong Luo in *Guanxi and Business* (University of Hawaii Press, 2000), it is still a form of corruption at the end of the day. Capitalism will only catalyze the forms of corruption present in the Chinese state and society and bring it to a different level. The lack of a tradition of clear regulatory laws governing business practices and the absence of liberal economic principles mean that much of what really goes on in the Chinese economy is not accounted or properly audited and this means a lack of control for a country that has survived for generations on central control. A director of an international merchant bank that I spoke to said that the reason why the US can't stop China or Japan from soaking up US long-term government bonds, i.e., the Treasury bonds in particular is simply because of the free market and a possible hedge against China's own intention to float its currency in several years. When the currency is eventually floated, there will be a fall in the value of the *Yuan* and having a large amount of reserves would help reduce the impact of a loss in value. However, I remain skeptical about the soaking up of such large amounts of Treasury bonds by a country that does not emulate the kind of liberal democratic values that are espoused by Americans and American government while still wanting to benefit from liberal capitalism in any event. In a sense then the communist leadership will continue to have the best of both worlds: authoritarianism with stock options.

INDIA AND US

The Hindu nationalist party in its decade of power failed to complete its globalization project. This has been the greatest election upheaval since Indian independence from its British master. The ethno-nationalistic politicking of the Vajpayee government is on the demise, and the rise of Sonya Gandhi's Congress Party, ostensibly through the new Indian president has turned the tables on the possibilities for continuing Hindu revivalism in the political and cultural history of modern India. The forestalling of Hindu revivalism has not solved other problems that continue to haunt the subcontinent. India has a highly charged racial and religious political culture where it is said that everyone has a political opinion, from the rich Bollywood moguls who produce hundreds of movies a year for the world's largest movie-going audience to the poorest homeless peasant roaming the Indian countryside. During the Cold War, India leaned towards the USSR, or as some Indian scholars would argue, India was politically more independent when it came to political relations with the US during the Cold War.

Nevertheless, the post-Cold War era has seen India being increasingly recognized as a regional player and a rising world economy. The Indian economy is also plagued by acts of god which make emergency responses to such disasters difficult given the size of its population and complex cultural systems. While many Indian ethnic nationalists see the work of the current Hindu nationalist Bharathiya Janata Party (BJP) led by former Prime Minister Vajpayee in a positive vein, there are some who would disagree with the economic prospects of India's future ability to provide jobs for one of the fastest growing populations in the world. There are deeply-set problems in agriculture and local commercial enterprises that are sometimes drawn into the political forays between Indian Muslims and Indian Hindus who constitute the largest religious and ethnic communities in the country. Natural disasters like the 2003 drought in Karnataka and the state of Andhra Pradesh that resulted in the death of close to a thousand farmers who would have rather committed suicide than face their creditors. The bourgeoning middle classes have split their support for Vajpayee's failed bid to return to office, and the rural-based peasants' political skepticism has triumphed. This is because they are the ones on the ground who are most likely to feel the immediate impact of negative consumer sentiment in the markets or suffer from a lack of proper national policy on disaster relief. Disaster relief is another Indian policy that is more talked about than operationalized. This is understandable given the limited resources and the resulting value of human life in the world's second largest population. Successive Indian governments have found it difficult to reform its ancient and fragmented agricultural systems and land policies.

Over the years, Americans have made ostensible donations to the country in cash and in-kind but this is insufficient and difficult to track. Because it is such a large country where there are more poor people for every working person, corruption is a significant factor in getting things done. It is not so much that people are unwilling to work and in fact they are most willing but the problem is that there simply isn't enough work to go around. So while Indian scientists, engineers and computer programmers woo the world with their expertise and while Southeast Asian and American corporations outsource their backroom activities to India's cities, there are many Indians who are starving and living "hand to mouth" or worse. Investing in India is a good way to make money for the major corporations because labor laws are weak and labor is cheap. Naturally, India's main economic competitor for FDI is China with whom they have had several border clashes. India's current annual FDI is only US$3 billion, about five per cent of the amount that China gets every year. India has also often been touted as the world's largest democracy. However this ideological situation has not let for consistently smooth political relations with the US. Rather, India is indeed a breeding ground for the kind of liberal differences that Americans take so seriously. "Oblivion," it is said, "falls upon the world navigated by the free slaves of the Ship of Fools" (Foucault [1965] 1988: 34). The political power of freed rural peasants living the life of economic slavery has helped shift the political mandate to govern the world's largest democracy to the unholy alliance between Left Wing splinter parties and Gandhi's dynastic Congress.

While liberalism in America has seen the marginalization and virtual wipe-out of socialist political parties including the communist party of America, especially after McCarthyism, the reverse appears to be true of India. Perhaps the large rural and urban poor make a suitable breeding ground for egalitarian-sounding socialist and other Left leaning parties. Hypothetically, why would the poor want to fight for free speech when they are starving to death?

India offers a fantastic array of investment opportunities for greedy capitalists because of its high level of first-rate engineers, computer professionals and emphasis on information technology. Unlike China, which has a different set of problems, India has a complex and complicated history of rising ethnic nationalism and religious intolerance between Hindus and Muslims. Mosques and temples will continue to be burnt and accusations and blame will continue to be hurled at both parties to the problem.

India is also burdened with the illegal but very subtle caste structure that stratifies Indian society across cultural, religious and social norms.

India is also known to reject MNCs that are not culturally sensitive to its needs as seen in the marketing problems of McDonald's Corporation in India and Coke's subsidary in India, Hindustan Coca-Cola Beverages (HCCB). McDonald's has perhaps found its nemesis in India because its basic product is the beef burger patty, and in India, the cow has been considered for the millennia as a sacred animal and not for making into beef patties. It is amazing to think that McDonald's (with its reputation for fast food serving up beef hamburgers as a main value meal) had not carefully considered this while trying to force open a new market where millions are vegetarian. Because of the value of the fast food industry in the US, and because money always draws attention, there are pending lawsuits against the corporation about allegations of concealing the use of animal extracts in their French fries:

> McDonalds reiterated that the french fries it served in India did not contain any animal extracts. "McDonald's India would like to assure you that French fries in India are a 100 per cent vegetarian product and do not contain any beef or animal extract of whatsoever kind," the company said in an advertisement in a newspaper on Saturday. The Press Trust of India quoted McDonald's Delhi Managing Director Vikram Bakshi as saying that all McDonald's outlets were open in Delhi after taking "necessary precautions." Earlier this week a vegetarian lawyer and native Indian, Harish Bharti, filed suit against McDonald's in the United States accusing it of "secretly" lacing its French fries with beef fat. A report on the case appeared in a leading Indian newspaper on Friday, stirring protests and attacks on the fast-food chain. "The cow is sacred to Indians. Foreign firms have made a habit of dumping things here without any regard to feelings of people," Goel said (*Indian Express Newspapers (Bombay)*, 2001).

The beverage giant Coke did not have the extent of the problems that McDonalds of India will have to do battle with for a long time to come. However, HCCB's own marketing secret reveals the nature of such MNC operations on the shop floor by providing bottles of Coke as the international and national alternative to popular beverages such as tea and Pepsi-Cola. The consumption of tea in India for example is an important and necessary traditional past-time. If one can get past these problems, one can access the wide variety and huge potential for investment but control and constant monitoring is essential for the greedy capitalist to take advantage of the huge labor pool. India is likely to see a net outflow of its best and brightest citizens to the United States and the UK where there are a growing number of diasporic Indian communities.

There is also increasing sentiment in India in terms of an improving investments and companies like Coke, McDonald's, and Ford who were among the first to invest significantly in India in the post-Cold War era. They are more likely than not to benefit from their pioneer status, if the Rupee does not go into another currency tailspin or get bogged in financial doldrums because of currency mismanagement, bureaucratic red tape and systemic corruption. Renewed investor confidence in such companies as *Reliance Industries*, and the *Indian Oil Corporation* are positive harbingers for the emerging Indian market. But the political mandate awarded to Congress (I) is limited by a forestalling of alternatives to Sonya Gandhi's party. This does not in any way lessen the burden on the ethnonationalist and ethnoreligious politics that have divided and continue to split India. It is doubtful that Congress and the Communists will be able to increase the voices of the political masses that have put them in power once again.

JAPAN AND US

The "liberal democratic" politics of Japan continue to experience deep links with the United States in order to discover new ways of making Japan's economy work. But there are also important political linkages between the politicians of both countries. In the third year of the Junichiro Koizumi administration, members of the Liberal Democratic Party (LDP) such as Shinzo Abe and Tetsuzo Fuyushiba of the New Komeito Party (NKP) hope to foster better relations with Washington (*Straits Times*, April 26, 2004). Meanwhile, political negotiations are going on to effectively deploy a USN Aegis-equipped destroyer with the SM3 radar system to the Sea of Japan "to jointly counter any missile threat. Plans call for radar information obtained in Japan to be passed on to the United States in real time" (*Asahi Shimbun*, April 22, 2004).

Like China, Japan is the other significant macroeconomic beneficiary from soaking up trillions of Yen worth of US Treasury bonds. Japan is taking advantage of the free market to increase its stake in the US and this will either cause increased investor confidence in the long-term economic power of the US, or if the critics have their way, will cause inflationary pressures on the US economy if Japan were to abruptly stop buying. The primary beneficiaries in the *international* (read US) bond markets are the governments, central banks, merchant banks and offshore banks. The major secondary beneficiaries would be the MNCs, while the major losers will be the US taxpayers should the demand for bonds fall dramatically.

Both China and Japan have mimicked each other in terms of large-volume buying of bonds but while China appears to benefit, Japan seems to be only just keeping afloat. Part of the reason for China's high economic growth over the last 10 years is due to the rapid and widespread industrialization and movement of foreign direct investment into what is supposed to be the largest single consumer market in the world. However, Japan is still suffering from a long hangover since the 1990 economic growth bubble was ballooned burst because of a lack of significant controls over the banking sector, the volume of bad loans, and Japanese companies having overextended themselves. At the national level, Japan also incurred a higher deficit because of the first Gulf War, which was supposed to have boosted the world economy (the US, Japan and their economic allies in particular) but this was thwarted by the Asian currency crisis. Let us now move to Japanese popular culture within Japan and examine the extent of influence that American popular culture has on this Asian country.

The idea of mimicry has clearly been seen in Japanese innovation and technology. There are more Japanese teenagers who have dyed-blond hair, wear clothing, and imitate the mannerisms of American Hispanics and African Americans from South Central Los Angeles and the Bronx. "[L]et us not be surprised to find it actually prowling through the streets" (Foucault [1965] 1988: 36).

But the imitative culture is also not a one-way street. Like the multiple passages between America and Asia that we described above, American entertainment and media have themselves begun mimicking Asian motifs as clearly illustrated in the movies by the late but acclaimed Japanese film director Akira Kurasawa, especially in his final film with the postmodern bent. There are many reasons to believe that the Japanese economy will bounce back, especially with modified versions of what has come to be called the "flying geese" theories of regional development through Japanese FDI in a manner similar to when West Germany was supposed to be the engine of growth for the European Community during the last 5–8 years of the Cold War until the FDR were stymied for some time by the social costs of political reunification with the German Democratic Republic (Communist East Germany).[23]

Japanese women have also come under increasing pressure to conform to traditional values that have been patriarchal for centuries. There is a desire among Japanese men for women to return to their traditional roles in late modernity despite advances in women's rights and feminist theory in Japan. However, if we read the map of Japanese political culture correctly, we will be able to recognize the differences between the younger generation of those in their teens to twenties, and those in their thirties and forties. While the older generation of Japanese women has its social and personal roles figured out, those in the youngest have not. Japan has one of the world's highest literacy rates and most comprehensives system of education in the world. This means that the younger generations are more willing to explore the world on their own— for example through the Internet and travel—rather than merely accept their fate according to custom and traditional family practices.

Like other places that have achieved high levels of material success, Japanese women are now more willing to challenge what has been "accepted gender practice and function" for centuries. This is causing a downward pressure on Japan's relatively homogenous social structure. Japanese popular culture is a mixture of both local inspired cults of personality in fantasy worlds and the importation of America's MTV culture. The blend that results is one where Japanese pop idols are powerful influences in their own right and bear the trademarks of an imitative and innovative popular culture.

These popular icons—whether they are real or animé or a mixture of reality in animé—have reversed the unidirectional manner of the American MTV culture and created their own unique innovations that are doing two things: (1) defining the uniqueness of their own popular culture; and (2) influencing American popular culture and other forms of Asian popular culture in Taiwan, Korea, Singapore, and China. At the aesthetic level, there are certain cues involved in the kind of export J-pop culture to America and the rest of the world. These include a (1) rejection of the idea that hard work will lead to employment stability; (2) a nihilistic view of a world in which only super heroes are able to compete across a moral terrain out of which there is never a clear winner; (3) feelings of disenfranchisement with the Establishment and rejection not only of traditional gendered roles but also a resistance against falling only into two gendered forms, male and female; (4) the centrality of materialism but the failure of it to satisfy individuals; and (5) a rejection of the traditional Japanese view of honor/dishonor in favor of individual differences such as "dating gaijin" rather than locals. While these artifacts of Japanese popular modernity are indeed reflected in many aspects of urban cultures across the globe, the high value of the Japanese *Yen* and the superior performance of the Japanese economy from 1970 to 1990 had created a large amount of relative wealth that has trickled downwards and across Japanese middle class society. The current generation of younger persons who occupy the Japanese middle class are now riding the products of that economic wave in the political culture and social changes that are gradually sweeping Japan.[24]

The Americans were there at the right time and the right place. The history of Japanese militarism in the early 20th century had ostensibly launched Japan into the modern period. But the forced modernization of Japan through a fine balance between a strong military cabinet and weak, non-military, traditional leadership resulted in greater damage to the region and to Japan itself. The wartime cabinet exhausted its own resources in its attempt to create the Greater East Asian Co-Prosperity Sphere. This made Japan invade China, occupy Mongolia and rape the rest of Southeast Asia. It was the acute and double military debacle in Hawaii and the Philippines that drew America deeply into the political and economic fray of Southeast Asia rather than South Asia which remained at that point in time the colonial purview of Britain's falling empire in the East. The creation of conditions of conflict by Japan (Katzenstein, Keohane, and Krasner, 1998: 652) ironically resulted in America's benefit in the longer term.[25] American support for the Japanese economy also engulfed its security dimension as seen in US support in the 1970s and 1980s.[26] This was the period where it became increasingly clear to members of the House of Congress and the US Senate that Japan, rather than being a mere relic from the Pacific War with a highly skilled and homogenous workforce was in reality a strategic economic partner for American globalization and security in the tension-filled days of the Cold War with the USSR.

Thus it was more than merely being the victor *victorious* at the end of the war in the Pacific, or McArthur's political rhetoric in Japan and Korea. The depth of America's links with Asia runs deep for example, to the time of Japanese reconstruction from 1946–56 in the vulnerable first 10 years of the fledgling Japanese economy. This gave American investors and overseas administrators first hand experience in dealing with re-building, in the case of Japan, an entire economy that had been decimated by the war from the ground upwards (Henderson, 1999: 206).[27]

America also has the highest number of scholars and research scientists in research and design (R&D) when compared to any other post-industrial country in the world. Only Japan came close but since the Japanese bubble burst in 1990, the Japanese brand of teamwork and company loyalty has had to undergo radical changes in its system of social and business values. Japan needs to address its status downwards from an international player to reassess its role as a regional economic giant.

MALAYSIA AND US

Malaysia's current Prime Minister Abdullah Ahmad Badawi wrote a letter to US President George Bush Jr. and other leaders of the UN Security Council and the Group of Four most powerful states in April 2004. Abdullah presented Malaysia's position on the meeting among Islamic states with a focus on the Iraqi and Palestinian issues. This is in contrast to the pronouncements of former Malaysian Prime Minister Mahathir Mohammed who never lifted an olive branch or any other kind of peaceful twig to the United States.

Recall the time of former Prime Minister Mahathir's embarrassment and bruised ego from former Vice President Dan Quayle's early 1990's visit to Kuala Lumpur, the Malaysian federal capital, during which Quayle lambasted Malaysia's human rights record and questioned its democratic record. Mahathir accused America of being dominated by Jews. He again said as recently as 2003 that America was indeed being run and manipulated by a small number of Jews who control everything from finance and broadcasting, to journalism and the print media. The powerful Jewish lobby was accused by the former prime minister for being the problem behind the Palestinian Question.

However, the events of 9/11 prompted the new prime minister who took over in October 2003, after fresh and clean elections, to extend the palm of cooperation and friendship. Was this motivated by fear or anxiety over US threats to eradicate terrorist cells wherever they may be found—in the world's largest Muslim state, Indonesia and its closest Muslim neighbor, Malaysia? This resulted in both countries seeking and offering intelligence-sharing strategies with US intelligence networks and through regular and legal American diplomatic channels. The Bali bombing and

133

reports of Al-Qaeda operatives and clandestine meetings in Indonesian and Malaysian cities have not boded well for the relationship between these predominantly Muslim countries and the US hegemon.

The arrest of the old Islamic cleric Abu Bashir and his incarceration and subsequent trial soon after the Bali bombing of a nightclub in the smutty Kuta Beach area—now left out of the "best beach resorts" program on the *Discovery Channel*—was another keen move by Indonesian authorities who, like their Malaysian counterparts, often have faced great difficulties in separating the sheep from the goats within the Islamic fold. Whenever a crisis erupts, the elite Indonesian and Malaysian anti-terrorists forces are often sand-bagged by a rush of emotion from genuine and peaceful followers and public threats and bombings from Muslim extremists with underground arms caches from Yala province in Southern Thailand, Kelantan in Malaysia's Northern territories, to Jogjakarta in Java. Little wonder that American embassies in the region bear a similar architectural face to its embassies elsewhere in the world, architecture that gives the impression of "Fortress America (Overseas Edition)." But Americans have short memories and American journalism and politics appears to thrive on their mnemonic lack. For instance, when Mahathir Mohamad made those anti-Semitic remarks, members of the diplomatic corps, republicans and democratic politicians themselves conveniently forgot the reality that is America.

When the National Archives released previously secretly classified videographic images of a conversation between Richard Nixon and Billy Graham in which Nixon made several anti-Semitic remarks and agreed that he could never repeat them in public, even though he firmly believed in them. Graham came under fire from left-wing liberals and from within the inter-faith ministries of America for his conversation as a young and rising popular preacher who agreed with Nixon that the Jews had a stranglehold over the media and that the situation had to be changed, as Nixon suggested, otherwise American would go down. Nixon was subsequently forced to resign in dishonor and was protected from Congressional indictment from his former vice-president who used his powers as a new president to absolve Nixon from his political sins over Watergate. Yet American politics seems to have forgiven and even resurrected Nixon's brand of racism, his hawkish demeanor, and his lying ways. He was to end his long and fruitful life as a kind of advisor-philosopher of sorts who wrote large tomes about his work and what he would have done, he said in his tours of US university campuses, had the situation been less difficult, or different, forgotten, or forgiven by Americans from his era.

THAILAND AND US

The structure of Thai society is best understood as a pyramid. At the top of the structure are the King and the royal family. They are considered very sacred and are supremely respected even when issues of politics arise. It is not uncommon for the king to summon political leaders in order to get them to resolve their differences.

A second tier consists of the ruling elite. The elite are made up of Thai people who are usually of Chinese descent and run many of the top companies within the country. For a traditional Asian society, Thailand is interesting because many of its top CEOs and corporate leaders are women. This is different from other Asian countries, and many Western countries, where the CEOs and top flight executives are usually men. The ruling elite comprises the highest military commanders within the Thai Army and the Thai Police, "in the precise sense that the classical epoch gave to it—that is the totality of measures which make work possible and necessary for all those who could not live without it" (Foucault [1965] 1988: 46). The reason for their dominance in politics is because of the combat power backing that they possess.

Since the end of the Pacific War, Thailand's politics has been dominated by military commanders who were raised on a diet of fear that Thailand was to be the next country to fall to Communism. As a result, there was an internalization of such foreign fears into the heart of the people themselves. Also, the dominant role of the military has not meant that there has been a clear and hierarchical politics among the generals themselves. In fact, since the absolutist king abdicated in favor of a Constitutional monarchy, Thailand has experienced 17 bloodless coups. However, the infighting has predominantly been contained within the military and the political parties and their supporters. The peasants have primarily remained outside this realm of politics. The only exception to this political model is in the southern provinces where there are militant Islamic enclaves, many based in Northern Malaysia, who are fighting for a separate state. This has been the case most significantly since the end of the Cold War. During the Cold War, there was greater news focus and media attention to the problems of communist insurgents and the activities of the Communist Party of Thailand (CPT) and the Communist

135

Party of Malaya (CPM). In the past, we can say that the peasant rebellions and insurrections in the South are primarily sporadic and politically motivated by religion or by ideology. However, these forms of political violence are indeed marginal to the larger corporate and business aspects of the Thai economy.

The third tier of Thai society's pyramid is made up of the peasant workers who are themselves predominantly engaged in Thailand's agricultural sector. Rice is continues to dominate as the main export of the country and is in fact the world's largest rice producer. While globalization has created a widening middle class of nouveau riche workers, the predominantly peasant farmers continue to bear the brunt of economic fall out and downturns. Like in all capitalist societies, these are the people who are hardest hit and mostly sacrificed in terms of having to suffer the indignities of no food, no home, no jobs and no future. Nevertheless, the problem of globalization in Thailand has spawned a deep, affective fissure between the minority elite industrial upper class and the majority peasant farmers and unskilled laborers who live for a pittance of what a waged salary worker earns in Bangkok. The reason Thailand has many social problems with globalization is because it embraced globalization with welcome arms in all possible areas of the economy.

The Thai people are known to be gentle and gracious in their demeanor as described by Orientalist perspectives of those who wish to believe in the exotification of Asian women, men and children. However, the reality is furthest from such images. As a Thai garment worker from Northern Chiang Mai once said to me, life is cheap in Thailand. And added that Thai criminal would think nothing of slitting your throat in front of your family if they wanted to make a point. In my estimation, Thai culture has been damaged by globalization inasmuch as it has damaged itself because of the nature of its traditional practices.

The concept of gift-giving, for example, is taken to extremes when there is much wealth or riches to be attained. Corruption and the human flesh trade are worth billions of Thai Bhat every year. The politicians, police, army and bureaucracy are filled with all kinds of corrupt practices. In a large sense, corruption is a way of life in a very overt sense in Thailand unlike America where corruption is considered something to be embarrassed about and is usually hidden from public view. This does not mean that Americans are any less prone to corrupt behavior than Thai people. Rather it is the rich and the super rich Americans and Thai persons who are corrupt. Most people in America and Thailand are indeed not corrupt and live by simple but strict moral codes of decency, honesty, and integrity. This is not the case in Thai corporate culture and neither is it the case in American corporate culture. Corruption is very much a large part of the process and experience of globalization for the elite in both countries. There is really very little that trickles down to the majority poor.

Corruption in Thailand is also clearly at the root of its tourism industry where ignorant and impoverished Thai people are drawn into a swirling pool of drugs, sex, pornography, and pedophilia in places such as Patpong Street 1 and Patpong Street 2 in Bangkok; in Pattaya, and in Hat Yai in the South. These are the markers that indicated to us the similarity between these Thai cities and those described by Foucault in Madness and Civilization:

> no doubt like the "decree of the *Parlement* dated 1606 ordered the beggars of Paris to be whipped in the public square [like the American prostitute caught in Tehran in the 1990s], branded on the shoulder, shorn and then driven from the city" (Foucault [1965] 1988: 47).

Sex tourists come from all over the world to Thailand as the globalization hub of Sodom and Gomorrah. Some estimates indicate that there were approximately 180,000 prostitutes in Thailand before the Vietnam War, but by the time America had established five military bases in pursuing the war in the East this number increased dramatically to about half a million.

Many of these women are lured into the underground sex industries of European capitals. Many are tortured, violently abused, and raped in the process. This is because globalization appears as a very large neon light to which many poor people, young men and young women, are drawn towards with the prospect of getting a job and earning enough money to send back to the villages. However, these simpletons are often ignorant of the entire vertical and horizontal efficiency of these underground networks that purchase young girls and boys from the hands of trusted relatives. Japanese sex tourism was a common feature in Thailand and the Philippines during the Japanese economic boom of the 1980s. However, such a cultural infestation ought to be understood against the backdrop of the major inadequacies of international organizations such as the IMF. Two books stand out as powerful indictments of the global and local structures of politics and globalization. One is by the Nobel prize winner in economics, Joseph Stiglitz's *Globalization and Its Discontents* (W. W. Norton, 2002) and the other is a neoWaltzian argument intricately made by another award-winning writer and Yale professor of law, Amy L. Chua, in *World On Fire: How Exporting Free Market Democracy Breeds Ethnic Hatred and Global Instability* (Doubleday, 2003).

THE BUSINESS OF MAKING MONEY IN ASIA

Most Americans since 1945 have not voted for the kinds of politician and the kind of foreign policies that have come out of American government but still pay the price for being American anyway. This is why Americans seem to believe in one thing but American government appears to be doing something else (Chapter 1, Introduction).

Being American in Asia has certain benefits in the sense that at the highest levels of industry and commerce, the Americans who are the members of the board, the CEOs, CFOs, and COOs get first class, red carpet treatment; however, those of us who have to work daily as the interface between the corporation and the customer or the corporation and other businesses, are vulnerable to different local and cultural norms in which one may either be sacrificed for the sake of the company or with good luck, poached with perks by another.

Investment opportunities in Asia abound for the Americans with information technology and communications skills who are young enough and possess sufficient drive and determination to work in places that are as foreign as any other place on earth. For example, there are many who have gone to Asia to begin work in their youth but have never left and have started families and social networks. There are Americans in Asia who are in fact more Asian than the Asians themselves. The long-time *kama'aina*, long-staying expatriates, serve as valuable contact points for quick launches into the local Asian marketplaces and know exactly what one needs to do in order to survive. Some are rather jaded, and others may be wary of newcomers, but many keep to the old, long celebrated traditions that were encapsulated in their youth in America. With the low cost of travel these days, it becomes much less problematic to make last minute changes to any itinerary. American investors need more than quick routes deep into emerging Asian markets.

Those Americans who want to make money in Asia often watch very carefully the kinds of programs that are aired over various Asian broadcast networks from CNBC, Star News Network, CNA, Sun TV, Zee TV, HKTV-B, The Nine Network, and others from the Asia-Pacific capital cities of Astana, Auckland, Baku, Bandar Seri Begawan, Bangkok, Canberra, Colombo, Dhaka, Dili, Islamabad, Jakarta, Kabul, Katmandu, Kuala Lumpur, Male, Manila, Nandy, New Delhi, Port Moresby, Seoul, Singapore, Sri Jayewardenepura Kotte, Taipei, Thimpu, and Tokyo. The money-making entertainment programs from many of these far-flung cities have a very distinct identity that is based on local and native or even regional languages but with very clear grandiose, Hollywood-style glamour. Look at the ways in which Indian popular culture promotes itself. Every single dance move is based on something that Michael Jackson created years ago, or something that John Travolta and Olivia Newton John (who is Australian by birth and citizenship) originated in *Saturday Night Fever* and *Grease*.

V. S. Naipaul may be considered by some as a great Indian, Trinidad-born novelist with keen observations about life, but being more colonial in his mannerisms than the colonials themselves, Naipaul did make at least one astute observation. He noted the idea of the way in which Asians and Africans like to mimic their former colonial masters, as seen in his brilliant *The Mimic Men* (Vintage, 2001). Naipaul's observation is similar to that imposed by Homi Bhabha's interstitial evaluation of "mimic man" but whose work is so densely sordid that it defeats plain language users from understanding whatever he might have to say, lost in ambivalence as he illustrates so well in "Of Mimicry and Man" in his *The Location of Culture* (Routledge, 1994). A far cry from the Nobel Prize winner Naipaul's work, or the clearly obtuse work of Bhabha lie alternative visions of mimicry in the Far East. The idea of mimicry is not limited to the Hong Kong or Taiwanese entertainment field that ranges from reality TV to soaps that are more extreme than *Days of Our Lives* or *Peyton Place*.

The mimicry between Asia and America is incredible. The Western images along the streets of Singapore, Bangkok, Kuala Lumpur and Tokyo make one think that you could be back home in the US. However, there are clear differences in the local customs in terms of business practices, interpersonal networks, and the recent history of MNC organizational behavior. Japan is too expensive for any one person to want to invest in a big way. It is better nowadays to have a Japanese product that is made anywhere else but in Japan.

However, Japanese innovation and creativity continue to be the main source of potential for the only country in Asia to have made it to the G-7 and in that sense, claims recognition and status. China is a great place to invest in if you can get by the language barrier. As a business executive intent on making money in China, it would be a great disadvantage not to know the language. Labor costs are low, but there are certain distinct features about *guanxi* and Chinese business practices that the intrepid executive ought to know before foraying into what will become the world's largest consumer market for low-value, low-yield but high volume domestic consumer products. The answer is not so much to make it in China for sale elsewhere in the world, but to make it in China for sale in China. This is however, harder to achieve than it seems. India, on the other hand, which had significantly lower FDI than China, has the clear advantage of having close to 289 million professionals who also speak the language of globalization.

The high levels of literacy make India a very promising place to be for the greedy capitalist be willing to immerse into a deep and ancient culture with one of the fastest growing economies in South Asia since 9/11. As a result of the large number of English-speakers, there continue to be many firms that have decided to outsource their backroom operations to this country. Outsourcing currently makes up between 2–5 per cent of foreign income earned by local Indian nationals. Remember that at this point in modernity, there are at least seven countries in South Asia and the word "Indian" is more about national identity than ethnic identity. India is also politically stable, a country where freedom of speech and the expression of such liberties are taken seriously. There are also many more languages spoken in India when compared to China where *Putonghua* gets you most places with ease. Both Indian and Chinese bureaucracies are full of red tape and tend to present problems for new investors and very often more red tape is created in trying to rid the apparatus of old red tape. Levels of corruption that might hinder business practices are high in both countries.

The Southeast Asian markets represent another set of valuable regional sites for investments where labor costs are relatively lower than in Europe and several in-roads have already been made in terms of manufacturing, banking and financial services, telecommunications, information technology, and tourism. Although Southeast Asia is gradually pricing itself out of the low-wage labor market when compared to Latin America, India, Africa and China, it continues to make up for this with highly-skilled and hardworking labor who appear to be very zealous about the language of globalization.

The business of making money in Asia works on a simple principle. This is the principle that revolves round the question of what can you bring into Asia to benefit both investor and the *invested*? The principle of business in Asia involves producing a good or service that is both cheap and functional that everyone needs every business quarter because it has a limited but value-laden lifespan. Examples involve printers and toners, toothbrushes and cosmetics, computer hardware and software, pharmaceuticals, food, and apparel. Perhaps with the exception of Japan, the rest of Asia does not possess sufficient a critical mass of experts in Research and Development to ensure a constant supply of creative products and services. Nevertheless, the edge that Asia has is in its wide markets, lower wage and start-up costs, and weak trade unions. Asian markets are also beginning to open up and become accustomed to the capitalist goods and services of neoliberal lifestyles so well-embedded in Western European cities and all across America. Another advantage that Asia has is its ability to innovate through reverse engineering and discovering alternative ways of acquiring product intelligence and consumer market knowledge and know-how. The possibility of developing Asian markets is a tremendous pull factor in attracting world-wide investments, if and only if (iff) the US continues to assert its presence as a benign military and economic hegemon in the Asia Pacific region.

ENDNOTES

1   J. Lodge Gillespie, Jr., "Rhetoric and Reality: Corporate America's Perceptions of Southeast Asia, 1950-1961," *Business History Review* 68, no. 3 (1994): 325–63. By way of a quick comparison, and a reminder of the earlier propandandistic nature of Americanism in Southeast Asia in the 1950s and 1960s, see Kenneth T. Young, "Asia and America at the Crossroads," *Annals of the American Academy of Political and Social Science* 384, (1969): 53–65; and contrast this with the work of Richard F. Doner, "Approaches to the Politics of Economic Growth in Southeast Asia," *Journal of Asian Studies* 50, no. 4 (1991), 818–49; and Susan M. Collins, Barry P. Bosworth, and Dani Rodrik, "Economic Growth in East Asia: Accumulation versus Assimilation," *Brookings Papers on Economic Activity* 2, (1996): 135–203.

2 Frederic L. Pryor, "The Impact of Foreign Trade on the Employment of Unskilled U. S. Workers: Some New Evidence," *Southern Economic Journal* 65, no. 3 (1999): 472–92.

3 James M. Griffin, and Weiwen Xiong, "The Incentive to Cheat: An Empirical Analysis of OPEC," *Journal of Law and Economics* 40, no. 2 (1997): 289–316.

4 Francesco Sisci, "La démaoization de la Chine," *Le Grand Soir*: *Asiatimes*, November 10, 2002.

5 Rafael X. Zahralddin-Aravena, "Chile and Singapore: The Individual and the Collective, A Comparison," *Emory International Law Review* 12, no. 2(1998): fn. 153.

6 "Reformasi" is the Malay word for 'reform' and is the battle-cry for the supporters of the National Justice Party that was founded by Anwar supporters including his wife Wan Aziza.

7 See for example, *BBC News*, Nov 23, 1998; and *The New Republic*, December 7, 1998.

8 *Italics* mine. See *BBC News*, November 23, 1998.

9 Abdullah Badawi is the man who replaced Anwar Ibrahim. Anwar was jailed for sodomizing his former family driver, Azizan Abu Bakar. Anwar believes that his former boss, Malaysia's fourth prime minister, the Singapore-trained medical doctor, Mahathir Mohamad, had framed him. In Malaysia the law states that sodomy is punishable by a maximum of 20 years imprisonment and whipping by a rattan cane. While he was incarcerated, Anwar was punched in the eye by the Inspector-General of Police Abdul Rahim Noor. See *International Herald Tribune*, March 3, 1999.

10 See also, Anne O. Krueger, "Meant Well, Tried Little, Failed Much: Policy Reforms in Emerging Market Economies," Roundtable Lecture at the Economic Honors Society, New York University, New York, IMF, March 23, 2004; and "IMF/World Bank Report Calls for Urgent Action on Poverty Reduction by All Countries," Press Release No. 04/85, April 22, 2004.

11 See for example, Peter G. Christenson, Lisa Henriksen, and Donald F. Roberts, "Substance Use in Popular Prime-time Television," Office of National Drug Control Policy and Mediascope Macro International, Inc., 2000; and "Monitoring the Future National Survey Results on Drug Use 1975–2002, vol. 2: College Students and Young Adults," *USDHHS*, BKD486, April 12, 2004.

12 Noam Chomsky, "An Interview with Noam Chomsky," *ZMagazine*, January 2, 2004.

13 In a "Letter from Iraq," see John Cassidy, "Beneath the Sand: Can a Shattered Country be Rebuilt with Oil?" *New Yorker*, May 11, 2004.

14 Note the US Supreme Court case number 163 U.S. 537 (1896).

15 Habibie, a German-trained engineer, was the interim president who served under Suharto and made his mark as Minister for Technology. As an Indonesian vice-president in Suharto's cabinet, Habibie was constitutionally appointed president after Suharto but was rejected by the MPR.

16 "Monas" is an acronym for *monumen nasional* or the National Monument in central Jakarta that is built on some tenets of ancient Hindu philosophy about the celebration of phallocentrism. See "Ex-military Chief Wins Suharto Party Nomination," *Agence France-Presse*, April 21, 2004.

17 See *Wall Street Journal*, February 12, 1998.

18 Tony Makin, "Preventing Financial Crises in East Asia," *Asian Survey* 39, no. 4 (1999): 668–78.

19 Henry Laurence, "Financial System Reform and the Currency Crisis in East Asia," *Asian Survey* 39, no. 2(1999): 348–73.

20 Robert A. Scalapino, "The United States and Asia in 1998," *Asian Survey*, 39, no. 1(1999): 1–11.

21 Vaclav Smil, "China's Energy and Resource Uses: Continuity and Change," *China Quarterly* 156, (1998): 935–51.

22 John W. Thomas, "Institutional Innovation and the Prospects for Transference. Part I: Transferring Singaporean Institutions to Suzhou, China," draft paper, Harvard University Kennedy School of Government, September 20, 2001. See also, John W. Thomas and Lim Siong Guan, "Using Markets to Govern Better in Singapore," draft paper, Harvard University Kennedy School of Government, August 15, 2001, written for the Kennedy School of Government's Visions of Governance in the 21st Century project.

23 With reference to the flying geese theories, see the compelling and interesting but outdated paper by Martin Hart-Landsberg and Paul Burkett, "Contradictions of Capitalist Industrialization in East Asia: A Critique of "Flying Geese" Theories of Development," *Economic Geography* 74, no. 2 (1998): 87–110.

24 For further reading, consider the useful but outdated book by Edwin O. Reischauer, and Marius B. Jansen, eds., *The Japanese Today: Change and Continuity* (MA: Harvard University Press, 1995) as a basis for understanding Japan; the creative work of Delores Martinez, ed., *The Worlds of Japanese Popular Culture: Gender, Shifting Boundaries and Global Culture* (Cambridge: Cambridge University Press, 1998); and the interesting counter-impressionistic argument made by Yoshio Sugimoto, *An Introduction to Japanese Society* (Cambridge: Cambridge University Press, 2002); and the terse but comprehensive work by Mark Schilling, *The Encyclopedia of Japanese Pop Culture* (NY: Weatherhill Publications, 1997).

25 Peter J. Katzenstein, Robert O. Keohane, and Stephen D. Krasner, "International Organizations and the Study of World Politics," *International Organization* 52, no. 4 (1998): 645–85.

26 This was clearly the case in terms of Foreign Assistance. See for example, William J. Long, "Nonproliferation as a Goal of Japanese Foreign Assistance," *Asian Survey* 39, no. 2 (1999): 328–47; and Dennis T. Yasutomo, "Why Aid? Japan as an Aid Great Power," *Pacific Affairs* 62, no. 4 (1989–90): 490–503. See also, John O'Loughlin; Luc Anselin, "Geo-Economic Competition and Trade Bloc Formation: United States, German, and Japanese Exports, 1968–1992," *The Journal of Economic Geography* 72, no. 2 (1996): 131–60; Brian Woodall, "The Logic of Collusive Action: The

Political Roots of Japan's Dango System," *Comparative Politics* 25, no. 3 (1993): 297–312; Roger W. Bowen, "Japan's Foreign Policy," *PS: Political Science and Politics* 25, no. 1 (1992): 57–73; and a more outdated but intuitive argument in Takashi Inoguchi, "Japan's Response to the Gulf Crisis: An Analytic Overview," *Journal of Japanese Studies* 17, no. 2(1991): 257–73.

27　Errol A. Henderson, "Neoidealism and the Democratic Peace," *The Journal of Peace Research* 36, no. 2 (1999): 203–31.

CHAPTER 4

Economy

The Business of American MNCs and their CEOs

Imagine a place so steeped in the tropics that it offers only heat exhaustion, malaria, yellow fever, and other tropical illnesses and diseases. A place that is so difficult for human life that the simple act of breathing in air was an act of conscious difficulty. A place that was so backward that for many years visiting seafarers believed that ghosts would consume and engulf people with a fatal fever from the swamps. Yet this place attracted no less than what was to become a series of political and economic intrigues that involved the youngest president of the United States (he was 43 years old when he took the oath of office), several Wall Street financiers, foreign experts, and ex-military specialists. Ironically, the case resulted in the creation of a new country, with its own national boundaries. And the CIA was not even involved (but only because it had not yet been established in those days) and therefore could not have, shall we say, complicated matters as it has in other parts of the world. This country even had a film that was shot entirely on its location between the Atlantic Ocean and the Pacific Oceans. This place is the Republic of Panama.

The Panama Canal was a result of the creative economics and the executive political will of the earlier American capitalists at the turn of the 19th and 20th centuries. Neil Postman believes that in order to save our future we need to build a bridge to the 18th century. He is half right. What Postman neglects to reconcile are the existing problems within modern cosmopolitan societies today. The problems of poverty, hunger, and the burden of state welfare systems continue to inflict the advanced postindustrial economies of the West. The roots of these economies are deeply embedded in the Industrial Revolution, but the speed and pace of modernization has resulted in an incomplete understanding of the economic lessons that were themselves partially understood. Modernity possesses and cannot be dispossessed of information overload, and is consequently faced with too little time to understand the real value of

145

the information being gathered. One lesson from the past was that the bourgeoning Western economies on which America had modeled itself were not designed to help the masses but to enrich the elites. This was the economic history that Nietzsche had warned us about in "Nietzsche's Preface to Constitutionalism," an article published in the *Journal of Politics* in 1963. In anticipating Postman's book by at least 36 years, Kariel argues that:

> We are distinguished, [Nietzsche] reasoned, by our capacity to remember the past, to recollect our past action. We are distinctively historical beings, as animals are not. Our experience, more properly, our consciousness of our experience—distinguishes us. And it rests upon us like a burden. Our consciousness of our past, our conscious knowledge, is our curse. Fully to take the past into conscious account—indeed, fully to take the future into conscious account—confounds all action. Full knowledge of the past, full knowledge of the future (including our inescapable death), produces either delirium or paralysis. Thus history, experience, consciousness, intellectual awareness, rational knowledge—all these are enemies of life. If we favor life we have no choice but to repress these (Kariel, 1963, 217).

We need to build the bridges to the 18th century but ones that are strong enough for us to return. But in building these bridges we seem to be merely going over previous ground, and that the seeds of the end of modernity as we know it today are so deeply embedded in the economic structures of Western societies that the full awareness of the present and a complete awareness of the future, as Kariel anticipates, will end in a consciousness about our own proximity to death.

The story of successful capitalism is therefore a long and twisted narrative that begins and ends with personalities. There was no real strategy of global economic dominance on the part of the US. The driving force and motivation during the Westward expansion towards California and against the Native Americans, the Spanish, British and French territorial possessions was the story of a seemingly unstoppable machine. Guided by the Monroe Doctrine and Manifest Destiny, the early Americans decided that they would be guided by shear synergistic economic conquest rather than by the classical economic theories of Adam Smith and his contemporaries. Indeed, it was the rejection by the early

146

settlers of such "classics" that made the growing American economy particularly robust and its war machine particularly confident, not so much of success, but of the possibility of failure. The Panama Canal is a case in illustration that represented an imbalanced mix of political intrigue, Wall Street financing, stubborn determination and a relentless physical geography. It was a good enemy to go up against. And I would like to argue that the likely company of politicians, economic czars, lawyers and ex-military men came together in a perfect concoction to establish what was to become a truly genuine American MNC.

This chapter explores and tries to make sense out of the successful capitalist narratives of several American CEOs. There is really no point or space in this book to assess narratives of failure because that would take several book series to even cover this year's cohort of failed entrepreneurs. The immediate answer is yes. This is provided that a caveat is added for example, that for every success story that one encounters, there are millions of failed stories that never get announced, never see the light of day. The reason for the focus on capitalism's success is twofold. It is a warning that sometimes when the Gods wish to punish us, they fulfill our dreams. The first reason for focusing on the importance of successful capitalism is that it gives us a sense of optimism. Perhaps for those who are believers, success stories motivate us to some higher plane. The second reason is that these successful MNCs and their successful leaders are themselves a product of failed chances. Not all of them were born with a silver spoon. Many rise from humble economic backgrounds. In reading success one must also read with peripheral vision. One must be willing and able to understand that globalization is not about a movement to make every one richer and must better off than the day before. Demographic research and the ethnographic record for example have shown clearly that there are problems of calculating what poverty, wealth or financial costs really mean.

THEORY AND CAPITALISM

Classical "laissez faire" economic theory involves two main assumptions. The first assumes that there are limited resources that are in demand. The second assumption is that these resources are potentially exchangeable by trade through a market mechanism. Economic models designed on the work of the Irish political economists developed *a priori* distinctions about absolute advantage and comparative advantage. Both forms of economic advantage revolve round the concept of production and the efficiency of production, that such goods can be produced from limited resources and that the production process can be sustained to support trade and the economy. But for any one economy to grow it has to take part in market exchange in order to satisfy a range of unlimited wants. One of classical economic theory's endowments to modern economic theory was the idea of unlimited wants outstripping limited resources.

Different aspects of demand and supply economic theory occupied the theorists of the Enlightenment era and the ensuing Industrial Revolution. The early theories such as Condillac's theory of commercial governance, Condorcet's theorem, Adam Smith's *Wealth of Nations*, Ricardian economics, and Malthus's work were too difficult and too complex for most ordinary people alive in the days leading to mercantilism. These early economic models were not immediately or directly helpful to ordinary folk except perhaps for providing simple economic models that could explain market functions and market competition. Classical economic theory seemed purely reserved for erudition and the work of the classical and neoclassical economists. But people still understood how economics worked. They did not necessarily have the language to express their knowledge and experience but they were able to make quotidian sense of living with economics and early business practices. Part of the reason for this intuitive trait of economics and the apparently natural extension from man's social interaction came from the work-life routine. The early merchants, craftsmen, apprentices, traders, their guilds and virtually anyone who participated in economic markets had some form of understanding of economics. Different parts of the economy were understood by different people. These were simple aspects of economic thought like the meaning of currency, the value of money, simple interest calculation, estimating stock values, the price mechanism, early state regulators, and the fact that money has time-value. Nevertheless, the models in theory and the theory in practice have come together to form what we understand as modern economic theory. These include some really intelligent and convincing models that help us understand business, society and capitalist culture in practice such as the Pareto effect, the Nash solution, the backward-bending leisure curve, the Lorentz curve, the concept of reciprocity, marginal utility theory, Giffen goods, bargaining and negotiation theory.

We have learnt different and compelling notions of capitalist economic theory from Smith, Pareto, Samuelson, Keynes, Milton, Reich, Stiglitz, Kahneman, Granger, Merton, Lucas and many others. Economic theory as we understand it today is particularly interesting because it builds on successive models of interpreting the business and economic world. It would appear that the ideal models that were created about the concept of markets, producers, households, consumers, the meaning of the firm, the meaning of technology, and the different types of market seem to suggest that economics as a discipline has learnt well from itself. The positivist or behavioral method particularly characterizes modern economics today. This is why many economic philosophers believe that the highest point of economic theory lies in mathematical formulae that go beyond the reach of most ordinary people who are not schooled in such languages and vocabularies.

There are two main problems with modern economic theory. The first problem is that most of its models are in fact idealized versions of the world that cannot be easily applied to real world situations. In the case where the explanatory models are used to explain economic relationships in real world settings, we discover that the contexts in which these explanations present themselves are so simple that it facts do not seem to fit theory. For example, graduate students in economics may have to study the General Equilibrium Theory of a capitalist market economy. Aesthetically pleasing to many scholars this general theory is very appealing, convincing and elegant. It has clear mathematical definitions and economic explanations of its constituent components. An excellent combination of mathematical logic and economic relevance. But because there are potentially so many different variables that constitute a real capitalist market it becomes virtually impossible to isolate the independent variable. But perhaps that was not one's intention. Perhaps, for example, if one wanted to understand how a simple market economy worked and the best picture that an economic theorist could give you would in fact be very limited. She or he would present you with idealized versions of two models: the perfect market mechanism and the imperfect market mechanism. Under the first, one would recount the basic assumptions of perfect knowledge, perfect competition, and perfect labor and resource allocation. In the second model, one would hold some or several of these assumptions constant and use proxies to determine the performance of a given good X or Y, or a given household A or B, or a production center, or a specific type of technology's performance under perfect and imperfect competition. Therefore what the questioner received was not a perfect and imperfect model explaining economic reality but two perfect or idealized models given to explain imperfect reality. Therefore we can conclude that economic theory is particularly exciting and captivating if and only if one understands the kind of vocabulary used and the language that carries its signs and symbols. Hence, at an advanced level, one could introduce different kinds of ideal states that seem to reflect or mirror the reality of capitalism such as welfare economics, international trade theory, convergence theory, and of course the neoclassical work of Vilfredo Pareto and the various careers and disciples that he has created along the way since the late 1800s and the rise of modernity in the wake of the Industrial Revolution.

We do not have to go far to get a glimpse of the kinds of economic theories that have become the signs and symbols of modernity. For each and every age of modernity there have been specific and different economic models and schools of economic thought. And each and every age seems to have had a different personality, perhaps even a Nobel Prize laureate in economics, at the center of some new paradigm of economic thought. One could say that someone like Bill Gates fits the picture of the kind of personality that has come to dominate the meaning of an economic paradigm such as the PC revolution, despite what his detractors might have against him. From him we have more modern applications in economic markets and virtual economic markets such as *eBay* on the Internet. The culmination of man's natural inclination to invent and to market goods and services by building on past experiences have led to the creation of Wi-Fi wireless platforms for PC notebooks that provide users the robustness or flexibility, PC notebooks that digitally record, store and transmit data through secured domains, and more ergonomic, intelligent, simple yet powerful personal computers from Apple.

AMERICAN CAPITALISM IN MODERNITY

When it comes to American capitalism we need to ask ourselves this question. Do all the MNCs and CEOs of America depend on in-depth knowledge of Pareto economics or post-Keynesian theory in order to make a profit? Why study when you can pay someone to do it right? If we examine the MNCs that have grown up indigenously in the United States we would find that there are very few economists and even fewer, if any at all, economic theorists, on their payroll. Why is this?

One reason is that economics is an extension of human nature's need to control the environment in the same way that Heidegger believed that technology was about controlling man's environment. Therefore, economics ought to be a vital technological tool for controlling the environment and if the intention of the MNCs was to dominate the capitalist and business environment with the aim of achieving monopolistic status. Yet economic theories about capitalism, the ideology that won the Cold War, do not seem to feature centrally in the modern MNC.

Perhaps this is because one does not need to have a Nobel laureate in economics to make rational market decisions. Any economics graduate should be able to effectively use the latest economic models to run specific alogarithms to determine the best possible outcome of a given problem. There is another reason why one does not have to be an economics genius or mathematically brilliant to determine when to make a stock purchase. Perhaps the greatest difficulty that economics as a discipline and economists as practitioners of their science is that they seem to come up with different predictions all the time for any one given problem. This is not the same as saying that one should do the direct opposite of the economic predictors and one would come out on top. This is also not necessarily true for all cases. There is a higher problem with economics in terms of economic philosophy which have tended to take a backseat in the modern universities across the globe. No one teaches economic philosophy and if it is indeed taught at the university, chances are that it would have been taught as a political ideology in the political science classrooms of the 1980s and 1990s. Perhaps this is where the problem lies. There is demand in modernity for straight and simple answers to the kinds of tricky situations are delivered by life in this age. As such the General Theory of Equilibrium involves recognition of a larger philosophical belief in a unified and balanced universe in which all things tend towards a symmetrical cadence, in a sense then, as an extension of the biology of man. Nevertheless, the latest research in economic theory revolves round econometric modeling, the use of algebraic formulae in computing market imperfections, applied economics, mapping of financial markets and stock indices, and computer programs that can track historical trends of market indicators, top performing investments and non-performing markets. This is where the economic modeling in modernity seems to be best employed: in the business of market analyses and prediction.

It would seem that the great western philosophers buried the treasure of the knowledge deep in complex and convoluted arguments that would take several lifetimes to distill. Some of the buried continental treasure continues to be researched by scholars interested in the aesthetic value, I think, more than making some practical link to Kantian Critiques in support of the Enlightenment. Kant's own contribution to economic thought was highly metaphysical. He believed that it was interpretation that creates the good rather than the good creating the interpretation. This would explain why there are many possible interpretations of an imagined or real concept across native speakers of the same language domain. But because Kant was so difficult to distill, his contemporaries interested in classical economics could not devote too much time to unraveling his transcendentalism and therefore a highly complex and abstract view of experience, subjectivity, and reality.

Nietzsche was more interested in warning us moderns about the damned thing called modernity and the dangers of event-filled historicism (and the doctrines that remind us of the importance of the so-called Wisdom of the Ages) rather than delving in perceiving and understanding economic models in modernity. Heidegger had something interesting to warn us about the dangers of technology. And he passed this message onto Arendt who squandered it on meaningful and accessible political theory. She demystified political philosophy, gave access to many, and lost some degree of the intrigued that had captivated scholars for the preceding 500 years. However there is an overlap of arguments on whether Arendt herself was a political philosopher or a political theorist. And it appears to me that she was more of a political theorist with training in political philosophy, a training system that she rejected in her work and experience of modernity, not in the least because of Heidegger's influence. But the world of these political philosophers and political theorists was one that was caught up with the great social, economic and cultural fractures of the time. It was an economic world that was limited and to an extent misdirected by the long staying power of European metaphysicians. Knowledge, both economic and political, continued to reassert itself in Hegelian terms of a dualistic universe. One that was set for the arrival of positivist social and political science where emphasis and appeal presented itself in terms of phenomena and explanatory models that were "applied," "practical," and "directed."

Most Americans however are less interested in the high abstraction of metaphysical theory and postmetaphysical speculation. Most Americans eventually came to accept the kind of neopragmatism that was associated with the observations of Thomas Paine and John Dewey. Ordinary American people were willing to settle for a much lower benchmark that explained economic life in simple terms. This benchmark is easily seen though not easily attainable. This currency involves making money work for you. So students who seem disinterested in philosophy and theory courses are indeed embarking on a pragmatic treadmill and will eventually discover that they are unable to keep up with the spinning and the speed. That is when they will rediscover the importance of reflecting on the ancient and medieval texts. But by then it might be too late. Yet armed with such knowledge, we should be able to avoid our minds becoming like the stories about Panama and acquire some kind of knowledge as best we can. Because knowledge is the real basis of power behind American MNCs and CEOs.

The case of Panama, the first genuine American MNC, is not such an unusual story that it stands out as a model for emulation. Rather, Panama seems to suggest a pattern among developing areas that would otherwise remain unused, infertile, perhaps even as dysfunctional as some of the crew on the *Ship of Fools*. But simply because places like Panama have been developed and its utility has been proven does not imply that it is a perfect story of success.

BUILDING CONFIDENCE

Accumulation theory details the fact that in order for a business strategy to work, there ought to be a unity of different aspects of the process (Jessop, 1990, 198–199; Rappa, 2001, 5–16). Any growth model requires arrangements, negotiations and business-like understanding between and among parties that intend to build a better society and perhaps a better world. The rise of the US as an economic hegemon reveals certain stories of successful capitalism that has been built on effective negotiations between politicians and business persons. The net effect of their work might severely be criticized as "collusion" at one end of the spectrum or "business acumen" on the other. In our story, we see that some aspects of building the organizational culture for American MNCs were born out of the Panama Canal (1870–1914). This involved a significant degree of collusion between the Chief Executive, Wall Street bankers and lawyers, and military men willing to do the dirty work of construction and coercion.

A nicer way of putting this would be creating a better understanding between government, businesses, and the army. In physical terms, the strange but functional idea of linking the Atlantic and Pacific Oceans goes back to the time of the Holy Roman Empire but a series of failures over almost four centuries resulted in the sale of the "site" by the French to the United States. While Ulysses S. Grant and William McKinley were the first two US presidents who were involved in this project, it was the youthful Theodore Roosevelt who pushed the canal works through after McKinley was assassinated. However, it was actually William H. Taft who saw the longest amount of digging work done on the project while the political scientist and war president, Woodrow Wilson, finally saw its proper end. It was a strange idea because of the immensity of the task but a functional one because if the idea could be achieved, communications would significantly be improved and the political returns would become enormous. One can therefore say that some analysts would argue that there was no collusion but instead the President was acting out of national interest and a deep desire to entrench US sovereignty.

Nevertheless, there was some degree of backroom dealing and secret meetings that enabled the US to take possession of the Canal Zone from Colombia through a third party agreement with a Frenchman designated to help out with the political processes required for eventual Congressional approval. The backroom political deal resulted in much hatred and antagonism toward the US but it seemed that only nature kept taking the lives of the construction crews through malaria and yellow fever. Nevertheless, the American MNCs such as the McClintic-Marshall Company, which was involved in the project, learnt much from the inept French attempts at creating a canal that was sufficiently wide and deep to allow ocean-going ships to pass through from the Pacific to the Atlantic and vice-versa.

There were also other secret deals in Wall Street that enabled the Canal's completion. The completion of the Canal was interrupted with the advent of World War I. Ironically, thousands of local inhabitants who were desirous of work and seeking employment anywhere they could find it would eventually die in the zone from various causes. And American workers died on the project that was operated and managed by former officers who received their professional military training from the US Corps of Engineers. This means that they had the expertise for moving and building roads, bridges, had knowledge of the use of explosives, and had practical training in war and peacetimes operations. This position of using former army officers ties in with anti-Marxist state theories of disciplining and controlling the police, military and other coercive state elements (Jessop, 1990, 279). The notion of control extends out from beyond the experience of labels. Hence military experience of individuals now converted to civilian occupations does not lessen the value of having shared those experiences in the first place.

The story of the Panama Canal is rationally described by David McCullough's *Path Between The Seas: The Creation of the Panama Canal, 1870-1914* (Simon & Schuster, 1978); Ulrich Keller *The Building of the Panama Canal in Historic Photographs* (Dover, 1984); and Ovidio Diaz Espino's *How Wall Street Created a Nation: J. P. Morgan, Teddy Roosevelt, and the Panama Canal* (New York: Four Walls Eight Windows, 2001). The creation of the Republic of Panama was the result of American neocolonialism and the strong-arm tactics of US president Theodore Roosevelt. In fact, Espino's intriguing book about the Panama Canal details the political duplicity, rhetoric, wheeling and dealing, and the gun-boat diplomacy that involved Theodore Roosevelt (the fifth cousin of the Great Depression Democratic president, Franklin D. Roosevelt); J. P. Morgan (the actual financier himself and not the corporation that took on his name); the Wall Street law firm, Sullivan and Cromwell; Philippe Bunau-Varilla; Charles P. Taft (the brother of the future president who was US Secretary of War); and Douglas Robinson (Roosevelt's brother-in-law) who helped finance the project.

Theodore Roosevelt believed in speaking softly and carrying a big stick. This does not mean that he was any more particularly powerful because of this style of leadership, but it does remind one of the kinds of political leaders who also used such a method. Rather than the fire and brimstone and charismatic political leader, Roosevelt was more akin to leaders like Deng Xiaoping rather than Mao Zedung. In other words, the leadership style required of politicians in charge of large economies does not necessarily have to be tied to their political ideologies. Roosevelt introduced many progressive policies that liberated America from its relatively insular, Western European-bound thinking. After all, America was still fighting to survive as a nation within a world where the UK and France were still considered Great Powers. Ironically, Roosevelt did not like the railroads and the stranglehold they had over large parts of the contiguous United States.

But Roosevelt's policies would prove too progressive for many Americans and he failed to get re-elected even after being shot in the chest (this was before Term Limits were imposed on the Executive Branch of US government, i.e., the President of the United States of America).[1] A Nobel Peace Prize-winner himself, Roosevelt believed that he would greatly expand the powers of the executive. This president believed that while one should not break the law, one ought to certainly go to the fullest extent of doing what the law would not *expressly* forbid. Perhaps because Roosevelt was a Republican president (though he switched to the Progressive label after the War) he appeared to have the "right" political ideals to move American liberal capitalism in ways that a democratic president could not. See for example, the arguments put forward by writers like Edmund Morris *The Rise of Theodore Roosevelt* (Ballantine, 1980) and Nathan Miller's *Theodore Roosevelt* (Perennial, 1994).

And ultimately, perhaps not by design or executive fault, American taxpayers paid the price. This was because, as the famous journalist Pulitzer discovered, it was scandalous how American taxpayers had not even known that they had paid 10 times the amount of money for a piece of property that was worth only US$4 million in 1914 dollars.[2] That is equivalent to about three-quarters of a billion US dollars in 2005. The Panama Canal, Theodore Roosevelt and (what is known in political science as) the rise of the "Imperial Presidency," Wall Street and "foreigners" set the basis for this chapter on the political power of American MNCs.

OUTSOURCING

Outsourcing is not new. It is a business technique like putting old wine in new wineskins. Outsourcing involves moving the more expensive "parts" and aspects of American businesses to someplace cheaper. Yet there seems to be a current trend in modernity where there is a need to label old activities with new names such as "convergence," "conveyance," "prospecting," "head-hunting," "downsizing," "right-sizing," "matrix," "flat hierarchy," "in-sourcing," and "outsourcing" for example. Outsourcing for US corporations is worth anywhere between US$58 billion to US$75 billion annually in savings.

Since the 1990s, at least ostensibly after the end of the Cold War, there was a rise in the need to outsource less productive sections of businesses. However, over the past three years, the tide appears to have changed. The current backlash against Business Process Outsourcing (BPO) might be attributed to a section of America interested in supporting xenophobic tendencies. American xenophobia, catalyzed by the tragedy of 9/11 and the recent public beheading of an innocent American hostage in Iraq is going to get much worse before it sinks even lower. Most Americans are not xenophobic, but those who do fear foreigners tend to direct their hatred towards them because they believe these foreigners are stealing American jobs.

Yet capitalist states appear to be able to survive the vagaries of neoliberalism very well through regulatory policy and a firm knowledge of the extra or external economic arena as Jessop argues poignantly in *State Theory* (1990, 309-310). For example, many US businesses feel that the best bet is with foreign labor for several reasons. Firstly, they are not paid in US dollars and are not domiciled (and hence not a burden on the US domestic economy) in the US. While Jessop's own brand of neoMarxism does not tally with the kind of critique that Sartre and others presented, his complex theories of descriptive capitalist accumulation strategies continue to make intellectual sense. Furthermore, because these workers are not living in America, the company doesn't have to worry about the high cost of medical insurance, cost-of-living allowances, income tax deductions, US laws and INS regulations governing foreign work permits, the problem of legal aliens becoming illegal aliens, cultural shock, and 401K pension schemes.

These foreigners are therefore not eligible under US law for medical, dental and other benefits. And so the companies do not have to and are certainly not obligated to resolve these social expectations of life in modernity. Also, foreign outsourced labor does not have to be unionized, which is a big headache for US corporations because workers are supposed to work and not to think in modernity.

MNCs resorted to the use of BPO for their backroom and frontroom operations in order to lower their cost profiles and rid themselves of unwanted social burdens involved in the production of goods and services in a given set of countries. Some pundits believe that outsourcing is a good thing for consumers and citizens alike. They say it is good for consumers because the lower costs enjoyed from BPO mean a cheaper product and the savings are then passed on directly to the consumer base. The reason, they go on, why outsourcing is good for the citizens is because while jobs are lost here in the United States, they result in higher employment levels overall since the overall returns mean a more profitable company or MNC that can then higher more locals to do more technically-demanding jobs at higher wages.

The problem with this argument is that it is false and misleading. MNCs exist for one purpose—to make money for their shareholders. As long as the MNC can find a better, cheaper, and more productive way of producing a good over a shorter time span, it will continue to do so. Lower costs are often not passed on to the consumer, and the citizens who need the lost jobs are often not the ones who are the same consumers of the given product. Nor are they able to fill the promised, more technically-demanding jobs at higher wages. This means that on average, outsourcing is good for the macroeconomy, MNC shareholders, its Board, and pretty much no one else. In fact, when more operations are moved overseas, the MNCs tax profiles are lowered significantly. This means that Uncle Sam can't tax the productive MNC anyway and the potential incidence of tax on such businesses may be lost for good.

Let's put some relevant numbers together to support this argument. Various risk analysts estimate the total projected costs of outsourcing by US-based MNCs, where the MNC is headquartered in any one of the fifty states including Hawaii and Alaska to fall within a range. That range of numbers *ceteris paribus* looks like this: between 200,000 and 500,000 new jobs created overseas; between US\$1.5 billion to US\$25 billion over the next five to eight years.[3] I know what you must be thinking right now. The numbers are insignificant when compared to the revenues that could be derived from in-sourcing backroom operations, et cetera. However, if we take the lower end of US\$1.5 billion, this would amount to much more money than most average American workers would receive in a given state in the US during a non-inflationary year, perhaps with the exception of Alaska, Hawaii, Illinois, New York, North Carolina, and Texas.

And, if we took just one half of the lower range of jobs created (i.e., 100,000 new jobs created) while the numbers represent an average, and a small one at that, the value derived from such numbers would not be something to scoff at during an election year. Also, outsourcing versus insourcing does not create more jobs for locals and foreigners alike. This is a trick that supporters of outsourcing use to confound the ignorant: the "if you move MNC jobs overseas you will create new jobs back home" argument really ought to be read as "let's hire foreigners to do the jobs locals could do because they're cheaper and less troublesome." So why should US MNCs cut back on outsourcing? Because there are totally employable Americans who are willing and able to do these jobs at equally competitive salaries without resorting to aggressive trade union tactics?

It's merely a matter of where the MNCs want to put their money and how much of a bottom line the management is thinking about.

This reminds us of the kind of neo-Gramscian theories that effectively mapped out the nature of the capitalist bottom line. In addition, readers can pursue the powerful arguments made by Niklas Luhmann, Michael Mann, and especially Ernest Mandel's *Late Capitalism* (1975). The desire and greed for wealth has resulted in a fall in offspring in developed countries with the exception of the US. We are aware that part of the reason for the graying populations of post-industrial countries is due to the fact that many people perceive having children as being an economic burden. And if a primary purpose of marriage is to have children, then many younger people seem to be putting this socially constructed arrangement off because having a family means that one cannot spend all one earns on oneself. Apart from the US, other developed nations are falling deep into the fertility trap where their most precious resource—their citizens—is not meeting their quota of offspring. This is the bottom line of fertility: there will be fewer younger people to support a larger number of older persons over the next 25 to 50 years.

One clear problem that besets modernity's advanced postindustrial societies is that the fertility problem knows no national boundaries. The replacement level of citizens who make up these countries keeps falling. Total Fertility Rate (TFR) is down. With some exception to the US, the rest of the developed world has failed in trying to raise the TFR to 2.1 for every woman of child-bearing years. It would also appear that it becomes increasingly more difficult to raise the level the closer one gets to the 2.1 threshold, which can be explained by Pareto's law where 80 per cent effort might be able to achieve at best outcome, a 20 per cent increase towards the target level.

Thus far, the literature on aging indicates that pronatalist policies have not worked comprehensively. And those policies that have worked are too deeply buried under other kinds of social policy that it becomes difficult to isolate the independent variable. But trying to isolate the independent variable in the case of pronatalist policies is like trying to predict who might win the 2008 US presidential elections. It is a needle in a haystack; everyone knows that it is in there somewhere but no one can safely say where it might be. The US is an exceptional case because of its liberal immigration policies that do not discriminate against ethnic ancestry as found in other countries. This means that people continue to find America an attractive place that is suitable to raise a family. Policy makers outside the US are searching for different methods and modes of resolving the issue of aging by changing essentialist and patriarchal policies, modifying in-migration laws, and giving bonuses and perks for those they want to produce more children. And the economic bottom line is that the economies with the larger number of younger people might be the ones that survive late modernity.

A CONVERGENCE THEORY OF POVERTY

There is a cautionary note from the *Global Monitoring Report 2004* that most developing countries will fail to meet their poverty reduction targets even those projected for as late as the next decade. This finding is not surprising because as neoMarxist theory tells us, there will continue to be a widening gap between the rich and the poor, between the haves and the have nots. As global population increases at an increasing rate especially in the developing countries, there will be more people who need employment, and hence more people in competition for potentially the same amount of occupations that are available.

The widening gap between the impoverished and the richest rich in countries (regardless of GNP per capita) will continue unabated. This is because there are significant indications from all financial sectors, business trend projections, and government policy analyses that the poor are here to stay.

Most poor persons will be unable to get back on the capitalist beltway to life, liberty and the pursuit of happiness. This is because of their hand-to-mouth existence and because they are likely to fall through the social safety net and hit the ground running from all the social pressures that keep them down there: illegal drug abuse, alcoholism, welfare dependency, racism, gambling debts, incarceration, prostitution, homelessness, demoralized attitudes towards neoliberal capitalism, and the neuroses and psychoses that prevent their minds from pulling themselves up by the bootstraps. Very often the poor are just poor because of bad luck, that catch all phrase exhibiting a category for those who are born at the wrong time, in the wrong place, and for the wrong reasons. Even the World Bank and IMF have projected dismal views of the future for the next decade.[4]

It seems clear to me that neoliberal capitalism requires a certain quota of poverty to exist at the bottom of the achievement-oriented society. Achievement societies can only do so much for people whose luck is always so bad that they can't seem to possibly recover from anything that is done to help them. This is what I call the "convergence theory of poverty." The operating principle here is that capitalist societies need many more poor and impoverished persons as a complement to the wealth and power of a few. The disparity between the two is concordant with the images and metaphors of ontological perceptions of being. In other words, human beings living under the so-called aegis of modernity are self-prescribed units that buy into the images created by the international mass media to the point that these images, however inaccurate, however sketchy or however partial, become the reality of the message that is being revealed. People believe in statistical support of poverty because the image of poverty exists as an important function of world capitalist domination. It is not so much that the urban and rural poor are uniting in some global undercurrent, because you know that they can't achieve this, but that there is a clear pattern of the poor—within all societies whether rich or poor—to converge and deepen their dismal livelihood. They look into the mirror and believe that the image is their own. And the call for change from social worker types is always the same: better policy planning, the government should do more, CEOs and other corporate big wigs are too busy chasing the almighty dollar, and a need for voluntarism in most societies. But how much is enough?

Could it be that the ideological nature of capitalism requires the presence of the poor? And that for the minority rich to remain in their wealth, there has to be a poor underclass of persons who simply cannot achieve or fit into any other part of the political and social system that they are branded outcasts from the onset?

Poverty is converging across all centers of capitalist development. It appears that there has to be a sufficiently large pool of impoverished people for the existence of a few wealthy ones. Perhaps Marx was right about the owners of the factors of production being callous authoritarian controllers of the "have nots." While he was certainly wrong about the historical determinism of revolution arising out of the internal contradictions between the base and the superstructure, he was quite right that there would be problems within capitalist societies that display great differences of wealth between the rich and the poor, between the workers and the owners of these workers.

No "real" Marxist or "Socialist" revolution is in the cards for America's future. But even if it did arrive later in American modernity, the poor will doubtless become cannon fodder for the movers and shakers of neoliberal global capitalism. So who are these movers and shakers and what kinds of salaries and bonuses do they expect to motivate them to higher levels of capitalist creativity? The next section examines with some empirical data the kind of expectations and results that the best American CEOs have achieved in recent years. This harks back to the wonderful quote from Thucydides's *History of the Peloponnesian War* where it is said that "we use riches rather for opportunities of action than for verbal contestation, and hold it not a shame to confess poverty but not to have avoided it" (Hobbes, 1959, "The Second Book," sect 40, 111). This means that we should not even be worried about using wealth to promote wealth while simultaneously having had previously experienced the depression and obstacle of poverty and its deep and dark cavern of remorse and regret. No one owes the impoverished a living, and successful CEOs continue to realize this as a reality throughout their lives. Capitalism and the neoliberal international economic system as we understand it today provides a deep and unending series of traps that serve to weaken and complicate honest and earnest attempts at accumulating capital. There is not an individual alive today who can remain secure with a total belief in the capitalist oeuvre. This is because the commitment to capitalism does not ensure or guarantee any thing more than one's participation in global process of greed and avarice.

Capitalism is both theory and practice in one, and cannot and should not be understood as being separable into Sophia and praxis, or any other Hegelian form of dualistic world view. It cannot be understood outside theory. In a throwback to the great thinkers of the Enlightenment, it becomes clear that capitalism is neutral in the sense of being callous and unfeeling. It is like that old and famous poem by James Shirley called *Death the Leveller*. That at the end of the road of modern life is a guaranteed end where one can not even bring one's accumulated wealth or poverty. It is an end where one will experience the total transformation of one's own biological matter as it is dispensed outwardly into the cosmos until the initial energy that exists is nothing that resembles the original mass. We are all moving towards that nothingness and will eventually have nothing to prove our existence, let alone, the achievements that we think we might have made in this single life. In a sense, there is a great degree of nothingness in capitalism and awaiting capitalists. A certain quality makes capitalists as a whole very driven and pragmatic people, unwilling and unbending to give much personal time to the study of political philosophy or the classics of economic theory as those espoused by the great Irish political economists. Perhaps if they did make space and time for such study there would be much fewer capitalists alive and well today. Thus in order for the convergence theory to work capitalism must work and Marxian economics must fail. So here we have a clear epistemological path, even if only temporarily grounded, at this stage in late modernity.

CEO HAVEN

If you consider yourself a true American capitalist, then you would want to be part of the top range CEO Haven that resounds with stories of successful American Dreams. But for every successful CEO raking in huge corporate bonuses there are stories of CEOs involved in corporate scandals, abusing executive privilege by taking personal flights on the company jet, and fully-paid vacations overseas on company expense in order to evade personal taxes and paying Uncle Sam. There are CEOs who get special perks such as housing allowances for relocating to another city or country, country club membership fees, children's education allowances, golden parachutes, and special signing bonuses that are not immediately revealed to the general shareholder or American public. Of course. Why would they?

Designating yourself as an American CEO is one thing, but getting into CEO Haven requires such skill and finesse that every single decision made by the board or by you or your top flight executives, or executives you inherited could result in falling through some IRS crevice that divides good business practice from bad. This would require you to have the passion of a Nietzschean superman who is willing and able to risk everything and challenge conventional wisdom and people who prefer to take the safe and cautious route to life. Rather than be held back by Platonic idealism, Cartesian logic, or Hegelian contortionism, the candidates for CEO Haven are indeed those who have not been affected by the influence of metaphysical speculations through directed study or indirectly through the mechanism we now understand as the system of liberal education.

When Ellen Smith, a writer for the Associated Press, claimed that the "the highest paid executives collectively enjoyed $30.9 million"[5] I did not believe this because it seemed that the figure was too small. While Smith was correct in arguing that the perks for American CEOs were clear and present to the public, she did not pursue the matter sufficiently.

For example, the CEO of Goldman Sachs, Hank Paulson, received US$21.4 million in fiscal 2003 that was almost twice his fiscal 2002 pay (which was a whopping US$12.1 million) excluding the US$5 million bonus for that year.[6] The headline news of such achievements drives and motivates capitalists to go to extremes in order to achieve top-notch status. Much has to be sacrificed. Unfortunately, this often involves breaking the law. Because capitalists are by nature very impatient with their own personal goals and often mix their personal goals with their corporate ability to achieve those goals, most forget that it takes most successful CEOs decades to get to where they are. The top earners in corporate America earn more than the US president could even think about making in two consecutive terms in office.

The youngest CEOs at the very top have a median age range of 38–43. Most have graduate training in business. Some are legally trained while others have degrees from prestigious Ivy League universities which as we all know are crucial for making network connections. The public is drawn to both the stories of success and failure of the CEOs. There is much applause and support for those on the ascent while those who fall quickly see their celebrity status disappear and their erstwhile colleagues scamper for cover from all forms of government agencies. Unlike many other countries, the anti-trust culture in the US is very strong and the public are often willing supporters of condemning corporate monopolistic culture as they are sometimes ready to invest directly and quietly in these giants themselves. A true capitalist CEO who desires to be part of American CEO Haven has to be able to walk the tightrope between shady deals that lead to financial perdition and ethical ones that can often lead to dismal returns to stockholders.

The problem for the people at the top is how to negotiate modes of going to the fullest extent of what the law does not expressly forbid, as Theodore Roosevelt did, without breaking it. But because shareholders and other greedy executives are often impatient to consider the magnitude of their personal wants and business objectives, they are willing to remain quiet and to elect CEOs who are both able and willing to bend the law to their own advantage. As long as people benefit within the neoliberal capitalist culture of corporate America, they will remain silent. If they feel that they have not benefited sufficiently, they will complain, and sometimes such complaints results in the fall of very highly placed public officials and corporate executives. Most shareholders are often not aware of the wheeling and dealing exercises of their CEOs. Most only want a

CEO who will take their company to new and profitable heights regardless of the consequences to the environment, the customer base, or the people working towards the bottom line.

However, there are many pitfalls along the way because for every honest business person on Wall Street, there are people who are watching and waiting for that honesty to dissipate into insurance fraud, tax evasion, backroom deals, abuse of company expenses, falsification of internal audit processes, and insider trading. *New York Post* reported on April 27, 2004 that a Long Island software manufacturer (known throughout the US as Computer Associates) had finally conceded its faulty accounting procedures that claimed US$2.2 billion in sales in 2000 and 2001. Legal suits were raised against Sanjay Kumar and his accomplices who posted negative results in order to collect US$1.1 billion in bonuses. Securities and Exchange Commission (SEC) investigators revealed discrepancies that eventually resulted in the demotion of CEO Sanjay Kumar, who is expected to be indicted by State prosecutors who are getting help from whistle blower Ira Zar, the ex-CFO of Computer Associates who admitted to accounting fraud. The IRS is sufficiently capable of monitoring the lifestyles of these people even long after they have served their prison sentences to ensure that whatever profits that could possibly be recouped would be done so in the most expeditious manner.

The money that is thrown at the capitalist "big boys" is so dazzling that it makes the decision-making process of many top flight executives seem to be all about the business of business risk. "Do I?" or "Don't I?" How much is it worth and how much can I get away with? American MNCs are not alone in the SEC investigations. Recently, China Life became the target of an SEC insurance probe into its IPO in New York and Hong Kong.[7] China Life is the largest assurance company in China and the probe will slow down the intention of gaining greater investments to speed up the growth of its local and foreign markets. There might be irregularities and omissions in the conduct of China Life's daily core businesses as reported in the *Financial Times* of London.

The view from above can sometimes be cloudy and therefore confusing and misleading and there are moves and ways forward that might be contentious but bring in more cash to the company than a tropical storm brings rain to a Panamanian jungle. But for those who are able to stay on that tight rope and see through the clouds, without getting on the wrong side of the SES, DEA, FBI, or private investigators, the bonuses and benefits are amazing. Not as amazing as the amount of money that *Amazon.com* CEO makes a year (in spite of the incredible success of his company over the past decade), but often better than his entire composite stock options in the company. The benefits and bonuses can only go upwards with the right CEO, in spite of gloomy business conditions.[8] Often times, the salaries of these high-flying CEOs contain such buffers as to be virtually recession-proof. *The top achievers in CEO Haven who can stay ethical and clean in their business deals stand to make the most money over time and to keep it even if the company's profits swan-dive.*

And I say recession-proof because it seems that these *guys*, because 90 percent of the top 15 percent of all capitalist achievers in this patriarchal world are men who get incredible amounts of money even when the company is doing poorly and has gone completely into the red. There is an even more interesting story to tell about the very top capitalist achievers. According to *Forbes*, the highest-paid American CEOs in 2002 were all men. Most had graduate training in business and related fields or at least useful ones like law and accounting. Most had been at the job for at least 10 years. And most were in their mid- to late-60s. In other words, CEOs right at the top do not appear overnight, nor does it take only a few years to make it to CEO Haven. The norm for achieving top flight CEO-ship is between 15 to 35 years on the job *and* to be in charge as a CEO. The *crème de la crème* include: Reuben Mark (Colgate-Palmolive), George David (United Technologies), Richard S. Fuld Jr. (Lehman Brothers)[9], Henry R. Silverman (Cendant)[10], Dwight C. Schar (NVR), Lawrence Ellison (Oracle), Richard M. Kovacevich (Wells Fargo), Howard Solomon (Forest Labs), James E. Cayne (Bear Stearns), and Todd S. Nelson (Apollo-Education Group). These were only in the 2002 cohort. They are very wealthy men even in 2005.[11]

The top achievers in CEO Haven who can stay ethical and clean in their business deals stand to make the most money over time and to keep it even if the company's profits swan-dive. For example, according to *Forbes*, the worst performer in their analysis was Richard A. Manoogian who has been the CEO of *Masco* for 36 years. His six-year average compensation amounted to nothing less than US$13,023,626 according to *Masco's* books. Another poor CEO who received an "F" grade from Forbes was Stephen F. Bollenbach, the eight-year-long CEO of Hilton Hotels, whose six-year average compensation was US$6,339,279. Take the famous name of Michael D. Eisner, the CEO of Walt Disney for 20 years. His six-year average compensation according to Forbes was a fantasy-world amount of US$121,170,940.[12] This is why the salaries of these high-flying CEOs contain such buffers as to be virtually recession-proof because no one else can fill their august positions given the political sensitivities of removing a CEO who knows too much or of replacing one to whom the political fortunes and life-long careers are indelibly tied to, and we wouldn't want the whole stack of cards to fall over.

The successful MNC must have capable drivers who always think only in the best interests of the company and not themselves. This matter is best illustrated in CitiGroup's current setting aside of US$6 billion towards legal costs in the pending law suits in the Enron case where the securities corporation engaged in shady deals that drove the company from dazzling and meteoric heights of capitalists' fantasy to the dustbin of the dotcoms. Another MNC characteristic is "drive and passion" for the company that equals long-term rewards. At least most of the time. The MNC must always outlive its CEOs and executive management. The business must go on in spite of the cracks that set in or in case of unforeseen circumstances. *The people want their goods. Or they will take their money elsewhere.* CEOs' successes, however, sometimes take their toll. Perhaps it seems just a little too ironic for the CEO of a fast food MNC who promoted healthier forms of fast food (like an expanded salad range) to die of a heart attack *at a fast food convention.* Take the case of Jim Cantalupo of McDonald's Corporation, for example. While Cantalupo's company was making one and a half times more than the previous financial year:

> CEO...Jim Cantalupo ... died of a heart attack while in Florida for a McDonald's convention, was replaced by the fast-food chain's 43-year-old president and chief operating officer, Charlie Bell. Bell paid tribute to Cantalupo in a news release accompanying McDonald's quarterly earnings report as "an incredibly inspiring and passionate leader" and said he is committed to strengthening McDonald's and 'continuing the momentum that began under Jim's leadership.' Net income for the first three months of the year was US$511.5 million, or 40 US cents per share, compared with US$327.4 million, or 26 US cents per share, for the same period a year ago. That matched the consensus estimate of analysts surveyed by Thomson First Call. Revenue was US$4.4 billion, up 16 per cent from US$3.8 billion a year earlier.[13]

It is sad to think that the amount of wealth we accumulate, like the Egyptian Pharaohs who had only one really big project, can never be taken with us when we die. All the good deeds that Cantalupo did for the poor and the needy in his lifetime have done nothing to extend the brevity that was his life. This is why capitalism is about greed and avarice, and not about being a nice guy. Because no matter how nice you are, as Jim Cantalupo was in his days in the sun, fate gets the better of us all in the end. And like a thief in the night, it is said, the grim reaper never stops working. Does it really matter whether you are a philosopher or a demagogue? And doesn't the sudden death of Cantalupo remind us all that no matter what we are in life, our legacy is only as long as the memory of the people who are still alive and maybe one day we might be featured in some footnote hidden in some unread text in a digital library. One thing is for sure, as the CEO of McDonalds, Cantalupo left a certain legacy that was politically relevant and socially necessary:

> McDonald's premium salad range was one of several innovations introduced in the US by [Jim] Cantalupo that drove sales and helped give McDonald's a healthier image in the face of rising concerns over obesity ... Charlie Bell, the 43-year-old Australian-appointed chief executive within hours of Cantalupo's death after a heart attack on April 19, pledged to continue the momentum of the changes begun by his predecessor ... McDonald's had served 2.3 million more customers during the first quarter compared with last year, the equivalent of adding 1,500 restaurants, but had added only 100 restaurants in the past 12 months.[14]

The new CEO was appointed within hours of the old CEO's death. The MNC must outlive its CEO and improve on what the CEO has done in order to continue to satisfy the legal requirements of its faceless shareholders. The heads of America's 500 biggest companies received an aggregate 8 per cent pay in fiscal 2003 and as a group their total compensation amounted to US$3.3 billion versus US$3.1 billion in fiscal 2002.[15] While the remuneration in CEO Haven is more money than ordinary folk like you and I will make in a thousand lifetimes, what is startling is the vulgar continuity of the process, and the willingness for some to be sad in one frame, and happy in the next. Like those broadcast journalists who can affect a smile when telling a happy story and show a serious look of concern when someone had been blown up in a car bomb somewhere.

HOPE: BACKGROUNDS THAT WORK

The top financial MNCs such as Goldman Sachs, Morgan Stanley, Merrill Lynch, Lehman Brothers, J.P. Morgan, Janus Capital, UBS, Citigroup, Deutsche Bank, Bear Stearns, Deloitte & Touche, PricewaterhouseCoopers, KPMG, Charles Schwab, Bank of America, Wells Fargo, and The Bank of New York all make their money the old fashioned way: "selling confidence about the future based on the present." But let's consider the person right at the top who pulls the team together and who make the politics of American globalization work the way it does. These are people who have usually gone through the right education system, possess the right values, and have an instinctive feel for taking the right business risk. What does it mean to be a successful CEO? Can we rely on a summary of their background interests to chart a course of understanding about the way commercial politics works? Were it possible, it would be interesting to create a clone distilled from the background of these CEOs to create a super CEO? Not possible. Nevertheless, some brief background notes on America's top CEOs is instructive to understand the power that motivates neoliberal corporate America.

Top on the list is Reuben Mark who has been CEO of Colgate-Palmolive for 20 years and with the company for over 43 years. *Forbes* ranks this 65-year old man as number one in terms of "Household & Personal Products." Mark was educated at Middlebury College, graduating with a BA in 1960 and holds a Harvard MBA dating back to 1963. He urged Colgate to help rebuild a school in Harlem and actually used to do community volunteer work on Manhattan island till he moved to his Greenwich, Connecticut home.[16] According to *Business Week*, "He rode a motorcycle … hunts game birds … and wants his company to be the superstar, not him."[17] Mark's total compensation package was US$148 million.[18]

Number two on the list is George David. For the past 10 years, George David has been CEO of United Technologies (UTX) and worked for the company for almost 31 years. David has been ranked number one in terms of "Conglomerates" was educated at Harvard and holds an MBA from the University of Virginia's Darden Graduate School of Business Administration. According to *CNNMoney*:

George David runs a company so diversified it makes products as small as air conditioners along with products as complex as the military's Blackhawk helicopters. With 155,000 employees worldwide, United Technologies has held its course and managed an impressive 28 billion dollars in revenue. Since David took over in 1994, the operating profit margin has jumped from four per cent to 14 per cent.[19]

David also believes in voluntary service, having served in the United Way in Hartford and in the American Red Cross. David's total compensation package was US$70.5 million.[20]

Number three on the list is Richard S. Fuld Jr., who has been the CEO of Lehman Bros Holdings (LEH) since 1993. Fuld Jr., is 58 years old and holds degrees from Colorado and NYU's Stern Business School. Fuld also chairs Lehman Brothers Executive Committee. He used to chair the Mt. Sinai Children's Center Foundation. His total compensation package according to *Forbes* was US$67.7 million.[21] Henry R. Silverman has been CEO of Cendant (CD) for almost 15 years in the same company that he founded. *Forbes* ranked this 63-year old executive number one in the "Hotels, Restaurants & Leisure Education" industry. He holds degrees from Williams College and is a Juris Doctor from the University of Pennsylvania. Silverman has made significant contributions to various buildings, scholarships, professorships, and other academic activities at the University of Pennsylvania. He was also awarded honors for his public crusade against discrimination by the US Hispanic Chamber of Commerce. The State of New York Governor's Office nominated Silverman to the Board of Commissioners of The Port Authority of New York and New Jersey.[22] A Yankees fan, Silverman, "is a study in contrasts. Formal, almost aristocratic in his bearing, he favors monogrammed shirts and a plush office that's sprinkled with Georgian antiques. But his speech is blunt, with a manner more like a street fighter than the prep school-educated son of privilege."[23] His total declared direct shares at Cendant tallied up to eight million in the summer of 2003 and his total compensation package according to *Forbes* was US$60 million.[24]

The next one on the list is Dwight C. Schar. He has been CEO of NVR for 18 years, and actually worked with the company for a total of 35 years so far. As a 62-year-old CEO, *Forbes* ranks him number one in "Construction." He was educated at Ashland University. Schar was a former teacher whose own story is a kind of latter day rags-to-riches narrative. He worked his way up very quickly and astutely made the right political moves that finally ended in his taking over the company itself. He currently is one of a 100 business persons who are the Northern Virginia Roundtable that represents the heart of the economic force of Republicanism in the state.[25] While the Roundtable is not really a pressure group, it certainly is a lobbying community of business-minded individuals who support political causes that put business as a top priority. Over the years, he has demonstrated that he is most capable at political networking. Apart from his political contributions in cash and kind that led him to become George Bush's Finance Chair for the state of Virginia, Schar has made other commitments. He has contributed to the local university, children's groups, youth groups and teen groups, and a cancer society. Schar is a generous donor to the causes in which he strongly believes. He and some of his friends also expressed their passion for the Redskins when they got together to make a controlling bid for that team.[26] Schar is now considered a minority owner of the team:

> The Redskins completed the sale of a minority stake in the club, to Dwight C. Schar, Robert Rothman and Fred Smith. Their purchase of about 20 per cent of the Redskins for a little over $200 million—with no say over operations—put the total value of the organization at over $1 billion.[27]

NVR is now found across 11 states and its total sales approximate US$3.7 billion.[28] Schar's total compensation package according to *Forbes* was US$58.1 million.[29]

Lawrence J. Ellison has been CEO of Oracle (ORCL) for 27 years. Ellison was born in 1944 and founded Oracle 27 years ago, when he was appointed CEO and director in 1977. He was also company president from 1978 to 1996. Ellison said:

> NT will earn more, but Windows CE may become the world's most ubiquitous operating system. And in each case, Microsoft is using its desktop monopoly and predatory tactics to … control the standards, eliminate competing access points, lock consumers into Microsoft products, and purchase competing technologies. With over $12 billion of monopoly profits in the bank, there are few markets Microsoft can't dominate. But it doesn't stop there. Microsoft is now aggressively moving to use its monopoly power to control online content. As more

and more Americans come online, the ability of Microsoft to favor its own content will have profound cultural, societal, consumer and economic implications. For your news go to MSNBC™; for financial services go to Microsoft Investor™; for travel services go to Microsoft Expedia™; for retail shopping go to the Microsoft Plaza™; to buy a car go to Microsoft Carpoint™; and to buy or sell a house go Microsoft Home Advisor™.[30]

It has always been Ellison's (and *Oracle's*) dream to be number one. Not surprisingly, Ellison is a close friend of Apple's Steve Jobs. While Jobs has had the most difficult of all the backgrounds in the sense that he was orphaned at a young age, and, like Gates and others, dropped out of college and hence took a big risk, Jobs is not on the rich CEO list. His own net worth of US$1 billion puts him very far behind his friend Ellison and others.

One person that has eluded both Oracle's Ellison and Apple's Jobs is Bill Gates. Perhaps one of the most influential man on the computing earth, Gates allowed Jobs to cut an Internet browser deal years ago that would save Apple. Bill Gates is just a cut above the rest. Always one step forward. Constantly just one move ahead. Consider his 1999 book, *Business @ the Speed of Thought*. Gates and his wife Melinda have donated over US$23.8 billion to charities on education and learning. After all, that is *Microsoft's* core business. Married in 1994, he and Melinda have three children and Gates plays bridge and golf to relax. Bill Gates is also one of the most controversial political figures in corporate America. He is like an almost indispensable interactive wood-carpenter of the 21st century. The majority of Americans and non-Americans worldwide use his benches and platforms to do work, it doesn't matter what kind of work, it is mostly done with Microsoft. When I was in graduate school, there was a strong movement against using Microsoft and IBM PCs. Many of us had no choice but to churn out term papers and finals on type-writers or Apple derivatives. What was political in the corporate world of computing software somehow traveled down to us all and not surprisingly. While many people actually learn to use a computer on old Apple II models, most end up with a PC.

Politically, the *PC* is less robot and more human. The Mac and its derivatives like the various *G-series, and the PowerBooks* are too ergonomic. Too pretty. You want to admire them for their plastics, colors and curvature. They are seemingly faultless. The PC, on the other hand is more like human nature because it breaks down. It has bugs. And it allows the user to tinker with it when it breaks down. If a Mac were to break down, you couldn't really fix it unless you were some stellar geek. But with a PC and with Microsoft, you could do so many things to fix it. To tinker around with its mechanisms. But there it is again. Political karma. My own students now use their PCs as an excuse for not turning in papers, or forgetting to make a back-up file, et cetera. The strong movement against Microsoft and the PC in our graduate school days ended in a division of hardware between, as you guessed, the PC cluster and the Mac cluster. The rest is history. Many of us thought that Apple sold out when there was talk of having an eventual merger with the PC and using Microsoft Internet browsers. Perhaps during the Cold War it was more important to have clear alternatives. We now return to the CEOs who themselves depend on the work of Ellison, Jobs, and Gates.

Lawrence J. Ellison, like Jobs, and Gates does not have the benefit of any college degree, or graduate school MBA. This might be the reason why they made it so far. Perhaps it was because they were not tainted by the education "system," and indeed created a system apart. Perhaps it can be said in American popular culture that the nerds do control the globalized, computing world. Ellison is a 59-year-old African-American CEO ranked number one by Forbes in "Software & Services." And for a man who taught himself all he needs to know, he earns a total compensation package of US$40.6 million.[31] *Forbes 400* cited him in 2001 as the third richest person in America with US$58 billion, while the second richest person was Bill Gates of *Microsoft Corporation* who clocked in at US$63 billion, while the ninth richest was Michael Dell of *Dell Computers* whose gross wealth is estimated at US$16 billion. Bill Gates has been the richest man in America from 1993–2003. But if Sam Walton of Wal-Mart were still around, according to *Forbes 400*, he would be worth about twice as much as Bill Gates. Sam Walton was born March 29, 1918 and died in 1992.

There are other top-notch CEOs, like Richard M. Kovacevich (Wells Fargo), who was educated at Stanford and receives a total compensation package of US$37.8 million.[32] Listed also as one of the most powerful individuals in America, Howard Solomon was born on August 12, 1927 in New York. Solomon is the CEO of Forest Labs.[33] This 76-year-old has degrees from CUNY and a Juris Doctor from Yale and is widowed with two sons, Andrew and David. Solomon commands a compensation package of US$36.1 million.[34] A Republican-supporter of the Bush campaign, James E. Cayne is the CEO of Bear Stearns (of diversified financials fame), 70 years old, and like Ellison has no degrees but commands a total compensation package of US$33.9 million.[35] Bear Stearns has twenty offices around the world and had 10,574 people on its payroll in 2002. The diversified financials' company has benefited significantly over the border wars between New Jersey and New York state, receiving tax incentives to stay on in New York and politically outwitting successive New York politicians, including the venerable Rudy Giuliani.[36]

The tenth best-compensated CEO is a young 44-year-old who was a former executive vice president and faculty member of the University of Utah. Todd S. Nelson, CEO of Apollo-Education Group, has degrees from Brigham Young University and UNLV, is worth US$32.8 million.[37] Running an MNC in America or at least from an American city with worldwide connections is not like building the Panama Canal. The tasks are now more urgent, with seemingly limitless possibilities, intense rivalry and competition, and limited resources. And the US president does not usually directly intervene to help out. There are some clear characteristics that all American CEOs share that make them the wealthy capitalists that they are today. All are willing to put in more energy than what they perceive are their nearest competitors by industry. All have a high degree of focus on a making a simple mission spectacular. Each has a specific inner ear that makes them very sensitive to potential changes in taste and market moods. They enable themselves with knowledge from the best person in the world for the job. They fight to get the best technical expertise and administrative managers to creatively contribute to the product. Successful CEO-ing in American involves dedication and ethics. They know exactly where the boundaries lie, and understand the political and organizational semantics of what the law does not expressly forbid them from doing. Being ethical is the way forward because if you do the right thing, you remain on the job in a way that makes you outlast your competitors who might fall by the wayside because of moments of intense greed. Successful American CEOs never see failure as a step back but a process and opportunity for renewal.

174

PROGRESS: TRUTH AND FALSITY

I always say that I landed on Omaha Beach, but I don't tell people that it was six weeks after the contested landing.[38]

The US economy is built on images of truth and falsity. These truths and falsehoods are complicated by a wide and deep and immense range of statistics and mathematical permutations from specialists in such highly specialized fields that sometimes no one understands what they are talking about. For example, high wages often mean low levels of employment for the average worker in the US, but low unemployment during critical election years may result in lower wages across the board for most middle class and lower class workers. But, as the World Values Survey claims, 60 per cent of Americans think that the poor are lazy. One might deduce from this finding that when you start getting lower wages, and perhaps when you finally lose your job you might become one of the poor. And if you are considered one of the poor, then people are going to think, six out of 10 times, that you are a lazy American. So, as the old saying goes, "get a job!" But how much of our self-worth or dignity should we be willing to lose when faced with occupational or career changes?

The images of truth and reality and the gap between the two becomes more complex and confusing when we add oil to the fire or add salt to the open wound: the ideological belief in individualism and the truism of achievement through hard work and personal sacrifice only worsens the self esteem of those who are indeed out of work and out of energy but full of responsibilities and commitments made during gainful employment. Therefore, it is one thing for academics and IMF managers to say that we ought to liberalize financial structures when the MNC that used to employ 250,000 Americans now only employs 2,000 because it makes more sense and a fist full of dollars to outsource or relocate BOP and backroom operations to several other countries where standards may be compromised, where cost-of-living is low, and where the CEO and the entire board can have their permanent offices in tax shelters where the sun shines all year round rather than in gloomy tax-burdened cities of snow, sleet, rain, and unionized strikes. Would you, as an individualist who might believe that a lot of the poor are lazy, not do the same thing so that when it comes to shareholder report time you can effectively say that you have done *your* job?

We have already seen in the preceding section the kinds of lies that are told by MNCs in order to outsource jobs. Outsourcing does not benefit everybody, but has different kinds of impacts on different people. How can anyone be convinced that jobs taken away from locals and given to foreigners in other countries will result in more jobs for the locals? If I have 50 people working as software programmers for me and I outsource all of them to China or Taiwan, how does it create more jobs locally in the US?

The reason why President George W. Bush supports outsourcing is because he is a Republican who wants to create more wealth for the wealthy Republicans. But he can't say this publicly so he has to use his words carefully such as "my fellow Americans" and "protecting American jobs." Also, most locals who lose their jobs to the backroom operators overseas are very unlikely to be employable. New jobs will be created locally but for different purposes and with different skills requirements. Do you think that a cost-cutting MNC is likely to send those who have recently been made jobless for training and upgrading? I don't think so. The image that is created around outsourcing is that it is a win-win situation, but the reality is that the local winners are the major shareholders who are laughing all the way to the bank because they have put in place a management team and a CEO who is not only able to reduce the total numbers on the payroll but also increase the numbers on the profit and dividend statements.

CONCLUSION: OPTIMISM

The political economy of the United States of America has a profound financial, social, cultural, and political influence on the process of globalization throughout the world. Anyone alive today probably knows more about America than the next nearest sovereign country to their own home nation. The ideals of Pax Americana and the American Business Dream are tantamount to the capitalist perfectionism of perfecting the US-led neoliberal international economic system. American MNCs and their CEOs are powerful machines whose personal drive and ambition cannot be easily or summarily curtailed, moderated, or circumvented in any series of academic discourses. But while scholars try to pin down their epistemological success stories, they themselves get caught in the economic rat race of research grant applications, research funding from government and private sources and the fight against those bureaucrats

176

who control the masses with their hypocritical use of regulations while hiding their own agendas for self-reward, self-promotion, and self-aggrandizement with the camouflage of neutrality and language of rationality—as if people did not know they were mostly undeserving. Yet this is nothing compared to the level of trickery and machination that goes into making profits in what the Fredric Jameson has called the "Cultural Logic of Late Capitalism."

How powerful are American MNCs? They are as powerful as their CEOs make them. There are specific characteristics in the background of the top performing CEOs but one must not mistake the difference between imitation and substantive drive. As we have seen, imitative behavior and the idea of the mimic man as described by Homi Bhabha and V. S. Naipaul, indicate a shallow copying of an original perception or impression with the view to achieving the same status and dignity of these origins. Going to the same schools and clubs, and having the same hobbies as these CEOs, does not make you likely to be as successful as they are. Rather, the politics of globalization in America demands, and indeed requires CEOs who are as dissimilar as possible. The key ingredient to their wealth is networking with a focus.

If you discover that your networking costs are more than your entertainment budget can withstand in any given year, something is not going right. Successful politics requires a certain disjunction, a rejection of the road well-taken and well-worn and is similar to the advice found in these titles: Robert D. Kaplan's *Warrior Politics: Why Leadership Requires a Pagan Ethos* (Vintage, 2003); the monastic-like life choices presented in the case study by Robert B. Catell, Kenny Moore, and Glenn Rifkin's *The CEO and the Monk: One Company's Journey to Profit and Purpose* (John Wiley & Sons, 2004); the earlier gender-specific, outdated, but no less inspirational logic of Laurie Beth Jones's *Jesus CEO: Using Ancient Wisdom for Visionary Leadership* (Hyperion, 1996); or, one book that I have not read but seems to be getting a lot of publicity and positive reviews, Eric Yaverbaum's *Leadership Secrets of the World's Most Successful CEOs: 100 Top Executives Reveal the Management Strategies That Made Their Companies Great* (Dearborn Trade Publishing, 2004).

However, the key remains contained in the puzzle presented earlier: how do the top achievers in CEO Haven who manage to keep ethical in their business deals stand to make the most money over time even if the company's profits swan-dive? Those who are ethical but callous, and driven by greed but cautious about being caught, are more likely to achieve success as a CEO. However, a comfortable (not luxurious), fulfilling life that is stress-free and uncomplicated requires some years of balanced hard work and a commitment to the ordinary work-life routine and the possibility of remaining bored for a long time. Most of the things we look forward to in retirement such as not attending company meetings, playing golf three days a week, fishing, bird-watching, camping, spending time with the family, watching *Monday Night Football*, playing pool, eating the finest cuisine without feeling sinful, and prayerful devotion can be achieved within the first fortnight of retirement. Some would argue that if you are a high achiever it is best to go the way of the McDonalds CEO and work yourself to death. Because when you work yourself to death, you know that you are doing something (hopefully) that you like to do. And even if you were to die eventually from not being overworked, there would probably be very many things that you could not have achieved in two or three lifetimes anyway. Better to die in the place that you love than in a foreign land and away from familiar surroundings.

Elisabeth Kubler-Ross's work on *Death and Dying* (Touchstone, [1969] 1997) presents a kind of distorted view of death and dying yet somehow became an invaluable text despite the books contortions. Like death, Kubler-Ross's book is very tricky. Nevertheless, there is another urban legend involving the belief that when death takes place, the point of exit from this life is crucial because that is the main memory that remains for eternity. Max Weber may have made many erroneous arguments but one thing he did get right was that work defines life. And therefore without work, human beings in modernity will only hasten their route to the next life, like the ancient Egyptians. Yet the fact of the matter remains that the tycoons who were involved in the Panama Canal project were themselves already very powerful and influential men who had close political connections with the powers of the day. Does anyone really bother about what their happiness or sorrows had impacted on the stock markets? Does any one really care when they are on their deathbeds whether their stocks will rise over the next quarter? Does any one think bother whether the economy will react to the notice of their demise? It might be too late as we eventually observe our former teachers, friends, enemies, relations, and most people we have never met disappear gradually, some instantaneously, with all the self-assurance and impressive confidence of Foucault's *Ship of Fools* as it sails quietly into the nothingness of the midnight of eternity. Nietzsche warned us that any single narrative and any particular origin were dangerous. And the knowledge of any one of these as a universalizing totality was an essentialist end in itself. The American economy is built on neoliberal assumptions that CEOs will never outlast some of the MNCs and some MNCs will never outlast their CEOs. American MNCs and their CEOs are powerful to a point, and that point being death.

ENDNOTES

1   This is similar to the shooting in the chest of Taiwanese president Chen Shui Bian in the 2004 election in Taipei. Chen, however, went on to win the election.

2   Ovidio Diaz Espino, *How Wall Street Created a Nation: JP Morgan, Teddy Roosevelt, and the Panama Canal* (NY: Four Walls Eight Windows, 2001), p. 6.

3   My own estimates from various business risk companies, interviews with bankers, and interviews with shareholders of American companies.

4   "IMF/World Bank Report Calls for Urgent Action on Poverty Reduction by All Countries" Press Release No. 04/85, April 22, 2004.

5   Ellen Smith, "Perks for American CEOs alive and well," *Associated Press/ Halifax Herald Ltd*, April 24, 2004.

6   Jenny Anderson, "Goldman Sachs CEO Paulson Joins JP Morgan Boss in Big Bucks Club," *New York Post*, February 25, 2004, 33.

7   According to FT's London sources, "The [American] SEC, looking at the circumstances surrounding the IPO, does not comment on individual investigations. An SEC inquiry becomes formal if investigators believe the case should go further and they gain powers to compel the delivery of evidence after a vote of the agency's five commissioners." See, "China Life Confirms It is the Target of SEC Probe," *Financial Times*, April 28, 2004.

8   Stephen Lynch, "Bankers Pay Headed Up: Survey," *New York Post*, September 13, 2003, 22. See "The Best Performers," *BusinessWeek Online*, April 5, 2004; and "Something Ventured, Something Gained," *CIO Magazine*, April 15, 2004. See also the television quote by Paul Solman, "Starting in 1998, when Enron's stock began to defy gravity, CEO Ken Lay exercised options on hundreds of occasions, pocketing over $200 million in gains. His successor, Jeffrey Skilling, exercised more than $100 million worth of options, many of them just before the company tanked. But why were executives given such huge options grants to begin with? According to Graef Crystal, it's because companies treated stock options as if they weren't an expense, didn't cost their companies a dime," in "Sharing the Wealth," *PBS Online News Hour*, January 6, 2003.

9   According to the Lehman Brothers' website, the "history of Lehman Brothers parallels the growth of the United States and its energetic drive toward prosperity and international prominence. What would evolve into a global financial entity began as a general store in the American South. Henry Lehman, an immigrant from Germany, opened his small shop in

the city of Montgomery, Alabama in 1844. Six years later, he was joined by brothers Emanuel and Mayer, and they named the business Lehman Brothers," and it is located at the prestigious address: 745, Seventh Ave., New York, NY 10019.

10   The Cendant Corporation describes itself as "one of the foremost providers of travel and real estate services in the world; one of the world's largest hotel franchisors, the world's largest vacation ownership organization, and one of the world's largest car rental operators; the world's largest real estate brokerage franchisor, one of the largest retail mortgage originators in the US, and the world's largest provider of outsourced corporate employee relocation services; the franchisor of the second-largest tax preparation service in the US and leading providers of travel information processing services worldwide." See http://www.cendant.com for details.

11   Data on the most recent wealth estimates accumulated by the latest cohort of top ten CEOs was not available before this book went to the printers, but I think you get the point made here: the top achievers in CEO Haven can stay ethical and clean in their business deals stand to make the most money over time and to keep it even if the company's profits were to swan-dive.

12   *2004 Forbes.com Inc.*

13   Dave Carpenter, "McDonald's Earnings Increase 56 per cent," *New York Post*, April 27, 2004.

14   Neil Buckley, "Cantalupo Recipe Rewards McD's," *Financial Times*, April 28, 2004.

15   *2004 Forbes.com Inc.*

16   See also "Colgate-Palmolive Co.—They Put a Smile on Your Face," *Corporate Board Member Magazine*, September/October 2002.

17   Nanette Byrnes, John A. Byrne, Cliff Edwards, Louise Lee, Stanley Holmes, and Joann Muller, "Reuben Mark—Colgate-Palmolive," *BusinessWeek Online*, September 23, 2002.

18   *2004 Forbes.com Inc.*

19   "George David, United Technologies, CEO and Chairman," *CNNMoney*, June 20, 2003.

20   *Forbes* defines total *compensation* package as "... total compensation as salary and bonus; 'other' compensation includes vested restricted stock grants, and 'stock gains', the value realized from exercising stock options during the just-concluded fiscal year." See *2004 Forbes.com Inc.*

21   *2004 Forbes.com Inc.*

22   George E. Pataki, Office of the Governor of the US State of New York, 2004.

23   Amy Barrett, Stephanie Anderson Forest, and Tom Lowry, "Henry Silverman's Long Road Back—He's Fighting to Restore Cendant's Reputation," *BusinessWeek Online*, February 28, 2000.

24   *2004 Forbes.com Inc.*

25   *Virginia Business Online*, June, 2001.

26 "Redskins report: Notes, quotes, anecdotes," *CBS Sportsline.com*, Aug. 28, 2003.

27 "Back to Washington," *St. Petersburg Times*, January 8, 2004.

28 Kenneth Bredemeier, "Rebuilding a Fortune: After the Early 1990s Bust, NVR Chief Dwight Schar Has Revived His Company, Bought Part of the Redskins, And Has Built Many Houses," *Washington Post*, March 1, 2004, E01.

29 *2004 Forbes.com Inc.*

30 Lawrence J. Ellison, "Competition in the Digital Age: Beyond the Browser Wars," *Statement of Chairman and CEO of Oracle Corporation before the US Senate Committee on the Judiciary*, July 23, 1998.

31 *2004 Forbes.com Inc.*

32 *2004 Forbes.com Inc.*

33 Robert Steyer, "Mixed Picture at Forest Labs," *TheStreet.com*, April 20, 2004.

34 *2004 Forbes.com Inc.*

35 *2004 Forbes.com Inc.*

36 Charles V. Bagli, "Mayor Rejects New Deal for Bear Stearns Jobs," *New York Times*, January 6, 2003.

37 *2004 Forbes.com Inc.*

38 Henry A. Kissinger, "Thayer Award Speech," *USMA West Point*, September 13, 2000.

CHAPTER 5

War

My fellow Americans ... We pray that peoples of all faiths, all races, all nations, may have their great human needs satisfied; that those now denied opportunity shall come to enjoy it to the full; that all who yearn for freedom may experience its spiritual blessings; that those who have freedom will understand, also, its heavy responsibilities; that all who are insensitive to the needs of others will learn charity; that the scourges of poverty, disease and ignorance will be made to disappear from the earth, and that, in the goodness of time, all peoples will come to live together in a peace guaranteed by the binding force of mutual respect and love (Public Papers of the Presidents, Dwight D. Eisenhower, 1960, 1035-1040).

The speeches of the US Presidents always seem to start with the phrase, "my fellow Americans." It is a kind of linguistic misogynism because language is used to incorporate and subsume women through a catch-all masculinist phrase, "my fellow Americans." "Fellows" indicate a brotherhood, a closed system, a buddy-boy culture of men getting on together on an essentialist ticket. The word "fellow" denotes camaraderie and unity of purpose, a special and selective group of men with a common destiny. There is already a double linguistic compression because the word "woman", as you already know, is believed to have been etymologically derived from the phrase "of man" and to subsume all American women and girls under "my *fellow* Americans" is really to do it a second time. Conservatives would say no. The American President uses fellow as a generic term for men and women. And there are so many instances out there about fellowships from the College of Surgeons, and other parts of academia, the professions, in business, and in industry.

War is life and death for mankind. War is the extension of human nature across man's environment. It has thus become a natural thing for men to kill other men for proprietary rights. It's about bravado and egotism. War is a masculine thing. War involves the venting of aggression and frustration essential to being human. But that which is greater than war is the state. The state is greater than war because it controls and determines the nature of war. However, the problem with war is that like fire, it is a good slave but a poor master. And hence war can lead to the destruction of the state. The state must therefore always remain in control of war and the potential for war. Like the pyramids of Egypt, war is symbolized by life and death. But in the late modern world, the soldier no longer lives a life that is separate from other forms of public and personal life. In other words, there is almost nothing that a civilian can do that a soldier cannot do too. Soldiers can incur debt and gain credit, and perform all other tasks that are common to civilian members of the American public. But there is an important difference in being a soldier, and that is the threat of death. For example a soldier can die during field training or on a local military proving ground. So what happens when an American solider is injured or even killed in battle? Can s/he sue the state that sent him there? The answer is no.

Consider the case before the US Supreme Court in *Feres v. United States* (1950) where the state is not "liable under the Federal Tort Claims Act" for injuries to soldiers in active duty and despite Feres having been burnt to death in the Pine Camp fire in New York.[1] In another case, *Jefferson v. United States* (1950), the plaintiff was not on active duty and had undergone an abdominal operation by an army medical surgeon who had negligently lodged a towel "30 inches long by 18 inches wide [and] marked *Medical Department U.S. Army* in Jefferson." Such instances where human life is altered at the point of discharge from military service or as a result of death resulting from inactive duty are indications of the seriousness of the nature of military activity and its bearing on the rights of the individual Americans who sign up for service. Unfortunately, the state continues to make very clear distinctions between active and inactive performativity that has resulted in an imbalance in the relationship between the state and the individuals presented to defend the state. The law needs to be amended and changed to keep up with the times and the military must initiate such problems so as to take care of their own service personnel, if only to raise the levels of confidence in and out of military training. The relationship between the state, the individual and military service should be given careful consideration in the politics of American globalization because of the global presence that the American military possesses. Withdrawing troops from a region a decade after the end of the Cold War is purely late symbolism. The Bush Administration's announcement in summer 2004 about withdrawing 70,000 troops worldwide is really a redeployment exercise. Pax Americana cannot continue without the presence of American military technology and hardware in terms of its current global distribution. Like Hermocrates, the son of Hermon who proudly announced in our continuing story of the Peloponnesian War as it relates to war in modernity:

> I am therefore of opinion that dismayed with this reckoning, they will either not put over at all from Corcyra, or whilst they spend time deliberating and in sending out to explore how many and in what place we are, the season will be lost and winter come; or deterred by our unlooked-for opposition, they will give over the voyage. And the rather for that as I hear the man of most experienced amongst their commanders hath the charge against his will and would take a light occasion to return if he saw any considerable stop by us in the way. And I am very sure we should be voiced amongst them to the utmost. And as the reports are so are men's minds; and they fear more such as they will hear will begin with them than such as give out that they will no more but defend themselves, because then they think the danger equal. Which would now be the case of the Athenians (Hobbes, 1959 'The Sixth Book' sect 34, 398).

The presence of active and inactive performativity was anticipated in the strategic considerations of the battles that constitute the vicious cycle of militarism in any age. This reality based on the essentialist nature of an unchanging and warlike masculinity demands that proper attention be paid with the full regard to prior diplomatic and civilian agreements that have constituted realpolitik. A postmodern reflexivity is not an option for those who seek to dominate and benefit from such dominance. This harks back to the realist balance of power theory that dictates a close watch be kept continuously on one's adversaries as one keeps an eye on one's enemies. After all, an interpolation of the passage above suggests that the enemy of my enemy's enemy is my enemy. Once America had decided to take lead in the war after the attack and massacre at Pearl Harbor in World War II, there was no way but forward as any other would invite a power vacuum that would be filled with adversaries. The cut backs on military spending from the Cold War days in relative terms has resulted in the increase in the confidence levels of terrorist cellular networks all over the world. These networks themselves keep a vigilant look-out to "how many and in what place we are" and plan very carefully now that much of their conventional tactical methods have been disrupted and exposed. The propensity for evil constitutes a major half of the other side of man. It is the half that needs to be disciplined and controlled. It the half that when exposed to the natural elements will, as Shakespeare wrote, "cry havoc, and let loose the dogs of war." That the evil and untrustworthy side of man would become so great and so powerful a force that once released would become untamable, intractable and therefore dangerous. "Where everything," as Hobbes reminds us, "from every place grieved them; and fear and astonishment the greatest that ever they were in, beset them round. For they were not only grieved for the loss which both every man in particular and the whole city sustained of every man of arms, horsemen, and serviceable men, the like whereof they saw was not left, but seeing that they neither had galleys in their haven nor money in their treasury nor furniture in their galleys, were even desperate at the present of their safety; and thought the enemy out of Sicily would come forthwith with their fleet to Peiraeus, especially after the vanquishing of so great a navy, and that the enemy here would surely now, with double preparation in every kind, press them to the utmost by sea and land and be aided therein by their revolting confederates" (Hobbes, 1959 "The Eight Book," sect 1, 504).

As we have seen, the nature of being human is political. Man, as Aristotle believed, is by nature political. And as long as there continues to be an imbalance of power within communities based on tradition, modernization, culture, gender, primordialism, circumstantialism, racism, religion, fossil fuels, and socio-economic class there will be a politics of control, a politics of discord, a politics of resistance, and a politics of subversion that feed into the global reach of American globalization. One has to be careful that the political power of those who are in charge does not go to their heads. No one would know about the horrors of uncommitted criminals holding high positions and beyond the reach of most ordinary citizens. This is especially true in military organizations where the prospect of civilian intervention is buffered by military "Standard Operating 'Procedures" (SOP). The horrifying, tragic, and darkly comedic images over the Internet and through *CNN* and the *BBC* about Iraqi Prisoners of War remind us of an earlier time of insanity, "At Bethleham, violent madwomen were chained by the ankles to the wall of a long gallery; their only garment was a homespun dress. At another hospital in Bethnal Green, a woman subject to violent seizures was placed in a pigsty, feet and fists bound; when the crisis had passed she was tied to her bed, covered only by a blanket; when she was allowed to take a few steps, an iron bar was placed between her legs, attached by rings to her ankles and by a short chain to handcuffs" (Foucault [1965] 1988: 69–70). The hope, optimism, and progress of American globalization in modernity has never escaped the tragedy of its political paradox that has misled Americans and cost American lives since World War I. The American public has more access to information today, because of technological advances, which has led to the political intensification of its tragic history in modernity.

AMERICA'S GLOBAL REACH

In the great discourse of America's global military reach, there is always an increasing propensity for American soldiers to die en route and on that same course that bears the symbols of those who are about to die and those whose deaths have already been preordained. This reminds us of the great Platean attack against the Thebans in The Second Book of Thucydides History of the Peloponnesian War by stealth and by night in a calculated and deliberate attack that would vanquish and exploit the enemy for all its worth without care for neither cost nor consequence of their military maneuvers. And this is what is happening in Iraq now, when no one really thought it would. American soldiers returning from Baghdad in flag-draped coffins. How sad. And how ironic that it is the same state in the 1980s had its Secretary of State George Schultz's emissaries cutting deals with Saddam Hussein's henchmen to ensure that Iran did not win the Iran-Iraq war, because the Shah had been such a good capitalist friend of America. Just like the Marcos from the Philippines. Didn't matter that the Shah's secret police tortured and maimed thousands of innocent Muslims as long as the great inroads of capitalism were being made into Iran of the 1960s and 1970s.

When the mullahs took over in the insurrection led by Ayatollah Khomeini and his militant clerics, the cycle of violence continued under the name of a different god, in place of the capitalist one.[2] Over 10 different nations sold arms to both sides of the Iran-Iraq War including the Soviet Union, France, Israel, and the United States. And now that Iraq has been illegally invaded by the US and its allies, the rest have restricted their comments to political rhetoric. And the UN under Kofi Anan, which had vehemently opposed the Bush-led invasion, has now been marginalized. The US still owes the UN money and will continue to get away with not making the payments since it is the biggest kid on the block. The reasons for the non-payments are political and politically motivated. Despite being in arrears, American presidents have continued to ensure they have a global reach even without UN support. While the UN flounders on matters such as the PRC and Taiwan, the US has continued with its back door support for Taiwan. The basis for the US-Taiwan relationship lies in the military provisions under the Taiwan Relations Act (1979) that empowers the US to assume a military position in the event of a PRC attack on the island. The US has also continued its policy of free-arms trade to Taiwan and other East Asian countries. America's military cannot continue its global reach without interfering in the politics of foreign governments. And many foreign government elites welcome the US presence in their region.

One example is Singapore. In 2004, for example, the Singapore prime minister had three meetings with George W. Bush. Singapore has for a long time officially maintained a 15-man American logistics unit on the island state. Singapore has often hosted USN naval aircraft carriers in its naturally deep harbor, much to the chagrin of Muslim-dominant countries such as Malaysia and Indonesia. The American interest in East Asia, which comes under the US Pacific Command, is overtly welcomed by its allies in the region—Singapore, South Korea, and Japan. Yet there have been widespread protests by opponents in these countries, with the exception of Singapore, against American military presence. Since the US pull-out from Clarke Airbase and Subic Naval base in the Philippines, the US had at first increased its naval presence in the South China Sea, then reduced it, and then sent in the fleet again. Why does the US need such a global presence and how is this achieved?

The answer is simple. America's global reach is tied to a global vision. Not the silly one proclaimed by Bush in 1990 but an earlier ideal that goes back to 1960.[3] In order to enjoy the universal freedom that Eisenhower used in his 1960 speech, it has to be imposed on others who do not believe in it. Or so it would appear. But picking a fight is important. You've got to discover something wrong with the men that you don't like. It doesn't really matter what it is that initially motivates your hatred, all that is important are the reasons that are given afterwards. 4,500 years ago there was a thriving civilization in Egypt. Before the desert sands engulfed the pyramids, the land surrounding it was fertile, green, and arable. It was the best land that the Nile offered. Exactly 10 miles from the center of modern Cairo are the pyramids. Most archeologists and research scientists think that the pyramids were created for symbolic purposes. That the ancient Egyptians believed that their Pharaoh was a God who had perfect control over the rising and setting of the sun. That the sun rose and set at the behest of the pharaoh and the death of the pharaoh would mean doom for the sun which they knew was crucial for the growing of crops in the Nile Valley. Therefore, the resting place of the king would allow his spirit to symbolically raise the sun each day. This is of course a spurious correlation as we understand it today. It cannot be accepted except as a kind of fateful belief of the Egyptians in that era. Other researchers believe that the pyramids were created out of a cosmic necessity, that the mathematic accuracy involved in the construction of the pyramids was itself a reflection of the presence of higher cosmological beings who guided the Egyptians in their 20-year quest.

The largest pyramid itself is built from over two million slabs of about a ton each. The ancient Egyptians were capable artisans who had hewn these huge slabs of limestone and emplaced them with such geometrical precision that they could withstand 23 centuries of erosion, and worse still, 2,300 years of human civilization. Yet these pyramids were built to serve a higher and more perfect purpose. That purpose, some modern researchers believe, involve astronomical calculations with regards to the position of the stars in the Milky Way, the galaxy to which earth belongs. While the researchers were right about the symbolism of the pyramids, their deductions about the purpose and function of these ancient tombs have all been wrong. The pyramids were more than symbolic places for the pharaoh to ensure the rising and falling of the sun each day. They were more than mere cosmological monuments to their dead king writ large across the universe. These monuments were created to celebrate the power of Egyptian kings over all men. They were a celebration of conquest and war over other men and other civilizations.

The US presence in East Asia provides an interesting study in comparison to the limited global reach of the ancient Egyptians. Take Taiwan for example. This island is home to the descendants and familial relatives of the Kuo-mintang (KMT) and those who escaped Mao's putsch in 1949. Despite being an avid supporter of the United States presence in China in the 1930s before the Pacific War, the KMT had been riddled with political corruption. All its leaders, including the wives of the top generals were on the take. This seems to be a pattern for the US support of foreign governments as seen in Marcos, Aristide, Saddam Hussein, and Taiwan's Chiang Kai-Shek much earlier on. Nevertheless, there continues to remain important strategic reasons for the US support of the democratic enclave of Taiwan. The US will continue to use its relationship with Taiwan as an alternative China in case Sino-US relations turn sour. The PRC has fired live artillery rounds across the Taiwan Straits several times since Mao called off an invasion of the island in the 1950s. It was only the US military presence in the region, in Okinawa, Tokyo, and the Philippines in the 1970s and 1980s that prevented a pro-Maoist attack to complete the Chinese Revolution's unfinished business. That was a major *faux pas* on the part of the PRC. Their window of opportunity has now grown smaller. However, there are two main items on the agenda. Firstly, the pyramidal relationship between the People's Liberation Army, the Chinese Communist Party, and the People continues to serve as the basis of "socialism with Chinese characteristics." Secondly, China is under pressure from the US and some other countries to float the Yuan, which will result in making the PRC's exports more expensive from the current fixed amount of US$1 to 8.28 Yuan. Because of the nature of Chinese politics that has evolved in its modern history, China will have no doubts about invading Taiwan if its president Chen Shui Bian continues with his political platform of "independence" and "democratic" rhetoric. Taiwan is the fly in the Chinese ointment. And America will doubtlessly use the island as a staging area should it come to war.

The Russians are unlikely to help the Chinese and will just wait to make corrections and advances along the 2,268 miles of difficult border-terrain with China. And the 2001 Sino-Russo agreement is merely an instrument on paper that is an agreement to remain non-enemies for the time being until both countries sort out their finances. Besides, it has never been in the US strategic interest for any Sino-Russo accords to materialize. This would potentially cut off one half of the US Pacific Command and result in the reconfiguration of NATO and perhaps even the newly-formed European Union that was launched on May 1, 2004 in Dublin. And the Indians have a 2,200 mile-long disputed border with China with which it is willing and waiting to have a grudge match. What is interesting here is that both the Chinese and the Indians use Russian-made, Soviet era weapons and are reported to spend close to US$100 billion annually on their large land armies. In other words, if China were to invade Taiwan, it would give the countries surrounding it an opportunity to resolve many historical differences with the country. China does not currently have the resources to defend its long borders from Russian or Indian incursion and has to configure all these in terms of any military calculus. The Taiwanese on the other hand continue to bait and annoy the Chinese PRC leaders with their calls for greater democracy. Internally, China has reneged on the Hong Kong mini-constitution with regards to the terms of the appointment of the Chief Executive of the Hong Kong Special Administrative Region (currently held by a pro-China, but former shipping capitalist Tung Chee Hwa). As a result, China has come under economic and political pressure from America, the UK and other interests in this former British colony to make these changes. But China merely told them to keep out of its internal politics.[4]

The year 2006 *Anno Domini* is the 230th year of American Independence. 2006 also marks the 9th anniversary of the handover to China from the UK. America will doubtless be in the thick of this war. It is only a matter of time before the US is drawn into a war in East Asia whether it is with the North Koreans (MacArthur's unfinished business) or with Taiwan and the PRC. It is only a question of time and money, and the US has both. The pyramid on the greenback is more telling a symbol than it immediately presents to the naked eye.

PYRAMIDS AS SYMBOLS OF WAR

The pyramids are symbols of war. The pyramids were reminders of man's mortality, about life and death. The Egyptian must have known that the earth was round a long time before the advent of Copernicus and Galileo. For the early Egyptians, the earth was the center of the universe and the pyramids were the central symbol of superior power. Egypt was the superpower of its day. The ancient Egyptian cities were among the most brilliant and most civilized places on earth. The pyramids were a reminder to all travelers visiting the center of the universe of the supreme power of the pharaoh over all men, and over life and over death. And these symbols of war were built to last. Despite the evil and horrific values of the Nazis, they did not destroy the pyramids. Neither did the Italians or the British during World War II. For these old armies, the pyramids were a respite from the horrors of the war and represented a sacred place built on values of honor and glory. By the time of the Yom Kippur War and the Six-Day War, both Israeli and Arab military machines did not destroy the pyramids. It is as if these lifeless stones possess some kind of spiritual power for the posterity of mankind. Perhaps, as symbols of war, these ancient tombs present a startling reminder to men about their own mortality and shortness of life. If Eisenhower's speech had been engraved in the Rosetta Stone it would have been just as appropriate a universal creed. A freedom expressed in the artisans who voluntarily built the pyramids as nationalist sentiment increased in ancient Egypt.

It would seem that Eisenhower's idealism will perhaps never come true as long as we have war. Because, sharper than a serpent's tooth, it exists in the *blood of men to kill and be killed*. Yet, we pray that peoples of all faiths, all races, all nations, may have their great human needs satisfied. Many hope that American globalization will bring with it peaceful overtures of a Keynesian-like exchange of goods and services, greater markets, innovative products, functional commodities at low prices. Better to trade than to war. As we have seen in Eisenhower's speech, "*those now denied opportunity shall come to enjoy it to the full; that all who yearn for freedom may experience its spiritual blessings; that those who have freedom will understand* ."

Yet Americans are hated around the world because they seem to want to have peace so earnestly that they are willing to go to war to get it. Look at Korea, Vietnam, Iran-Iraq, the Cold War and the arms race, the proxy wars between the former superpowers, the first Gulf War, and over a decade later, the second Gulf War. Now look at the war on terrorism. Many of the terrorists were trained by the Americans and their various special forces during the Cold War. Our century now is the playing out of the vestiges of the Cold War, and of 9/11, where former allies, foreign military Special Forces and other paramilitary units trained by Americans have refused to lay down their arms. This is similar to the Malayan People's Anti-Japanese Army in 1945 that refused to surrender their weapons and turned towards communism as they led a jungle-based military campaign against the former British colonies of Malaya and Singapore while operating from covert bases along the Thai-Malaysian border. Soldiers who were supplied with weapons and training to suit one purpose cannot easily be told to lay down their weapons after hostilities are over or after the political victory has been achieved. Because they who were trained to kill and assassinate always need an enemy. How many more American lives will have to be sacrificed in the cause of the

191

tragic mimicry of the American Dream on the global *Ship of Fools* by 2010? Americans must learn to admit that many of the problems that are associated with globalization's terror are the result of a building up of decades of hatred. Hatred for US foreign policy. In Nicaragua, the Philippines, in the Pacific, Japan, the Middle East, Afghanistan, Haiti, Panama, Colombia, and other parts of the world as we shall soon discover. And in the absence of a clear enemy, they have turned on those who once taught them. The process of war is a deep and penetrating part of globalization. It is the way of man, to command and to conquer. What would happen if from tomorrow the US disbanded its offensive military units; if the USN and USAF *stood down* its naval submarines and jet fighters; if Delta Force, the Green Berets, the Special Forces, Navy Seals and the Secret Service stopped all their *black operations* tomorrow morning 0600 hrs EST? Would there be massive insecurity? Would America be able to protect its own citizens? Has America been able to protect its citizens in the first place? This situation will not happen. But if it did, it might change the course of history and perhaps even save more lives than the current scheme of bombing the hell out of Fallujah.[5]

If any more Americans are held hostage by Iraqis fighting in their *own* homeland, would the president withdraw all the ground troops? Of course not. Because America cannot stay out of other peoples' businesses. American does not negotiate with terrorists. Look at the increasing number of flag-draped coffins that are being returned to these United States. How many more young Americans in the prime of their lives must fight and die for the sake of oil, or MNCs or free trade, or the Japanese, or the Europeans? How many more American lives must expire before their time for the sake of the militaristic egos of the political brass in Washington? How many more families must be torn apart and left with empty rooms filled only with silent memorabilia, photographs of smiling faces in happier times?

Unlike our modern buildings in a post 9/11 world, no one feels threatened by the Egyptian pyramids in the sense that terrorists had been threatened by the presence of the twin towers of the World Trade Center in New York pre-9/11. The pyramids are political symbols of death, power, and tragedy over all other races. The pyramids are huge sand castles that have ironically long survived the immediate threats to the Egyptian dynasties. We don't make them like we used to anymore. The globalized world today, created by neoliberal capitalist energy generators called MNCs has built non-permanent structures that remain unprotected and vulnerable to the enemies within and the enemies without. "My fellow Americans" is a phrase that contains in itself the masculinist hostilities that men inflict upon men, where women are not merely subsumed but considered irrelevant. There were cases in the American Civil War, for example, where fighting was considered such a time honored, masculinist convention that at a few points on the battlefield, women and children would gathered together from a safe hillock to watch the ceremonial killing of Americans by Americans. There is something else, a different and more ominous structure that has existed in tact and in perfect condition as a relic from the Cold War that continues to dominate the directional frontiers of all kinds of science, and kinds of experimental technology from physical matter to the manipulation of nanomatter and the artificial creation of genetic codes through mutation. These structures have become so embedded in the American way of life, and constitute such a great portion of the American Dream that the silent anti-war protestors of the 1960s have all but remembered them as distant and dissatisfying memories of victories that were never achieved and Pyrrhic battles that were never won.

THE MILITARY INDUSTRIAL COMPLEX

James Madison once said that if men were all angels we would not need the state. Unfortunately, this statement was taken to the other extreme. And this extremity came in the form of the military-industrial complex (MIC). The MIC comprises a huge interstate network of military bases, security structures, and affiliated industries that have been created to fulfill their complementary needs. The MIC serves three main constituencies: the "name of the people," "big business," and the "military establishment."

> ... the US is basically a one-party state—the business party with two factions, Democrats and Republicans. Most of the population seems to agree. A very high percentage, sometimes passing 80 per cent, believe that the government serves "the few and the special interests," not "the people." In the contested 2000 election, about 75 per cent regarded it as mostly a farce having nothing to do with them, a game played by rich contributors, party bosses, and the public relations industry, which trained candidates to say mostly meaningless things that might pick up some votes. This was BEFORE the actual

election, with the accusations of fraud and selection of Bush with a minority of the popular vote.[6]

The natural evolution of American politics has resulted in the gross engulfment of the American polity by the military industrial complex. As we have seen in the previous chapter, a minority of the population directs the majority thinking; the minority-popular vote therefore determines the outcomes for the majority of American citizens. This was what Madison had cautioned his peers and the American people in the *Federalist Paper Number 51*. He called it the "tyranny-of-the-minority." That the minority wields so much power as to be able to control the rest of society through its social, cultural and political institutions. And if Madisonian man was indeed angelic, there would be no need for government. We would perhaps even be able to accept a kind of anarcho-syndicalist politics that was the entire rave in the early 20th century. But what if the state itself was not made up of angels either? The MIC is made up of a pyramidal structure of military academies that come under the direct control of the Office of the Secretary of Defense. These are the civilian structures that control the military units. Each year, the Department of Defense (DoD) (that comes under the direct purview of the Office of the Secretary of Defense) devotes close to US$1 billion to academic institutions that are involved in military-type research an amount that is larger than most sovereign state economies the world over, yet an amount that was unable to foresee nor forestall 9/11.

There are several important academic institutions that continue to receive major military grants such as the California Institute of Technology (CIT), Columbia University, Dartmouth College, Harvard University, the Johns Hopkins University (JHU), the Massachusetts Institute of Technology (MIT), RAND Graduate School (RGS), Syracuse University (in New York), and the University of California. There are other military institutes that form part of the larger militarist culture that rides like a cultural undercurrent within society. These include the Air Force Institute of Technology (AFIT), Air University (AU), the Defense Acquisition University (DAU), the Defense Language Institute Foreign Language Center (DLIFLC), the Information Resources Management College (IRMC), the Industrial College of the Armed Forces (ICAF), the Joint Forces Staff College (JFSC), Joint Military Intelligence College (JMIC), the Marine Corps University (MCU), the Naval Postgraduate School (NPS), and the National War College (NWC) among many other units.[7] Each is a recipient of huge multimillion dollar defense budget grants that could run a few Central American republics without cocaine exports.

The importance of the entire military industrial organizational culture is determined by the kind of enemy that is being fought. In the past, the enemy was clearly seen and visible to the naked eye. The enemies of the United States go back a long time in history. It began with the British Red Coats in the 18th century; then the German Nazis, the Italians, and the Japanese in World War II; the Koreans, and the Vietnamese from the 1950s to the 1970s; the Soviets from 1955 to 1989; and now the enemies of the post-9/11 era. But if we look at the kinds of funds and the extent of the research done within the MIC the major work involves conventional warfare and technological application. In fact, such research institutes as RAND, for example, have been designed towards a specific purpose and a specific enemy. Unfortunately, the new enemy of the post-9/11 era is very different from the historical enemies of modern American history.

Ever since the Berlin Airlift, America has developed its own view towards assuming the role of a global policeman. This role of global policeman transformed into a global military combat force capable of annihilating the Soviets at the height of the Cold War. However, the post-9-11 era has created another new kind of enemy for the American global combat force. It is no secret that the new enemy is international terrorism where no one is without suspicion, even American citizens themselves who have aided and abetted fundamentalist Islamic reactionary terrorists in their fight for what can only be a cause against human life itself. Yet there is another enemy perhaps that is just as malignant and latent as the international terrorist. *Madness.* And because of this a "whole security system against the violence of the insane and the explosion of their fury" (Foucault [1965] 1988: 73), may have to be created to incarcerate those who had been doing the incarceration all the while along the way.

This kind of enemy might be much worse because it is entrusted with the nation's safekeeping and well-being. This is a very serious situation because we are talking about the new kind of enemy who is a renegade "American" trusted with defending the nation but hidden among 1.4 million active duty personnel[8], 654,000 civilians, 1.2 million national guards and reserves, 2 million retirees and families on benefit. All these personnel are operating within the MIC and from 6,000 locations across

30,000 acres, 600,000 buildings and structures, involving 145 countries and over half a million stationed overseas.[9] These personnel come under five commanders with geographical oversight and four commanders with worldwide responsibilities.

The globalized world under the lens of America's military professionals is divided into the following five unified commands that form part of the global geography: Pacific Command (PACOM) Northern Command (NORTHCOM), Southern Command (SOUTHCOM), Central Command (CENTCOM), and European Command (EUCOM). The largest is PACOM, and the smallest is CENTCOM. Therefore, we are talking about a global military force that is highly structured, highly politicized, and hierarchical, and contains different subcultures and values and emphases that have generated and evolved over the past 200 years.[10] The MIC also has an annual DoD budget of US$371 billion and 2.036 million personnel. Compare this to the largest American MNCs, such as Wal-mart (US$227 billion with 1,383,000 employees), Exxon-Mobil (US$200 billion and 97,900 employees), General Motors (US$181 billion with 365,000 employees), and Ford (US$160 billion with 354,000 employed).[11]

We will now examine the pyramid of military education that has evolved over the years in the politics of American military globalization. This will generate the context in which the minority of service personnel can be shown to be the new enemy of the American people.

THE PYRAMID OF MILITARY EDUCATION

Military education for children in the US has a long history dating back to the time of the civil war. Parents send their kids to these places for two reasons: firstly, the parents or at least the father was educated there. Secondly, but not exclusively, the parents feel that a military education early in life will instill discipline and patriotism for the country. It also keeps the kids off the streets and off drugs and out of the house. Many of the schools are themselves stepping stones for ascendance into the higher military academies run by the DoD and serve as a purposeful career path for the future. Ninety-eight percent of these military institutions are coeducational.

If one can imagine a pyramidal structure with an apex made up of five academies and lower level educational colleges, junior colleges, boarding schools, and other preparatory schools with a military dimension, then you would have the impression of a clear set of educational institutions geared specifically towards creating a military culture. This culture represents an important dimension of what Eisenhower, Williams and Moos called the military-industrial complex (MIC).[12]

There are currently five fully-fledged military academies run by the DoD across the contiguous United States. These are the United States Air Force Academy (USAFA) in Colorado Springs, Colorado; the United States Coast Guard Academy (USCGA) in Connecticut; the United States Military Academy (USMA) at West Point; the United States Merchant Marine Academy (USMMA) in New York; and the United States Naval Academy (USNA) in Annapolis. President Eisenhower signed the USAFA into law on April 1, 1954. Officer Cadets at the USAFA earn a base pay of US$734.10 per month plus a range of between US$100 and US$315 for their "class" pay. Naturally, the USAFA shares the same core values inspired by General Michael E. Ryan, which are "Integrity," "Service before Self," and "Excellence in All We Do." There has been a tradition of executive interest in these military academies that has bolstered the art and science of war since the 1800s. For example, the USMA at West Point was itself established through executive concurrence by President Thomas Jefferson. The mission of this academy is, "To educate, train, and inspire the Corps of Cadets so that each graduate is a commissioned leader of character committed to the values of Duty, Honor, Country; professional growth throughout a career as an officer in the United States Army; and a lifetime of selfless service to the nation" (USMA, 2004). In addition to the cadet honor code, cadets at USMA share the army's seven core values: "Duty," "Honor," "Integrity," "Loyalty," "Personal Courage," "Respect," and "Selfless Service.". It isn't easy to get admitted to West Point. To do so, a prospective candidate has to be nominated by a member of the US Congress or a member from the Department of the Army. For over 200 years, the motto of USMA is "Duty, Honor, Country" and this has been imbued in 50,000 graduates that include Stonewall Jackson, Mahan, Polk, Whistler, Ulysses S. Grant and Robert E. Lee (the Confederate general during the American Civil War, and a former USMA superintendent), Sherman, Omar N. Bradley, Eisenhower, MacArthur, Patton, Pershing, Buzz Aldrin (astronaut), Schwarzkopf, Westmoreland, Alexander Haig (former president of United Technologies Corporation, and US Secretary of State), and Brent Scowcroft.

The twice-wounded, decorated, military tactician and strategist, Colin Luther Powell, who served no fewer than three US presidents and was the first African-American to assume the 12th Chairman of the Joint Chiefs of Staff, was from the ROTC and not a West Pointer. *Tragic*. Yet not so tragic because when Colin Powell conducted and controlled the First Gulf War through Norman Schwarzkopf, there was no ritualized beheading of an American civilian hostage. His fault was that he did not push hard enough to destroy Saddam Hussein then, because of some silly political strategy that the Bushes had for the future and current president. They did not want to create what is known in realism as a "political vacuum." Not since Hoover has America ever worried about political vacuums when cleaning up the messes that it has created overseas.

Naturally, at the end of his military career before he became a Republican politician, Powell was awarded high honors from USMA at West Point. But one should also consider his own outdated book, *My American Journey* (1995). He has changed his views of Republicanism significantly since the 1990s because there isn't really a concerted political ideology in practice that supports what is generally perceived as republicanism.

Powell is one of only 41 Americans over the past 200 years who have been honored at West Point. The unusual bunch of awardees includes John Foster Dulles, Cardinal Spellman, Bob Hope, Dean Rusk, Barry Goldwater, Ronald Reagan, Paul H. Nitze, Walter Cronkite, Henry Kissinger, and Daniel K. Inouye. Not too bad for Colin Powell. He was someone who was not allowed in the Academy and had to be invited. At the end of his almost tearful and tragic acceptance speech, Powell said in all humility, with a hint of regret in its tone, "… And thank you for letting me visit once more."[13] Like an outsider who was never welcome as a young cadet hopeful, and who had risen to the highest military rank that the military could offer, it appears that the United States has come a long way in its war on racism and ethnic segregation. Powell was a young man during the time the Jim Crow laws were in effect, long before *Brown v. Board of Education of Topeka*, and the enactment of the Civil *Rights Act* (1965).

American military culture has evolved through a process of distillation for over 200 years. Yet it continues to have its misogynistic, anti-African American organizational walls eroded but not destroyed. African-Americans were only allowed into the USMA at West Point in 1948. West Point was "occupied in January 1778 as an American

Revolutionary War outpost ... and the home of the United States Corps of Cadets since 1802" (USMA).[14]

There are seven state military colleges with old historical links to the American civil war in South Carolina, Georgia, Vermont, Texas, and Virginia. Additionally, there are seven maritime colleges across the US. These include the California Maritime Academy; Great Lakes Maritime Academy; Maine Maritime Academy; Massachusetts Maritime Academy; New York Maritime College; Seattle Maritime Academy; and the Texas Maritime Academy in Galveston. Finally, there are also 47 military high/preparatory schools with various military training options across the contiguous United States with ROTC and JROTC programs. Not all the military programs are compulsory: two in Georgia, three in Alabama, one in New Mexico, one in Pennsylvania, three in Missouri, three in Florida, three in California, one in South Carolina, one for Pennsylvania, another for Mississippi, three in Indiana, six in Virginia, four in Texas, one in Kentucky, another in New York, two in North Carolina, one each for Kansas, Wisconsin, Minnesota, Oregon, and Delaware, four in Illinois, and two in Maryland. The roles of these military educational institutions compliment the DoD's Academies for the various military services. The military boarding schools act as feeder institutions that groom and prepare many of its students for life-long careers in the military.

Despite such a grand military tradition and honorable military culture in the US, there has been a growing series of disjunctions that have begun to unravel a more sinister side of the military itself. This involves examinations and the problem of gender in a male dominant culture:

> Ultimately, hundreds of cadets had received unauthorized assistance, or cheated, on an electrical engineering assignment and more than 150 cadets were separated for honor violations. The large numbers of cadets involved led to unprecedented congressional and public scrutiny of academy policies and programs. Ultimately, due to the large numbers of the cadets involved and indications that certain institutional practices may have facilitated this behavior, many were permitted to reapply. In the end, nearly 100 returned, and 85 ultimately graduated.[15]

Women now make up about 15 per cent of the population at US military educational institutions. And while women personnel have been sailing for at least two decades in the USN, they are still not allowed on

US submarines.[16] No Western male political philosopher who genuinely holds Plato in reverence would ever consider training men and women together in the same institution. It would be a recipe for disaster. There continues to be an organizational culture within the US military, specific to each of the services, perhaps created to inculcate a certain degree of creative inter-service rivalry. Such cultures and subcultures impose specific rituals, traditions, and values on servicemen and service women. These values are often based on mythical beliefs or irrational modes of understanding gender differences or perceptions of women through misogynistic and patriarchal lenses. That is why in a sense, the Tailhook incident (where over a hundred USN and USM officers allegedly abused over 80 American women in Las Vegas in 1991), the "Sergeant Delmar Simpson" case, and the "Sergeant Major of the Army Gene McKinney" case were "eye-openers" and perhaps a kind of dysfunctional "blessing-in-disguise" in exposing the extent and depth of the problem of "gender silence" and "engendered non-silence."[17]

Also consider the USAFA report on sexual improprieties at that academy, or the case of Maj. Gen. David R. E. Hale a graduate of the USMA. Also consider the following quotation that was carried by the *Marine Corps News* originating from an article from the *Associated Press*:

> Statistics on assault cases at the schools are incomplete and difficult to compare. West Point has had 15 reported cases, ranging from unwanted kissing to rape, since August 1999—or about 4.3 per year. 10 of the 15 accused cadets resigned or were forced out of the academy, three received lesser punishments, one was cleared by DNA evidence and one case is pending. Annapolis had 11 cases reported during the last three academic years, an average of 3.6 per year. Charges were substantiated in four cases, a finding that generally leads to expulsion, three are pending and four cadets apparently were cleared, based on the fragmentary information the institution provided. The Air Force Academy says it has had 56 cases of sexual misconduct since 1993, an average of 5.6 per year. Six cadets have faced courts-martial during that time, resulting in five convictions. At least eight others were dismissed from the academy, and seven others were reprimanded after disciplinary hearings. Not all the cases involved cadets as victims. Those figures don't reflect a central accusation in the Air Force scandal—that women cadets avoid reporting assaults for fear it will hurt their careers.[18]

If this is what is considered a tradition then it is a very ominous one. It is particularly foreboding because the American military and its personnel are posted all over the world for all kinds of military and non-military activities. If the US armed forces are to continue to be the global force of peace in the fight for freedom and justice, perhaps they should consider very seriously what they have been doing to their fellow Americans. If the lives of minority Americans and American women are taken for granted by the American military itself, what about the US as a global force? Even across prevailing theaters of operations from Iraq and Kuwait to Afghanistan and Bahrain there were at least 129 reported cases of sexual assault of US military men on US military women. According to Scott Berkowitz, the President of the *Rape, Abuse & Incest National Network*, "They rob our country of the services of many we have trained and nurtured to protect us."[19] The US as a global military force of supreme dominance must seriously accept the role it has chosen for itself and for imposition on the rest of the world.[20] While the US has not militarily threatened most foreign states, and only invaded a few, the reputation of the US military in all its forms will continue to be tarnished if prevailing realities are not addressed in ways that prevent recurrence. If the US military wishes to prevail as a global peace keeper, it must ensure that all its military and non-military personnel behave themselves while overseas or locally. Since the information and communications' revolution, the bad news of military impropriety travels further and reaches a wider audience. If the US cannot treat its own men and women with human dignity, how can it expect any one else to respect the entire organization? A US military culture that incubates fear and psychological repression among its own personnel will result in the emplacement of time-bombs that will go off at some point in time in the future. Some US serviceman or US servicewoman will eventually complain.

How can the US possibly accept itself as a global force if it mistreats its own citizens? Given the power and politics of American globalization, more thought and consideration ought to be given to this matter. Not surprisingly then we have a situation where the American military has performed well in some areas but a minority of American personnel have performed some dastardly tasks too in Iraq, Korea, Vietnam, Thailand, Okinawa, and even in the 50th state of Hawaii. Even Bush showed "deep disgust" for the recent American abuse of Iraqi prisoners. Katharine H. S. Moon, an assistant professor of political science at Wellesley College argues that the allegations of scandals go much deeper than meets the public eye. She provides evidence of the systemic use of Korean women prostitutes in various "security arrangements" since the 1970s in her original work titled, *Sex Among Allies Military Prostitution in U.S.-Korea Relations* (Columbia University Press, 1997). The *Marine Corps Times* ran a news article on what was described as the US military support of a flourishing sex trade:

> ... the US military supports a flourishing trade in sex slaves in South Korea. Hundreds of trafficked women, mostly from former Soviet bloc countries and the Philippines are forced by local bar owners to work as prostitutes in bars that cater to American servicemen. The women are typically lured to Korea with promises of high-paying jobs but end up being held against their will and coerced into working as prostitutes in circumstances that both the State Department and the United Nations condemn as a form of sexual slavery. The US military leadership in Korea says it is powerless to put a stop to the practice, which they claim is the responsibility of the Korean police. But the top Korean police expert on prostitution said it is unlikely Korean police will do anything to halt the trafficking because of widespread police corruption. While US troops continue to be the sex-slave racket's best customers, US commanders turn a blind eye.[21]

How can we create a community of power if the prevailing personnel entrusted with power are themselves the power abusers? If an American civilian or a foreigner looks at a military serviceman or service woman, how can s/he tell if the service man or service woman falls into that small minority of power abusers?

The US military overseas has a culture where nothing is done unless something blows up. If the servicemen need to "let off steam" from military training, and there are local women to support such a venting of taught "aggression," then the system will work. Thus we see Russian and Korean women forced by Korean men and Korean women into accepting sexual overtures from US servicemen in this "under ground economy." We also see the same patterns surrounding the activities of US military personnel in Okinawa, Japan.[22] The US military is therefore a highly efficient and organized global force with a mission to impose peace and stability across the globe for the sake of neoliberal capitalism and "free-trade." Nevertheless, the motto that is accepted by all US military services,

"Duty," "Honor," "Country" is perhaps better understood as an optimistic ideal. There is no duty to perform oppressive sexual abuse of Americans by Americans. There is no honor in denigrating foreign men and foreign women who come under the gaze of the US military presence in Iraq, Korea, Okinawa, or Hawaii. There is no "Country" to defend if it is already being weakened on the inside. The seeds of destruction are sown when you don't respect your own citizens. Otherwise America will go the way of the Roman Empire, the Spanish Conquistadors, and the imperial Japanese militarism of previous centuries. This is why, if America is to continue its self-imposed mission of global domination through military intervention—be it in Taiwan, the Philippines, Okinawa, Hawaii, Pakistan, or perhaps even India—then it has to get its act together at home. The abuse of its own citizens is a harbinger of the kinds of abuse that can be expected of innocent foreigners who are caught in the crossfire between the US and whomever it considers its enemy-government targets.

CONCLUSION

The Egyptians built the pyramids as monuments to their kings, and symbols of their ability in supreme warfare. There is an urgent and pressing need for the MIC in America which is both alive and well, to take cognizance of what its role actually is within the globalized world. Businesses, academies and military units within the MIC have to realize that their research and activities have a great impact on the nature of globalization as emanating from the USA. The laws and military guidelines that have been put in place, and the high ideals of the pyramidal military educational culture appear to have been all but tossed aside. There is a need for Americans to return to the politics of military globalization and take a long hard look at what is being done within these centers of military work.

We saw at the beginning of this chapter the important message that Dwight D. Eisenhower had for Americans in 1960. In his prayerful speech he urged not only Americans but people of all faiths and races and nations towards the importance of freedom and the heavy responsibilities that came with it. He went on to talk about the various ideals that could be removed like poverty, disease and ignorance so that people can live together in a binding force of "mutual respect and love" (*Public Papers of the Presidents*, Dwight D. Eisenhower, 1960, pp. 1035–

40). Almost a century after Eisenhower mentioned those words, we can say that we are perhaps more knowledgeable about the planet, about different societies, about racism, about poverty, and disease. We are perhaps more knowledgeable now that at any other point in human history. But the politics of globalization has taught us that no one, not even America or Americans, with its dual-pronged spirited mission of converting all peoples towards world peace, and imposing free-trade on all those who would accept it *with force*. We can see that the gap between the rich and the poor, between rich people world and poor people in every country, with the exception of North Korea, Cuba, China, Libya, Iran, and Myanmar because their political institutions are incapable of making sense of poverty, is growing at an increasing rate. Eisenhower's idealism almost sounds like he was preaching from some Holy Book. That he was some kind of prophet who was envisioning a world that could not be achieved. Like Malcolm X and Martin Luther King. Like Richard Nixon, Elvis Presley, and Billy Graham. The world today is more informed of its class distinctions, despite the ending and in spite of the end of the Cold War. The world today is also more informed of the racial divide between and among people. The world today is more knowledgeable about disease and disease-control mechanisms. But the globalized world of America and its Allies, America and its enemies, America all alone is not better off than it was when Saint Eisenhower mentioned those words.

Perhaps a more thoughtful comment at this junction would be the one reiterated by the old political scientist and president of the United States, Woodrow Wilson, who spoke when America was not a hegemonic power but had some idea of what it would be. Wilson had some sense of the "destiny of America" when he spoke of not wanting "a rivalry of power, but a community of power."[23] Today that phrase seems equally apt. While Wilson was fearful of other powers such as the Soviets, Chinese, French and the British, his fears have all but disappeared today. Yet his phrase is equally apt because this is exactly what America needs to do today: to lower its military sights, to get its military *houses* in order, and to view the world as communities of empowerment if only to realize the later Eisenhower idealism in the politics of American globalization. Perhaps Chomsky's left-leaning politics might be right after all, that America is indeed a one-party state: a business party with two factions— Republicans and Democrats and with party bosses to steer the way forward. Thinking Americans have a duty to prevent the party bosses from leading the way too quickly towards disaster.

The next chapter deals with a different global reach that the politics of American globalization possesses: American popular culture. The American political culture of neoliberal individualism has created a large middle class which tends to "look-down" on the poor while remaining "politically correct" by reserving their genuine and personal feelings about the widening gap between rich and poor and the continuing impoverishment of the American underclass—for social scientific analyses drawn from instruments such as the World Values Survey—it seems easier for Americans to associate poverty with ethnicity. But there remain many questions about success and failure under the American model because it seems that many African-Americans have been so psychologically scarred that they are unable to advance in the greedy capitalist manner or the sophisticated admissions standards used by American academic institutions that new immigrants to the metaphorical Ellis Island such as the Koreans, Vietnamese and Indian Americans are able to achieve without much trouble. Perhaps it is because the divide between Black and White is do deeply ingrained and so manifest that it is a fissure like the Grand Canyon that cannot be closed within geological time. The next chapter will examine how popular culture acts as a channel for venting the frustrations of being—African, Anabaptist, Anglo-Saxon, Buddhist, Chinese, California, Canadian, Catholic, Christian, Columbian, Czech, Dutch, Episcopal, English, Eskimo, French, German, Greek, Hindu, Hispanic, Indian, Irish, Italian, Japanese, Jewish, Korean, Lebanese, Mexican, Micronesian, Mormon, Muslim, Navaho, Native, Pacific North Western, Panamanian, Polish, Rastafarian, Russian, Scandinavian, Vietnamese, West Indian, or White—American. Neoliberal capitalism in America has had the positive effect of creating a milieu where even the most racist comments emanating from influential talk shows over network television and syndicated cable broadcasts; the anti-Semitic Louis Farrakhan; the resistance politics of a former director of the *Kamakakuokalani* Haunani Kay Trask; the White-racism of David Duke; the political ineptitude of George Bush; the saintliness of Francis Cardinal Spellman; and the antagonism of Michael Moore's inverse racism can exist in an uneasy plural "balance."

The world is in America inasmuch as America is in the world. This is why there continues to be a politics of American globalization. The plural political culture of American politics is designed on a rejection of the older European pluralistic model that is based on proportional representation (with the exception of the UK, of course). While the European model affords a greater extent of political representation, the younger American model is designed as political expediency and policy efficiency. It appears that the American plural model supports the thesis that might makes right, and this not only makes all the three constituencies of the MIC very satisfied customers who are smiling all the way to the bank, it also means that the American hawks continue to win over the softer power of the American doves.

ENDNOTES

1   Note the US Supreme Court case number 340 U.S. 135 (1950).

2   See for example, the case of *Saeed Rezai v. Immigration and Naturalization Service* (1995); *United States of America v. Oliver L. North* (1990); and *People's Mojahedin Organization of Iran v. United States Department of State and Madeleine K. Albright, Secretary of State* (1999).

3   Several political scientists specializing in "American politics" were discussing the reasons why George Bush didn't win a second term despite his stellar performance in the first Gulf War in 1991. Most concluded that it was because even the Republicans didn't think too highly of his ability. One did not have to look far. The cable television commentators, talk show hosts, and comedians had a field day mimicking Bush.

4   In 2003, over half a million pro-democracy demonstrators took to the streets of Hong Kong in support of a democratic Hong Kong. Doubtlessly supported by the capitalists who are reaping in billions each year from this tiny capitalist nodal point. It ought to be pointed out that the British held Hong Kong on a lease from China for 150 years but did nothing for democracy until it was time to hand Hong Kong back to China in 1997 and gave this impossible task to its last British governor Christopher Patten, the former chair[person] of the Tory party (the British Conservatives). The diplomatic fracas and embarrassment that ensued after the return— the UK reneged on granting British citizenship to thousands of Hong Kong pro-British loyalists—saw Patten elevated to EU commissioner and now, Chancellor of Oxford University as a face-saving gesture for the darkened British empire of islands.

5   "In Fallujah, Marines adjust to changing plans," *NavyTimes.com*, April 7, 2004.

6   Noam Chomsky, "History of US Military Involvement: An interview with Noam Chomsky," *ZMagazine*, January 2, 2004.

7   See also "Office of the Secretary of Defense, Joint Chiefs of Staff, Military Departments, Unified Commands," *US Department of Defense*, 2004. The military departments under the Office of the Secretary of Defense include the US Army, US Air Force, US Navy, US Marine Corps, and the US Coast Guard.

8   This figure for the regular service personnel is not as large as the People's Republic of China's *People's Liberal Army* (PLA) total land unit-components, but the US Armed Forces are certainly more technologically advanced, better equipped, better fed, and much better paid. The question remains for Americans is whether or not they can be better trusted with American lives.

9   "An Introduction," *US Department of Defense*, 2004.

10   See also the pro-government, US-centric report by Walter F. Ulmer Jr., Joseph J. Collins, T. O. Jacobs, eds., *American Military Culture in the Twenty-First Century: A Report of the CSIS International Security Program* (Washington, DC: Center for Strategic and International Studies, 2000).

11   "An Introduction," *US Department of Defense*, 2004.

12   William D. Hartung, "Eisenhower's Warning: The Military-industrial Complex Forty Years Later," *World Policy Journal* 18, no. 1 (2001).

13   Colin L. Powell, "Thayer Award Acceptance Remarks," *USMA West Point*, September 15, 1998.

14   "West Point Bicentennial," *USMA*, 2002.

15   "West Point Bicentennial—The Long Gray Line Changes Formation," *USMA*, 2002.

16   Andrea Stone, "Navy Resists Idea of Opening Submarines to Women," *USA Today*, September 14, 1999, 14A.

17   The work on sex scandals in the US military is growing larger by day as more information gets revealed or is leaked out of the system, either deliberately or not deliberately. See for example, Andrea Stone, "Women See Smoother Sailing in the Navy," *USA Today*, January 12, 1998, A01; Andrea Stone, "Army Orders Trial in Sex Case. Top Sergeant Could Face 56-year Term," *USA Today*, October 9, 1997, A03; Tom Curley, "Sergeant convicted of 18 rapes," *USA Today*, April 30, 1997, A01; and The Office of the Inspector General, *The Tailhook Report* (NY: St. Martin's Press, December 1993).

18   Robert Weller, "West Point, Annapolis avoid Air Force Academy's travails," *Associated Press*, March 30, 2003.

19   "Military Sex Assault Likened to 'Friendly Fire'," *China Daily*, May 1, 2004.

20   Kathleen T. Rhem, "Bush Shows 'Deep Disgust' for Apparent Treatment of Iraqi Prisoners," *American Forces Press Service*, April 30, 2004.

21   "Sex slaves and the U.S. military," *Marine Corps Times*, 2002.

22   Eric Johnston, "Okinawans' Anger Inflamed Rape Case Stokes Anti-US Fervor," *USA Today*, July 9, 2001, A10.

23   Henry A. Kissinger, "Thayer Award Speech," *USMA West Point*, September 13, 2000.

6

American Popular Culture

The body and the traces it conceals, the soul and the images its perceives, are here no more than stages in the syntax of delirious language.[1]

This chapter is about another part of the politics of American globalization that has often not been covered by the literature on globalization because it is not considered "political" or "economic." An element of the reason why it is not considered political is because it does not seem to be the "stuff" of high politics. Because its label—popular culture—appears too be too frivolous for most "serious" work on "international relations theory" and "globalization." As a result, such serious work is denied the insights of an invaluable aspect of American politics because it prefers to conform to prevailing misperceptions of conservative political scientist-gatekeepers of international relations theory within the academic discipline of political science. This represents another tragedy of uncanny errors in the American idiom. Perhaps because people who are sad tend to be more aware, more attuned, more sensitive to the inner mysteries of unnatural nature, and that Aristotle was manic depressive.

This chapter is about the different popular and mass cultural activities of that phenomenon collectively known as "American popular culture." The competing number of academic books and articles on popular culture is as diverse as the definitions that come with them. Popular culture has similar characteristics all over the world. One such trait is currency. Not the kind of currency that we saw in the previous chapter but a certain fashionableness and trendy set of consumer goods and services. Popular culture is a global industry simply because it is a money spinner. Therefore, popular culture in America and elsewhere in the world constitutes both a currency of fashion and the currency arising out of the sale and purchase of fashionable goods. While this chapter explores *some* of the different kinds of American popular culture and attempts to show how these cultural tropes inform the politics of American globalization, it cannot possibly encompass all the different kinds of popular culture that has made America what it is today. Some of the more prominent tropes of American popular culture that have been omitted include American Cuisine, American Pulp Fiction, American Television, Broadcasting and Networking, and Syndicated Networks, and American social sciences as a form of global tertiary popular culture. There are also other aspects of American popular culture that deserve more in-depth treatment such as the metaphorical use of Urban Legends, the myth of the Cowboy, the Big Apple, Manifest Destiny and the Monroe Doctrine, the American Red Indian, the Superbowl and the Sugar Bowl to name a few. The inclusion of these different modalities would have increased the weight of the book tremendously but were left out because of the limitations of the writer's own time and space considerations.

HARLEY-DAVIDSON AND GLOBAL POPULAR CULTURE

The Harley-Davidson Motorcycle Company almost went broke in the 1970s but was eventually revived as an important pillar of American popular culture. This was the beginning of a global popular cultural ethos that commemorated at least two levels. One dimension was the celebration of freedom, individualism, and self-expression; the other aspect was the celebration of anti-Establishment ethos, renegade youthfulness, drug abuse, sexual promiscuity, and a gangster culture that challenged all forms of social propriety and commonsense. Ironically, many state and federal traffic police units all over the world use Harley-Davidson motorcycles. The Harley-Davidson brand is now a worldwide entity with an MNC that provides the continuity of an old American tradition of the cowboy on his horse with the freedom of the open road to anyone of any color, age, gender, size, sexual orientation, socio-economic class, or religion with the skill to operate a 1,000 cubic centimeter (twin-cam 88) motorcycle. The negative dimension associated with these powerful machines and the Hell's Angels group has become so diluted over the past half century that they have become an urban legend across the world. Harley-Davidson motorcycles at the annual pilgrimage to Sturgis, South Dakota, for example, no longer pose a threat to society any longer. In fact, the popularity of the Harley-Davidson culture has become so ingrained over the past 62 years that it now seems to be a rite of passage for high-flying CEOs, young executives, and middle managers who still wish to recapture the nostalgic moments of their youth so aptly captured by Marlon Brando in *The Wild One* (1954), Steven McQueen in *The Great Escape* (1963) and the ultimate classic *Easy Rider* (1969) that starred Peter Fonda, Dennis Hopper, and Jack Nicholson. Later versions of the bad boy image on a Harley include Arnold Schwarzenegger in *Terminator 2* (1991) and Mickey Rourke and Don Johnson in *Harley Davidson and the Marlboro Man* (1991). The popular culture of Harley-Davidson motorcycles and the images that they evoke has become a global industry found on every continent and virtually every city and street. It is perhaps one of the most well known names in global popular culture like *Coke* and *McDonald's*.

COUNTRY AND WESTERN POPULAR CULTURE

Many Americans love Country and Western (C&W) music in the songs of Hank Williams, Patsy Cline, Johnny Cash, Randy Travis, the Judds, Garth Brooks, or Charlie Pride. The popular cultural attributes in their songs derive from a history of living out, literally, in the country where self-reliance and hard-work were key features of quotidian life. Unlike non-C&W music, there is a much lower emphasis on material gains or the "bling-bling" resistance movement in African-American Rap.[2] Some believe that C&W music only began in the 1930s. This is untrue, and supports too narrow a definition given the genealogical history of C&W music in America today. C&W music history dates back at least 200 years to the time of the American Civil War.

C&W music is known for its misogyny and for the greatest part of its history, most C&W singers were indeed men. This could be part of the reason why there are many people who believe that C&W continues to be the last preserve of Western Male dominance in America, with the rest of America having been taken over and overtaken by feminists and feminist-supporting males. This is untrue of course for two reasons: one is that the primordial division of labor and allocation of resources continues to remain strongly in favor of men. The second reason is that feminists are not necessarily male, and to say that most feminists are women would be to place too fine a point under extremely essentialist terms. Besides, most statistical estimates point towards the fact that while "women" make up about 50 per cent of the world's population, they only

210

receive 10 per cent of its wages. I don't think that this is a true reflection of the situation for American "women" but it is certainly true of certain constituencies of American "women." But then again, this places too fine a point on *what it means to be a "woman."* This led Judith Butler to re-question the noun (of the word) and suggest that it be left out of feminist discourse because of its proclivity to the word "man." I think that Felix Guattari and Phyllis Turnbull would certainly have supported Butler's position.[3] However, a good way to explore Butler's position is to look at Kathy E. Ferguson's *The Man Question: Visions of Subjectivity in Feminist Theory* (University of California Press, 1993) where the idea of a temporary grounding of the subject helps us move onwards, perhaps even upwards, in discovering our own ontological positions in life.

The epistemological position about C&W music for this book is that it represents C&W popular culture. On the other hand, the study of the meaning of the self is potentially discoverable in C&W music because of its reflection of what is perceived as "natural," "in nature" and "of nature." This is because C&W music is made up of a diverse reflection of different selves, and different approaches to the self turned inside out. This is seen in the variegated genres of C&W music subtypes such as Bluegrass, Dixie, Country Rock, Country Blues, Country Folk, Country Pop, Hawaiian Slack Key, Southern Gospel, Gospel Blues, Hawaiian Gospel, and New Age Country Gospel. C&W music is ostensibly tied, but not exclusively, to a kind of Christian ethos. This is why there aren't many C&W singers or songs that celebrate Jewish feast days or Islamic prophets or Buddhist days of fasting and abstinence.

Perhaps the most interesting thing about C&W music is that it is easily recognized by people all over the world as being a genuine American invention. C&W music is so well recognized that there are many people all over the world who can actually sing C&W songs without ever having set foot in America. Such is the politics of globalization. If the politics of globalization is about influencing people who aren't even in America then this is certainly one example. The global appeal of C&W music—again, as only one example of American popular culture—is in its humility, its simplicity, and its shared "values." The strength of C&W music comes from the use of simple and straight forward themes that are easily recognized almost any where there has been access to free radio waves. C&W music also touches the hearts of people with its simple themes about family, losing someone or something, about the "good-old-days" and nostalgia, emotional wrangles, gambling, alcoholism, success, and joy.

Another aspect of C&W music's popular appeal to the consumers of America is that it has a constant set of working metaphors: the "cowboy," "backroads, country roads," the "Lonesome Somebody," "Unrequited Love" and many other metaphors that are presented in a non-threatening, easy-listening, non-challenging, and conventional manner. There are no heavy political messages, no politics of resistance, no deep emotional angst, no "hatred of the White Man"; "Let's lynch the nigger"; "I've been to prison so I know what life's about"; "kill this person or kill that person because of some power trip" syndrome. There's a certain absence of audio-listener *abuse* that is common in another kind of American popular culture—"Gangster Rap" music promoted by performers like Ice-T, Two Pac and other "gangsta rappers." Because being notorious emits an image of being "cool" for people with low self-esteem, desiring to mimic the tragic image of being "bad" because it is "good." Gangster Rap invokes the shameful violence of the Italian Mafioso. It mimics a violent Sicilian "negative tradition." And more. Gangster Rap is a form of aggressive political resistance against the Establishment. Gangster rappers are shameful of the social status accorded to them because they believe that society's prejudices and hatred of Black America is immutable and unchanging. They find it futile to devote time and energy towards improving poverty among Americans, the police abuse and profiling of Black Americans, and the criminalization of Blacks on Black communities that want out of the vicious cycle of violence. Extreme rappers prefer to instill and provoke violence while bringing violence on them. Gangster Rap music is for those with fragile egos who wish to terrorize Americans of all ethnic persuasions through music.

In fact, Gangster Rap and C&W music are very interesting areas of research because their characteristics are in direct opposition to each other: Gangster Rap music often represents the angst, hatred, the suffering, and the power struggles within America's decaying inner-urban cities. Gangster Rap Music portrays the paraphernalia of alcoholism, drug abuse, sexual abuse, sexism, misogyny, prostitution, misogamy, gang rape, hatred, racism, in-your-face verbal abuse, stealing people's property, treating women as property, and the extended use of expletives in place of adjectives, nouns, and adverbs. Ordinary Rap Music uses more instruments and complex variations in the musical score than C&W music. But Gangster Rap politicizes the music in more overt ways than C&W music.

Ordinary Rap Music certainly has more "depth" and "soul" than C&W music. C&W music tends to be overly "simplistic," "monotonous," and "boring." True enough, Rap Music as a whole seems to be "more real" than C&W music when rappers listen to its *booty beat*, while C&W music appears as "realistic" when cowboys listen to it *melodious tunes*. Both Gangster Rap and C&W music represent popular genres that are equally real. It is just that one emphasizes the violence in human nature and the other doesn't. All things considered and remaining constant, which of course is never the case, Gangster Rap emphasizes hard-hitting and thumping violence. It is a reflection of political power and subordination. It is about insubordination. It is about *bling-bling* blinding lights and rapid heart beats. Gangster Rap is the music of political resistance in a way that C&W music is already the music of the empowered and the leisure class (but only to a certain extent because C&W music is quite non-confrontational and rather pro-establishment). Ordinary Rap Music is not "laid back" or less politically powerful. But it sends the message without resorting to violence. It refuses to lay down and smell the folksy green *green* grass of home, bother about "yellow ribbons" round "old oak trees," or "the misty taste of moonshine" and "tear drops in my eyes."

It is unlikely that many American parents would allow their children to listen to extreme versions of Rap. Overseas and away from America, however, Rap may be more acceptable by the local Establishment because they simply can't read it. Although both C&W and Rap are clearly recognizable as genuine American popular cultural inventions, when sent away, Rap tends to be more displaced by time, space, language, and social memory than C&W. This is exemplified in the plausibility of a young Thai teenage consumer of extreme rap music who has never visited America, doesn't speak Spanish or American English, has no knowledge of "jive" or "street slang," never lived in a *'burb* or a *'hood*, doesn't know anyone living in the decaying inner cities, nor has ever watched MTV. This is a teenager who will have a *highly* distorted view of Rap. If the teenager's parents were also in the dark about Rap, it would serve no less to ameliorate the perception of what Rap might mean. This kind of feature of globalization makes it political in the sense of a politics of apathy. Another example of political apathy follows.

In the early 1990s, over a period of several months I noticed some young male teenagers in Singapore and Malaysia wearing T-shirts with a symbol emblazoned boldly on the front. But there was a problem with the symbol. At first I thought that it was the Buddhist swastika which is common in Southeast Asia where there are relatively large Chinese populations. There is even a "Red Swastika School" in Singapore[4] that belongs to the *Tao Yuan* Sect also known by its philanthropic arm as the "Red Swastika Society" (Smith, 1970: 586; Freedman and Topley, 1961: 16). However, the symbol in question was the Nazi Swastika. But the teens did not know what the symbol of the swastika meant. Had these "non-Aryan" teenagers been alive at the time of the National Socialists they would have been considered one of the lower races and subjected to the usual atrocities of the "non-chosen" people. They would have very quickly realized that the swastika was the symbol of Aryan supremacy and White-racism under Adolf Hitler.

One day, out of curiosity (and the kind of frustration that only substitute high school teachers can understand) I asked a young teen loitering along Singapore's Orchard Road whether he knew what the symbol meant. He said that he did not. I politely gave him a brief history lesson about the dangers of (what I later learnt in graduate school to be) primordial and essentialist views of the world. And then I carefully explained what the symbol represented. What made *it* political? At the end of my explanation, he merely smiled, shrugged his shoulders, and said that the Jews "deserved" it for killing innocent Palestinians.[5] But because his mind was made up, there was nothing else I could possibly have done for that individual stranger. Over a decade has passed since that incident. The fad of wearing such T-shirts has long gone. I only worry when it might come back in time, in a different form. This is the kind of problem that globalization presents when the youth of the world are callous about events and aren't willing to bother to discover "the truth" on their own.

Globalization's reach within the popular culture of "trendy fashions" are part of a political problematic that teachers and social scientists need to continually engage.[6] The situation described above may indeed be an isolated episode and is not representative of any one entire distinct minority. But there was a strong undercurrent of anti-Semitism among the Malaysian political elite under Mahathir Mohamad. The former prime minister blamed George Soros and other currency speculators for the 1997/8 Asian currency crisis. While this was indeed true, it was Mahathir's suggestion of Soros' Jewish identity that pointed to the former prime minister's anti-Semitism. Mahathir could have simply said that Soros was a greedy speculator who preyed on the structural vulnerabilities of developing states. Mahathir did not have to emphasize Soros' "Jewish identity" (See also, Groth, 1971: 89).

There has also been a history of Mahathir's anti-Semitism since he became prime minister in 1981. Known for his outspoken views and harsh criticisms of the West, Mahathir has earned great respect and influence in the region from other Southeast Asian states. He did not have to racialize issues to score points with the Malaysian Muslim population. His racialization of such issues clearly had not benefited Malaysian politics in general, nor BN's and UMNO's performance in the elections.[7] All this is being done while a whole generation of Malaysians, both Muslims and their non-Muslim friends, are enjoying the latest American movies, in legal and illegal formats, the most up-to-date American rock musicians and singers, and American popular fashion, trends and linguistic styles. Some examples of American trendy brand names that are popular in Malaysia include Marlboro, and Marlboro Lights, Levi's denim jeans, Starbucks Coffee, and fast food "restaurants" like McDonald's, Burger King, and Kentucky Fried Chicken. While the government is saying one thing about globalization and Western values, the people are doing something else about popular culture.

It was only when Mahathir stepped down in October 2003 and handed power over to his deputy, Abdullah Badawi, that there were significant changes in the political platform. BN and UMNO regained Trengganu and narrowly lost to PAS in Kelantan. Malaysians also seem to be more accepting of the conservative, MOR Islam provided by Abdullah's Islam Hadhari. There were other instances of Mahathir's anti-Semitic remarks. When Israeli president Chaim Herzog visited Singapore in 1986, Mahathir temporarily withdrew the Malaysian High Commissioner from Singapore. In a speech to the 26-member Non-Aligned Movement (NAM) in 1986, Mahathir condemned the Jews. In 1994, the Malaysian authorities censored *Schindler's List* because it seemed to "tarnish the other [German] race."[8] Later that year, Mahathir went to another extreme by supporting China's stand on human rights against the American onslaught which he referred to as being "badgered and hectored by the Clinton Administration" (Sikorski, 819). The "Jewish Question" is quite different from the time that Marx analyzed it in his famous essay bearing the same title. The problem has clearly become a global problem that is waiting to be used as an excuse for political violence, revenge killings, or Holy Wars. Globalization may promote trendy-beliefs through its empty and meaningless symbols but it also sponsors, perhaps unwittingly, ethnic hatred between Jew and Muslim, between Christian and Jew, between African-Americans and Jews, between Korean Americans and African-Americans. The list is long and too bloody to complete. But I think you get the picture if you realize that there are so many innocent Christians, Jews, and Muslims out there in the "silent majority" who do not deserve to have their beliefs pushed from pillar to post for the sake of propagating some politicized discourse. We need to turn away from such negativity and towards more positive things. But the real issue with Mahathir's anti-Semitic remarks was that there was little if any sustained criticism from the Opposition or from Civil Society groups. This is why we said that the undercurrent was strong in Malaysia under Mahathir. This is why Singapore, its Southern neighbor, has an undercurrent problem among some members of its youthful generation under what is perceived by some as an authoritarian, personality-based government. Such as the real story about the teenager with the trendy and popular symbol among his friends. Then there is the problem of rock music and a heavy metal rock music that poses different sets of problems to different constituencies across the globe. Teenagers are particularly vulnerable to the products of pop culture—whether these are made around C&W music, Rap, MTV, California Rock remixes, or the "blue-eyed soul" of Daryl Hall and John Oates. The producers of popular cultural goods and services must themselves be made more socially aware and thoughtful about what they make, even though their ultimate desire is to make more money.

On the other hand, C&W music appears much less threatening to many American parents than the extreme versions of Rap. But I cannot do justice to this genre of music and would urge you to read the work of Pamela Hall, especially her article titled, "The Relationship Between Types of Rap Music and Memory in African American Children" (1988) and Tricia Rose's excellent "Fear of a Black Planet: Rap Music and Black Cultural Politics in the 1990s" (1991).[9]

Yet, the attraction of C&W music to many Americans and to people all over the world is found in its predictability, simplicity of themes and values, and association with a certain "Southern, Confederate culture" that has survived the overwhelming Union victory so many years ago. There apparently is a cowboy in all of us. Even in Elvis Presley, according to the research of David Emblidge in 1976.[10] C&W music may not be able to mesh with American rap music but it certainly has had its share of

216

related criticism. This is seen for example, in the "satire" and jocular diatribes of entertainers such as Jeff Foxworthy. He has indeed made a very good living out of taking the Mickey out of American "Southern culture" and what is generally understood as the "Redneck" subculture. Foxworthy's success as an entertainer reflects a careful blending of a subcultural trait with his own familial history.

In many extreme cases, an African-American person may unintentionally instill fear in an outsider who is lost in the inner cities, while the reverse would be true for an African-American person getting going astray in the Deep South, the Everglades and other parts of the old American Confederacy. What is interesting is not the fact that you could say this about any other district minority in the world and still come up with examples, but that if you told this to a foreigner in Japan or in Taiwan, chances are that this foreigner, unless s/he has been a complete recluse, would know more about the "Americans getting lost story" than Americans would know about the hill tribes people such as the *Ali Shan* living in the remote mountains of O' Luan Pi in Southern Taiwan who come into town every once in a while and also get lost.

The interesting thing about the politics of American globalization is that foreigners often know more about America than Americans know about foreigners. Perhaps because America is more interesting to more people, or perhaps because there are more geographically challenged people in the US. But this is only a hypothesis because a positivist social scientist in modernity would support the need for the construction of a proper survey instrument, by asking the "right" questions, and by operationalizing the concepts for a representative survey, backed up by ethnographic focus group activities for the absence of a normative bend in qualitative analyses.[11]

THE POPULARITY OF AMERICA

On thing has to be said about the nature of the popular culture of American music: what is considered radical today will become out-dated and old-fashioned tomorrow. Unless the songs and the music are elevated to the level of classic chart toppers. It is hard to believe that the gold-gilded music of legends like Bing Crosby, Frank Sinatra, Dean Martin, Louis Armstrong, were once the radical set. As a young man, Sinatra received much adulation from "bobby-sock wearing high school girls" and together with Sammy Davis, Jr., and Dean Martin were known collectively as the "Rat Pack."

American popular culture has been a constant that has continued to invade and occupy the time and space of all social classes, all ethnic communities, and all religious persuasions. This has happened all over the world in an uneven manner. How has the phenomenon of American popular culture come about and why has it continued to stay. More importantly, how is the phenomenon linked to the politics of American globalization? The phenomenon of American popular culture is built on three main ingredients: (1) The American Dream and the Anti-American Dream (2) the creation of legends, myths, and stories about America's past such as those found in the fictive truths of—*A Horse With No Name*, Abraham Lincoln, American Cowboy, American Pie, Babe Ruth, Big Apple, Big Easy, California Dreamin', *Casey and the Sundance Kid*, Davy Crocket, Easy Rider, From Here to Eternity, *Harley Davidson*, Hotel California, JFK, John Lennon, Johnny Appleseed, Marilyn Monroe, Marlboro Man, *Miss Saigon*, Paul Bunyan, Route 66, Tom Sawyer, Uncle Sam, Uncle Tom's Cabin, *West Side Story*, Westward Ho! Woodstock; and (3) the commodification of these legends, myths, and stories into bite-sized bits that can be consumed—through images on television, movie characters on the silver screen, in computer games, in hand-held computer games, in animated films and cartoons, and the export of these to the rest of the world.

It is important at this junction to note that there cannot be a single comprehensive definition of American popular culture. The best kind would be the broadest, something that sounds like 'the culture that is readily accepted by the masses, easily commoditized, subject to imminent changes in taste, and has the potential to return as retrospective culture or "retro." However such a broad definition is not very useful when we consider that American popular culture by nature is about challenging that which is defined and definitive, that which seeks to remain stable and constant, and like the Rat Pack of Sammy Davis Jr., Frank Sinatra and Dean Martin, designed to ostensibly reject in a politically non-violent way that which is considered to be part of the Establishment culture.

ESCAPE FROM TERROR

It is one thing to have important quotes from the work of Theodore Adorno, Herbert Marcuse and Max Horkheimer in addition to the specifics of the Authoritarian Personality but it is quite another to deconstruct the work of Eric Fromm. The wars in late modernity have depleted the human mind and challenged its adaptive capacity to face its biggest enemy, itself. There are peaceful means of using technology but because they are human inventions—as are nuclear power plants, the Internet, and bio-chemistry—they contain the seeds of death and destruction. The dangers of mass consumption were indeed anticipated by Adorno while Heidegger before him had already warned and taught Arendt about the problems that Jaspers had raised the notion of technology in modernity.

The threat to human life and civilization as we know it comes in the shape of a political paradox. Unlike the paradox that continues to confront Americans that we saw in Chapter two, this paradox comes from living life itself. Most threats are either biological, environmental, or associated with communications. It is a paradox because the sharing of information in the globalized world means that we have solved some problems of disease and certain aspects of food distribution. We have improved our knowledge in the physical sciences, in pharmaceutical products, and in psychological, clinical and emergency medicine. We have also learnt to develop different lifestyle choices that help us deal with unexpected loss. However, because of globalization's access and speed, modernity has also brought with it the scourge of those who are alienated. Thus it is a paradox because the vehicle that has brought good had also brought bad. And we have to accept the good with the bad. It is a political paradox because those who feel that they have been alienated for whatever reason feel the need to use modern technology for destruction. Nuclear maps and explosive devices can be built with the help of the Internet. The ingredients for demolition devices can be purchased discretely and separately over the Internet. Our modes of communication—train travel, sea travel, and air travel—all move us towards efficiently getting there faster in comfort. Yet these modes of communication are themselves targets of alienated persons hiding under the camouflage of religion, race, or language. The micro technology used to perform cardiac surgery can also be used to create hidden explosive devices. And soon, nanotechnology's advantages will be put to bad use. Our greatest achievement has resulted in our worst fears. Globalization is therefore a political paradox of raking in the good and bad without being able to tell the what from the which, *quid pro quo* within the promise(s) of American life as suggested by Walter Michaels and his discussion of "classes" and "masses."[12]

The world as we know it has increasingly become a tinder box of terror. The rates of political and social change brought about by globalization's increasing access (to information, resources, talent) and speed (it takes a shorter time to travel, to cook, to write a book, to complete a university education) have also been taken advantage by terrorists planning on destroying for the sake of destruction. The tinder box of terror might be ignited by people who have the same access to the information and resources with the same speed. In addition to Connolly's analysis of depth in his article 'Cosmopolitanism, Speed and Concentric Cultures' we continue to be confronted by people who have spun out of the circle of modernizing cultures. And to have spun out of control is to be made redundant and insignificant.[13] They want attention. That is what the terrorists desire. But they want it the easy way. Rather than going through the political process, rather than employing means that will extend bridges of communication, these marginalized groups want to blow them apart.

There appears to be little respite from the threat of someone somewhere plotting to destroy what American families may have been taking for granted for years. It is one thing to consider such a prison mentality as a kind of Gramscian hangover, and a thing of the past. It is quite another thing to consider the prison in a Foucauldian sense that encompasses our modern modes of organizing politics, economics, culture, and society. However, it is because human kind is continually beset and under siege by one form of terror or another than we cannot completely rule out a proto-alarmist position on the possibility that the people we know in a quotidian sense could be the next victim of a terrorist attack. War it seems follows the human being like a shadow. And the faster we go, the faster the shadow follows. The Communists used the nuclear threat on Americans for the greater part of the lives of most people who are likely to read this book. America, in retaliation, called its own nuclear program nuclear deterrence. The McCarthyism that followed did not achieve anything but make Americans fear the threat was imminent. There was Korea, Vietnam, Afghanistan, Iran, Iraq, Libya, Lebanon, Kuwait, Haiti, and the indefatigable mess created in the Middle East between the Palestinians and the Israelis. There was also the problem of OPEC's oligopoly and the threat of depleted fossil fuels that were driving the industrialization plans of developing countries, and the post-industrialization of America and Western Europe. The world has become so small and so interrelated that any problem occurring in a distant part of the globe soon becomes an issue of concern for the rest of the world, such as the resurgence in Islamic fundamentalism in the 1970s, AIDS, ozone depletion, global warming, the Savings and Loans scandal, environmental disasters caused by super tankers like the Exxon Valdez, SARS, avian or bird flu virus, Mad Cow Disease, the election of George Bush instead, the threat of chemical and biological warfare, Enron, and the horrifying destruction of World Trade Center's twin towers (9/11), the Bali bombing, the Madrid train bombing, scourge in Southern Thailand, and the continuing problem of latent terrorists trained by the CIA, international waterway piracy, a weakening UN, the rising strength of the Euro and the increasing sentiment of European unity and potential protectionism since May 1st, 2004. Americans need to escape.

And American popular culture is part of an important machine within the neoliberal capitalism of America that helps provide that means of escapism. But how does one avoid the real terror exposed to America within its borders as Michel and Herbeck reminds us in their *American Terrorist: Timothy McVeigh and the Oklahoma City Bombing* (Regan, 2001) or an earlier harbinger by Raphael S. Ezekiel in *The Racist Mind: Portraits of American Neo-Nazis and Klansmen* (Penguin reprint, 1996). There will always be a number of Americans devoted to terrorizing the rest. Despite Madison's cautionary prose in *Federalist Paper Number 51*, and in spite of the peaceful efforts of world renown academics, thinkers and scholars who are too many to detail and too old for us to remember. How do Americans escape from being incarcerated by their own educational, social, and religious institutions and avoid the prison-induced madness of Antonio Gramsci, Friedrich Nietzsche's metaphorical madman in the market place, Michel Foucault's prison of society, and Max Weber's Iron Cage? How does one out-think the irrationality of fear(s) that terrorize us from wanting to be over prepared for terror that we inadvertently stultify our own mechanisms for growth and creativity? We need popular culture to escape the horrors of our own images, our own species, and our own world. Popular culture is there at the heart of the social fabric. It could be that popular culture presents itself so instantaneously and on such a vast scale that it helps keep hope alive. Popular culture might be the only thing left for the masses who think they are individuals and are searching to escape the scorching reality of clear and present threats, and vague and future anxieties.

ENTER CULTURE

Unlike Alvin Gouldner's rather tame and richly brilliant work titled *Enter Plato*, the cultural considerations of modernity require and often demand that people accept popular culture whether they ideally accept it or not. There is no real choice. The influence is subtle and overt, noisy and quiet, hard and fast, soft and slow, entering and exiting as we pass time towards the kind of nihilism that Jean Paul Baudrillard experiments with in the last chapter of *Simulacra et Simulacrum*. We consider and question the sacred cows of modernity's popular fictives and their illusory and captivating devices that project us backwards into the immediacy of existence. Autonomously, these become canons of combat, created to fill spaces of modernity's boredom and languish within late capitalist consumption behavioral patterns that clog up the streets in Greenwich Village with the ardor and stench of neo-radical perspectivism. And the *New York Times*. Let us consider some of the more favorite canons of popular culture the world over: (1) popular culture works because of *peer pressure*; (2) popular culture is promoted through *mass mediated advertising and marketing*; and (3) popular culture is about creating instantaneous *cultural icons* of television, movies, drama, sports, war, philosophy, and science. Examples of *cult figures* or personality cults in popular culture over the years include Simone De Beauvoir, Hannah Arendt, and Judith Butler (American feminism), Henry Miller (forbidden novels), Toshiro Mifune (Japanese Samurai monochromatic television), John Travolta (American disco), Alec Guinness (British drama), Mika Hakkinen (Formula-1 sports), Carl Von Clausewitz (war), Michel Foucault and postmodernism (philosophy), Stephen Hawking (physics), Josef Stalin and Mao Tse-tung (Communism), Antonio Gramsci (Italian neoMarxism), Eleanor Roosevelt (American icon), Il Duce (Italian Fascism), Martin Luther King, Jr., (American icon), John F. Kennedy (American liberalism), and Fidel Castro (Cuban socialism). This is perhaps the poorest list of names that I can come up with because there are so many more possible areas of popular iconography that could perhaps include Bollywood actors who are watched by hundreds of millions of fans across South Asia and the rest of the Indian Diaspora; Chinese cinema, drama, and television stars made and featured almost exclusively in Taiwan and Hong Kong for the Chinese Diaspora throughout the world; African-American rappers who influence young Japanese schoolgirls in Tokyo and young Malay school boys in Singapore; famous

222

Superbowl quarterbacks; astronauts; cosmonauts; and stand-up comedians like Ellen DeGeneres, Brett Butler, Robin Williams, Sinbad, Jay Leno, Jerry Seinfeld, David Letterman, Bill Maher, Drew Carey, George Wallace, and legendary ones like Sammy Davis Jr., Bob Hope, and Dean Martin. As we proceed we will encounter different discursive elements within American popular culture that have developed and resonated over the years with others fading away in an instant or over several instances. This is why it seems easier, perhaps even better, to consider the notion of American popular culture that is viewed from today as a genealogical trajectory away from the past rather than a single monocotyledonous root tied to the past.

COUNTER-CULTURE

A large part of American popular culture is represented by the Counter-Culture of the 1960s. Americans have a finite ability to hark back to that time of their youth and the celebration of that specific zone of leisure and carefree consciousness that evolved out of Woodstock and the anti-Vietnam War sentiment. Perhaps this is another genuine and unique kind of American popular culture. But because of all the violence involved, I am not sure that it ought to be promoted as such.

The Counter-Culture was itself the popular culture of the era but it had such a much large politically profound effect on Americans of that generation as embedded and displayed in American music, drama, Broadway, musicals, movies, television, radio, sports, and public life of that era. The Vietnam era is so distinctive that there are permanent Hollywood sets that have been erected for the precise purpose of capturing another Vietnam War movie. We just have to go down to Florida, or Panama.

The American counter-culture of the 1950s and 1960s also saw the rise of American rock music mainly from Southern California. Unlike the Cowboy Culture that predated it by almost 200 years that had created "country and western music," the Counter-Culture of the 1960s was different because it brief as it was bloody. The Counter-Culture was the political uprising of a young generation of Americans who did not want war. And who lived in the shadow of its fear, ironically, resounded in that Rap song "Gangsta's Paradise" that begins with the lines, "as I walked through the valley of the shadow of death …".

Perhaps, at some level, we have to thank the American social scientists for this fact, for provoking a certain consciousness among the youth of the day. The Counter-Culture was about battling peaceably against the government. It wasn't about toppling the government, but it was about being anti-Establishment. This meant that the youth were rebelling against their parents, in a way that Mao orchestrated the movement of Chinese youth against theirs in the Great Chinese Cultural Revolution of the 1960s. However, there was no dictatorial hand in the case of the American Counter-Culture. Unless you consider the indirect hand of the Frankfurt School, and the rising attraction of neo-Marxism and the increasing disaffection with Western liberalism. The American Counter-Culture was about turning away from American middle class values. The American middle class believed in monogamy, frugality, filial piety, religious conviction, and a proper education. The Counter-Culture presented to youthful Americans a channel for asserting their individuality. It was also a form of political resistance against the domestic and foreign policies that had made America into a new nation up till that point in time. In fact, there was a degree of fear among the middle class that the popular culture of rock music would erode the social fabric that had held Americans together. In hindsight, we understand that this was not to be the case and that in fact, the popular culture of the 1960s was indeed a phase which many Americans if not most at that age had to go through. This was a type of passing phase that would be passed on down to the next generation of young Americans who had not been old enough to have been present at Woodstock or who had been too sheltered by their parents and guardians who did not subscribe to these values. Eventually, the values of the counter-culture of 1960s popular culture would be used as a turning point now called "retro"—a cultural benchmark of what was formerly fashionable. The interesting twist here is that "retro" is also considered current and updated. It's like the fashion industry. Old fashions keep showing up like old wine in new wineskins.

In countering the Establishment, the ideal composition of the populist Counter-Cultural ethos was one that was made up of three main ingredients: (1) a radicalization of how America was being viewed; (2) a systematic critique of the Establishment policies that had dominated the US since the end of World War II; and (3) a bourgeoning distrust of made-in-America political institutions. Implicit within these three ingredients was a rejection of the materialism of the American Dream; a proto-nihilistic and alienated view of American life; and a fear that

American politics overseas would continue to haunt future generations of Americans by taking their youth and the blood of the youth for the sake of national interests. While the last two characteristics of the American way of life are consistent with much of the feelings that Americans have today in the first quarter of the 21st century, the first characteristic did not come true. In fact, as we have seen in Chapter one of this book, Americans have embraced materialism and replaced the gods of religion with the gods of wealth and material goods.[14] Whenever a sports star suddenly "makes it big" s/he will begin thinking of what s/he can buy. Material goods have therefore taken center stage in American popular culture and the more luxurious the good, the greater its appeal in terms of the perceived social status that is attributed to the consumption of such expensive labels. Here we see a collapse of two things: expensive merchandise on one hand and social status on the other. Americans have come to associate particular branded goods and labels with the rich and the powerful. By making purchases along such branded labels, one mimics the purchasing choices of the various target idols—movie stars, sports figures, political celebrities, CEOs.

The social mimicry of the consumer behavior of the *minority* rich and famous by *majority* the not so-rich and unlikely to be famous is highly political. The reason why it is highly political is because identity formation is crippled by a need to project images of stability, success, wealth, and power when these are not genuine identities. Only means towards an end.

American social scientists and American social science was at the forefront of this revolutionary counter-culture. Almost every American politician, captain of industry, social scientist, researcher, or social worker who grew up in the 1950s and 1960s has been influenced by the counter-culture of the day to some degree. Whether one was a conscientious objector to the Vietnam War draft, a highly decorated veteran, a communal-living protestor of "Love Not War," or a draft dodger, the influence of the popular counter-culture was present and had influence one at some point in that stage of life. The influence of this formative phase of American popular culture would come in three forms: it may have influenced people to go to extremes in experimentation, for example with the effects of psychedelic-inducing drugs. Secondly, it may have resulted in the repression of non-conformist attitudes that would resurrect decades later. And thirdly, it might push some to go to the other extreme of withdrawing totally from the counter-cultural iconoclasms. This means that three kinds of people, in their fifties and sixties are alive today: those whose minds were fried when they were hippies; those whose careers took a boost when they realized that "free love and fresh air got no one anywhere"; those who became withdrawn and manic-depressive because of over-experimentation with the counter-cultural revolutionaries.

Peer pressure continues to be an important factor in making individuals conform to particularistic group behavior such as smoking marijuana, consuming alcohol to the point of excess; sexual experimentation at a young age, below that which ordinary people and the law would find acceptable; and the difficulties associated with stereotype-casting from one's peers. While the discussion so far has dealt with the psychological impact of the counter-culture, it is important to note that these effects persist over time and may be considered unique for each generational change but in effect retain certain similarities. Peer pressure and hazing in high schools are a common phenomenon that people are forced to adjust to. There is only so much avoidance of one's peers that can be achieved in a given school year for example. Sooner or later one has to maintain a particular stand and become part of some sub-cultural group, listening to its sub-cultural music, dress, values, outlook, accent, and "slang." There is a clear politics of the counter-cultural era and the subsequent periods because people desire to be part of a group but in trying to achieve that goal become beholden to the prevailing expectations of the group's sub-cultural gatekeepers.

PUBLIC SPACE

The idea of a public contingent on its participants is the analogue of resonance to music because neither would make sense without the other ... [and where] the Legal-Autonomous Public Model, and the Multiple Public Model in the work of John Dewey, Walter Lippmann, and Kenneth J. Arrow [exist in the] great contest between Lippmann and Dewey in the 1920s signified a clashing of the two interpretations of the public with one arguing about the need for a return to a constitutionally guaranteed, left-of-centre public philosophy that would entertain the elite while taking care of the poor, and the other a plea for a rationalistic recourse that surmised and envisaged rational public discourse as only one of several possible publics. The article concludes with the notion that the constructions of public space defined by Dewey, Lippmann, and Arrow promote distinct yet related interrogations of public space that is more than an agora of resonating ideas, but includes a kind of automatic reverberation on its own axes.[15]

American popular culture in public space is about a debate over social equations. This is also a political equation because there are some who do not fit in completely because they suddenly discover a consciousness or a mind of their own. There are those who do not fit in because they were coerced in the first place. And then there are those who eventually assume the roles of the new generation of the sub-cultural gatekeepers and their proxies. There is politics because someone gains power and influence over another or over others within the group. Group identity formation and group identity decay are thus central to our complex idea of American popular culture. The wallpaper of popular culture in America is therefore made up of its counter-cultural ballast, "retro," and intergenerational transfers of group identities in public space. Habermas constructed his notion of the theory of communicative action on his reading of the bourgeoisie in 19th century Europe. For him, individuals are unable to come together in the revolutionary spirited manner described by Marx because of the structuration of society. In this sense, Habermas must have drawn some inspiration from Gramsci's notion of hegemony. Thus, while Habermas stressed the importance of language dynamics within his theory of communicative action through iterative politics as a way of achieving freedom, Gramsci emphasized the controls designated within society that prevent individuals and imprison them from achieving freedom. The intergenerational transfers from one generation of American pop cultural consumers to the next therefore cannot employ Habermas's outdated theory of communicative action because it does not allow for revolutionary change.

In fact, it is Gramsci's notion of the soft power of hegemony that presents the challenge for popular culture's consumers. Unlike Joseph Nye's position on soft power, and very much like the US military, the consumers of popular culture as a whole desire an Establishment "adversary." And this comes in the form of the kind of hegemonic control explained in Gramsci's political thought. But Habermas may be useful because he noticed the importance of language dynamics in his theory of communicative action as a way towards freeing the self from social and political constraints (but not from cultural ones). Any theory of communicative hegemonic action in American popular culture must address the existing mix of ingredients created during the counter-cultural revolution against the Establishment which as we have previously discussed involves: (1) *the radicalization of the view of America by Americans*; (2) *a systematic critique of the Establishment policies*; and (3) *a bourgeoning distrust of made in America political institutions*. Elements of the counter-cultural mix of ingredients found in retro can be observed in situation comedies made in the late 1990s but harking back between twenty-five to thirty years through flashback sequences of cast and characters such as *Seinfeld*, *Third Rock From the Sun*, *Fraser*, *Friends*, *Grounded for Life*, *The Simpsons*, *That Seventies Show*, and *The King of Queens*. Examples of these retro-flashbacks help anchor the viewers and the characters with truisms of the past through the reproduction of fictive unions between what actually occurred as fact and what is being presented as a *simulacra of that fact*. While these sitcoms are themselves mediated monuments to the modern history of popular cultural norms, they also serve as a way of filling leisure time and occupying space that has been freed-up for television broadcasts and receptions. The successful sitcoms of the late 1990s that captured the retro fever in different episodic moments were predated by such prequel sitcoms as *Step by Step*, *Married...With Children*, *Home Improvement*, *Caroline in the City*, *Ellen*, and *Mad About You*. Thus retrospective iconography through situation comedies, television soaps, drama, and even musicals popularized by Andrew Lloyd Webber instinctively assume the presence of an Establishment antagonist. The political structures of control in the public sphere therefore create the poles of disaffection towards which the angst and frustration, satire and Black comedy, love and anger can be directed towards and against as a cultural sounding board. Gramsci's advocacy of the soft power of hegemonic control on one hand and his ideas involving subordinate behavior enable a theoretical understanding of how such consumers are able to transmit (iteratively) *popular cultural values* over time, and across generations within the public sphere through retrospection.[16]

THE POWER OF COMEDY: FANTASY AND ESCAPISM FOR ALL

One of the greatest comedic enterprises and creative talents ever to be generated within American popular culture as a potential *school of thought* is Black Comedy. Bill Crosby's family-centered comedy routines are an excellent example of centrist Black Comedy. Despite some sarcastic comments about White people in some interviews, the character of Bill Crosby in the vintage *The Crosby Show* adroitly uses his wit and charm to exploit what is known as the "White comfort zone" (Inniss and Feagin, 1995: 708). My treatment of Black Comedy here is different from *black comedy* (as many readers are already as keenly aware about the political and social implications as most African-Americans would be expected). Black Comedy is usually "funny—Ha! Ha!" encapsulating serious social, political and economic messages. The difference in function between Black Comedy as a narratival exposition of Black life and death through satire, slapstick, or soliloquy is stridently different from the black comedy that focuses on the dark side or the evil side as seen in McFadden's view of Nietzsche (McFadden, 1981: 338). Black Comedy does overemphasize its moral position. Its morality and ethics are therefore not considered central to its expository themes as an American popular culture. Shakespeare, for example, used black comedy as dark comedy, but his *weltanschauung* addressed a different kind of audience that the Black Comedians of American popular culture are addressing in today's globalized world. In my estimate, Black Comedy as a globalizing force of American popular culture is likely to have a greater impact on late modernity than the anachronistic Shakespearean dark comedy or the literary texts of Ben Jonson (1572-1637).[17] More people of the world are likely to empathize with Black comedic routines if only because of the sublimated and subordinated positions of their characters. But the total effect remains to be seen.

As Inniss and Feagin suggest, White people would be more willing to accept knowledge of Black people through a certain level of comfort. And the segue into that zone of comfort is comedy. But they also make the important point that such access to Black life, Black problems, and Black happiness are not considered important and hence can be taken lightly. I think that they are wrong about such a hypothesis because they assume too much on behalf of the White audience's level of tolerance and they perhaps misdirect the readers' attention away from a "White" ability to understand the Black problems. The world is not so clearly divided, although many people live life that way because it is easier without complications. It is certainly less tiring, and less enervating to think in simplistic terms. Consider the classical Black Comedic routine of Sammy Davis Junior and the genuine king of Classic Black Comedy, Richard Pryor, who even made fun of his own setting himself on fire by accident. In a film with Gene Wilder titled *See No Evil, Hear No Evil* (1989) Pryor plays a blind African-American man who is self-opinionated and angry at the world for the accident that caused his blindness. In a leap of sudden realization, he stands up in the middle of a crowded commuter train and shouts at the top of his squeaky voice, "you mean, I'm not White?!" Also consider the up-and-coming comedy stitches of Jamie Foxx in *Breakin' All the Rules* (Screen Gems, 2004), Snoop Dogg in *Soul Plane* (MGM, 2004), the expletive comedy of Chris Rock and the milder versions displayed by Chris Tucker, and Martin Lawrence in *Martin Lawrence Live: Runteldat* (Paramount, 2002).[18]

The power behind Black Comedy lies in the systematic historical and political suppression of Black rights to the point where they were led to believe that they were not responsible for thinking like the White Man was responsible for thinking. Black Comedy is distinguished from other forms of comedic presentations because of the sustained levels of emotional and cultural abuse that the Black people have received since their ancestors were forced into labor. The transatlantic slave trade between Portuguese Brazil and West Africa, between West Africa and the British isles, and between the Americas and Africa from the 14th–19th centuries would have broken the spirit of any one culture. Furthermore, the internal slavery issues and racism that were systematically implemented in these colonial countries and in the America of the day resulted in the complete denigration and mnemonic erasure of the different "origins" of various Black cultures. Consequently, the lost cultures that were destroyed by mercantilist trade resulted in the re-creation of new American cultures. These new cultures were themselves caught in the political economy of the day, the social and civil strife of the frontier world and a vicious cycle of impoverishment and political control by the White elites over the Black slave-underclass.[19] There is a clear master-slave dialectic that continues to draw its resources from the Black American experience and I have suggested that Black Comedy as a powerful type of American popular culture—provides such an avenue of escapism for the spectatorialism of the sociological problematique of leisure within the American public.

PUBLIC SPACE AND LEISURE

The active pursuit of leisure in public space leads to a construction of modes of lifestyle choices in real/reel life that become mimicked over generations through the broadcast media (such as television, radio, the

Internet, and film) so that audiences can laugh at themselves while laughing at these characters. The ability to laugh is not limited to the American media but is a reflection of a global and very human phenomenon that requires skill, dedication, focus and hard work to achieve the effect of laughter. This is partially what Neil Postman was darkly trying to convey about the public sphere in *Amusing Ourselves to Death*. Coming close to Lippmann's views on the public, Postman's notion of laughter becomes political when we realize that perhaps in laughing at the characters on TV, those with whom we easily identify, they are indeed a reflection of our own achievements and lack of achievements. Perhaps, this might be why these situational comedies are designed so as to un/cover as wide a range of the social structure as possible.

There is always one sitcom that makes fun of the gentile upper classes and those who desire to be part of that class but fail trying (*Fraser*, *Dharma and Greg*, and *Just Shoot Me*). There are also sitcoms for those who identify with the working class misery of having to walk the picket line, work on three different shifts, wear a uniform, punch a clock, deal with callous bosses, and fight the problem of being overweight (*The King of Queens*). Also, a third category of sitcoms deal with the life of "yuppies" (young upwardly mobile professionals) and "dinks" (double income, no kids) with a limited social circle (*Friends*, *Herman's Head*) or gender-based ones on television such as *Sex and the City*. A fourth category often deals with teenage and marriage problems that tend to draw audiences from both ends of the spectrum (*That Seventies Show*, *Grounded For Life*, *Third Rock From the Sun*). These different presentations of the lighter side of life constitute important images of temporary escape. The audience identifies with one or several characters. The process of identification invites the audience to participate in a fantasy of escapism. There is a politics of escapism in the public space of leisure in these comedic situations because laughter lightens the load of the laden; laughter frees the mind; laughter distracts the audience from the onerous routine of daily work. However, one could make this observation about almost any form of entertainment in the public arena.

So what exactly is unique about these sitcoms? The answer is in the idea of political satire. Most of the sitcoms make sense to the viewer because they take ordinary everyday situations faced by many Americans and place them at the center of the frame. The focus on one particular event out of many highlights the chosen scene through slapstick routines, exaggeration and hyperbole, or pushing the limits to its logical extremes.

This is part of political fantasy but the comedic element prevents the violation of the viewers' choice of the fantasy. Comedy is a means of political escapism because it provides a fantasy of retreat and escape that does not infringe on the rights of the next individual. The moment that comedy goes beyond its bounds it ceases to have its original effect and loses power.

THE AMERICAN DREAM IN PUBLIC SPACE

The American Dream involves "life," "liberty" and the pursuit of "happiness" but it is also made up of a very specific set of historical images that mixes fantasy of fact and fiction to produce a global phenomenon that has changed the way people all over the world perceive themselves, their own cultures, and their own histories. Like its *political culture*, the novel event that *is* American popular culture is a deliberate attempt to create a 'culture' in a hurry. This is because of the US' relatively shorter amount of history as a modern democratic state. People travel to Europe to "see," "feel," and "experience" culture. There is a clear cultural presence in Europe because of its long and bloody history of romance, religion, philosophy, languages, and war. These ingredients have evolved into different sovereign states themselves such as France and the lower countries. In Europe we have cultural production houses that have emerged through violence and conflict over 2,500 years, at least since the time of the classical Greek period. American culture is a breakaway culture, a break from the English colonial traditions that were settled in the first 13 colonies of the Atlantic seaboard. American culture is a culture in a hurry because the speed of modernization and the need to survive in a rapidly changing world environment has led to less time and space for culture to evolve. This is why many Europeans, perhaps unfairly, criticize US Americans for not having a culture. Given the temporal and spatial constraints, there was a clear need for Americans to create its own cultural space within a shorter period of time. The result was a two-pronged effort that began with the Founding Fathers and the rise of the Pioneer culture. The 17th and 18th centuries were particularly crucial for the development of something out of nothing. As a result, the foundations of American popular culture may be best understood in terms of two strategies of (1) cultural borrowing, and (2) the symbiosis of location.

Cultural borrowing meant the copying and mimicry (again we note this important and useful phrase used so effectively by Naipaul and then some by Bhabha in different contexts) of so-called original cultures in England. Cultural borrowing also involved the transplantation of migrant cultures from other parts of Africa, Europe, and more recently Asia and the Pacific in three stages. The first stage was the transfer of the software through reading material, oral histories, nutrition and dietary habits. The second stage was the amplification of such motherland or "old country" practices and taboos in the new cultural site, with the gateway eventually being called Ellis Island. The third stage involved what is known as the codification of such practices within the first and second generation of migrants who serve as the cultural gatekeepers of these old traditions in the new country through local histories, the oral tradition, entertainment and leisure activity. The pioneering spirit and the frugality of the early settlers with their year-end celebrations of harvest and Thanksgiving are considered important anchor points for these cultural stake-points.

A cultural stake-point occurs in the public arena. It is the place one might understand to be "ground zero," in the parlance of late modernity. Therefore any values and norms that are created, e.g., "pioneer spirit," "frugal," "hard work," or "team effort" as seen in the Anabaptists of yesteryear during a barn-raising or at Thanksgiving are making use of a cultural stake-point at which to locate the activities that lock in its members. Membership therefore requires participation. Popular cultural traits then begin forming on the fringes of these cultural stake-points not in a subordinate manner but in a way that engages and re-engages those on the public fringe towards the center, and therefore inwards to the central concerns of the given culture, which in this case is American popular culture. This highly Aristotelian persuasion is nonetheless moot when one considers that cultural anchoring and gate-keeping are concomitant activities that bind members of a community together while promoting their feelings of group solidarity and demoting emotions of insecurity. Consequently, we can see how the cultural stake-points in public space pave the way forward towards a political strategy that I call the symbiosis of location.

The symbiosis of location is the second strategy from where popular culture can be said to truly originate. This symbiosis involves the mixing up and sharing of cultural resources between and among cultural groups and subgroups in the third and subsequent generation of migrants. The sharing of resources includes (linguistic) accents, dietary and nutritional habits, taboos, the function of women, the function of men, and the place of children within the fabric of the new nation. The symbiosis is a result of people of different migrant cultures who have been forced into a new situation where they have no other choice but to live with people of different colors and languages. Over time, a nexus of symbiotic relationships develops among the co-ethics of each community. The resultant product of such cultural mixing is what some call the "melting pot." However, not all co-ethnics within a given community will support the idea of a melting pot and therefore there is a return to the old ways of doing things and of surviving the pressures of urbanization, regionalization, and now, globalization. The symbiosis of location takes place across time and space and involves the marked definition and redefinition of cultural boundaries that change over each generation. Within a given population of Irish-Americans, for example, there will be those who seek to preserve the past for posterity while there are those who completely reject this in favor of the national identity we call "America" and "American." In between the cultural preservationists and the cultural rejectionists are those who prefer to keep a little of the old ways while being happy to adapt to changes that take place in the public sphere. The public sphere is where the cultural showcase of ethnic pride is displayed ever so often to keep hope alive. In constructing these real displays of culture, one gets an immediate Foucauldian view that involves the construction of discursive formations within society. The public sphere is that container where there are plural cultural activities giving and taking, consuming and producing, demanding and supplying events and activities, action and non-action, upon which the symbiosis of location can settle and take deeper root.

Both cultural strategies that form the basis of American popular culture are understood in my reading of the texts to have matured by the 4th and 5th generation of migrants therefore compressing migrant culture into a system of shared Diasporic values over a brief period of 40–60 years. Here, in addition to the Counter-Culture of the 1960s, C& W music, Rap music, and Black Comedy, we discover the other stake-point of American popular cultural celebrations. Consider the commodification of Kwanza, Christmas, and Hanukah. Other examples are seen in the fictive/fact Christian practice of All Souls' Day and the pagan ritual of Halloween, the neo-animistic Chinese practice of the Hungry Ghost Festival, and the mythical shamanism depicted by some American playwrights.[20] All these festivities represent mixtures of foreign and local, borrowed and invented traditions of filling the chasm devoted to leisure. Celebrations through festivals, parades, song, drama, music and stories are broadcast across the spectrum of public space. Like Kant's notion of tutelage, the level of creativity rises with the determination to succeed in play as in work. This is all part of the routine that populates the idiom of the American Dream. The Dream is volatile and interpretive, enhancing and sublimating texts that rise through history channels of American social, economic and political institutions. The Dream is a fantasy world made real in endeavoring to attain and understand liberty. Freedom comes in the form of denial to others. In America, the cultural popularity of the exercise of capitalist choices over goods and services can exist only when these choices are denied to others who do not share the ideological beliefs of neo-liberal capitalism. If countries other than the US and its Allies are willing to give up their traditions and differences with American popular culture, they too can share in the hegemonic conquest that is the United States of America; they too can share in the American Dream provided that they use the right currency, stand in line, and get their tickets at the door. And there area a wide variety of films to view at the box-office. For example, there are the American classics that celebrate the American Dream of success through perseverance, and hard work despite the presence of total calamity that saw the successful launch of such careers as Clark Gable, Olivier De Havilland, Leslie Howard, and Vivien Leigh in *Gone With The Wind* (1939). Classic American movies about Americans wedged in a social class they seemingly cannot escape include Frank Capra's *It's A Wonderful Life* (1946) or a battle of personalities in Elizabeth Taylor's role in a *Cat on a Hot Tin Roof* (1958), and, Marlon Brando and Vivien Leigh in Tennessee Williams's *Streetcar Named Desire* (1951). Some American movie classics involved deeper psychological terror skirting a kind of Nietzschean abyss, as with Jimmy Stewart in Alfred Hitchcock's *Vertigo* (1958) and Hitchcock's *Shadow of a Doubt* (1943). In America, there has always been a set of films that depict the savior-slave metaphor where a marginalized Black Southerner accused of raping a White woman is finally saved by a brilliant White lawyer (Gregory Peck in *To Kill a Mockingbird*, 1962). Could the American civil rights movement have proceeded without the help of real life Atticus Finch personalities or could it have purely depended on the powerful political resistance of real-life Rosa Parks refusal to sit in the White folk's section of a public bus?

We understand now that these "classic" films have become the source for new generations of actors to mimic and hone their own acting skills but there is more to it because many new films often use the

American classic movie in a "cameo" piece to add depth or to capture the attention of an older segment of the audience. The entire American movie industry as a popular cultural economy of escapism through war movies centered on John Wayne (who never had any war experience) and a young Elvis Presley (who was posted to Germany and returned an army sergeant to much aplomb) and Cowboy movies called Westerns that were easy to understand because the bad guys usually wore black, had little clothes, made whooping noises, or threatened White civilization. And then the Cavalry returned to decimate the entire Native village. The political economy of American film also provided an avenue for rich acting talent that depicted a Sartre's psychological hesitation (Richard Burton and Elizabeth Taylor in the 1966 film *Who's Afraid of Virginia Woolf?*); Bertolt Bretch's tempestuous self-inflicted politics (Orson Welles in *Citizen* Kane, 1941; Robert Redford and Mia Farrow in *The Great Gatsby*, 1976; and Robert Mitchum and Gregory Peck in [the original] *Cape Fear*, 1962); Edward Said's *Orientalism* (Errol Flynn in *Captain Blood*, 1935); and Henry S. Kariel's widespread desperation (Henry Fonda in John Steinbeck's *Grapes of Wrath*, 1940; and perhaps eventually, Cervantes' *Don Quixote*). While most actors get involved in some kind of social movement or take up some public challenge voluntarily to boost their careers, Gregory Peck was an exception. Peck openly challenged the impoverishment of American values during the civil rights movement when many actors were under intense pressure to stay away from defending "Negroes." He also spoke out against the Vietnam War. He was the most outspoken American liberal actor who believed he could put into practice what he said on film. Peck's movies and the others above are only a few of the movies that constitute the local and global power of the American moving picture industry. The American Dream in the popular cultural political economy of film endeavors to present and represent prevailing versions of truth. Doubtlessly, there will be a war film based on the atrocities of American soldiers in Iraq in the second Gulf War, but would probably end with American forms of justice and fairness where the good preside over the punishment of evil.

The American Dream is defined as "life, liberty and the pursuit of happiness." The materialistic component is one heavy aspect of the Dream and the other heavy aspect is individualism. And all ideological forms of individualism need political heroes and cultural anti-heroes. "We understand the tragic hero … can never be mad; and that conversely madness cannot bear within itself those values of tragedy, which we have known since Nietzsche and Artaud. In the classical period, the man of tragedy and the man of madness confront each other, without a possible dialogue, without a common language; for the former can only utter the decisive words of being, uniting in a flash the truth of light and the depth of darkness; the latter endlessly drones out the indifferent murmur which cancels out both the day's chatter and the lying dark" (Foucault [1965] 1988: 111). If the tragic anti-hero of Gregory Peck were still alive in this racist world, he would have uttered on screen more depths of darkness and more truths in light while looking into the distance at the end of the dénouement, and saying, "it would have been a great adventure...but remember it's a sin to kill a mockingbird."

CONCLUSION

We saw at the beginning of this chapter how Americans desire to escape the problems of modernity through the creation of popular cultural activity in public space. And that such leisure activity over generations is transformed into cultural anchor points or stake-points around which acceptable norms of popular culture can grow and spread for the benefit of its members. The examples we provided at the start involved publicly overt illustrations of genuine American popular culture such as Country and Western music, Rap music, and the politically charged Counter-Culture of the 1960s. We showed how such popular cultural programs are generated through television which has been both a boon and a bane for the promotion of American values overseas and locally. The recreational "sport" of popular cultural activities are part of the politics of American globalization because of the powerful influence over foreigners, strangers who have never set foot on US soil or are ever likely to do so. The political dimension of American popular culture represents a kind of soft power of hegemony where the cultural theory of Gramsci (more so than Habermas) ignites a certain attraction to America, to its genuine cultural activities, its situation comedies, its war movies, through classic American film, via powerful MNCs that promote Hollywood as an American capitalist idol. Americans have been influencing the world through their popular takes through the broadcast media in ways that are more powerfully residual than gross invasions that lead to undesirable consequences such as the mockery of naked Iraqi prisoners of war dovetailed in homoerotic coils of naked and vanquished flesh. The dark comedic non-value of the minority of American soldiers poking pornographic fun at faceless Iraqi captives represents the repressed homosexuality of the military itself on one hand. But on the other hand, the notion of homoerotic and homosexual empowerment through military invasion and conquest is not something new. Rather than remaining merely the preserve of the nobility and the upper classes or those with more time to devote to leisure, to read and develop axioms from the Marquis de Sade's *Philosophy in the Bedroom*. Once the masses get control of a thing, as they say, it never goes back up and never gets concealed. Look at the end of the Louis XIV, and the ultimate political insurrection in the three French Revolutions. Look at what the deterioration and end of the corrupt upper classes had unleashed, despite having lived lives *plaisir a tout prix*. The formal off-loading of the elite control of special leisure activities at the end of the Ancient Regime led to a rapid distribution of work otherwise inaccessible without the Guttenberg Press and other earlier forms of mass printing. It was however, the education received by the masses desirous of understanding the written word through the formalization of educational systems across Europe and its colonies as a form of religious expansionism and political control that enabled the rise of crude forms of popular culture. Rameau's Nephew was no longer to remain the idle chatter of a circle of *philosophes*. And schools of philosophy that had held intensely to their cherished works from Plato and Aristotle began wavering under the weight of the Enlightenment theorists and their disciples.

Suddenly anyone could listen to Brahms, Beethoven, or Tchaikovsky. Suddenly anyone could read musical scores without having to go through long and arduous training in Switzerland. No one needed to be of Teutonic stock, a German or Russian to create classical music. Consider Lang-Lang, a 22-year-old music prodigy from China. He is one of two great prodigies, the other being a 21-year-old Russian. Now not only can the rich and the swanky afford to listen to Chopin's *Scherzo E Major*, Opus 54, his wonderfully sullen funeral march *Sonata No. 2* in *B flat Minor*, Opus 35, or Mendelssohn's *Allegro brillant* in *A Major* but anyone who can afford a CD and a Sony CD Walkman can do so.[21] The counter-culture of American rock has indeed created such a demand that it is now more expensive to listen to hard rock bands than classical music ensembles, the tickets of which sometimes cannot be given away even free of charge, not even when one reconsiders the centrality of popular forms of cultural dominance *vis-à-vis* the practical and functional aspects of the late modern life as suggested by Shusterman,[22] Shapiro, Street, and Docker.

We recall how easy it is for political violence and war to lead to the creation of a weakened human spirit; how the positive aspects of human-made globalization are secret carriers of human destruction. The political paradox of globalization means that for every step forward we make there are co-human beings out there willing and able to force us three steps back. Terrorists motivated by psychosis, childhood-abuse, religion, race, or plain madness have made humankind collectively more stupid. The illegal American invasion of Iraq ended many atrocities of the former US-backed regime of Saddam Hussein. However, a small number of American soldiers have caught the headlines. This time within the frame of photographic images showing at least one woman soldier ridiculing a naked and bound Iraqi prisoner. Apart from the obvious living out of some perverse fantasy involving men of color, we see the resurrection of a long existing form of popular military culture common to many if not most military units across the globe. But these wayward soldiers have forgotten the importance of their sacred motto, "Duty, Honor Country." What happened to that? The system is not working perfectly.

The previous chapter showed clearly how an American military intent on harming, hazing and violating its own American troops on American soil. Chapter six has illustrated have such politics has come full circle by re-inventing the dark comedy of a situation that is not "Funny Ha! Ha!" in Iraq. The invading army has become the enemy they were on a mission to vanquish and eradicate. In a wider sense, America is in danger of becoming the kind of regime it seeks to destroy. Engulfed in the flag of evil, these American soldiers have lost all sense of reality. They have brought grave dishonor to the dead Americans in the Iraqi desert of 2004 inasmuch as they have brought the good deeds of the US military to the grave. As the US DoD struggles to resolve this issue of POW abuse, we see that there are other issues that the DoD has left unresolved. In Chapter five we noted that the systemic and widespread abuse of American soldiers by American soldiers could only be a bad thing for US-occupied foreign cities like Najaf and Fallujah. It would seem that for every million women and men that follow the Lord of Good Things, there are another million following the Lord of Evil Things. There is no going beyond good and evil, as Nietzsche tried to persuade us. There is only residing in good and in evil. The world needs

239

to escape from itself or find a way to let escape be our philosophical guide. The American public reprisal and House minority calls for the resignation of the 21st US Secretary of Defense (who was a former Chairman and CEO of the General Instrument Corporation) have sealed the fate of Rumsfeld's folly. The scandal has also significantly lowered American popular voters' approval ratings of US President Bush. This has worsened the spilt within the Bush Cabinet. For example, the former Chairman of the Joint Chiefs of Staff and current US Secretary of State Colin Powell (did a Shakespearean *et tu Brute* when he) drew an unsolicited parallel between the Iraqi debacle and the *My Lai* massacre in the Vietnam War on *Larry King Live*. This is the Republican realpolitk of American globalization. It is the drama of soap opera performed wildly across US media networks. A reality television show that makes American day time soaps and reality TV appear as pathetic as the keys to their voyeuristic master-slave menageries. After a while, if social scientists were to conduct a survey of what really happened in Iraq, it would not be surprising if someone said in all honesty that s/he thought it was another reality TV show to make money for the media moguls. What will be considered politically correct and acceptable as popular culture then? Which persona are we to believe? And what does it say about America and Americans? It says for sure that some things are better read in private and sold in public rather than being read in public and sold in private. It points towards a district minority of citizens confined by their own popular *political culture* of correctness and popular culture of indiscretion. The tension between the two is the reason why teachers exist.

The popular culture that is circulated by the media also plays to another audience. The public's need-to-know is itself a form of arbitrary justice that has evolved ostentatiously since the time of Lippmann and Pulitzer. The media will always reveal, for whatever reasons of professional ethics, what the world has always known about the fault lines in the American military as a global organization of coercion. Whither human rights abuse? Wither American hegemonic control or the lack thereof? And it seems to be a grave shame that the conduct of American businesses overseas and the conduct of American foreign policy supports American life at the expense of non-American life. This statement would be considered true at the onset, and at the surface, and in the eyes of the State. However, Korea, Vietnam, Afghanistan, and Iraq are all examples of how American foreign policy has gone awry and astray. As we have seen, *the nature of being human is political. Man, as*

Aristotle believed, is by nature political. And as long as there continues to be an imbalance of power within communities based on tradition, modernization, culture, gender, primordialism, circumstantialism, racism, religion, fossil fuels, and socio-economic class there will be a politics of control, a politics of discord, a politics of resistance, and a politics of subversion that feed into the global reach of American globalization. The extension of life through individualism is a very popular in the US. The entire economy is geared towards the maximization of individualism and the fulfillment of life through materialism. The entire meaning of popular culture may be contained within the spirit of material achievement and the desire for more goods and services that advance instant gratification and promote a wide array of temporary but real options (Rappa, 2002). Life is contained within the popular culture of coffee consumption—Starbucks is a spectacular success and has many clones to prove its world wide undisclosed value of over US$5 billion per annum clones included—nicotine consumption, alcohol consumption, and the rest of what used to be prohibited in the Progressive Era of 1930s America. It certainly is popular culture now.

An understanding of the politics of American popular culture is important because it continues to have a strong impact on the nature of public culture and public choices across the globe. This in itself makes American culture "political." Consider the acceptability of such displaced persons as Larry Miller whose own sober provocation of Americans (in general) and African-Americans (in particular) seem acceptable because he is an African-American. Or Michael Moore's thrashing of American social problems across the broad backs of White American men as being legitimized and made acceptable to many simply because he is White. But what if the populist roles were reversed? Would the media remain as mere descriptors of the event? Would we read in the *Atlantic Monthly* or the *New Republic* about how wonderful it is to see White folk rise up again in strength and pride?

It seems that the support gained in America for every problem blamed on African-Americans finds similar support on the other side that tries to understand the African-American problem. After a while no one can tell if it is genuine concern and *reason* that motivates retelling the histories of racial abuse and violence (towards African-Americans and the Jewish holocaust) or that it is all a sensational popularity contest filled with political correctness and pure hypocrisy.

"Melancholia is madness without fever or frenzy accompanied by fear and sadness" (Foucault [1965] 1988: 121). Are Americans trying too hard? Is American trying to win the support of the world by being the *most* popular kid on the block, even if we have to beat everyone else up to remain "King of the Hill"? Are Americans trying to make a big show-and-tell of repressed feelings of hate, fear and suspicion (of men, women, Blacks, Whites, Hispanics, Koreans, foreigners, etc.) displayed across the world's stage like a public confessional? Or does America's genuine popular culture truly exist elsewhere? Could it lie under layers of Botox-injected, nicotine-patch wearing, and Viagra, Prozac, and Zoloft, etc., representing many citizens who live from one sensation to another? "Delirious themes that remain isolated and do not compromise reason's totality. Thomas Sydenham would even observe that melancholics are people who, apart from their complaint are prudent and sensible, and who have an extraordinary penetration and sagacity. Thus Aristotle rightly observed that 'melancholics have more intelligence than other men" (Foucault [1965] 1988: 118). Pill-popping Republicans and Democrats, who like their political leaders, can't really tell the difference except through hints and life-line public votes. Have we not become increasingly led by powerful advertisements and market researchers who prod us from one pillar to the next post of information that is broadcast by syndicated columnists and cable television? Is popular culture about crunching crackers on a retractable sofa-bed while watching ridiculously emaciated models with their plastic smiles pumping away under the cash-line currency of infomercial America? As we have seen, the American popular culture is indeed a political phenomenon. It is one that is built and designed like General Motors, on the concept of the American Dream. And why shouldn't it? American popular culture has three main legs: (1) The American Dream and the Anti-American Dream (2) the creation of legends, myths, and stories about America's past such as those found in the fictive stories of—Paul Bunyan, Tom Sawyer, Johnny Appleseed, Uncle Sam, the American Cowboy and the Marlboro Man, Harley Davidson, and Easy Rider (3) the commodification of these legends, myths, and stories into bite-sized bits that can be consumed—through images on television, movie characters on the silver screen, in computer games, in hand-held computer games, in animated films and cartoons, and the export of these to the rest of the world. Sometimes known as mass culture, popular culture is perhaps a more accurate term because it conveys the popularity of the instant gratification society while mass suggests a certain lack of discernment and the absence of choice as in the politics of mass mobilization, but you can see why the distinctions between

242

mass and popular continue to be a moot point. The phenomenon of American popular culture(s) continues to maintain a stranglehold over the nameless, faceless, and sometimes masked masses. American popular cultures need to keep filling a widening canyon of political apathy among its citizens. And a growing number of Americans and their allies are moving steadfastly towards becoming dispossessed of leisure space in chasing the American Dream and knowing full well that for every successful CEO there are a hundred thousand, perhaps more, unsuccessful ones. The time is ripe, like the *Grapes of Wrath*, for heightened levels of distrust of one another, suspicion of newly settled migrants, and a greater predilection for contemptuous human behavior in late modernity. The late modern world needs popular culture to order and simplify its grotesque demands for filling in the holes of leisure that are complicit with the neo-liberal capitalist world economy guarded by increasingly uncontrollable military units and their solutions to problems on the ground.

ENDNOTES

1   Foucault [1965], (1988): 97.

2   Or street code for living a flashy, ostentatious lifestyle with glittery trinkets and baubles than shine and reflect light thereby giving the impression of overflowing wealth. Naturally, such "bling-bling" behavior correlates with low social status because of its "in-your-face" quality. This is a logical extension of the problem of centuries of repressive political violence that no other community possesses and cannot simply be eradicated by education, affirmative action, coercion or force.

3   We do hope that we can temporarily accept the use of the word "woman" and "women" otherwise we might not be able to proceed with the rest of the book. Apart from "women", no other ethnic community has been so systematically repressed historically, culturally, politically, economically, culturally, and psychologically than African–Americans. Even the Native American cultural position was much higher, as they were perceived as the enemy within the Cowboy metaphor, and never enslaved in the way that African–Americans have been. The problem becomes a highly-charged political one as we have seen in the previous chapters with regards to the statistical percentages of Black people in US prisons, Black people perceived as another American "social problem"; Black people returning to US prisons, Black people living below the poverty line, Black people committing crimes, Black people falling behind the newest migrants, Black people being ostracized by White Flight when they move into some predominantly White neighborhoods, police brutality and Black people, crimes committed against Black people by Black people, the overflowing number of conspiracy theories that the other ethnic communities from the Jews and the Koreans to the Whites and the Chinese are out there to

destroy decent Black folk. All this is much more than singular articles on political symbolism or Blacks in sports can bear, or do justice to, no matter how much they try. See for example, Steven C. Dubin, "Symbolic Slavery: Black Representations in Popular Culture," *Social Problems* 34, no. 2 (1987):122–40; and John C. Gaston, "The Destruction of the Young Black Male: The Impact of Popular Culture and Organized Sports," *Journal of Black Studies*, 16, no. 4 (1986):369–84.

4　The "Red Swastika Society" was the philanthropic arm of the Tao Yuan Sect—formed in 1921 in Tsin-an with the intention of uniting Christianity, Buddhism, Taoism, Confucianism and Islam. According to Smith, the Tao Yuan Sect spread to Nanyang in the 1930s, and claimed to have a supreme spirit above all the five religious deities called the *Tai-i Lao-jen*. R. B. Smith, "An Introduction to Caodaism II. Beliefs and Organization," *Bulletin of the School of Oriental and African Studies* 33, no. 3 (1970): 573–89. See the earlier work, by Maurice Freedman, and Marjorie Topley, "Religion and Social Realignment among the Chinese in Singapore," *Journal of Asian Studies* 21, no. 1(1961):3–23.

5　How would people such as Mahathir Mohamad or Gregg Easterbrook dispel such criticism? Are Jews being too sensitive? Or, as Groth correctly notes, are people using anti-Semitic stereotypes for political/material gain? Consider the important paper by Alexander J. Groth, "The Politics of Xenophobia and the Salience of Anti-Semitism," *Comparative Politics* 4, no. 1 (1971): 89–108.

6　It is one thing to spread democracy and to support its ideological precepts but it is quite another thing to popularize democracy itself as a culture to be transplanted to foreign places where there is no tradition of democracy. Western countries cannot expect newly-democratizing countries to achieve the same level of democratic change that took the West over 200 years to achieve. The West must learn to control its urges to interfere. I can anticipate what my colleagues would say as social scientists. But if you are a jaded doctoral student somewhere in Oxford, Baltimore, New York City, Auckland, or Toronto, what might you think would happen to American popular culture if China becomes a superpower and begins to export Chinese socialism to Middletown, USA. What would be your reaction? And what would you do if the Chinese announced unilaterally that it was going to invade your country because of all the alleged torture and impoverishment of African–Americans whom "they" were trying to save on humanitarian grounds, and to save American kids from the authoritarian US president's regime?

7　For example, the 1990 general elections saw the loss of Kelantan State to the right-wing fundamentalist political party, PAS. The subsequent 1995 general elections saw another loss in the state of Trengganu to PAS. This had never happened previously in the history of Malaysian politics in late modernity. Mahathir was now under severe pressure to perform because he had no choice but to explain to UMNO why it has lost two of its Northern States to the right-wing Islamic political party, PAS, or Parti Islam Se-Malaysia. Strangely enough, Mahathir's fast-rising and long-serving deputy Prime Minister, the youthful Anwar Ibrahim, was suddenly sacked in 1998 on allegations of sodomy and other criminal offences. Anwar had gradually incurred the wrath and secret hatred of senior Malaysian politicians he had passed over in his meteoric rise to power because he was considered Mahathir's "blue-eyed boy". By that time there already were many rumors circulating about Anwar's alleged sexual "flings". And there was also talk about the "bad-blood" that had developed between Mahathir and Anwar. However, my hypothesis is that there was no real proof of Anwar's alleged homosexuality and sodomization of his wife's chauffeur. And that the real reason was tied to the former prime minister's performance in the 1990 general election and 1995 general election where BN and UMNO had suffered the loss of two states to PAS. In other words, Mahathir took the moral high ground and Anwar took the fall. He was the political scapegoat sacrificed to appease the Malay–Muslim right, and to demonstrate Mahathir's commitment to Islamic beliefs. But I have no evidence to support this hypothesis yet. For background to the complexities of BN and UMNO politics, see William Case, "The UMNO Party Election in Malaysia: One for the Money", *Asian Survey* 34, no. 10 (1994): 916–30; and Audrey R. Kahin, "Crisis on the Periphery: The Rift Between Kuala Lumpur and Sabah," *Pacific Affairs*, 65, no. 1 (1992): 30–49.

8 See "The Protocols' Malaysian Style: The Case of Prime Minister Mahathir Mohamad," *Policy Dispatches* 24 (December 1997); Diane K. Mauzy, and R. S. Milne, "The Mahathir Administration in Malaysia: Discipline through Islam," *Pacific Affairs* 56, no. 4 (1983–84), 617–48; William Case, "Comparative Malaysian Leadership: Tunku Abdul Rahman and Mahathir Mohamad," *Asian Survey* 31, no. 5(1991): 456–73; James Chin, "Malaysia in 1997: Mahathir's Annus Horribilis," *Asian Survey* 38, no. 2 (1998): 183–89; and for example, David Camroux, "State Responses to Islamic Resurgence in Malaysia: Accommodation, Co-Option, and Confrontation," *Asian Survey* 36, no. 9 (1996): 852–68; Philip Bowring, "Malaysia After Mahathir," *International Herald Tribune*, October 28, 2003; Douglas Sikorski, "Effective Government in Singapore: Perspective of a Concerned American," *Asian Survey* 36, no. 8 (1996): 818–32; and Denny Roy, "Singapore, China, and the 'Soft Authoritarian' Challenge," *Asian Survey* 34, no. 3 (1994): 231–42.

9 Pamela D. Hall, "The Relationship Between Types of Rap Music and Memory in African American Children," *Journal of Black Studies* 28, no. 6 (1998): 802–14, and Tricia Rose, "Fear of a 'Black Planet': Rap Music and Black Cultural Politics in the 1990s," *Journal of Negro Education* 60, no. 3 (1991): 276–90. See also, Errol A. Henderson, "Black Nationalism and Rap Music," *Journal of Black Studies* 26, no. 3 (1996): 308–39; and Houston A. Baker, Jr., "Handling 'Crisis': Great Books, Rap Music, and the End of Western Homogeneity," *Callaloo* 13, no. 2 (1990): 173–94.

10 David Emblidge, "Down Home with the Band: Country-Western Music and Rock," *Ethnomusicology* 20, no. 3 (1976): 541–52.

11 See for example, the work of William S. Fox and James D. Williams, "Political Orientation and Music Preferences among College Students," *The Public Opinion Quarterly* 38, no. 3 (1974): 352–71.

12 Walter Benn Michaels, "An American Tragedy, or the Promise of American Life," *Representations* 25, (1989): 71–98.

13   William E. Connolly, "Speed, Concentric Cultures, and Cosmopolitanism," *Political Theory* 28, (2000): 596–618. See also William E. Connolly, *Neuropolitics: Thinking, Culture, Speed* (MN: University of Minnesota Press, 2002) where he makes a relatively similar argument as Henry S. Kariel in the early 1990s about the value of the interface between society and images in the screen versions of *Vertigo, Five Easy Pieces,* and *Citizen Kane.* Both Kariel and Connolly approach the problem of different ontological paradigms from different angles, meeting at the apex, and then coming away separately. More specifically, Henry S. Kariel rises from the ashes of his *Desperate Politics of Postmodernism* (MA: Massachusetts Press, 1989), Connolly advances his position based, I think, on the context that the provides his earlier work. See William E. Connolly, *Ethos of Pluralization* (MN: University of Minnesota Press, 1995).

14   Alternatively, consider Daniel H. Levine, "Popular Groups, Popular Culture, and Popular Religion," *Comparative Studies in Society and History* 32, no. 4 (1990): 718–64.

15   Antonio L. Rappa, "Modernity and the Contingency of the Public," in "Modernity and the Politics of Public Space," *Innovation - The European Journal of Social Science Research* 15, no. 1 (2002): abstract.

16   One cannot expect to draw immediate inspiration from a literal reading of Gramsci's political work because it would seem immediately outdated. This is with regards to the notion of education, unions and freedom in his political writing of the 1920s. For an understanding we need to turn to the work of Gramsci scholars such as Paul Piccone, "Gramsci's Hegelian Marxism," *Political Theory* 2, no. 1 (1974), 32–45; Paul Piccone, "Gramsci's Marxism: Beyond Lenin and Togliatti," *Theory and Society* 3, no. 4 (1976), 485–512; Walter L. Adamson, "Beyond 'Reform or Revolution': Notes on Political Education in Gramsci, Habermas and Arendt," *Theory and Society* 6, no. 3 (1978): 429–60; James P. Hawley, "Antonio Gramsci's Marxism: Class, State and Work," *Social Problems* 27, no. 5 (1980): 584–600; Joseph V. Femia, "Gramsci's Patrimony," *British Journal of Political Science* 13, no. 3 (1983): 327–64; and the excellent piece by Nadia Urbinati, "From the Periphery of Modernity: Antonio Gramsci's Theory of Subordination and Hegemony," *Political Theory* 26, no. 3 (1998): 370–91.

17   Brian F. Tyson, "Ben Jonson's Black Comedy: A Connection between Othello and Volpone," *Shakespeare Quarterly* 29, no. 1 (1978): 60–6. There is much reference to race in the interpretive and performative aspects of Shakespeare's work and texts but it would go beyond the ballpark to attempt any deconstruction of this poet laureate's work at this juncture, tempting though that it is. See also James Shapiro, *Shakespeare and the Jews* (NY: Columbia University Press, 1997).

18   See also Leslie B. Inniss, and Joe R. Feagin, "The Cosby Show: The View from the Black Middle Class," *Journal of Black Studies* 25, no. 6 (1995): 692–711. Compare the difference in the use of black comedy versus Black Comedy in terms of how McFadden uses black comedy as dark comedy. See George McFadden, (1981) "Nietzschean Values in Comic Writing," *Boundary* 2 9, no. 3 (1981): 337–58.

19   Therefore despite the so-called advances in politics, law and cultural sensitivity among Americans of all ethnic persuasions, it is impossible for anyone to lift themselves up single-handedly by their bootstraps. One cannot deny that the purchasing power of Black America and the leisure time devoted by Black America to leisure activities has increased significantly. But it is another thing to say to a person of color that another person of color, for example, the color White, freed you and your family. Perhaps because no human being should be enslaved in the first place? Rather than freedom, there should be apology and that is precisely what Affirmative Action has tried to do and had floundered on "emotive" grounds of "cultural pride" and "politics by the back-door" for many people of color.

20   See, for example, V. A. Lucier, "'Offrenda' on All-Souls' Day in Mexico," *Journal of American Folklore* 10, no. 37 (1897): 106–07; Elsie Clews Parsons, "All-Souls Day at Zuni, Acoma, and Laguna," *Journal of American Folklore* 30, no. 118 (1917): 495–6; Arnold Perris, "Feeding the Hungry Ghosts: Some Observations on Buddhist Music and Buddhism from Both Sides of the Taiwan Strait," *Ethnomusicology* 30, no. 3 (Autumn, 1986): 428–48; Ernest Ingersoll, "Decoration of Negro Graves," *Journal of American Folklore* 5, no. 16 (1892): 68–9; and Mae G. Henderson, "Ghosts, Monsters, and Magic: The Ritual Drama of Larry Neal," *Callaloo* 23, (1985): 195–214.

21   Bruce Tucker, "Tell Tchaikovsky the News: Postmodernism, Popular Culture, and the Emergence of Rock 'N' Roll," *Black Music Research Journal* 9, no. 2 (1989): 271–95.

22   Richard Shusterman, "Pragmatist Aesthetics and Popular Culture," *Poetics Today* 14, no. 1 (1993): 99–100.

CHAPTER 7

Norms and Values

WHAT IS A "NORM"?

A norm is a widely accepted social practice. Norms serve to guide a community's members along what is considered acceptable behavior. Because there cannot be specific rules for every single form of human activity, norms provide an important means of social interaction that enables a given society to get on with life in modernity. Norms develop over time and there are always more people in favor of a norm than not. There are also always some people who go against the norm. Sometimes, this is considered abnormal behavior, and at other times this is considered anti-social behavior, both not always meaning the same thing. Acceptable practice .usually becomes the norm. and there may be several accepted ways of satisfying social norms.

A norm also reflects the average performative actions of a given community. The *American Heritage Dictionary* (4th edition, 2000) states that a norm is "a standard, model, or pattern regarded as typical [such as] the current middle-class norm of two children per family." Nouns are etymologically derived from the Old French word *norme*, and from the Latin root, *norma*, meaning a "carpenter's square." Therefore, the metaphor "to square away" an entity is to get work done, and norms help us organize our lives by getting work arranged into neat compartments to be pursued at a later time or for future reference. Norms are not a priori or universal and tend to be dynamic and moderated by such factors as economics, culture, technology, and philosophy. Norms help regulate and contain the social actions of individuals in the private and public spheres. Norms are a means of controlling human emotions and keeping people in check *vis-à-vis* acceptable standards of behavior. Norms that are accepted in one community are not necessarily acceptable across other communities within societies and across societies. The appealing value of a particular set of norms in one community might be repulsive to another. Traditional societies that subscribe to the killing of

248

old persons and young children would be considered morally reprehensible in modernity and in late modern societies. But this does not mean that the killing of the old and young universally acceptable. Nevertheless, the United Nations Declaration of Human Rights is a global document that represents a legal putsch towards basic norms that are considered universally applicable. But as we are aware, the problem of universal human rights is that they are not always universally acceptable. Thus norms require time, space, and cultural space before they can be accepted. This makes the creation of global norms particularly difficult an objective to achieve, and as difficult as achieving the moral categorical imperatives of Immanuel Kant.

Norms are an integral part of the world today and function at all levels of human interaction. Some scholars of modernity would support the Aristotelian formulation that human being are by nature "political." This hypothesis was corroborated 2,313 years later by the political sociologist, Seymour Martin Lipsett in *Political Man: The Social Bases of Politics* (Double Day, 1963). However, there is no certainty in regulating all instances of human interaction through specific rules and regulations.[1] We need norms to help govern, guide, and *process* the interstitial aspects of human interaction. Hence computers require programmers to create specific syntax for a computer program to work in terms of generating specific binary instructions for each miniscule step. But human interaction is much more infinitely complex and faster than any current computer such that it is not possible to construct a computer that can provide the norms for individual human interaction except through virtual mimicry. One example is IBM's *Big Blue* and its cloned-derivatives that were designed to play chess against Russian and American international chess grandmasters. The computer most often lost to the human challenger/defender though not all the time. At the given level of global technology, there does not appear to be any software that can effectively compute all the different variations and permutations that can mirror the human brain. It therefore becomes virtually impossible to create a human artifice to mimic the humanity in terms of the norms that help govern human interaction. Perhaps there is no superior computer software or language currently available that can govern the psychological and emotive norms of the human being. Computer science needs to move away from the binary languages that dominate its mathematical formulae and computing paradigms in order to reconstruct nominal modes that mimic human-to-human interfaces.

Therefore, norms exist as important modes for facilitating the interstitial relationships between a minimum of two human beings. Now that we understand that norms are integral to the human world, we can understand why they are important in globalization. This is because they perform simple tasks that are difficult to mimic or artificially create despite the advances in nanoscale engineering, science, and technology,[2] cloning science, and the advances that are claimed by the Human Genome Project and consortiums like the Integrated Molecular Analysis of Gene Expression (I.M.A.G.E.) Consortium.[3] Nevertheless, human civilization can look towards the creative sharing of information across the globe as increasing numbers of think tanks and research institutes approach the nether regions of the frontiers of science. We all wait in anticipation of that big break that will cause the next paradigmatic shift.

HOPE

What Americans do not want are politically-charged scientific "rhetoric" claiming that there is life on planet Mars because it insults the public memory. These ill-conceived statements appear more like ploys to gain public support for ensuring continued federal funding. The public norms that led to the continuation of the Space Shuttle program have in effect led to a higher incidence of tax on the individual tax payer than the so-called normative returns from space travel. The program has also wrought unnecessary death and misery while cunningly reproducing snippets from the US space programs of the past. The only achievement apart from placing a man in space was placing a man on the moon. Everything else pales in comparison to the photograph of the world that changed the face of philosophical and theological musings across the centuries about what planet Earth really looked like. The competitive norms that arose out of the space race between the Soviets and the Americans seemed to have created significant gains and pay-offs during the Cold War. Since the end of the Cold War however, there hasn't been much achieved in this light. Despite these norms, there are significant numbers of people who believe in the possibility of life outside planet earth despite a clear lack of evidence at this point in time with current levels of technology. There is always hope. The hope of the possibility of alien life encourages exploration into the unknown and motivates people to do conventional norms might consider abnormal.

OPTIMISM

Norms may be governed by optimistic outcomes to situations. So if scientific researcher discover evidence of life on Mars, this might serve to modify and change the norms about alien life in other places and cultures. Man is driven by optimism in modernity to seek and fathom the unknown and the unknowable. Man is the only species on earth that has developed a highly complex regime of norms and values with the power to change life on earth. However, man's power to protect other species on earth derives not from some universal belief in the security of other species but from man's ability to destroy and even obliterate other life forms. The prevailing scientific norm on other species is highly optimistic in the sense of creating the belief that all species are part of a larger ecological system. And that the destruction of one part of that system will result in negative repercussions on the system as a whole. This has not been proven to be true, but who is willing to risk going against the norm? Can we justify the presence of global norms that might satisfy alternative imaginations that enable creative worlds where man alone is at the center and no species exists outside or along the periphery?

PROGRESS

Globalization is the key to increasing the possibility of global norms because the knowledge that other cultures perform certain activities in certain ways might in reality become acceptable practice in an otherwise non-globally connected environment. Globalization breaks down the political, social, and cultural barriers to the exchange of local norms for global ones. Part of the problem is the fear of losing out on a set of arranged and agreed practices that a given community has come to live comfortably with and a set of norms that a given community has also come to depend and rely upon in past practice.

How do we progress from localized norms towards global ones when there are so many differences that prevent the optimistic creation of universal norms? What impedes the possibility of man's desire for universalizing human norms about the ethics and morality with regards to other species that share planet earth? Man himself cannot agree because man has consistently been characterized by differences of opinion rather than singularity of thought. Singularity of thought usually breaks down after a while, and cultures that possess frameworks that allow differences to exist in non-violent ways tend to survive much longer. Differences in approaches to global survival techniques also seem to command the most formidable obstacles to the possibility of global norms.

DIFFERENCE AS LAW

For example, the differences in the norms between America and Asia exist to prevent a unity of opposites. These "normal" cultural differences facilitate different interaction between and among people from different cultural backgrounds. Being armed with the knowledge of local norms will save the global traveler from potentially embarrassing situations or from finicky customers who might be overly sensitive to the words or phrases used by a person from a different country and ethnic identity.

For example, in Asia, it is the norm to remove one's shoes before entering someone's home. It is *not* the norm to remove the shoes upon entering an office or public environment. It is also the norm *not* to talk to strangers on the bus or train. A foreign person who strikes up a conversation with a complete stranger might later discover the extent of his or her embarrassment as time goes by. There are also norms governing the payment for a meal, which depend on whether the guest is a personal friend, an office colleague, or a distant relative. There are norms in which one may sometimes have to make the gesture of payment as politeness even though one did not make the dinner reservations. There are norms for social behavior at restaurants in Asia that often depend on four main factors: (1) the kind of restaurant—French, Italian, Japanese, Korean, Muslim, or vegetarian; (2) the kind of company—family, friends, colleagues, total strangers; (3) the purpose of the dinner or lunch; and (4) the cost of dining. After a while one will begin to realize that the norms of dining in Asia and the rest of the world are very much the same with the exception of a few subtle differences. Wine, for example, is not "drunk" in the same manner that one would drink beer. Even the glasses are different.

Unlike Paris, pets especially dogs, are often not allowed in restaurants throughout Singapore, Bandar Seri Begawan, Jakarta, and Kuala Lumpur, since this will cause offence to many Muslims who believe that dogs are unclean animals. In Asia it is also considered impolite to offer a Muslim food or drink during the daylight hours of *Ramadan*, the fasting month.

Neither does one place one's legs on top of a coffee table as a guest in someone's home. In Asia, it is common to ask someone if s/he has eaten. It doesn't mean that the person "looks hungry" or appears to be in need of food. And it is customary to answer yes or no without necessarily pursuing the matter. This is just an example of phatic communion, such as phrases surrounding the tropic, "predictions on the likelihood of rain" or questions like "how is the weather?" between strangers.

In Asia, it is a norm to bring a small gift when visiting a friend after a long while in a different part of the city or country, just as an American may bring wine to a dinner party. It is customary for many Asians to eat while sitting crossed-legged on the floor, such as in the Bidayuh, Dayak, Iban, Japanese, Kadayan, Malay, and several Southeast Asian communities. Apart from the Koreans, Japanese and Chinese, it is also a norm in Asia and Africa for many people to eat with their right hand rather than using utensils. The left hand is usually reserved for ablutions and therefore not thought of as being "clean" to ingest food. The non-use of utensils for consuming food is not something normal in North America, Latin America or Europe. Military units on the other hand are an exception to this norm although an inspection of the types of Western army combat food rations such as the US Army's meals-ready-to-eat (MRE) usually includes some form of utensil.

Something that is seen on a wide scale in Asia is the exotification and pedestalization of Asian women, with it having become a kind of business norm to expect to be pampered by Asian women. The alleged subservience of the Asian woman is marked by essentialist characteristics such as remaining "quiet," being "attentive," and acting "gentle," and "submissive" to men. Such stereotypes find real evidence all across Asia, Africa, and the Pacific. This can result in a grave misconceptions and even may result in cultural shock for those who are ill-prepared or those who possess an essentialized version of women (and men) in their minds. For example, a few Japanese business travelers often mistake the "exotic allure" of the "Singapore Girl" of SIA fame for something else and end up being charged in Singapore courts for criminal molestation. While the flight attendants of United Airlines, Southwest, or other Western airlines may use a no-nonsense approach when it comes to dealing with passengers who have had too much drink, the "stewards" and "stewardesses" of many Asian airlines tend accept the norm of adopting a more "gentle, caring" and relatively "submissive" approach towards their passengers. This is clearly not the norm in the behavioral patterns of Western flight attendants. However, a person raised in the West who then works for an Asian airline, for example, might adopt quite quickly to Asian norms and behave in the stereotypical Asian fashion. Stereotypes therefore represent norms at their worst because it ill-informs the person about the kinds of social expectations prevailing in a given community. American students for example tend to be very outspoken and will speak up in university lectures but it is the norm for Asian students not to speak up, or to "speak when they are spoken to". This norm is changing because of globalization.

Business-driven, norm-changing behavior sometimes leads to ironic situations. The stereotypical image is sometimes larger than reality, and then, becomes the reality. The "Singapore Girl" for example, is required by company policy to wear a figure-hugging, curve-accentuating "kebaya" (a traditional Malay dress). This design is based "an original" outfit by the French designer, Pierre Balmain. This makes the SIA girl's job not only difficult but also tends to create a different kind of impression on some of its customers. The Singapore Girl is perhaps the best example in the world of the exotification of the Asian woman, this ironically, by a local Singapore MNC that has made it the best airline in the world for the past three decades because of its new fleet of American and European aircraft, timely schedules, excellent service, and periodically troublesome pilots. However it seems surprising to me that the Singapore Girl story has not received the kind of critical comments from feminist groups in Singapore for the past 30 years despite entrenching stereotypes of Asian women. The management believes that it is all about service.

GLOBAL NORMS

What are the norms that exist in globalization? There are many norms that continue to exist in globalization and that have survived the rapidly changing social, political, and economic world. These norms exist for the precise reason of promoting or facilitating quotidian human activity. Norms may be created out of political violence, coercion, peace treaties, confidence-building measures, the work of NGOs, the work of the UN, or an agreement between and/or among several states, parties, or communities in order to facilitate the way in which the parties to the norm might proceed over a given matter. The noun "norm" is related to the idea of normalcy, i.e., what is considered the normal thing to do in a given context. A norm may also reflect the "traditional" or "conventional" method of doing something. Norms are geographically located and determined so that what is considered a norm in one place would not be the norm in another. In other words there are different regimes of norms that vary from region to region and are informed by ethnicity, culture, religion, economics, and politics.

One such regime norm exists in the corporate world. There are different norms that make up different corporate structures; they are modified and informed by the demographic makeup and the ethnic, cultural, religious, economic and political dimensions of place and time. For example, McDonalds' failure to adhere to the religious norm against the consumption of beef and related products in India created obstacles and marketing problems despite their PR endeavors at correcting misconceptions and disinformation created by their competitors who were perhaps more "norm savvy."

Japanese companies used to instill the need for group exercise before the start of the work-day shift in many of their subsidiary companies overseas until the bubble burst and they realized that their group-norm behavior was perhaps not quite appropriate for all countries. While some Japanese firms continue with these exercises, especially in the manufacturing sector, these norms have become all but diluted versions of their predecessors. Another norm that was discovered about American companies overseas was the fact that they had really fancy-sounding titles. Almost everyone appeared to be a vice-president or senior manager. In the European and Japanese models, the hierarchy and rank-structure remained fairly rigid and high-sounding titles formed no part of their norm.. However, the successes of many American MNCs and the contacts that were made in the buying and selling of European and Japanese companies, goods and services, resulted in a degree of pressure on non-American firms to change with the times. Very soon there were all kinds of high-sounding titles everywhere in the corporate world. It seemed that customers preferred to have their problems resolved by a senior engineering executive rather than a customer salesperson; or that vice-presidents of marketing and research preferred to deal with people of similar if not greater stature than their own.

There were also new management styles that developed over time because of the intense interaction between MNCs and other businesses the world over through three phases. Phase I: post-World War II (reconstruction); Phase II: Cold War models of developmental corporate behavior; and Phase III: post-Cold War regenerative corporate management models. These management styles in general saw the flattening of management hierarchies, the broadening of specialist tasks, and the importance of creating a better after-sales services for those businesses that were in the corporate competition for the long term. Phase I was distinctive because the old colonial powers continued to possess the management and resources to develop and hone their homegrown industries while being set up as models for "Third World" countries to mimic. Phase II was a result of intense competition between and among corporate styles of management within the 'free world' that came under the protection of pro-democratic countries. This phase in particular saw the rise of American norms of management across Europe and the acceptance of the US as the leader of the free-democratic capitalist world as well as d the meteoric but momentary rise of the Asian Tiger or Dragon economies. Phase III saw the rise of Japan as a potential superpower that had the backing of US government and other multinational corporate giants. But there was also a decline in domestic confidence within the US amidst rising expectations of the alternate possibility of a European resurrection.

The New World Order that supported a multi-polar world scenario with large free-trade areas hardly had time to take root before 9/11, and then Bali, Madrid, and Southern Thailand began having trouble with terrorists. Even before the terrorists began making headway into the heart of neoliberal capitalism based on MNCs and the sleepless financial markets, there were already signs of other problems. These problems centered on the outdated norms, and the inefficient and illiberal financial structures of the advanced developing nations in Asia such as Thailand, Singapore, Malaysia, Taiwan, and South Korea, as well as the lesser developed nations of the Philippines, Indonesia, and Vietnam (to a much lesser extent). The problems in Phase III also demonstrated the weaknesses of the world financial support system modeled after the European Bank for Reconstruction and Development (EBRD) and the International Bank for Reconstruction and Development (IBRD). In addition, there was trouble with the norms that the WTO had tried to implement resulting in worldwide demonstrations at every important summit.

Therefore, the New World Order did not turn out to be a democratically free-trade world but one with several poles that have come under threat from international terrorism. This has led to the creation of new norm regimes such as the need to police airline, shipping, and train travel with anti-terrorist measures. This has resulted in a heightened sense of insecurity as a kind of international norm.

However, the political paranoia created by terrorism seems to be at its highest point in the US. This was illustrated in the treatment of its own citizens through curb-side checks; deliberate 24-hour delays for international parcels coming into the US through international courier services such as FedEx, UPS, and Airborne Express; long queues at all airports and major hubs resulting in long-delayed departures of scheduled flights; new regulations for all travel centers and points of entry/exit; individual checking of domestic passengers; 100 per cent bag checks, removal of attire and shoes; and the profiling of suspected people who turned out to be quite normal after all. In September 2004 American Customs and Excise officers began fingerprinting and photographing everyone visiting the United States. If this is not paranoia, then it must be a ploy by Big Business to ensure that Kodak or Fuji or some popular brand of film maker remains marketable and in power. This is only the beginning of the commodification of terrorism. Recall that during the days of McCarthyism people began building underground shelters in preparation for a Soviet nuclear attack.

Therefore, 9/11 and the following string of terrorist acts against non-Muslims and Muslims alike from New York City to downtown Jakarta and Jeddah, have created a new kind of international norm: the fear that anyone at anytime could be a terrorist. This has also led to zero tolerance of non-normal behavior within the travel industry and especially among airlines themselves. New norms are created each time a specific event causes the previous norm regime to blister and break apart. On May 9, 2004, a Swedish student on a Singapore Airlines flight jumped off the air plane through its emergency door before the Airbus plane could disengage from the passenger terminal. This caused a two hour delay as the authorities made several kinds of checks. A week earlier, the anti-terrorist beacon on a Singapore Airlines plane that was scheduled to land at LAX was set off accidentally resulting in the plane being escorted by a USAF fighter to a remote runway where various anti-terrorist troops stormed the plane to complete their anti-hijack drill. It appears that only the captain can key in the code of the anti-hijacking beacon, but the captain of the aircraft said that he did not. It would make more sense if indeed the crew could activate the beacon from the rear of the aircraft. The news report sounded more like a cover-up for a live anti-hijack drill on unsuspecting passengers. This illustrates the level of preparedness by the authorities on one hand and the level of paranoia that goes into such preparation. Therefore, the breaking of one set of norms from a previous norm regime usually requires the ending of that regime before a new set of norms can come into play. At the individual level, there is need for knowledge of such new norms before the norm regime can work efficiently.

Norms arrive at the doorstep of the corporate world because they are brought in by people who practice and perform other norms in the private world outside of the workday. Take for example the need to greet a fellow employee in your business organization. In the conduct of daily business, if you pass by the same person 10 to 12 times before lunch and another 15 times after lunch, and you both notice each other, how are you supposed to behave? Does a single greeting of "good morning" at the start of the work day suffice or is there a need to greet this person all the time?

Much depends on the kind of organizational culture and the kind of personalities of the people about whom we concerned. It might also depend on the organizational status of the other person involved, such as a senior vice-president, a junior manager, the mailroom person or the janitor. What is the norm for your organizational culture? There are also group norms in business organizations that devote certain times to group activity and other times to individual ones such as tea-breaks (in Commonwealth countries, i.e., ones that were formerly British colonies), coffee breaks (in America) and lunch breaks. In Europe, it is not uncommon for Mediterranean workers to take a siesta in the afternoon and to continue working till late at night. The norms for the business day also range widely across the globe. In many "Western" nations, the idea of the business day begins late at about 11 am and ends early at about 4 pm. Workers may also only work five days a week, though not necessarily beginning and ending on Mondays. This means that the shops remain open for a very short and specific period of time when compared to many Asian cities in which the shops remain open from 10 am in the morning till 10 pm at night, seven days a week for most days in the year. The "workday week norm" across the globe is influenced by several factors. These include the historical performance of the economy; the kind of product or service required; the number of workers skilled in the given area of work; the kind of work ethic that prevails; the impact of unionized labor versus non-unionized labor practices; and the importance placed on leisure time by the workers themselves. Singapore workers, for example, are seen to be hardworking and in great support of their companies and business bosses.

The reason there are no strikes in Singapore is because it is illegal to strike, even peacefully, in that country. The norm for strikes simply does not exist any longer since the end of the British colonial period. Therefore, it is common for the law to determine the kind of norms that exist in business practice, and in industrial and labor relations. Another example of a "norm" influenced by regulations in Singapore is what Sim Wong Hoo, the CEO, chairman, and founder of Creative Technologies calls the "No-U turn syndrome." Sim is a prominent Singaporean and an international entrepreneur because his company invented the original Sound Blaster card that you probably have on your PC right now. Sim's basic argument is that Singapore has too many laws and regulations that stifle creativity. And he uses an example involving driving in Singapore, which like the British system, is on the left side of the road with a right-hand drive. The U-turn rule in Singapore is a reflection of the regulated society that has been modified from one and a half centuries of British colonial rule from 1819 to 1959. Drivers in Singapore are not allowed to make a U-turn on the road unless there is a sign that permits such a turn. Sim compared this to the United States where one is allowed to make a U-turn unless there is a regulatory sign expressly forbidding it. What Sim did not mention of course was that the American case was a clear demonstration of President Theodore Roosevelt's belief in *going to the extent of what the law does not explicitly prohibit*. And apparently, the absence of regulations such as these make Americans "more creative" and "unlike Singaporeans." The latter group usually find themselves in need of someone to tell them what to do. Letters to the forum page of the largest local daily for instance often carry the phrase, "will the relevant authorities" do something about this or about that. Of course, Sim is not entirely correct about the situation in the US and in fact, many Americans themselves find that there is simply too much bureaucracy and red tape in America.

So where is the norm in this situation? The spirit of the law determines the norm which determines the law in the US, however, in Singapore, the letter of the law appears to determine the spirit of the norm in daily practice. Not surprisingly, there are now two kinds of road signs in Singapore for U-turning vehicles. There are now two kinds of signs in place. An old sign that instructs drivers to make a U-turn, or, a new one that tells them that they can't. Rather than accept a single principle, there are now two principles at work where one says you can U-turn here, and another that says when you cannot. This is how the minds of some Singapore civil servants work. When they face a problem, such as Sim's comments in the local papers, they create another set of regulations to control those problems. This is also an example of a Singaporean norm called *kiasu-ism* which is a Chinese Hokkien word for a psychological state of "being afraid of losing" or "being afraid of being outwitted by another person."

Corporate culture often involves business norms that become beholden to the activities of other corporations within globalization. As a result, global norms of dress, etiquette and behavior develop and arise over time, despite differences in language, capital size, or the kind of goods and services produced. Also, in order to project the image of success or professionalism, many corporations require their male staffers to wear at the very least, a long-sleeved shirt and tie, and probably even a two piece suit when meeting clients. What is ridiculous is that in the tropical heat of Asia, one can find busy executives wearing such ridiculous apparel out in the hot sun. Part of the ability to withstand such a corporate norm is the presence of air-conditioning, without which the business world would have a very uncomfortable environment to work in tropical Asia and tropical America. One would assume that since the tropics are so hot and humid that the people would wear clothes that afforded comfort rather than style. This is clearly not the case in many capital cities in Asia and the Pacific that support the neo-liberal corporate culture. Hawaii is one exception to this norm where the accepted office attire for men is a short-sleeve shirt and slacks, while women have greater latitude of choice.

When the British still ruled in Southeast Asia, the standard dress for male civil servants was a stiffly-starched white uniform usually made out of cotton drill material. The belief was that it was fabric that was "cool" for the tropical heat. Corporate culture therefore determines the type of dress in the tropics as a norm. It is also a norm to dress down on Saturdays where dressing down involves wearing of a polo tee-shirt and jeans.

There are also certain personality traits that result in non-normal behavior. For example, there was once an executive from the European arm of an MNC who wore the same shirt, tie, and slacks everyday while at work in the Singapore headquarters of the MNC. You can imagine the stench if you walked by his cubicle. After a while, everyone was making fun of him. What made matters worse was that he never wanted to have lunch with anyone, unless it was some "big wig" from senior management (which was rare in any case). Rather, he used to raid the division pantry for lunch and consume all the free beverages provided until the "tea-lady" complained to one of the managers that someone was pilfering the beverages meant for all staff. Our spies from the HR department informed us that the executive was very well paid, not suffering from any known psychological disorders, and did not have to care for an elderly person or for any other family. He was single, and lived in a secured apartment with squash courts, a swimming pool and other amenities paid by the MNC. He also didn't have lunch or dinner with the local staff because he told us all that local food was disgusting. This, of course, coming from someone who had poor personal hygiene and who was stingy beyond belief. Not surprisingly, he did not last long in the company and was ostracized because of a non-adherence to corporate norms.

Certain elaborate idiosyncrasies existing in the psychological world become apparent after working for a while in any business corporation. Basic standards of personal hygiene are common the world over in any corporate environment and often form part of the expected norms of behavior.

Another element of corporate norms includes gift giving. For example, in Asia, there are different forms of gift-giving according to the rank and status of the prospective client or business partner. These may take on the form of an expensive dinner for the whole company or the giving of a "Rolex" watch at retirement. This is a considered a norm that is built on a value. However, the material value has become too much of a burden over time. So changes are made to norms over time and space. For example, some MNCs in Singapore try to save money on corporate gifts, anniversary gifts and retirement gifts. One cannot always expect a "Rolex" on retirement. We now turn to the meaning of the norm in US law.

"NORM" AND THE "LAW"

We have examined the nature of the concept of the "norm" in globalization and have ascertained its unique and functional position in daily life, and perhaps, death too. We also understand that the US political system is built on a system of "checks and balances" and the "sharing of power" between the legislative (law-making), juridical (arbitration and interpretation), and executive (implementation) arms of American government. History has shown that all three arms of government are taken very seriously by their defenders and those who occupy the respective seats. The US system of justice is built round a very specific set of legal terms and definitions that are used to guide the officers of the law in their daily work. In other words, the law is something that has to be very precise and what are considered ordinary definitions of words and phrases often mean something quite the opposite in legal terms. This includes the law of tort, the law of evidence, and power of attorney. Jurisprudence or the theory of justice has evolved over time to adjust to the changing nature of human civilization whether it is under US common law and constitutional law tradition or the British natural law tradition. We are also informed that natural law underlies both the US and UK traditions with American law having evolved from British common law and then adding its constitutional dimension. Despite the gravity of the situation and in spite of hundreds of years of evolution, there is a compelling need to have norms in the search for justice. In other words, there are many situations where the law is unable to specifically dictate what is to be done and hence the judge has to interpret the law according to existing legal norms. The clearest example is in the norm of consensus by the Supreme Court of the United States of America.

The norm of consensus may arguably involve a non-majoritarian decision that is arrived at by the Court in its interpretation of the law and the events surrounding the case in question. And therefore, in most cases, it seems that there continues to be a need for the court's majority position and the court's minority report that are themselves based on these legal norms. Some examples of this may be found in *Mutual Life Insrance Company of New York v. Harris* (1877),[4] *First Security National Bank v. United States* (1965),[5] and the case of *Maryland v. United States (1965).*[6] The norm of consensus is politically charged because it is a reflection of society's values and the impression that the American public (is assumed to) projects as discussed by Epstein, Segal, and Spaeth.[7] Apart from the idea of norm of consensus, there are also unanimity norms that arise out of Supreme Court decisions that guide and inform the norms practiced by the lower courts, as discussed for example, by David A. Skeel in "The Unanimity Norm in Delaware Corporate Law" (1997).[8]

There are additional situations when the norm of the law also provides for resolving disputes between the federal government and former elected officials of the federal government and local businesses as illustrated in part by the following cases between the *United States v. Glaxo Group Ltd.* (1973),[9] *Nixon v. Warner Communications* (1978),[10] *Department of the Army v. Blue Fox Inc.* (1999),[11] and the case of the *National Federation of Federal Employees v. United States* (1999).[12]

The US federal system of justice has also become the arena for settling international issues and the differences between MNCs that are headquartered in different countries. It is a political decision on the part of the business corporation because there are compelling reasons for fighting a case on neutral territory or on territory that gives one's position a legal advantage. Some examples of the use of American legal norms in the settlement of business disputes between and, or, among different parties internationally including foreign aliens: *Alfred Dunhill of London, Inc. v. Cuba* (1976),[13] *Hampton v. Mow Sun Wong* (1976),[14] *Wilson v. Omaha Indian Tribe* (1979),[15] *United States v. Sioux Nation of Indians* (1980),[16] *Wolrdwide Volkswagen Corporation v. Woodson* (1980),[17] and *United States v. Vernanzuela-Bernal* (1981).[18]

Similarly, the politicization of the law may also arise out of the interaction of legal and public norms that exist in the first instance, to generate new legislation such as the *Voting Rights Act* (1965) and in the second instance the changes that arise within the public arena as a result of normative responses to the initial act that result for example, in the *Voting Rights (Amendment) Act* (1976).[19] Most of the norms can be traced to the Constitution which is seen by many scholars as a brilliant document. I have always held that it has been a misleading and deliberately broadbased document that has caused more trouble for America and Americans in its interpretation than in its philosophy. There are many examples that could fill several hundred book-length manuscripts. However, a useful example for the sake of brevity and in order to further explain norms in US law can be traced to the Second Amendment within the Bill of Rights (i.e., the first fifteen amendments to the US Constitution). The US Supreme Court decision to stay within the latitude of a dry bones, literal interpretation of the Second Amendment, despite the advance made by the Brady Act (1993), resulted in more gun-related deaths.

The Second Amendment states that, "A well regulated militia, being necessary to the security of a free state, the right of the people to keep and bear arms, shall not be infringed." This decrepid Amendment dating back to the year 1791 contains the primary subject phrase, "necessary to the security of a free state." Therefore, the adverbial phrase, "the right of the people to keep and bear arms" is in support of the "subject phrase." The right to "keep and bear arms" was a reflection of the time when America was still very much an undiscovered frontier, vulnerable to Native Americans who were fighting in defense of their *own* homeland against the internal colonialism of the American settlers. There were also fears of Spanish and British invasions. But today, almost 200 years after the Second Amendment was passed, are the British marines in the Gulf of Mexico? Is the Spanish Armada threatening the port of New York? Currently, the US Supreme Court's judges—the great legal minds of that esteemed bench—and Americans who have a romantic attachment to pro-gun legislation of the American Frontier culture are only making the politics of American globalization worse. Repealing the Amendment would prevent more domestic gun-related violence like that of the Attica-incarcerated Colin Ferguson, who pleaded temporary insanity with the tragic but innovative defense called "Black rage" for killing six fellow American citizens and shooting 25.[20] Making personal weapons, concealed or otherwise, illegal will prevent the kind of violence that killed 12 students and one teacher at a high school in Columbine, Colorado in 1999. The norm-regime created by the Second Amendment and the egotistical pride of those who support its presence has resulted in the death of more than a million Americans over the past 45 years. There are also situations that are potentially norm-blind. This refers to a situation where norms are absent in a given social, economic, or cultural context. In such cases, and in the absence of precedent, US judges may be compelled to arrive at a politicized form of "norm-creation" as illustrated in part by the case of the *National Farmers Union Insurance Companies v. Crow Tribe of Indians* (1984),[21] the *United States v. S.A. Empresa De Viacao Aerea Rio Grandense (Varig Airlines) et al.* (1984),[22] *Air France v. Saks* (1985),[23] and the case of *Chan et al., v. Korean Air Lines Ltd.* (1989).[24]

The collective norms of the Warsaw Convention and the Montreal Agreement were brought into play to resolve this last international incident. This is, in a sense, a form of norm-creation by an institution that was not designed for norm-creation in specific terms but is not dispossessed of an administrative cum legal framework capable of such a function within the set of given statutes. The US system of checks and balances and the sharing of *powers* among the three arms of government have given rise to a unique context in which we have described and explained: (1) unanimity of norms, (2) norm-consensus building, and (3) norm creation in situations which are norm-absent or norm-blind. The politics of American globalization in terms of norms and the law serves as a platform for arbitration of not only local and federal issues but also issues that involve foreign aliens and businesses with or without a legal relationship with a US business or US government agency.

American approaches to the problem of globalization involve the use of legal and rational norms within the public and private spheres. The US as a sovereign political entity is also becoming a stage for the arbitration of foreign-domestic disputes which result in what may be perceived as increasing neo-liberal state confidence in the US as a arbiter of the last resort in a manner that one day might replace the work done by UN justice tribunals and commissions, the International Court of Justice at the Hague and the smaller European Courts of Justice.

Since the beginning of this chapter, we have seen the various kinds of norms and norm regimes that exist with some degree of illustration from the US and Asia. This does not mean there are not norms elsewhere in the world, nor does it mean that the norms that were highlighted are superior in any way. Chances are that norms and norm regimes the world over share several basic and common characteristics such as: adaptation to place; being modified and informed by ethnicity, religion, culture, society and politics; dynamic; and easily replaced when the previous norm regime implodes due to an unforeseen event that interrupts its normal continuance. Those who are part of a given set of norms or a norm regime are also expected to understand the prevailing norms for the efficient running of a norm regime.

WHAT IS A 'VALUE'?

The *Merriam-Webster Online Dictionary* (2004) defines a value as deriving from the Latin root *valuta* meaning "to be worth," some thing or to "be strong." "Value" may also be defined along the following lines: (1) a fair return or equivalent in goods, services, or money for something exchanged; (2) the monetary worth of something or its marketable price; (3) the relative worth, utility, or importance of a good; (4) a numerical quantity that is assigned or is determined by calculation or measurement; (5) the relative duration of a musical note; (6a) relative lightness or darkness of a color; and (6b) something (as a principle or quality) intrinsically valuable or desirable. On the other hand, the *American Heritage Dictionary of the English Language* (4th edition, 2000) explains value through its adjectival variants: *nominal* value, *face* value, *numerical* value, *R*-value, *expected* value, *surplus* value, *absolute* value, *truth* value and *market* value.

To the list of definitions from these two dictionaries, we can add the following modifiers: *political* value, *cultural* value, *sacred* value, *global* value, *economic* value, *social* value, *pedagogical* value, *consequential* value, *subsequential* value, *spiritual* value, *complementary* value, *residual* value, and *marginal* value. The two patterns that arise from these definitions is that value is a relative term and highly subjective. However, we are concerned with the concept of value in politics of American globalization.

What do Americans hold dear, that it is also generally considered valuable? This chapter began with a reference to the work of Lipsett on the political nature of human beings. It is this political nature that gives birth to the upholding of the Constitution as a sacred document. But the sanctity of the Constitution comes at a cost. This book has shown so far that many Americans clearly hold on to a romantic notion of keeping changes to the US Constitution restricted to a minimum. This tragic "value" has resulted in the death of many Americans abroad and overseas. Millions of Americans have died from hand-gun violence since World War I on US soil. It is one thing to die for one's beliefs, but quite another to accept the prospect of early, painful, and excruciating death in the defense of anachronistic laws. Similarly energized by such Constitutional "safeguards," America sends troops and private sector building contractors, oil engineers, and social workers to rebuild Iraq. This is a country that America invaded over a decade ago during the First Gulf War under the current US president's father. Iraq is the country America has been trying to destabilize after the American oil puppet, the Shah of Iran, was rooted out of Teheran by Islamic revolutionaries led by the Ayatollah Khomeini. After the fall of the Shah in 1979, the US-aided Iraqi attacks on Iran while secret government aides eventually revealed the Western European interests in the region and the covert "Allied" plans between the Americans, the French and the British that were supposed to be put into practice in the aftermath of the decade-long war. The Iraq-Iran War of the 1980s was fought southwest of the Great Pyramids at Giza on the West Bank of the Nile. This was where the ancient ancestors of Americans of Iraqi and Iranian descent fought over lands belonging to the ancient Babylonian Empire. In American popular culture, the old song, "By the Rivers of Babylon" by that popular musical group, *Boney-M*, was about that Empire. We assume that song ran an interesting parallel with the Old Testament Jewish flight into the Land of Milk and Honey after being persecuted by their ancient enemies. This was empire-building at the center of ancient civilizations that predated the Iran-Iraq War by millennia. The *Ship of Fools* has come full circle along the Wheel of Tragedy, mistaken so often as a Wheel of Fortune in popular American television.

There must be seven to eight generations of Americans whose ancestors successively killed foreigners in the American wars against the Native Americans, the British, the Hawaiians, *themselves* (American Civil War), the Spanish, the Mexicans, Latin Americans, Koreans, Vietnamese, Afghans, Iranians and Iraqis. There are many more Americans who have been killed in these countries. There are in fact more Americans who have died in defense of this tragic value that has permitted what we have been socialized to believe as America's role as the world's policeman, the global peace-keeper, the defender of liberty, and the benign hegemonic superpower in the post Cold War.

The value of the nation and the sanctity of the Constitution as a sacred document are held in the greatest esteem for many Americans. With the exception of conscientious objectors and those in peaceful and non-violent organizations, there continues to remain a sacred and tragic episode in American life. In order to protect this idiom of American sovereignty, many Americans have been beguiled into believing that there is honor in dying for their country. The metaphor of the American Hero and the images created by consolidations of centuries of giving death for liberty are deeply ingrained in the American public psyche. J. Peter Euben's endeavor at addressing the theoretical implications of our discipline of political theory is a case in point. Euben's work on the democratic roots of America's heritage points towards the tragic narcissism of sacred and traditional "values." Euben ideas support the post-Nietzschean philosophy of engaging the abyss of horror and the enigma of embracing its tragic comedies. This was admirably but foolishly reiterated in Vietnam War epics that mimicked World War II movies constructed on Union Armies sweeping away the widepread Frontier belief in the anti-hero represented by 'savage' Native Americans.

The anti-hero worship common in the popular cultural literature feeds and informs the stereotypical commodification and museumization of the Old Frontier West. Cowboys and Indians was the management idiom and business metaphor used to express the value of these brave warriors defending themselves against the internal colonialism of White

267

America. The old American chieftains have mostly been erased from memory. Those whose memory remain because they were not afraid of being photographed or ethno-museumized are remembered for enhancing the value of American liberal democratic *ex post facto* overtures of peaceful co-existence. The men of War must have at least included Chief "Cochise," Chief "Red Cloud," Chief "Little Wolf," and Chief "Sitting Bull." The Federal State's constrictive amount of time accorded to Native American integration into the urban cultural milieu of America has compressed their cultural space while delimiting their temporality as a resource for ethnic remembrance and political remonstrances. This challenges the naïve arguments made by Dobyns, Stoffle, and Jones in their 1975 article.[25] My criticism is supported by David Henige's 1989 reply titled "On the Current Devaluation of the Notion of Evidence: A Rejoinder to Dobyns" in the journal, *Ethnohistory*.[26] The next step in the urban planners' calculus has shown to be the cultural warehousing of Native Americans in the Southwestern United States and elsewhere once the subjects have surrendered to the capitalist enclave of the urban town and city.

Such internal colonial politics hastens the ethnic-bankrupting of Native American cultural values. The revaluation of ethno-Native traditions become vulnerable targets for the commodification of the surviving co-ethnic Native American settlers. They have to do this to survive the neo-liberal impasse of American modernity. The Pacific Northwest is replete with such interesting cases thanks to the wonderful methods provided by American Social Science. In a similar historically famous case, Chief "Jeronimo" was forced to appear in a state parade after his surrender. Like a modern American puppet without the appropriate paraphernalia of nobility, the Chief was forced to take part in the Louisiana Purchase Exposition in St. Louis. He died, broken of his ethno-cultural values, in an old and dingy American prison thousands of miles away from the sacred lands. Jeronimo was nominally chosen as a showpiece, an anti-heroic icon for Hollywood. He became the Savage Chieftain made malleable into a "token freak" to be put on display as a show to impress upon the new citizen conquerors that their cultural values had vanquished the Savage, and their cultural norms were safely in place. And they were solely in charge of discharging normalcy and the normal death dances in modernity (Rappa, *Sincronia*, 1998).

The politics of internal colonialism places a high cultural value on the museumization of ethno-cultural epitaphs to indigenous tribes.

Because they hope that the preservation of such ethno-history, ethno-music, and ethno-culture under Plexiglas in modern and expensive architectural buildings will not only enhance but legitimize the internal colonizing effort over time and space. The speeding up of time by internal colonial post-structural museumization results therefore in the compression of ethnic space in American modernity. According to Wilmer, Melody and Murdock, such inclusiveness extends Almond and Coleman's 1960 work (Wilmer, Melody, and Murdock, 1994, 269). But the authors are incorrect to suggest that including Native Americans in Political Science courses extends the kind of liberal inclusiveness arguments of the great positivist era supported by Almond and Coleman's own belief in general systems theory. [27] Rather, the value that is derived from such ethno-inclusion leads to the legitimization of the US liberal democratic norm regime. If this is their intention, then it makes sense otherwise it works against the larger multi-universal picture that is postmodernism. Chief Crazy Horse (also known as Tashawanka) was stabbed in the back by the American soldier sent to protect him while under US Army guard. Can any one really wonder if American troops can be trusted after stabbing a Native American Chief in the back? Is the picture of a modern American soldier mocking the naked, homo-erotic stance of a hooded Iraqi Prisoner of War a similar reminder in late modernity? Is history repeating itself or is this just a point at the tip of the apex of the top of a new modernity that has made it increasingly difficult to prevent secret and embarrassing information from leaking out into the torrential broadcast stream of CNN, BBC, CNBC, and CNA? How many more lives must American globalization destroy before Americans themselves are considered free? What value is there in words of "Duty," "Honor," and "Country," when scores of US and UK troops defile the prisoners covered under the Geneva Convention but uncovered and forced to perform hideous and barbaric acts that cut across their own and their captors' religious beliefs? Let us return to the contiguous United States for another aspect of American made liberalism.

The hooded cloak and dagger past of David Duke is a grim reminder of the kinds of cultural values that American liberalism entertains from a distance simply because it is part of "the deal of liberalism." Permitting someone like Duke free speech continues in support of a principle, rather like those people who refuse to change the Constitution because it is a sacred cow. People willing to save a sacred and mythical cow despite the human lives that might be lost in the sacrifice of not having sacrificed it in the first place. Duke's widespread anti-Semitic, anti-Black, pro-White Unity racism is the result of liberal ease. He was the prime mover in the reinvigoration of the *Knights of the Ku Klux Klan* during the 1970s. The American liberal democratic system allows for people such as Duke to stand for political office and make a nuisance in the public domain. He travels widely, like all racist leaders, to promote the international racist network that exists in the neo-Nazi mind. Duke blames 9/11 on the Jews.

The US Constitution forbids the establishment of an official religion. This means that any religion can be practiced in the US as long as it remains within the ambit of US federal and state law. Religion is a global value and even though the US Constitution expressly forbids the creation of an official religion, it has indirectly sanctioned liberal religious development. At the "Million Man March" in October 1995, the "reverend" Louis Farrakhan's personal bodyguards were dressed like they were going to a Michael Jackson concert. But the man they were protecting was certainly not like the child-loving Jackson. Farrakhan mentioned Jackson in his speech for being a "drawn out" Black man, but by 2003, neither Michael Jackson nor the Nation of Islam wanted to have anything to do with one another (*Nation of Islam* Press Release, 12-29-2003; *Fox News*, April 2004).

The Nation of Islam is an American Muslim activist group that was "re-established" by Farrakhan in 1977 as a political realignment with the teaching of a former Nation of Islam leader, Elijah Mohammed. Farrakhan (also known as Louis Eugene Walcott), a kind of religious celebrity who loves the populist limelight. He has great self-confidence in his knowledge of Islam, of his creativity with numerology and the importance of "19" and "440" in representing the political icons of previous American presidencies. Farrakhan's speeches are usually emotive and provocative. The former virtuoso, Calypso singer and dancer (who attained fame in Boston) attacks the primordial instincts of African Americans and provokes them by reminding them of their misery. It does appear that his mannerisms mimic Martin Luther King, Jr., but unlike King, he is afraid to die. That is why Farrakhan has so many bodyguards to protect him from the people he speaks to, from the people he believes in, from the people that he claims to love. These are the people he fears. Unlike Martin Luther King, Jr., who not only had a dream but also stood publicly against racism, Farrakhan is comfortable with rhetoric as some critics believe:

We cannot be sanguine about the fact that the most ardent and widely listened to voice of unchurched Black Americans is probably Minister Louis Farrakhan. Farrakhan is a separatist who has no commitment to racial reconciliation. He is a persuasive speaker who evokes and manipulates black rage with ambiguous intent and consequences. I believe that tens of thousands of African Americans turn out to hear him, in part, because they are hurting and angry, and they crave the therapy of having those powerful emotions ventilated with style, bombast, and defiance[28]

The Million Man March was designed for the purpose of Black unity, which was well served. There was no racism or hatred in Farrakhan's speech, despite what former majority leader Senator Bob Dole, Rep. Gary Franks (R-Connecticut), Rep. John Lewis (D-Georgia), and other US political leaders have said about Farrakhan's anti-White, anti-Semitic views. While the march appears to have been planned at some level to elevate Farrakhan into the national spotlight, many Black Americans attended because they wanted to share in the value derived from a sense of unity, a sense of purpose and a sense of being part of America. Farrakhan reminded the audience that if the Jews were held captive by the Egyptians for 400 years, the Black Man had been oppressed for 440 years. The October 16th march was meant to be a turning point for Black men, to turn back on their social ills (BBC News, 1998).[29] The liberal democracy of American politics enables vast differences, racially charged and provocative to take place within the same agenda. This is why in the aftermath of 9/11, Farrakhan could say in a speech that the attack was "a crime against all humanity." He went on to add:

> When Timothy McVeigh committed the worst act of terrorism on American soil, the first persons accused of this were members of the Nation of Islam and immigrant Muslims. Many followers of Islam were attacked, and then it was found that the perpetrator of this crime was a White American, a soldier who professed to be a Christian. But no Christian of his denomination was attacked ... [*later, in response to a question from an American Muslim journalist, he said:*] I myself know who and what I am. I know I have never hated Jews. I'm critical of aspects of Jewish behavior in relationship to Black people. I'm critical of the government in aspects of their behavior toward

Black people. It doesn't mean I hate America. I'm critical. And because I have the freedom, because of that great constitutional guarantee, to speak even if people do not like what I say, it is the freedom to speak that guarantees America a greater future.[30]

This does not sound like a speaker who is an anti-Semitic, White-hating Muslim preacher that the media and the UK have painted so vociferously. There are two possibilities. Either there is a "great White conspiracy" against Farrakhan within the politics of American liberalism, or Farrakhan is himself is a liar and playing a highly-charged politicized game. Where is the evidence? Where is the public groundswell against Farrakhan's anti-White, anti-Semitic, and sexist comments? So far, the public domain seems content to keep their views on Farrakhan politically "contained" and "non-violent." Perhaps Farrakhan's case is one that seems to illustrate the working value of American democratic liberalism. Nevertheless, Farrakhan continues to be banned from entering the UK because of his anti-Semitism.

The liberal/conservative divide in American domestic politics has itself raised doubts about what is politically achievable apart from empty political rhetoric. Neo-realists have never seemed as fashionable as neo-liberals since the end of the Cold War. Neo-liberals run the world capitalist economy that is intricately tied to though not dominated by America. Inside the US itself, the political ideology of liberalism was supposed to create and support individual rights and protect individual freedoms in the light of hope, optimism, and progress. Yet the tragic mimicry of these end-goals seem to have been outplayed, outlasted, and outwitted by the very people it was designed to protect. Like the so-called reality TV series, *Survivor*, America up close is armed to the teeth and dangerous. Neil Postman was correct about amusing ourselves to death. So was Michael Moore's book with the essentialist title that catches attention but serves no real purpose in the end.

The servant of liberalism, as we shall continue to revisit, is already incarcerated by the Constitutional rejection of desperate changes to the political institutionalism of the US Federal System of Government. Liberalism in America was the "answer" and "solution." It is now more of the problem that enhances the gravity of the American political paradox:

Like the critical theorists, Adorno, Horkheimer, Lefebvre, Berman, Latour, and Kariel, Postman warned of the dehumanizing potential of technologically-based societies. Public and private spaces become increasingly enmeshed as meaningless symbols with worthless teleologies. Postman, however, failed to consider the impact of the internationalization of American media; that the same paradigmatic shift from print to television as the main interface between media producers and media consumers in America of the early 1980s would consume Latin America, Africa, and Asia. These modern cultural masks of death are totems for social normality, and political correctness in society, a correctness that prepares us as we prepare for that last gasp, that last breath, that final rush, "[t]here was no sleeper more elegant than she, with her curved body posed for a dance and her hand across her forehead, but there was also no one more ferocious when anyone disturbed the sensuality of her thinking she was still asleep when she no longer was" (Rappa, *Sincronia*, 1998).

The master of neo-liberalism that has engraved the Native American into the iconography of American popular culture remains limited to areas outside of Washington DC. Chief Sitting Bull has no place near the Lincoln Memorial. When US Marines invaded Hawaii on January 16, 1893, they went unceremoniously looking for the Queen Lili'uokalani who was forced to surrender at gunpoint so that the sugar plantation proto-MNC owners could flourish. These men were hateful of Lili'uokalani's stoppage of the (forced) import of Chinese labor from Shanghai to work on their sugar cane plantations. Because of the unhygienic conditions involved in the long trip, the Chinese laborers were forced to live with malaria, dysentery, and other tropical diseases. This made them vulnerable to sickness and disease. When a smallpox epidemic began in the Chinese population, it came to no one's surprise.

The Queen closed the harbor, well before the invasion of the US Marines, in order to prevent further death among the Hawaiian community from the smallpox disease brought in by the forced migrant labor. It is a well-documented fact that the US government and Big Business helped destabilize the local economy, naturally with the help of some support from the Native elite that they were grooming with promises of entitlement, wealth and other trinkets. The Bishop Estate today has an endowment fund that is larger than the Harvard Endowment

Fund. Americans have taken many sovereign nations by force for hundreds of years and the American values and norm regimes that are recognized today, like other colonial powers transformed into postcolonial democracies, are afraid of remembering the horror that they brought down onto innocent people because of the greed and avarice of Big Business. Panama was nothing compared to Hawaii. The result of political liberalism is the disenfranchisement of people of color, women, and minorities.

There is little wonder that the primordial backlash from White America continues to find support among a minority of Americans in the racism of David Duke. Is this to be considered a value, when some American citizens consider this to be their Constitutional right? I do not think that the families whose relatives were killed or shot in any case of gun-violence—such as the ethnic riots in Los Angeles ("Rodney King Riots") that ostensibly began because of police brutality but erupted into Korean-African American violence, the high school kids shooting one another in Columbine, or the African American New Yorker who hated White people in the Long Island Railway shooting—all have to politically acquiesce to the (deliberate linguistic misinterpretation, as I have demonstrated earlier, of) individual right to keep and bear arms guaranteed under the Second Amendment. All this done and in spite of James Madison's clear warning about this form of tyranny in *Federalist Paper Number 51*.

NORM, VALUE, AND THE AMERICAN GLOBE

We have seen that the primary difference between a norm and a value is that one is mainly for functional reasons while the other is for both ideational as well as sacred reasons. Values also take a much longer time to distill and while a norm may be created almost instantaneously between two parties that agree on a prescribed mode of carrying out a task. A value requires much debate and consensus before it is informally adopted. There is a great difficulty in formally adopting values because one cannot implement values through the legal-rational framework of political, social and cultural institutions. For example, a society like Japan may value hard work, but if the value called hard work were raised as a Bill before the Japanese Diet, chances are that the Bill would not pass into law and if it did it would merely be window-dressing or valuable only in a legalistic sense. Another illustration might be to show how the line between the meaning of a value and the meaning of a norm may be vague. Japanese workers are known for their hard work. This is something that is considered a Japanese value. It is not unique to the Japanese but it is something valuable to them anyway. Doesn't matter who invented hard work at this point. How does one operationalize hard work then? Or at least measure hard work? One way that is often widely accepted is through time, i.e., the number of hours on the job. The Japanese salaried worker knows that the value of hard work means that he has to work the complete eight-hour day and not any less. To work less than eight hours is to be considered letting the team down. But most Japanese workers do more than spend eight hours a day at work. Let us take a norm of 10.5 hours. After which we know from social scientific studies that more work after such a norm is merely counter-productive. Yet because of the importance of the position of hard work in the Japanese system and because of the emphasis on common behavior by the working group, the Japanese *salarymen* cannot merely leave their desks after 10.5 hours of work a day. This is when a value turns into a norm. The Japanese *salarymen* pretend to work for more than the 10.5 hours, sharpening pencils, staring at the computer screen, making coffee for the boss, and reading, and generally pretending to do work without working. But once the boss or immediate superior decides that he (and his superiors) have worked "hard enough" he decides to leave the office. This is when there is a sudden and mad scramble for the after office *tête-à-tête*. The value is hard work but the norm is to pretend to keep at the place of hard work, i.e., the desk, while waiting for the right time to leave the office. Therefore the time spent idling away at the desk rereading material or surfing the net or pretending to work is known as a norm. However, to the casual observer it seems like hard work. How can we take our example of the Japanese worker to the American workplace? The Japanese *salarymen* example is not too different from the American worker who also values hard work but the norms are quite different.

POLITICS AND PHILOSOPHY: QUESTIONING VALUES AND NORMS

Hard work and company loyalty are considered part of the norm regimes implicit in Weber's *The Protestant Ethic and the Spirit of Capitalism*. But the philosophical intrigue goes deeper.

We saw at the start of Chapter seven that norms are needed to help govern, guide, and *process* the interstitial aspects of human interaction. The interstitial aspects refer to those "dimensions that exist between spaces" of two points where there are no laws, rules, regulations, or norms to guide human behavior. The concept of "norm" and "value" in the politics of globalization is centered on the idiosyncratic work of Western political philosophers. But there is a clear pattern of political empowerment and disempowerment in the history of the specific kind of globalization that we have been examining. The idea of the politics of American globalization has been reiterated politically through its repeated histories of inflicting violence and committing crimes against other sovereign nationalities. Since 1776, after a long and hard-fought war against the British colonial masters, the American form of global dominance has been its strategy of empowerment and control over the security of its future. America has survived because it has learnt that globalization means conquest and control of resources through military conflict and political violence. The politics of American global survival is vested in the extension of its political strategy platform in the *Monroe Doctrine* and *Manifest Destiny*.

The philosophical commitment and the incarceration of good and bad ideas, right and wrong norms, are genealogically linked to the Western "tradition." Each generation of divergent philosophies constructed different theoretical positions based on their limited observations of the Western World. Very much like we do today, but at a more naïve level, one would like to think. Marx made racist comments about India. Mill and his father, both British MPs, similarly made racist remarks despite the differences in their philosophical positions. Naturally, current conceptions of the democratic transition and transformation accorded to the universalism, utilitarianism, and pragmatism of the Enlightenment theorists persists forcefully within the American idiom of conquest, command, and control.

The work of Immanuel Kant and G. W. F. Hegel, the British empiricism of John Locke, as well as George Berkeley and David Hume are also often cited and indicted by postmodern theorists as the philosophical culprits of the past. These culpable constructions of the liberal democratic world have impinged on the direction of the social and political sciences and the humanities over the past 250 to 300 years.

The earlier days of these academic disciplines in the late 19th and early 20th centuries saw the legitimization of liberal democracy while

276

remaining short-sighted, or perhaps blatantly ignoring the violence that was being inflicted outside the Academy, and across the Great White Plains and prairies of the Western Frontier to the conquest of what is now the modern American colonized State of Hawaii, and New Mexico to give two examples. The problem was that the Western philosophical view of the world, according to the Enlightenment theorists co-located the political realism of American conquests with the expansion of the freedom of rights arguments. This led to the belief that a country or people ought to be conquered, if they could not be bought, to force them to accept liberal democratic freedoms. This is exemplified in the "purchase" and "annexation" of the Philippines at the end of the Spanish-American War; the Louisiana Purchase; and the Alaska Purchase. The Western philosophical tradition has come under attack by many American philosophers, theorists and social scientists—modern and postmodern alike—for setting the philosophical pace of survival through violence. After all, they believe that this is in the nature of political man and hence cannot be helped or changed.

A tentative resolution to the problems of democratic liberalism may appear in detailed studies of the politics of philosophical globalization that revolve round the post-Enlightenment, post-Nietzschean narratives of Husserl, Wittgenstein, Hypolite, Sartre, Arendt, Beauvoir, Foucault, Deleuze, and Guattari.[31] The influence of Fanon, Conrad, Blumenberg, Butler, McClintock, Millet, Cantalini, Narayan, Rushdie, and Gusmao (which some will doubtlessly essentialize by highlighting the superficiality of their Irishness, Japaneseness, Indianness, Whiteness, Jewishness or Frenchness, while exposing the gravity of their ignorance) provides a series of overlapping arguments about the individual and the individual's relationship with other individuals. In other words, they have begun paving the way off the *Ship of Fools*. Before the Founding Fathers founded anything, we discover other nascent problems in the Western tradition that gave birth to American democratic liberalism. Hegel likened women to plants. Nietzsche was a misogynist and a hyper-elitist. Yet these were the formulators of the Western philosophical tradition whose debates and intellectual criticism, responses, and counter-criticism paved the way for the contortions of the democratic verve that we have received, and inherited today. The point here is to keep interrogating the so-called philosophical foundations that are often taken for granted. And then we can begin to understand the violence and the political paradox of the politics of American globalization.

ENDNOTES

1   That is, 2313 years if we start counting from the time that Aristotle wrote the eight "books" of the *Politics*, some "books" of which are closer in style that others. See for example the argument in Book VII where Aristotle suggests that, "those who are in a position which places them above toil have stewards who attend to their households while they occupy themselves with philosophy or with politics". Does this not foretell much about the politics of globalization as it is today? See also Books V and VI of Aristotle [350 B.C.], *Politics* (NY: Penguin, 1992).

2   See for example, a brief update by Patricia Dehmer, "The Beauty of Nanoscale Science," US Department of Energy, occasional paper on the study of matter at the atomic scale; see also Ivan Amato, (1991) "The Apostle of Nanotechnology," *Science* 254, no. 5036 (1991): 1310–1; Michel Hehn, Kamel Ounadjela, Jean-Pierre Bucher, Francoise Rousseaux, Dominique Decanini, Bernard Bartenlian, and Claude Chappert, "Nanoscale Magnetic Domains in Mesoscopic Magnets," *Science* 272, no. 5269 (1996), 1782–5; P. M. Ajayan, J. C. Charlier, and A. G. Rinzler, "Carbon Nanotubes: From Macromolecules to Nanotechnology," *Proceedings of the National Academy of Sciences of the United States of America* 96, no. 25 (1999): 14199–200; and Karen L. Wooley, Jeffrey S. Moore, Chi Wu, and Yulian Yang, "Novel Polymers: Molecular to Nanoscale Order in Three Dimensions," *Proceedings of the National Academy of Sciences of the United States of America* 97, no. 21 (2000): 11147–8.

3   See also, "Gene-Rich Human Chromosome 19 Sequence Completed," Department of Energy, Joint Genome Institute, March 31, 2004.

4   Note the US Supreme Court case number 97 U.S. 331.

5   Note the US Supreme Court case number 382 U.S. 34.

6   Note the US Supreme Court case number 381 U.S. 41.

7   Lee Epstein, Jeffrey A. Segal, and Harold J. Spaeth, "The Norm of Consensus on the U.S. Supreme Court," *American Journal of Political Science* 45, no. 2 (2001): 362–77.

8   David A. Skeel, Jr., "The Unanimity Norm in Delaware Corporate Law," *Virginia Law Review* 83, no. 1 (1997): 127–75.

9   Note the US Supreme Court case number 410 U.S. 52.

10   Note the US Supreme Court case number 435 U.S. 589.

11   Note the US Supreme Court case number 121 F. 3d 1357, reversed and remanded.

12   Note the US Supreme Court case number 132 F. 3d 157, vacated and remanded.

13   Note the US Supreme Court case number 425 U.S. 682.

14   Note the US Supreme Court case number 426 U.S. 88.

15   Note the US Supreme Court case number 442 U.S. 653.

16   Note the US Supreme Court case number 448 U.S. 371.

17   Note the US Supreme Court case number 444 U.S. 286.

18   Note the US Supreme Court case number 458 U.S. 858.

19   Alan Howard, and Bruce Howard, "The Dilemma of the Voting Rights Act—Recognizing the Emerging Political Equality Norm," *Columbia Law Review* 83, no. 7(1983): 1615–63.

20   "Pistol Bought Legally," *Chicago Sun Times*, December 9, 1993, 7.

21   Note the US Supreme Court case number 468 U.S. 1315.

22   Note the US Supreme Court case number 467 U.S. 797.

23   Note the US Supreme Court case number 470 U.S. 392.

24   Note the US Supreme Court case number 490 U.S. 122.

25   Henry F. Dobyns, Richard W. Stoffle, and Kristine Jones, "Native American Urbanization and Socio-Economic Integration in the Southwestern United States," *Ethnohistory* 22, no. 2 (1975): 155–79.

26   David Henige, "On the Current Devaluation of the Notion of Evidence: A Rejoinder to Dobyns," *Ethnohistory* 36, no. 3 (1989): 304–7.

27   Franke Wilmer, Michael E. Melody, and Margaret Maier Murdock, "Including Native American Perspectives in the Political Science Curriculum," *PS: Political Science and Politics* 27, no. 2 (1994): 269–76.

28   Robert Michael Franklin, "Response to Leonard Lovett's The Problem of Racism in the Contemporary Pentecostal Movement," PCCNA National Conferences, October 17–19, 1994, Memphis, Tennessee, "Pentecostal Partners: A Reconciliation Strategy for 21st Century Ministry."

29   See "Low Turn Out for Black Awareness March [in London]," *BBC Online*, October 17, 1998. Published at 15:17 GMT 16:17 UK.

30   Official transcript, *Nation of Islam*, September 16, 2001.

31   Consider also Wittgenstein's rejection of Husserl; Sartre's resistance against vulgar Marxism; Einstein's response to Newton; Hawkings' bridge to Einstein; and Skinner's defense of conservative liberal thought.

CHAPTER 8

End Thoughts: The Business of Thinking Broadly

THE PARADOX OF POLITICS

It would seem that some of our greatest achievements in this century have also resulted in our worst fears: poverty, terrorism, viruses, diseases, psychoses, clinical dependency, future uncertainty, cultural insecurity, unemployment, failure, debt, and loss. It would appear that Foucault's description of the *Ship of Fools* represents an uncanny and at times unlikely metaphor for globalization. But seen from the perspective of Asia, and viewed from as far away from the United States as possible, the picture of reality seems to meet the perception of the metaphor. Jean Baudrillard extended this metaphor in his *Simulacra et Simulacrum* when he wrote about the "end of the panopticon." The French cultural historian who died almost 20 years ago, Michel Foucault, treated the idea of the panopticon as a structural device, a functional method of keeping up a permanent gaze over the prisoner in *Discipline and Punish: The Birth of the Prison*. Further back in history, John Stuart Mill's invention of the panopticon enabled a single gatekeeper with the all-seeing eye of a demigod that controlled and watches over us all. Baudrillard, Foucault, and Mill all have one theme in common—they come together in making a distinction between two types of people in modernity. One type desires exhibitionism, and the other desires voyeurism. Globalization is political because it is the net effect of gazes that enhance the meaning of exhibitionism and the voyeurism across the world. We see this in marketing, advertising, public calls to attention for beheading, mock beheading, talking heads, weddings, funerals, baptisms, and birthday parties. We are knowingly and often, unknowingly held victim to the public gaze of authorities and the coercive structures that we invent to protect us from our own kind.

In attempting to promote peace, life, liberty, happiness, hope, optimism and progress across the world, America's role since the Louisiana Land Purchase and the acquisition of Alaska from the Czarist Russia in 1867 has seen the unintended consequence of promoting war, death, incarceration, sadness, hopelessness, pessimism, and regression across the globe. American men and women have paid the ultimate price for American involvement in defending the free world but in that defense, in Korea, Vietnam, the Middle East, and in Latin America, the world has not always accepted the kind of democratic practices that the US has imposed upon these places. Czarist Russia offered to sell off Alaska to the Americans in 1859 and with the defeat after the Crimean War it became even more imperative that the Czar stave off burning a candle on both ends. The balance of power in those days was highly tilted towards the British as a world naval power. British power was so extensive in those days that I would eventually be educated at a Christian missionary school as a result of British power as far away from the British Isles. The school was set up by the Christian Brothers in 1852 and named St. Joseph's Institution, on the tiny, back-water island called Temasek (Singapore) that most people had not heard about since its "discovery" by Stamford Raffles in 1819. The year 1819 marked the end of the Xhosa War with Britain, the end of the Seminole War with America, and the American decision on the Florida Purchase. There are many Americans who prefer to forget the horror and death that was brought about by America in its neo-Imperial quest. The ideals of life, liberty and happiness that brought the early Americans together against the Red Coats of King George would ironically be pursued under America's quest for global supremacy. This is not to say that the world has not benefited from Pax Americana. And there are many reasons for remembering that neo-liberalism in the post-9/11 era is a much lesser evil than the kind of political ideology that the Soviets were espousing had they won the Cold War. Another book should perhaps explore why many Americans are not aware of the political power that brought it into existence and the kinds of atrocities that were done in the name of the American Dream.

GLOBAL GAZE

The power of the Foucauldian gaze is itself a reminder of the other kinds of political derivations that we have experienced in modernity and continue to experience as experience itself, the being of being as an anthology of the arrested self. The deference to expert counsel, the importance of the scientific event, the mercy killing of medical science, the need for pharmaceutical drugs that dominate through the false camouflaged of highly-paid public relations executives who guarantee turning water into wine. The old modernity's dependence on science and technology that Martin Heidegger anticipated and Henry S. Kariel warned us about reveals much about the extent and depth of the new modernity's tentacular forms of control over our daily lives. There are uppers and lowers, drugs to make you high, drugs to make you stoned, drugs to make you forget, drugs to make you remember. There are so many kinds and variations within the global political economy of drugs that after two decades of exposure to the international pharmaceutical giants, we have become as much dependent on them as they are on us. The gaze of the giant pharmacies have been returned with the blank and empty stares of people in late modernity who have been over-medicated, self-medicated, and over-dosed their boredom-filled lives with the reckless cacophony of competing streams of information. How many of us now alive and well in the late urban, post-advanced industrial suburbs of a luxurious life really care about the wondering and suffering masses whose own lives hang on a thin thread of our decisions; whose worthless lives disappear vapidly into the swirling pool of Nietzschean cultural abysses sometimes mistaken for a balanced life of work and play? If you actually managed to have watched television last night it would really be remarkable if you could recall the main stories that were headlined on the screen. It would remarkable if you could recall the pain or the anguish that you might have felt at seeing innocent lives being wasted, or the joy of witnessing youthful playfulness with hope and promise in the local kindergartens and classrooms. It would even more remarkable if you even remembered telling yourself that tomorrow was going to be another and a better day. But it would have been most remarkable if you said that you did not recall anything at all, and did not bother to remember because you believe that there really isn't anything good on television. And that Neil Postman was really amusing himself as he thought of our cultural ends dipping their feelers into the quagmire of a Nixonian death dance— perfectionism till the end. Kant and Hegel may have anticipated the great cosmological motifs that they believed dominated the universal and moral landscapes of philosophy. And they must have gone happily to death because they thought that they were on to something really powerful, and really unique, something that had never had an original starting point, or an image of a simulated past.

But is there hope in late modernity and can all the convictions of past practice convince us that we ought to return to ourselves and know where we stand, know what grounds us and are sufficiently knowledgeable about our own weaknesses and strengths to want to embark on that journey of optimism, hope, and progress? It is one thing to think that the postEnlightenment world is a large and duplicitous deceit; a matrix of confusion that has been cunningly concealed and contrived to convince us of the plausibility of reality and the certitude of truth. But it is quite another to take the urban and legendary bull by the horns and admit to ourselves that we are indeed the inheritors of a great destiny, a great people, a positive and a real future that admits no boundary or structure can bend us from living life to the fullest. We do not really need to build bridges to the 18th century as Postman argues, but bridges that can withstand the weight of late modernity as we know it today. We do not need the textbook histories and confidence tricksters who would have us believe in solid ground but in the kind of controversial and interrogative methods used by Foucault and less ordinarily and more conventionally by writers such as Marshall Sahlins, Henri Lefebvre, David Harvey, and Zygmunt Bauman. Similarly, one would want to consider carefully before being convinced by the latter day prophets in the work of Aldous Huxley, Michael Mann, D. H. Lawrence, Zhang Yimou, George Santayana, George Orwell, Louis Hartz, Gabriel Garcia Marquez, Akira Kurosawa, Paul McCartney, Carl Sagan, and especially Salman Rushdie. We ought to be forewarned about these prophets of modernity because their moral epistemologies—through fiction, film, or fact—are genuine, too authentic, too clever, and too believable. Their work has come to be too readily accessible to the mass marketplace of modernity and consumption. And each of these writers has savagely vindicated the possibility of man's propensity for failure at his own hands, all by himself. In other words, their books are too optimistic to really be read in broad daylight, and are therefore too blinding for globalization viewed from any other part of the world. Yet they continue exist at the top of the trade and in fact revealed interesting values about globalization through their stories and methodical disjuncture. The Asian perspective would warrant a longer list of non-English sounding names whose ethnic ancestry would gravitate towards syntax and symbols that trace the global picture for East Asia, the Pacific Rim, New Zealand and Australia. There are simply too many books that try to explain the view of America from the outside with in qualitative terms or through quantitative analyses. These books share the clear and purposive direction of all modern texts, aims, objectives, definitions, frameworks for analyses, charts, diagrams, illustrations, and conclusions. How can we be so confident as to conclude anything in life? Globalization appears to be shifting us periodically, knowingly, incrementally towards some predestined place and time. We are not necessarily in agreement with the direction of the globe because we really have not many choices for all that is said and done in modernity. There are problems in the *Ship of Fools* because everyone thinks that someone is steering the ship, some people have noticed people steering the ship, and still, others think that someone ought to be steering the ship. But there may not be anyone at all in the wheelhouse, and the ship is really moving fast and purposefully with all the verve and deliberateness of a newfound faith. These accounts were demonstrated through the various quotes on Sahlins argument on the multiple searches for the origins in the apotheosis of a colonial sea-master to the death and Harvey's Weberian-influenced linear delineation of the condition of postmodernity contrast heavily with Lefebvre's contentious predictions about terrorism in his *Everyday Life in the Modern World* (Transaction, 1984) and Zygmunt Bauman's reinvention of modernity from gas, to solid to its liquid states are all remarkably detailed and well-thought out conceptualizations of globalization from within the "United" something or other. These works bear the imprint of powerful diatribes against the urban legends that have returned from the rapid turning of pages over the past 60 years into a political reality that confronts us in life-like images in the newspapers on a daily basis. Globalization appears to center on a political paradox of taking in the good and bad without being able to tell them apart. Like the philosophical moralism of Aldous Huxley, or the first and last postmodernesque film of Akira Kurosawa. It is like voting for the Republican or Democratic parties and hoping that some of our grassroots ideals will be attained and some of our fears vindicated. Globalization involves the sexual innuendoes of Lawrence's wicked novels that have been recast incorrectly and by mistake in the films of a Michael Mann intoxicated with the beauty and power of love in the time of cholera in a soliloquy about the directionless textual motifs of late modernity. The central paradox of the politics of American globalization is that American citizens are left responsible and vulnerable as targets because they have been continuously betrayed by their own governments that they never really elected except through some neutralizing platform and dehumanizing mechanism. Some people call this the Electoral College. Others blame the Senate or the House of Representatives. Most recently, especially since the 2000 President so-called elections, the Judiciary has come under question from legal experts and independent interpreters of the law throughout the US.

Let us recapitulate the paradox of American politics that has impacted modernity. Most Americans since 1945 have not voted for the kinds of politicians and the kind of policies that have come out of American government but still pay the price for being American anyway. This is why Americans seem to believe in one thing but their government appears to be doing something else.

THE POWER OF AYN RAND

Ayn Rand was very influential in New York among the socialites and Republican *crème de la crème*. Her "analytical philosophy," camouflaged under the guise of "objectivism," belied her libertarian economic beliefs. And the Republican Party supporters loved it. Rand lived through the people that she influenced most and of those that she influenced most seemed to have attained high positions in American life. If there was anyone who has tried to achieve greatness as her ideal man in *Atlas Shrugged* (1957), it was Alan Greenspan. Greenspan was to work under many American presidents and became one of her most ardent fans, and a cherished and favored supporter. The problem is that Rand by all accounts is an economic idealist. Like the idealist hero in *Atlas Shrugged*, Rand's vision of the ideal could only be attained through rationality. For her, objectivity is best promoted through economic libertarianism. Rand was great at understanding some parts of the big picture of business but poor on its mathematical aspects. Perhaps this was why she was such a convincing novelist, as seen in *The Fountainhead* (1943) and the bestseller, *Atlas Shrugged*. This means that a significant aspect of her philosophy lacked making sense of the kind of data available to her when she was alive. But this was not even a big problem in her philosophy. The biggest problem was her trust in the kinds of assumptions that she made about economic markets, more specifically, the free market. Her philosophy has been twisted out of its weakness to support what is ostensibly touted as the free market, but what is in effect a democratically controlled,

285

regulated and contrived market. The "free" aspect of the market has nothing to do with that dubious phrase, "the invisible hand." The "free" dimension of the free market refers to neo-liberalism and neo-liberal capital across the globe. But how do we get to go across the globe? This is where the democratically controlled aspect rides into the arena. In other words, as long as a country is willing and able to accept the fable of the democratic free market, it can join the club or remain in fear of being bamboozled, coerced, intimidated and bullied into opening up its markets. To wit, Atlas merely shrugged. He could not get rid of the weight. But what kind of democracy does neo-liberalism offer? We can see that the absence of a proper training in philosophy has misled Rand and her disciples, who have tried vigorously to promote her as a philosopher in ways that Arendt never needed help. Rand is not on the compulsory reading lists of the major centers of philosophy, not even economic philosophy. But her name was raised in this concluding chapter to revise the value of her street-worthiness as a philosopher of sorts. Since Greenspan and others seemed so taken in by her, she has indirectly influenced the nature of the American political economy and hence the politics of its causeway to globalization.

ONE MAN, ONE VOTE

The politics of American globalization is not about the "one-man, one-vote" system. Instead, the democratic dimension of American globalization revolves round the "one-dollar, one-vote" manifesto popularized by the former pro-Republican satirist Arianna Huffington.[1] Money buys votes and as long as players within the public politics of American globalization are willing to remain within the idiom of the American Dream—dramatically supported by its variegated global popular cultures, a willingness to wage war, defended and propped up by the US military in the pursuit of life, liberty and the pursuit of happiness—and to go to the fullest extent of which the law does not expressly forbid. But Huffington is being too harsh. People need hope optimism and progress in this postEnlightenment world, but not the kind of so-called objectivism that Rand provided. Yet ironically, Rand gave to the world a kind of street-level philosophy of elitism that enabled the layman to think that he actually had a hand in changing the economy through free-market libertarianism when in fact all they were doing was buying her popular novel(s). If Rand had not influenced Greenspan's conservatism, America would have taken bigger risks and would have achieved much more materially than it has today. Part of the problem of the politics of American globalization is that no one knows who is going to become the next power holder, and no one can predict the next set of elites that will take hold of political power or economic power in America.

> How do we know when irrational exuberance has unduly escalated asset values which then become the subject of unexpected and prolonged contractions as they have in Japan over the past decade? (Greenspan, 1996)

The Chairman of the US Federal Reserve Board admits that he was very concerned about speculation in the stock market in 1996. A few months later in the summer of 1997, the Asian financial crisis struck. He does have some sense of the impending gloom of the immediate future. In testifying before a Congressional Committee in mid-April 2004, Greenspan said that no one knows the number of illegal immigrants in the country. What they have at best is an estimate. However, they do know that the payroll data and the family income data surveys have matching results. He deduced that the value of the illegal work must be captured by either survey since both surveys have the same result. He also said that it would be a major step ahead in their statistical methods if they manage to figure out the illegal migrant issue. This is clearly a situation where there are problems with the statistical methods used, and perhaps the wrong instruments are being used to compute something that these instruments are not designed to capture. Greenspan also said that there are no indications of wide scale inflationary pressures. And he did support permanent tax cuts in 2002. He also suggested that Social Security be cut in order to solve the problems that the Republicans and the Democrats have created since the end of World War II. What does it mean when influential economic proctors like Greenspan represents both the problems and the solutions of American neo-liberal capitalism?

VAIN GLORY

Certainly, there are political and economic institutions for controlling the Foucauldian gaze. But an intimate knowledge of these formal institutions flowing from the checks and balances system and the structure of shared powers that were created by the Founding Fathers only leads to higher levels of bureaucratic knowledge. Bureaucratic knowledge is limiting because someone who is intimately knowledgeable about the red tape in a system can only quote more red tape. This was what Foucault meant when he referred to the de-centering of the author. Foucault did not mean that we should do away with authors because they were clearly part of the entire set of discursive formations that reveled in society. Rather, that the author—whether s/he was armed with the power of bureaucratic knowledge or not—should take a side-step and not be made the focal point of power relations. Yet if we look at any of the talking heads in Washington, from high powered attorneys and MNC CEOs with Wall Street accomplishments, to the senatorial class of regenerative political families, we immediately know that the author is surviving well in spite of public necessities and public problems. Each vain-glorious politician and political hopeful, to borrow a phrase from Thomas Hobbes's *Leviathan* (1651), hopes to achieve more than the 15 minutes of fame prophesized by the twisted brilliance of Andy Warhol. Each political author and his or her entourage of emotive supporters desire stretching those 15 minutes for as long as the media networks can bear. This makes alignment with popular but nonsensical and elitist authors like Rand a clear strategy in itself doesn't it? However, the politics of American globalization and its norms, values and rules have been influenced more directly by other writers than Rand. Rand's fame came from her book-buying public of unseen and unnamed masses, and her strident students of the elite (like Greenspan). Her effect on the politics of American globalization was indirect. And she received no professional support from any philosopher of merit in the Academy. However, there are those within the Academy who have directly affected America's process of globalization. One of them never even saw America. Adam Smith's highly influential book, *An Inquiry into the Nature and Causes of the Wealth of Nations* (Oxford University Press, 1975) also available as the *Wealth of Nations* (Penguin, 1982; Modern Library, 1994) presupposes the continuing existence of an inordinate mechanism known as the "Invisible Hand." Naturally this phrase also fits in with the views of the governing elite and those of the amicable citizens of his day who wished to perceive this in a spiritual sense that economics was undoubtedly guided by the invisible hand of the Christian God. Regardless of its spiritual roots, the "Invisible Hand" seemed politically resolute. Its role was to resolve all the problems and questions of the economy and hence of civilizational survival. If you needed food, the market mechanism and the "Invisible Hand" would provide it for a fee. If you needed clothing or exotic wares, same thing, you'd go to the market. The idea of the "Invisible Hand" and the "free market mechanism" became so popular among the elite that it actually seemed to work. The culminating point of these successes, inventions and economic activities in the West was called the Industrial Revolution. The "Invisible Hand" of Smith of course is felt throughout the neo-liberal capitalist world. Smith's ideas have in fact outlasted many of the criticisms of his peers, and of critics who have come after him but are not remembered in public by name because they have become so insignificant. Apart from his economic idealism as the *economic advent* of over 200 years (and counting), the most important reason why Smith has become so influential is that his work is so old and crusty that it has been whittled down to its very bare assumptions and continues to be twisted this way and that by economic libertarians, Republicans, Democrats, and greedy neo-liberal capitalists on the ascent.

Therefore Smith's work impacts the process of politics in American globalization because of its idealism and its distance from today's global macro-economy. He achieves this effect in a way that Rand could not. Rather than the value of his microeconomic theories and concepts, Smith's far-sighted vision provides the politics of American globalization with "hope," "optimism," and "progress." These are the three central values of the politics of American globalization. These are the three values that will propel America to selfish individualism and vulgar material achievement regardless of how many times the Al-Qaeda, the CIA-trained Osama bin Laden, the Abu Sayyaf, and the Jemaah Islamiah rears its ugly head. But like the Frankenstein of Mary Shelley's novel of the same name, America has to come to terms with the monster that it has been mainly responsible for creating. The sooner that Americans realize that these terrorists are Cold War relics who now have personal grievances to resolve, the faster will the paranoia that is clouding the US subside and fade away. The terrorists are not as organized as Americans think they are. It is the media that gives some semblance of organization and cohesion in their incredibly irritating, up-to-the-minute updates to ensure that they too survive the politics of American globalization.

The terrorists have to be made redundant so that the focal point of debate and discussion can continue to center—not on the authors and talking heads—but on the three values that are propelling America towards greater selfish individualism and vulgar materialism. Greed is very important, according to the neo-liberal capitalists, for without which there would be no American global economy and political scientists would have a significantly smaller amount of work to do. It would appear that there are significant reasons for giving moral support to these neo-liberal capitalists, since there doesn't seem to be any viable alternative in modernity thus far. Neo-liberalism is like the war in the Middle East. It will never end as long as the oil is there. And since the only viable alternative, socialism, exploded in ethnic violence across Eastern Europe at the end of the Cold War, and only manifested unaccountable greed and corruption among the top flight Communist leaders. Over the past 15 years since the end of the Cold War ostensibly with the fall of the Berlin Wall, the former communist cadres are slowly reinventing themselves as neo-capitalists of a new American age. Human beings have achieved so much failure up till now. And it is sad to think that no one has truly come up with a viable and practical alternative to it. But life must go on despite the drawbacks of the system. Perhaps by understanding its core values, its norms and rules, and its main weaknesses we can create a newer and better system. If you think that this is the case then you certainly are an optimist. I am less than optimistic about such certitude.

AGAINST TERRORISM

Terrorists are wrong because they do not know what they want except to destroy what most sane people desire. They hate the ideals of hope, optimism and progress and are entirely against Big Business in America because they can never be part of that American Dream. They are callous and unfeeling not because they possess some superior political philosophy but because they have marginalized themselves through stupidity and idiocy.

Nevertheless, what seems more interesting despite all that pessimistic funk is that the three values of "hope," "optimism" and "progress" are also central to motivating the rest of the neo-liberal capitalist world as we know it today. This represents the politics of global economic mimicry writ large. The world today is about innovation, reverse engineering, blatant imitation of ideas, concepts and products that seem original. The global village concept has been one that continues to grow and give birth to new ways of getting round government restrictions, loopholes in regional and international agreements, copyright laws, and new ways of making great imitations of overpriced and overvalued merchandise. Modernity no longer needs the management advice of Peter Drucker and his failed attempt at explaining anything when he wrote *The End of Economic Man* (Transaction, 1939) and the *Age of Discontinuities* (1968). Modernity needs to listen more carefully and attentively to the politics of Noam Chomsky. Look for example, without prejudice, at his work titled, *Hegemony or Survival: America's Quest for Global Dominance (The American Empire Project)* (Metropolitan, 2003) and you will understand better the meaning of America's sorrow.

One could also say that despite his age and celebrity status, Drucker has managed something really well. He has reinvented himself repeatedly to the signs of the changing times, unlike the reinvented loopholes that present themselves in other work. One such work is in the politics of reinventing government and economic productivity by Ted Gaebler and David Osborne in their aptly misnamed, *Reinventing Government: How the Entrepreneurial Spirit is Transforming the Public Sector* (Addison-Wesley, 1992), or the myopic, self-aggrandizing, and repetitive journalistic modalities of Thomas Friedman's *Lexus and the Olive Tree: Understanding Globalization* (Anchor, 2000) and his recent *Longitudes and Attitudes: The World in the Age of Terrorism* (Anchor, 2003) were no less than US-centric, capitalistically self-serving, and onerously preachy. And not the much vaunted brilliant guides to globalization and everything else on earth by someone who does not hesitate to draw on the things and activities in modernity that support "hope," "optimism," and "progress." Thomas Friedman is like Milton Friedman but without the academic clout. The younger Friedman is, for want of a better term, a current poster boy for *globalization American style*. But I have a feeling that he is about to be replaced because the second book is not selling as well and hence not making its investors as rich as they could possibly become.

So what could be worse than the attractiveness of the glossy covers of Friedman's books despite his manipulative victimization of the American public? Enter Samuel Huntington's remarkable best-selling *Clash of Civilizations and the Remaking of World Order* (Touchstone, [1996] 1997) that paved the way for more Fukuyama-type work. Huntington proved finally to the American public that he was capable of glossing over minority cultures and zoom in on what he thought were the preeminent cultures that would dominate the world. However, many of the problems of the simplistic arguments in his *Clash of Civilizations and the Remaking of World Order* were glossed over and perhaps even corrected by a more intellectually convincing version that he co-edited with Peter L. Berger called *Many Globalizations: Cultural Diversity in the Contemporary*

World (Oxford University Press, 2003). Based on the work of less than prominent authors (I mean they are not as well known in the US as Huntington), Huntington illustrates once again his prowess as an editor, and of work done for his functional array of books, as seen in the Kovacs chapter on Hungary and the Kellner one on Germany. The most provocative aspect was the final part of the book by Hunter and Yates. Perhaps if we could recommend a book that contains some interesting views this might be the book. Although readers are warned that it repeats its own caution about globalization's steadfast promise of remaining with us from here to eternity.

Globalization is indeed not here to stay forever. But the politics of globalization and the politics of American globalization will continue to manifest itself across the globe for much longer than Smith, Rand, Friedman, Huntington and others think it will. The secret is that neo-liberal capitalism has finally found its new enemy, now that the Soviet bear is gone, while China and India look too promising as neo-liberal markets to destroy militarily through an arms race. The new enemy of neo-liberal capitalism is in fact a bugbear from the Cold War. "International" terrorism is the new enemy. And despite its Islamic front, it isn't an Islamic-only organization. There are many marginalized Americans who have converted to Islam despite being raised on a diet of American popular culture and who have now come under the shadow of suspicion of the American public. This is not surprising. Who else is the American government supposed to suspect? Richard Pryor, David Duke, Oprah Winfrey, Larry King, Jay Leno, Howard Stern, David Letterman, Martha Stewart, O. J. Simpson, John Travolta, Queen Latifah, Michael Moore, Jerry Seinfeld, Arnold Schwarzenegger, Drew Carey, or John Kerry? We all know that the Greenspans, Rumsfelds, Powells, and Bushes are definitely on "our" side. Aren't they? The politics of American globalization and its influence on the world stage can only make it legitimate if the American leadership takes cognizance of the extent of the real problems that plague the world today: poverty, the widening divide between the rich and the poor, terrorism, AIDS, and environmental degradation through the burning of fossil fuels.

COUP DE VILLE

On August 19, 1953, the United States sponsored a *coup d'etat* against Mohammed Mossadeq, the prime minister who was known for being pro-democratic in favor of the Shah of Iran. The US was also involved in the one in Guatemala in 1954, and the one that toppled Salvador Allende Chilean government in 1973. In Nicaragua, the Sandinistas overthrew the US-backed Somoza regime in 1979. Three months after Ronald Reagan took office in 1981, the US announced that it was suspending aid to Nicaragua and allocating US$10 million for the organization of counter-revolutionary groups known as Contras. The Iran-Contra scandal (1983–89) was another exercise that involved congressional hearings and the statements of marine Lieutenant-Colonel Oliver North. The US has also been involved in the CIA's overthrow of democratic governments in Guatemala, Brazil, Chile, Guyana, Iran, Indonesia and Congo (*Lonely Planet*, 2003). There are also publications that allege that the CIA conducted training and support of death squads and repressive secret police in Iran, Indonesia, El Salvador, Chile, Guatemala and Vietnam. However, one might also wish to consider the alternative views offered by MIT professor Noam Chomsky in *Media Control: The Spectacular Achievements of Propaganda* (Seven Stories, 2002), *9-11* (Seven Stories, 2001), and Understanding Power: The Indispensable Chomsky (New Press, 2002).

THE OILY ROOTS OF WAR

The chapter on War in this book examined the problems associated with American global commitment to its neo-liberal ideological design that ostensibly facilitates the democratic transformation across the world. How far true can this be from an America that is struggling to keep its international debt down, its currency afloat and its citizens safe? To what degree can Americans themselves trust their own governments when it takes years if not decades for the system of checks and balances and the work of thousands of university professors daring enough to do original research on topics that would challenge the dominant norms and values that occupy the American mind? What do we really know about the war in Iraq today and how might it be related to oil and the Cold War? The following story tells us about the CIA involvement in propping up and bringing down foreign governments. But it also reveals much about what has been taken for granted about the American way of life.

Honest, hardworking, taxpaying Americans who dutifully vote for their governments have little control over the kinds of decisions that their democratically elected representatives take on their behalf. The primaries are often considered standard benchmarks for the outcome of presidential nominees but the extent to which these nominated leaders are capable of effectively marshalling the resources of political office is an entirely different ball game from the process of getting elected. This is why the distance between idealistic promises and actual political delivery in policy terms appears to be both wide and at times misleading. The American voter ought to expect clarity and purposefulness during the hustlings. The most idealized versions of any political mandate ought to be articulated in the run-up to the polls. However, as we have seen, this is much more complex a problem than it appears on the surface. The political candidate in American modernity has to satisfy the basic funding issues to gain sufficient exposure in the public space. But such exposure also means that long forgotten events and incidents in the candidates life are subject to scrutiny. At the level of presidential candidates, there are considerably greater pressures on the person in question to take a stand about, for example, the foreign policy direction towards the Middle East. Or the real military and economic threat posed by the People's Republic of China. The presidential political candidate has also to be aware about past and present political benefactors and those politicians already in the milieu who might support one aspect of a program but not others. There are many aspects to any one Bill before the Houses of Congress. And there are many miniscule aspects to the way in which a bill passes into law. Even in the construction of bills to be passed, or the meaning of a law might be debatable. There are variances in interpretation by the candidate, the senior senators, congresspersons, chairs of congressional committees, ordinary members of the candidate's political party, and the mass media. This is one reason why Senator John Kerry appeared to be flip-flopping over foreign policy issues in the run up to the November election. And then there is the opposition. Republican Senator Bob Dole, the former Republican presidential nominee believes that Kerry, whom he calls his friend over national television, raised the issue of the legitimacy of Kerry's three purple hearts. Dole recounted his own media fight fest with Clinton where Dole was up against someone who did not even serve. And Dole therefore thinks that it is the issues before America today that are important and not the values held in the 1960s.

Then there is the American public and the perceived demands of the American people. Different people with different views, changing across time and space. Since 2002, Kerry showed himself to be a democratic hawk. However, when word got out that the democratic caucuses wanted an anti-war candidate, he began back-paddling. This resulted in his flip-flopping on whether he was for or against the War in Iraq. There was no consistency of statements in terms of whether he was for or against. He was for the war and then against the war. He was at first against the US$87 billion supplementary budget for the war and then voted for it. On the other hand, the administration of the Republican incumbent George W. Bush misled Americans with regards to the weapons of mass destruction. No wonder Americans prefer to uphold the old adage, "In God We Trust, Everyone Else Pays Cash." But does Kerry or Bush know about the real history of American business and political interests in the Middle East?

In 1979, the Shah of Iran was forced to go into exile by a revolutionary Islamic groundswell against his 57 year old regime. The "Shah" or "Emperor" had virtually ruined the Iranian economy through a systematic squandering of national resources on cronyism and nepotism; torturing of dissidents by the Savak or Iranian secret police; acrimonious business deals with British, French, and US oil companies; and widespread corruption among Islamic leaders, local and foreign businessmen, family members of the Shah, the military, and the government of the emperor. Two years after the fall of the Shah, US Executive Order 12284 raised "Restrictions on the Transfer of Property of the Former Shah of Iran" as noted in the *American Journal of International Law* 75, no. 2 (1981): 431–2. This indicated the extent and depth of the wealth owned by the former monarch in America.

During his reign, the former Shah was caught in a complex political triangle involving the US, the UK, France, and several Arab nations. He was also torn by growing disaffection within his autocratic regime and haunted by his own indecision and political compromises that dogged him till the very end. At one point in the mid-1970s it appeared that he was courting the French with a US$4 billion deal that would resolve some of France's economic problems and in return France promised delivery of five nuclear reactors. Ironically, France was also home to the Islamic ideologue and widely respected Islamic cleric Ayatollah Khomeini who would eventually be swept into power by the pressures from the Islamic ground against the Shah's regime. Mohammed Reza Pahlavi thought he had the Americans in the palm of his hand, but the Americans thought that it was the other way round. So did the French. And the Soviets had their own agenda. In many ways, so did the CIA. American intelligence agents were already been deeply embedded in Iranian society after World War II. The Americans also feared that without the Shah, the special relationship between the American economy that was virtually built on oil would be irrevocably disrupted. This was also the Cold War era. The Soviets hated the fact that American interests could be protected by the Shah so close to their long geographical border with Iran. The Shah ultimately was a Cold War pawn but his fall saw the rise in more problems for America and confirmed the death knell for many future American soldiers who would fight in the two Gulf Wars in 1990 and in 2003. The Shah himself had other plans. He toured India, Pakistan and Singapore to establish warm ties with countries that needed oil. He lived in great splendor in the tradition of his ancestors. He was adored and loved by many within Iran and across the world. Even President Jimmy Carter praised him lavishly to the very end despite tear gas being decanted across the White House lawn.

The British government had continued to control much of the Iranian economy since 1945. The popular Islamic lawyer, Mohammed Mossadeq, was perceived as a threat to US and Allied oil interests and this resulted in their plot against him. The plotters involved anglophile Iranians, clerics and businessmen as well as members of the British intelligence agencies. Both Conservative Party leaders Anthony Eden and Winston Churchill suggested an Anglo-American strategy against Mossadeq. By the mid 1950s, American economic interests were higher than any previous point in history. Iran was also increasingly being courted by Soviet intelligence agencies given its proximity to the Soviet Union. CIA operations were already in place since the end of World War II and were in position to conduct black operations on behalf of US national interests. British MI6 was also involved in kidnapping and coup plotting. Despite these invidious conditions, the Shah continued to rule through the 1970s with the aid of US special advisors and the formation of the notorious secret police called the Savak in 1954. Naturally, in the months that led to the fall of the Shah, attacks against American citizens domiciled in Iran increased. The details of the 1953 coup are detailed in Mark J. Gasiorowski's 1987 article, "The 1953 Coup D'etat in Iran" that was published in the *International Journal of Middle East Studies* in 1987.

Henry Kissinger met with the Shah to negotiate oil prices. The Shah antagonized the other Arab countries by saying that Iran would sell oil to Israel in 1976. Rockefeller's meeting with the Shah involved future business deals that both were planning on implementing. On July 8, 1977, *New York Times* headlined a shouting woman who had disrupted traffic on Fifth Avenue at a luncheon in honor of Empress Farah, the Shah's wife. The writing was on the wall. On September 13, 1977, a car carrying the Shah of Iran's twin sister in Paris, Princess Ashraf Pahlevi, was attacked by gunmen on the French Riviera. Her lady-in-waiting was killed. In November 1977 Jimmy Carter, a wealthy peanut planter from Georgia who became the Democratic president to succeed Republican president Gerald Ford, assured the Shah of the strong relationship between the US and Iran. He praised the Shah for the "strong, stable and progressive Iran." By January 12, 1978, *New York Times* reported an incident where several hundred police officers had to protect the Waldorf-Astoria Hotel where Empress Farah Pavlevi was at a party. There were 200 demonstrators outside, across Park Avenue that shouted "Shah is a fascist butcher, down with the Shah!" Apart from Jimmy Carter, support for the Shah also came from Richard M. Nixon. In 1978, *Time* magazine carried an article where the Shah accused the CIA in 1978 of using dirty tricks since the 1960s to destabilize his regime. On January 16, 1979, the Shah landed at Reese AFB in Texas and by February 12, 1979, the Soviet Union recognized the government of Ayatollah Ruhollah Khomeini. By February 16, 1979, Iran's Islamic Revolutionary Council executed four of the Shah's generals, including the head of Savak by firing squad.

CONCLUSION

Herodotus' view of the ancient world is a romantic beginning for many who subscribe to the ideals of western civilization. The romance of these ancient ideals provides a sense of realism because it creates the possibilities for original starting points. The globe then and the globe now are geographically very similar. But the process of globalization in modernity would be vastly unrecognizable by Herodotus and his contemporaries. Yet the tragedy and the sadness of the past seems to permeate our late modern world. We seem to have come closer to Nietzsche's willingness to break with the past despite the pressures by cultural gatekeepers to retain historical validity, as if that could preserve the future. The role that America plays continues to be fantastic because it returns the complementary and contradictory phenomena of neo-liberalism with its images of hope, optimism and progress. We saw how America is both real and unreal. How it remains one of the most peaceful countries in the world yet is not dispossessed of a history of political and economic violence. America suffers poverty on its own shores, while the richest of the rich bask listless on the widening shores of the almighty greenback. The longest chapter in this book was the third one, as if sixty-odd pages could effectively deliver any view of American modernity from Asia. And yes it did by describing the responses of both large and small nations in Asia towards America. For example, we could have divided it into two separate chapters but I think that the internal consistency would have changed dramatically. The chapter on Asia examined how the US had influenced, directly or indirectly the kinds of global models of successful business models. The subsequent chapters on economy, culture, norms and values tried to reveal the relationships between these aspects of American life and politics in late modernity.

This book has been about the politics of American globalization and how it has manifested itself through its use of military power and cultural norms. In a sense, it is a book that has shown how the world celebrates American successes while simultaneously condemning America's failures. The book is about the need to readjust the formal and informal institutions that constitute the political culture of American globalization, like a large leprosarium where the leper runs the colony and the entire village of lepers all suffer from the same dysfunctional inability to get rid of their diseases, their viruses, and their essentialist paradigms. The *Ship of Fools* metaphor is steered by the criminally insane and mastered by the psychotically disturbed and motored by the neurologically impaired. It therefore has no relationship to American way of life, or the global future in which America plays a powerful role.

PROLOGUE: THE SHIP OF FOOLS

Then a familiar stranger turned and insisted that he listen to the rest of my story about that Black Prison Ship aptly named the *Courageous and the Highly Valiant*. The *Ship of Fools* where prisoners are their own wardens. And sheep look like goats. Insanity rules norm while value steers forward. The *Ship* is moving tremendously as if it were on *speed*. There is a cacophony of voices from various wooden crosses recessed on board that are saying this or arguing about that, and trying to convince each other of the differences and the similarities about *Being and Time*. In the time being, the wooden sailing ship speeds on famously. It has 12 Main Decks made of wrought iron from a little known foundry. There are seven Minor Decks, 77 Cabins, 12 masts, a little known Masonic Lodge, and cotton white wide sails that stretch across thousands of nautical miles.

The entrance to the ship is guarded by Joseph Conrad's two women knitting wool with a funereal air and smoking really expensive Cubans. Yes, sometimes, there is a fire on board the ship. Or someone cuts down the mizzen mast and *replaces* it with 3M duct-tape. But because its imaginary pine furniture is sponsored by *Ikea*, no one can hope to realize that they are being incarcerated by their own vanity, and ego. Sometimes it takes a few years, sometimes centuries. Eventually the memory is erased and the *SMS Courageous and the Valiant* speeds along. It goes on anyway because the *Ship* is much bigger than one can stretch one's eye-balls. One needs at least six days to complete the tour while resting on the seventh day. Millions die on its revolutionary year-round voyages especially in Tourist Class. But at least they serve good Portuguese Port. People are committing suicide from the Crow's Nest, hurtling themselves into the Pacific, making nuclear bombs, killing and maiming one another, surfing the Internet, making small holes in the plywood sideboards, setting fire to the sails, and running naked amok through the narrow passageways with scissors. But there is also loud singing and rejoicing. And old people shaking their heads. Some people look bright-faced and illuminated, smiling while pointing skywards. They hug and embrace each other. There are happy campfire songs, as a stuttering Johnny Mathis wannabe sings A Ray of Hope. Old salts shove people overboard after torturing them for hours. Many watch in horror. And then go back to their shopping at Borders. Karen doesn't allow rubbernecking for more than two seconds. Others return to the football game played across a colossal plasma screen on a high definition television. Those who believe that they are steersmen and oarsmen work strenuously. An original, but friendly slave-driver who looks like a cross between Lawrence Olivier and Joseph Stalin beats a battle drum while Robin Williams tells really good jokes to the rhythm of Gloria Estefan's *The Miami Sound Machine*. In a dark and wet corner of the Lower Deck is a sacred shrine where pilgrims pay homage to an old picture of Dean Martin and Sammy Davis Jr. while drinking cheap tequila and vodka shooters. On the Quarter Deck, Woody Allen hums the Battle Hymn of the Republic of the Galapagos because *Manhattan* was okay, *Annie Hall* was too real, and *Mighty Aphrodite* was a canvass mop. No one leaves their *Post* even when the fast food Galley begins flooding from tropical torrential rains that are a common feature in these parts. The Grand Council of Economic Advisors is made up of the original cast of *Monthy Python* and a fiercely armored rabbit wearing a wire with sharp, pointy teeth. Meanwhile, anadromous Sturgeons work quietly in the ship's General Infirmary, cutting away flesh that causes pain while extending life *For a Few Dollars More*. Don't worry. It's only a flesh wound. Sometimes a miracle happens. But there is only room for one more waiter behind Mel Brooks' reprise of the Last Supper. The National Dance is called the "Fish Slapping Dance." The State Crest is missing, and the State Bird was mugged by a taxi cab driver in a New York Borough. Every Halloween, millions wear Montezuma's death masks and gather under the moonlight to watch Major League Cow Acrobats. The dead are heaped overboard after a quick ceremony involving flowers, wire mesh, chanting, and some police brutality. The Prophet tells them that it's okay, because they've put a Man-in-the-Moon, the cat-in-the-cradle, a dog-in-a-manger, and a pig-in-a-poke. Parts of the floorboards are made of marble chips from fallen boulders along the Pacific Coast Highway. Ancient temples in late modernity are inhabited by carpet-weaving, peace-loving, Persian-tourists while taking a break from acting as suspects for the terrorism police. Other parts of the Main Deck feel like sinking cabbages and sealing wax that the Hunchback of Notre Dame got for Christmas from the walrus and the carpenter's shopping trip to *Jiffy Lube* and *Home Depot*. The staple drink is Lewis Carroll's *Diet Soda* but some concoct their own brews while hiding from anal retentive bureaucrats wearing horn-rimmed glasses and cheap leather shoes. The Upper Deck is carefully regulated and lined with pictures of David Hasslehoff, Sidney Poitier, and *The Third Rock from the Sun*. This Deck is outfitted with security cameras, false mirrors, disappearing stairs, inappropriate mid-drifts, foreign accents, and glass ceilings. People everywhere are dying for TV, while more promises made by used car salesmen are broken by small-time teamster politicos. Unfortunately, the *Ship's* only library near the only 7-11 was burnt down by the First Emperor in a tantrum because the Turtle Dove Soup caught Cold. Ancient Greeks throw decaying philosophical monuments at wondering Bands of Brothers. All of a sudden, six characters from Pirandello's shallow sea chest decide to rest uneasily against the creaking Mizzen Mast while spying another author walking hurriedly. Women and animals, as usual, are "known" in common at the Upper deck, while Men stand in line for years waiting to contract gonorrhea and syphilis. There is blood in the urine and piss on the beer-nuts at all 77 "all-day, all-night" taverns. There is an abundance of food and pornography. Shoes that are made for less than 10 cents on the Upper East Side are sold for 300 times that amount in Greenwich Village. The Port Side dwellers don't know why the Starboard-siders get all the Sun.

The Starboard-side complains that the Port-siders stole an ancient effigy of their God who claimed to have killed as many people in the name of religion as Attila the Hun. Once in a while, some approved communities see God and commit mass suicide. Other communities are charged with writing letters, sewing, and feeding stray cats for *their* dinner. There is one major disease on board the *Ship*. There is also an annual Pride Parade (PP). The PP seems long but in fact is very brief. The route always taken is from the Port-side to the Starboard-side. They navigate by the hot air balloons sponsored by MetLife filled with Sports Commentators and energy watch dogs eating Ruffles Potato Chips (even though McDonald's fries taste better) and chugging huge vats of pink Champaign while the Eagles are forced to replay *Hotel California* on air guitars, or need to travel to faraway places like Bangkok's Impact Center (October 15, 2004), Singapore's Indoor Stadium (October 18, 2004) Hong Kong's Coliseum (October 19, 2004), Sapporo at the Sapporo Dome (October 24, 2004) and Tokyo at the Tokyo Dome (October 30–31, 2004) in order to drum up support for their final years. The PP takes place at the same time each year except for heavy flow days when tropical torrents flood Main Street. Reviewing the PP is a must for the Eco-tourist. For as far as the eye can see, there are rich people, poor people, child molesters, murderers, Saints, agnostics, democratic aristocrats, the Queen, her deceased mother, and Howard Stern standing behind them. There are Republicans, winos, straight talkers, backstreet walkers, David Soul, the Pope, Liv Tyler, Communists, Grand Central Station, and the CEOs of all the major food groups. There are comedians, a milk powder factory, a war-time *consigliere* (plural: *consiglieri*), Billy Bob Thornton's acting debut, the *Young and the Restless*, *ACDC*, *Lavern and Shirley*, Satan, one million marchers from Cambodia's holocaust from 1975–79, an image of the Pharaoh Akhenaton in drag, all the second runners-up of the Miss World Pageant, 1929, and *My Favorite Martian*. The PP is watched by hundreds of millions all over the ship, some from the portholes, some from the decks, some from the mast heads, from under the rotting wood, under milkwood, and under cover. Some watchers watch through tiny holes in their log cabins, while others become scurrilous when they think that they've been caught on poorly-made rip-offs of *Candid Camera*. Sometimes during the PP, prophets dressed in sequins appear. They often sound like the character played by that John Travolta-look alike in *Pulp Fiction*, speaking truthfully but duplicitously while looking at Demi Moore's acting double in *Striptease*. So they drag one across the *Arc De Triumph* and sell pictures

301

of him taken on digital cameras to the locals, as the *Courageous and the Valiant* turns once again into the sunrise, I said to the once-familiar stranger.

ENDNOTES

1   See also Arianna Huffington, *How to Overthrow the Government* (NY: HarperCollins, 2001) and her *Pigs at the Trough: How Corporate Greed and Political Corruption are Undermining America* (NY: Random House, 2003). It has become clear to me that there are really very few differences, if at all, between the Republican Party and the Democratic Party. In their scramble to win over the traditional voters and swing voters on either side. Over the past fifty years, nominees from both parties have conceded so much ground that traditionally fell under the purview of the other side that there aren't any real differences that can be discerned nor measured. I would like to thank Deane E. Neubauer for reminding me that the two parties are like Tweedle-Dee and Tweedle-Dum. The predominance of the Democratic party in the South for example has been eclipsed by the presence of strong Republican support. The national voting public is really not voting along party lines but along personalities as subsequent presidential electioneering contests continue to demonstrate. This means that if Alice in Wonderland were part of the voting public, and she met the Tweedles in the forest, they would be of exactly no help to her at all.

References

Adamson, Walter L. "Beyond 'Reform or Revolution': Notes on Political Education in Gramsci, Habermas and Arendt." *Theory and Society* 6, no. 3 (1978): 429–60.

Aghion, Philippe, and Jeffrey G. Williamson. *Growth, Inequality, and Globalization: Theory, History, and Policy* (Cambridge: Cambridge University Press, 1999).

Ajayan, P., M. J. C. Charlier, and A. G. Rinzler. "Carbon Nanotubes: From Macromolecules to Nanotechnology." *Proceedings of the National Academy of Sciences of the United States of America* 96, no. 25 (1999): 14,199–200.

Alesina, Alberto, and Edward Glaeser. *Fighting Poverty in the US and Europe: A World of Difference* (Oxford: Oxford University Press, 2004).

Althusser, Louis [1968]. *For Marx* (Verso, 1996).

Amato, Ivan. "The Apostle of Nanotechnology." *Science* 254, no. 5036 (1991): 1,310–1.

American Heritage Dictionary of the English Language. 4th ed. (Houghton Mifflin, 2000).

Aristotle [350 B.C.]. *Politics* (NY: Penguin, 1992).

Axelrod, Paul, and Michelle A. Fuerch. "Flight of the Deities: Hindu Resistance in Portuguese Goa." *Modern Asian Studies* 30, no. 2 (1996): 387–421.

Bacchetta, Paola. "When the (Hindu) Nation Exiles Its Queers." *Social Text* 61 (1999): 141–66.

Baker, Jr., Houston A. "Handling 'Crisis': Great Books, Rap Music, and the End of Western Homogeneity" *Callaloo* 13, no. 2 (1990): 173–94.

Bell, Daniel A. "A Communitarian Critique of Authoritarianism: The Case of Singapore." *Political Theory* 25, no. 1 (1997): 6–32.

Berger, Peter L., and Samuel P. Huntington. *Many Globalizations: Cultural Diversity in the Contemporary World* (NY: Oxford University Press, 2003).

Bolce, Louis, and Gerald de Maio. "The Anti-Christian Fundamentalist Factor in Contemporary Politics" *Public Opinion Quarterly* 63, no. 4 (1999): 508–42.

Bowen, Roger W. "Japan's Foreign Policy." *PS: Political Science and Politics* 25, no. 1 (1992): 57–73.

Bragg, Steven M. *Outsourcing: A Guide to Selecting the Correct Business Unit, Negotiating the Contract, Maintaining Control of the Process* (John Wiley & Sons, 1998).

Burks, Arthur W. "Icon, Index, and Symbol." *Philosophy and Phenomenological Research* 9, no. 4 (1949): 673–89.

Calvo, Guillermo A., and Enrique G. Mendoza. "Capital-Markets Crises and Economic Collapse in Emerging Markets: An Informational-Frictions Approach." *American Economic Review* 90, no. 2 (2000): 59.

Camroux, David. "State Responses to Islamic Resurgence in Malaysia: Accommodation, Co-Option, and Confrontation." *Asian Survey* 36, no. 9 (1996): 852–68.

Case, William. "Comparative Malaysian Leadership: Tunku Abdul Rahman and Mahathir Mohamad." *Asian Survey* 31, no. 5 (1991): 456–73.

Case, William. "The UMNO Party Election in Malaysia: One for the Money." *Asian Survey*, 34, no. 10 (1994): 916–30.

Chin, James. "Malaysia in 1997: Mahathir's Annus Horribilis." *Asian Survey* 38, no. 2 (1998): 183–9.

Chomsky, Noam. *9-11* (Seven Stories, 2001).

Chomsky, Noam. *Media Control: The Spectacular Achievements of Propaganda* (Seven Stories, 2002).

Chomsky, Noam. *Understanding Power: The Indispensable Chomsky* (New Press, 2002).

Chomsky, Noam. *Hegemony or Survival: America's Quest for Global Dominance (The American Empire Project)* (New York: Metropolitan Books, Henry Holt and Company, 2003).

Chomsky, Noam. "An Interview with Noam Chomsky." *ZMagazine*, January 2, 2004.

Clarke, Susan E., and Gary L. Gaile. "Local Politics in a Global Era: Thinking Locally, Acting Globally." *Annals of the American Academy of Political and Social Science* 551 (1997): 28–43.

Cnudde, Charles F. and Deane E. Neubauer (eds.). *Empirical Democratic Theory* (Chicago, IL: Markham Publishing Company, 1969)

Collins, Susan M., Barry P. Bosworth, and Dani Rodrik. "Economic Growth in East Asia: Accumulation versus Assimilation." *Brookings Papers on Economic Activity* 2 (1996): 135–203.

Connolly, William E. *Ethos of Pluralization.* (MN: University of Minnesota Press, 1995).

Connolly, William E. "Speed, Concentric Cultures, and Cosmopolitanism." *Political Theory* 28 (2000): 596–618.

Connolly, William E. *Neuropolitics: Thinking, Culture, Speed* (MN: University of Minnesota Press, 2002).

Crafts, N. F. R. "Some Dimensions of the 'Quality of Life' during the British Industrial Revolution." *Economic History Review* 50, no. 4 (1997): 617–39.

Deeb, Mary-Jane. "Militant Islam and the Politics of Redemption." *Annals of the American Academy of Political and Social Science* 524 (1992) 52–65.

Dobyns, Henry F., Richard W. Stoffle, and Kristine Jones. "Native American Urbanization and Socio-Economic Integration in the Southwestern United States." *Ethnohistory* 22, no. 2 (1975): 155–79.

Doganis, Rigas. *Flying Off Course: The Economics of International Airlines* (Routledge, 2002).

Doner, Richard F. "Approaches to the Politics of Economic Growth in Southeast Asia." *Journal of Asian Studies* 50, no. 4 (1991): 818–49.

Drucker, Peter F. *The End of Economic Man.* (Transaction, 1939).

Drucker, Peter F. *Age of Discontinuities* (Transaction, 1968).

Dubin, Steven C. "Symbolic Slavery: Black Representations in Popular Culture." *Social Problems* 34, no. 2 (1987): 122–40.

Earman, John. "Causation: A Matter of Life and Death." *Journal of Philosophy* 73, no. 1 (1976): 5–25.

Emblidge, David. "Down Home with the Band: Country-Western Music and Rock" *Ethnomusicology* 20, no. 3 (1976): 541–52.

Epstein, Lee, Jeffrey A. Segal, and Harold J. Spaeth. "The Norm of Consensus on the U.S. Supreme Court." *American Journal of Political Science* 45, no. 2 (2001): 362–77.

Eribon, Didier. *Michel Foucaul,* trans. by Betsy Wing (Cambridge, MA: Harvard University Press, 1991).

Espino, Ovidio Diaz. *How Wall Street Created a Nation: JP Morgan, Teddy Roosevelt, and the Panama Canal* (NY: Four Walls Eight Windows, 2001).

Euben, J. Peter. *The Tragedy of Political Theory.* (Princeton, NJ: Princeton University Press, 1990).

Fanon, Franz, [1952]. *Black Skin, White Masks* (MacGibbon and Kee, 1968).

Fanon, Franz, [1961]. *The Wretched of the Earth* (MacGibbon and Kee, 1968).

Farazmand, Ali. "Globalization and Public Administration." *Public Administration Review* 59, no. 6 (1999): 509–22.

Femia, Joseph V. "Gramsci's Patrimony." *British Journal of Political Science* 13, no. 3 (1983): 327–64.

Fernea, Elizabeth Warnock, and Basima Qattan Bezirgan, eds. *Middle Eastern Muslim Women Speak* (Austin, TX: University of Texas Press, 1978).

Foucault, Michel, [1965]. *Madness and Civilization* (NY: Vintage, 1988).

Fox, William S., and James D. Williams. "Political Orientation and Music Preferences Among College Students." *Public Opinion Quarterly* 38, no. 3 (1974): 352–71.

Franchot, Jenny. "Unseemly Commemoration: Religion, Fragments, and the Icon." *American Literary History* 9, no. 3 (1997): 502–21.

Franklin, Robert Michael "Response to Leonard Lovett's The Problem of Racism in the Contemporary Pentecostal Movement" PCCNA National Conferences, October 17-19, 1994. Memphis, Tennessee, 'Pentecostal Partners: A Reconciliation Strategy for 21st Century Ministry'.

Freedman, Maurice, and Marjorie Topley. "Religion and Social Realignment among the Chinese in Singapore." *Journal of Asian Studies* 21, no. 1 (1961): 3–23.

Friedman, Thomas. *Lexus and the Olive Tree: Understanding Globalization* (Anchor, 2000).

Friedman, Thomas. *Longitudes and Attitudes: The World in the Age of Terrorism* (Anchor, 2003).

Gaebler, Ted, and David Osborne. *How the Entrepreneurial Spirit is Transforming the Public Sector* (Addison-Wesley, 1992).

Gasiorowski, Mark J. "The 1953 Coup D'etat in Iran" *International Journal of Middle East Studies* 19, no. 3 (1987):261-286.

Gaston, John C. "The Destruction of the Young Black Male: The Impact of Popular Culture and Organized Sports." *Journal of Black Studies* 16, no. 4 (1986): 369–84.

Gillespie, Jr., J. Lodge. "Rhetoric and Reality: Corporate America's Perceptions of Southeast Asia, 1950–1961." *Business History Review* 68, no. 3 (1994): 325–63.

Griffin, James M., and Weiwen Xiong. "The Incentive to Cheat: An Empirical Analysis of OPEC." *Journal of Law and Economics* 40, no. 2 (1997): 289–316.

Groth, Alexander J. "The Politics of Xenophobia and the Salience of Anti-Semitism." *Comparative Politics* 4, no. 1 (1971): 89–108.

Hall, Pamela D. "The Relationship Between Types of Rap Music and Memory in African American Children." *Journal of Black Studies* 28, no. 6 (1998): 802–14.

Harrison, Bernard. "Judaism." *Annals of the American Academy of Political and Social Science* 256 (1948): 25–35.

Hart-Landsberg, Martin, and Paul Burkett. "Contradictions of Capitalist Industrialization in East Asia: A Critique of 'Flying Geese' Theories of Development." *Economic Geography* 74, no. 2 (1998): 87–110.

Hartung, William D. "Eisenhower's Warning: The Military-Industrial Complex Forty Years Later." *World Policy Journal* 18 (2001): 1.

Hawley, James P. "Antonio Gramsci's Marxism: Class, State and Work." *Social Problems* 27, no. 5 (1980): 584–600.

Hehn, Michel, Kamel Ounadjela, Jean-Pierre Bucher, Francoise Rousseaux, Dominique Decanini, Bernard Bartenlian, and Claude Chappert. "Nanoscale Magnetic Domains in Mesoscopic Magnets." *Science* 272, no. 5269 (1996): 1782–5.

Henderson, Errol A. "Black Nationalism and Rap Music." *Journal of Black Studies* 26, no. 3 (1996): 308–39

Henderson, Errol A. "Neoidealism and the Democratic Peace." *Journal of Peace Research* 36, no. 2 (1999): 203–31.

Henderson, Mae G. "Ghosts, Monsters, and Magic: The Ritual Drama of Larry Neal." *Callaloo* 23 (1985): 195–214.

Hobbes, Thomas (trans.) *Thucydides' The Peloponnesian War* (Chicago, IL: University of Chicago Press, 1959). Notes and introduction by David Greme.

Howard, Alan, and Bruce Howard. "The Dilemma of the Voting Rights Act—Recognizing the Emerging Political Equality Norm." *Columbia Law Review* 83, no. 7 (1983): 1615–63.

Huffington, Arianna. *How to Overthrow the Government* (NY: HarperCollins, 2001).

Huffington, Arianna. *Pigs at the Trough: How Corporate Greed and Political Corruption are Undermining America* (NY: Random House, 2003).

Huffington, Arianna. *Fanatics and Fools: The Game Plan for Winning America Back* (Hyperion, 2004).

Huntington, Samuel P., [1996]. *Clash of Civilizations and the Remaking of World Order* (Touchstone, 1997).

Hussaina J. Abdullah, and Ibrahim Hamza. "Women Need Independent Ownership Rights." Paper presented at an international workshop on *Women and Land In Africa*, Emory University Law School, Atlanta, Georgia, in collaboration with Associates for Change, Kampala, Uganda, at the Entebbe Beach Hotel, April 24–25, 1998.

Ilinitch, Anne Y., Richard A. D'Aveni, and Arie Y. Lewin. "New Organizational Forms and Strategies for Managing in Hypercompetitive Environments." *Organization Science* 7, no. 3 (1996): 211–20.

Ingersoll, Ernest. "Decoration of Negro Graves." *Journal of American Folklore* 5, no. 16 (1892): 68–9.

Inniss, Leslie B., and Joe R. Feagin. "The Cosby Show: The View from the Black Middle Class." *Journal of Black Studies* 25, no. 6 (1995): 692–711.

Inoguchi, Takashi. "Japan's Response to the Gulf Crisis: An Analytic Overview." *Journal of Japanese Studies* 17, no. 2 (1991): 257–73.

Jackson, Bernard S. "The Prophet and the Law in Early Judaism and the New Testament." *Cardozo Studies in Law and Literature* 4, no. 2 (1992): 123–66.

Jessop, Bob. State *Theory: Putting Capitlist States in their Place* (University Park, PA: Pennsylvania State University Press).

Johnson, D. Gale. "Population, Food, and Knowledge." *American Economic Review* 90, no. 1 (2000): 1–14.

Jorion Philippe, and William N. Goetzmann. "Global Stock Markets in the Twentieth Century." *Journal of Finance* 54, no. 3 (1999): 953–80.

Juergensmeyer, Mark. "Christian Violence in America." *Annals of the American Academy of Political and Social Science* 558 (1998): 88–100.

Kahin, Audrey R. "Crisis on the Periphery: The Rift Between Kuala Lumpur and Sabah" *Pacific Affairs* 65, no. 1 (1992): 30–49.

Kariel, Henry S. "Nietzsche's Preface to Constitutionalism" *Journal of Politics* 25, no. 2 (1963): 211-225.

Kariel, Henry S. *Desperate Politics of Postmodernism* (MA: University of Massachusetts Press, 1989).

Karliner, Joshua. *The Corporate Planet: Ecology and Politics in the Age of Globalization* (Sierra Club Books, 1997).

Katzenstein, Peter J. "Regionalism in Comparative Perspective." *Arena Working Papers*, 96/1 (1996).

Katzenstein, Peter J., Robert O. Keohane, and Stephen D. Krasner. "International Organizations and the Study of World Politics." *International Organization* 52, no. 4 (1998): 645–85.

Kissinger, Henry A. "Thayer Award Speech." *USMA West Point*, September 13, 2000.

LaFleur, William. "Points of Departure: Comments on Religious Pilgrimage in Sri Lanka and Japan." *Journal of Asian Studies* 38, no. 2 (1979): 271–81.

Landsberg, Marge E. "The Icon in Semiotic Theory" *Current Anthropology* 21, no. 1 (1980): 93–5.

Laurence, Henry. "Financial System Reform and the Currency Crisis in East Asia." *Asian Survey* 39, no. 2 (1999): 348–73.

Levine, Daniel H. "Popular Groups, Popular Culture, and Popular Religion." *Comparative Studies in Society and History* 32, no. 4 (1990): 718–64.

Levy, Gidon, and Udi Adiv. "The Jew the State Thinks is an Arab." *Journal of Palestine Studies* 13, no. 2 (1984): 176–8.

Liebman, Charles, and Bernard Susser. "Judaism and Jewishness in the Jewish State." *Annals of the American Academy of Political and Social Science* 555 (1998): 15–25.

Long, William J. "Nonproliferation as a Goal of Japanese Foreign Assistance." *Asian Survey* 39, no. 2 (1999): 328–47

Lucier, V. A. "'Offrenda' on All-Souls' Day in Mexico." *Journal of American Folklore* 10, no. 37 (1897): 106–7.

Makin, Tony. "Preventing Financial Crises in East Asia." *Asian Survey* 39, no. 4 (1999): 668–78.

Martinez, Delores, ed. *The Worlds of Japanese Popular Culture: Gender, Shifting Boundaries and Global Culture* (Cambridge: Cambridge University Press, 1998).

Mauzy, Diane K., and R. S. Milne. "The Mahathir Administration in Malaysia: Discipline through Islam" *Pacific Affairs* 56, no. 4 (1983–84), 617–48.

May, Brian. "Memorials to Modernity: Postcolonialism and Pilgrimage in Naipaul and Rushdie." *ELH* 68, no. 1 (2001): 241–65.

Maynard, Patrick. "The Secular Icon: Photography and the Functions of Images." *Journal of Aesthetics and Art Criticism* 42, no. 2 (1983): 155–69.

McFadden, George. "Nietzschean Values in Comic Writing" *Boundary 2* 9, no. 3 (1981): 337–58.

Merriam-Webster Online Dictionary. Available online at http://www.webster.com/.

Michaels, Walter Benn. "An American Tragedy, or the Promise of American Life." *Representations* 25 (1989): 71–98.

Miller, David B. "Legends of the Icon of Our Lady of Vladimir: A Study of the Development of Muscovite National Consciousness." *Speculum* 43, no. 4 (1968): 657–70.

Moen, Matthew C. "The Evolving Politics of the Christian Right." *PS: Political Science and Politics* 29, no. 3 (1996): 461–4.

Neubauer, Deane E. "Some Conditions of Democracy" *American Political Science Review* 61, no. 4 (1967): 1002-1009.

Neubauer, Deane E. "Hawaii State Budget: Budgeting in the Year of the Shortfall" *Proceedings from a Comparison of Thirteen Western States*, Budget Roundtable, Western Political Science Association, Center for Public Policy, University of Utah, March 1996.

Neubauer, Deane E. and Kastner, Lawrence, "The Study of Compliance Maintenance as a Strategy for Comparative Research," *World Politics*, July (1969):629-640.

Neubauer, Deane E., and Robert Alan Dahl. *Readings in Modern Political Analysis* (Englewood Cliffs, N.J.: Prentice-Hall, 1974).

Norton, R. D. "Industrial Policy and American Renewal" *Journal of Economic Literature* 24, no. 1 (1986): 1–40.

O'Loughlin, John, and Luc Anselin. "Geo-Economic Competition and Trade Bloc Formation: United States, German, and Japanese Exports, 1968–1992." *Journal of Economic Geography* 72, no. 2 (1996): 131–60.

Parsons, Elsie. "All-Souls Day at Zuni, Acoma, and Laguna." *Journal of American Folklore* 30, no. 118 (1917): 495–6.

People's Mojahedin Organization of Iran v. United States Department of State and Madeleine K. Albright, Secretary of State (1999).

Perris, Arnold. "Feeding the Hungry Ghosts: Some Observations on Buddhist Music and Buddhism from Both Sides of the Taiwan Strait." *Ethnomusicology* 30, no. 3 (1986): 428–48.

Peterson Indira V. "Singing of a Place: Pilgrimage as Metaphor and Motif in the Tevaram Songs of the Tamil Saivite Saints." *Journal of the American Oriental Society* 102, no. 1 (1982): 69–90.

Pfaltzgraff, Jr., Robert L. "The Emerging Global Security Environment." *Annals of the American Academy of Political and Social Science* 517 (1991): 10–24.

Piccone, Paul. "Gramsci's Hegelian Marxism." *Political Theory* 2, no. 1 (1974): 32–45.

Piccone, Paul. "Gramsci's Marxism: Beyond Lenin and Togliatti." *Theory and Society* 3, no. 4 (1976): 485–512.

Postman, Neil. *Building a Bridge to the 18th Century: How the Past Can Improve Our Future* (New York: Vintage Books: 2000).

Powell, Colin L. "Thayer Award Acceptance Remarks." *USMA West Point*, September 15, 1998.

Pryor, Frederic L. "The Impact of Foreign Trade on the Employment of Unskilled U. S. Workers: Some New Evidence." *Southern Economic Journal* 65, no. 3 (1999): 472–92.

Ra'Anan, Uri. "Soviet Strategic Doctrine and the Soviet-American Global Contest" *Annals of the American Academy of Political and Social Science* 457 (1981): 8–17.

Rappa, Antonio L. "Modern Death Dances: The Irreverent Politics of Postmodernism." *Sincronia* (Spring/Primavera, 1998).

Rappa, Antonio L. "Urban Political Theory and the Symmetrical Model of Community Power," *Innovation: European Journal of Social Science Research* 14, no. 1 (2001): 5-16.

Rappa, Antonio L. *Modernity and Consumption: Theory, Politics and the Public in Singapore and Malaysia* (Singapore and New Jersey: World Scientific, 2002).

Rappa, Antonio L. "Modernity and the Contingency of the Public" in "Modernity and the Politics of Public Space." *Innovation—The European Journal of Social Science Research* 15 (2002): 1.

Rappa, Antonio L., and Lionel Wee. *Language Policy and Modernity in Southeast Asia* (forthcoming, complete proofs available from authors)

Reischauer, Edwin O., and Marius B. Jansen, eds. *The Japanese Today: Change and Continuity.* (Cambridge, MA: Harvard University Press, 1995).

Romm, James S. *Herodotus* (New Haven, CT: Yale University Press, 1998).

Rose, Tricia. "'Fear of a Black Planet': Rap Music and Black Cultural Politics in the 1990s." *Journal of Negro Education* 60, no. 3 (1991): 276–90.

Rosenfield, Sarah. "Factors Contributing to the Subjective Quality of Life of the Chronic Mentally Ill." *Journal of Health and Social Behavior* 33, no. 4 (1992): 299–315.

Roy, Denny. "Singapore, China, and the 'Soft Authoritarian' Challenge." *Asian Survey* 34, no. 3 (1994): 231–42.

Roy, Parama. "Oriental Exhibits: Englishmen and Natives in Burton's Personal Narrative of a Pilgrimage to Al-Madinah & Meccah." *Boundary 2*, no. 22 (1995): 1, 185–210.

Rushdie, Salman. *The Satanic Verses* (Viking, 1989).

Rushdie, Salman. *The Moor's Last Sigh* (Vintage, 1997).

Sawyer, Darwin O. "Public Attitudes Toward Life and Death." *Public Opinion Quarterly* 46, no. 4 (1982): 521–33.

Scalapino, Robert A. "The United States and Asia in 1998." *Asian Survey* 39, no. 1 (1999): 1–11.

Schilling, Mark. *The Encyclopedia of Japanese Pop Culture* (Weatherhill Publications, 1997).

Schlosser, Eric. *Reefer Madness and Other Tales from the American Underground* (London: Penguin Books, 2003).

Scholte, Jan Aarte. "Global Capitalism and the State." *International Affairs* 73 (1997): 3.

Shapiro, James. *Shakespeare and the Jews* (Columbia University Press, 1997).

Shusterman, Richard. "Pragmatist Aesthetics and Popular Culture." *Poetics Today* 14, no. 1 (1993): 99–100.

Sikorski, Douglas. "Effective Government in Singapore: Perspective of a Concerned American." *Asian Survey* 36, no. 8 (1996): 818–32.

Sisci, Francesco. "La démaoization de la Chine." *Le Grand Soir*: *Asiatimes*, November 10, 2002.

Skeel, Jr., David A. "The Unanimity Norm in Delaware Corporate Law." *Virginia Law Review* 83, no. 1 (1997): 127–75.

Smil, Vaclav. "China's Energy and Resource Uses: Continuity and Change." *China Quarterly* 156 (1998): 935–51.

Smith, Adam. *An Inquiry into the Nature and Causes of the Wealth of Nations* (Oxford: Oxford University Press, 1975).

Smith, Adam. *The Wealth of Nations* (NY: Penguin, 1982).

Smith, Adam. *The Wealth of Nations* (Modern Library, 1994).

Smith, R. B. "An Introduction to Caodaism II. Beliefs and Organization." *Bulletin of the School of Oriental and African Studies* 33, no. 3 (1970): 573–89.

Song, Xue. "American Poverty and Welfare Reform." *Perspectives* 2, no. 6 (June 30, 2001).

Spieser, J. M. "The Representation of Christ in the Apses of Early Christian Churches." *Gesta* 37, no. 1 (1998): 63–73.

Stark, Oded. "Altruism and the Quality of Life" *American Economic Review* 79, no. 2 (1989): 86–90.

Sugimoto, Yoshio. *An Introduction to Japanese Society* (Cambridge: Cambridge University Press, 2002).

Tucker, Bruce. "Tell Tchaikovsky the News: Postmodernism, Popular Culture, and the Emergence of Rock 'N' Roll." *Black Music Research Journal* 9, no. 2 (1989): 271–95.

Tyson, Brian F. "Ben Jonson's Black Comedy: A Connection between Othello and Volpone." *Shakespeare Quarterly* 29, no. 1 (1978): 60–6.

Ulmer Jr., Walter F., Joseph J. Collins, and T. O. Jacobs, eds. *American Military Culture in the Twenty-First Century: A Report of the CSIS International Security Program* (Washington DC: Center for Strategic and International Studies, 2000).

Urbinati, Nadia. "From the Periphery of Modernity: Antonio Gramsci's Theory of Subordination and Hegemony." *Political Theory* 26, no. 3 (1998): 370–91.

United States of America v. Oliver L. North (1990).

Wacker, R. Fred. "Assimilation and Cultural Pluralism in American Social Thought" *Phylon* 40, no. 4 (1979): 325–33.

Weiss, Anita M. "Women's Position in Pakistan: Socio-cultural Effects of Islamization." *Asian Survey* 25, no. 8 (1985): 863–80.

Werbner, Richard. "The Suffering Body: Passion and Ritual Allegory in Christian Encounters." *Journal of Southern African Studies* 23, no. 2 (1997): 311–24.

West, Cornel. "A Matter of Life and Death." *October* 61 (1992): 20–3.

West, Cornel. *Keeping Faith: Philosophy and Race in America* (New York: Routledge, 1993).

Wilmer, Franke, Michael E. Melody, and Margaret Maier Murdock. "Including Native American Perspectives in the Political Science Curriculum." *PS: Political Science and Politics* 27, no. 2 (1994): 269–76.

Witkin, Robert W. "Constructing a Sociology for an Icon of Aesthetic Modernity: Olympia Revisited." *Sociological Theory* 15, no. 2 (1997): 101–25.

Woodall, Brian. (1993) "The Logic of Collusive Action: The Political Roots of Japan's Dango System." *Comparative Politics* 25, no. 3 (1993): 297–312.

Wooley, Karen L., Jeffrey S. Moore, Chi Wu, and Yang Yulian. (2000) "Novel Polymers: Molecular to Nanoscale Order in Three Dimensions." *Proceedings of the National Academy of Sciences of the United States of America* 97, no. 21 (2000): 11,147–8.

Yasutomo, Dennis T. "Why Aid? Japan as an Aid Great Power." *Pacific Affairs* 62, no. 4 (1989–90): 490–503.

Young, Kenneth T. "Asia and America at the Crossroads." *Annals of the American Academy of Political and Social Science* 384 (1969): 53–65.

Zahralddin-Aravena, Rafael X. "Chile and Singapore: The Individual and the Collective, A Comparison." *Emory International Law Review* 12, no. 2 (1998): fn. 153.

Author Index

Achebe, Chinua, 99
Adorno, Theodore, 218–219
Aghion, Philippe, 18, 303
Ali Farazmand, 71n2
Arendt, Hannah, 12
Aristotle, 34, 185
Arrow, Kenneth J., 226–227
Avineri, Schlomo, 5
Axelrod, Paul, 41–42n12, 303

Baudrillard, Jean, 222
Bauman, Zygmunt, 5, 283–285
Berkeley, George, 25, 276
Bhabha, Homi, 139, 177
Bosworth, Barry P., 141n1
Botwinick, Aryeh, 5
Burke, Edmund, 107
Burks, Arthur W., 42n12
Butler, Judith, 5, 211, 222, 277

Calvo, Guillermo A., 40n5
Case, William, 245n8, 304
Cassidy, John, 110
Chan, Heng Chee, 76
Chan, Sewell, 71n3
Chomsky, Noam, 104, 142n12, 204–205, 206n6, 293, 304
Chua, Amy L., 138
Clarke, Susan E., 21, 40n6, 304
Cohen, Joshua, 5
Conrad, Joseph, 26
Connolly, William E., 5, 18, 220, 246n13, 304
Crafts, N. F. R., 40n7

D'Aveni, Richard A., 40n6
Derrida, Jacques, 24
Dewey, John, 226
Dittmer, Lowell, 116
Doganis, Rigas, 83, 304
Doner, Richard F., 141n1

Earman, John, 41n8
Eastburn, Kathryn, 72n6
Emblidge, David, 245n10
Euben, J. Peter, 1, 5, 40n2, 267
Ezekiel, Raphael S., 221

Feagin, Joe R., 246n18
Femia, Joseph V., 246n16
Ferguson, Kathy E., 33, 211
Foucault, Michel, iii–ix, 20, 45, 50, 64, 66–67, 73, 178, 221–222, 242, 243n1, 280, 281, 305
    Bethnal Green, 186
    oblivion, 127
    prisoners of the passage, 40
    values, 90
    Western modernity, 33–34
Friedman, Milton, 291
Friedman, Thomas, 291, 305
Fromm, Eric, 219
Fuerch, Michelle A., 41–42n12
Fukuyama, Francis, 12

Gaile, Garry L., 21, 40n6
Gillespie, J. Lodge, 73, 141n1
Gilpin, Robert, 14–15
Goetzmann, William N., 13, 40n5
Goldenberg, Suzanne, 42n14

Gouldner, Alvin, 222
Gowa, Joanne, 15
Gramsci, Antonio, 220–221, 227, 246n16
Groth, Alexander J., 244n5

Habermas, Jurgen, 5, 24, 227
Hall, Pamela D., 245n9
Harvey, David, 5, 283
Hegel, G. W. F., 152, 276–277, 282
Heidegger, Martin, 12, 219, 282
    and technology, 29, 74–75
Henderson, Errol, 144n27
Henderson, Mae G., 247n20
Herodotus, 1, 297
Hobbes, Thomas, 288, 306
    Corcyra and Hermocrates, 184
    Corinthians, 65
    Miletus in the Peloponnesian War, 49
    opportunities for action, 162
Homer, 27
Horkheimer, Max, 218–219
Howard, Alan, 279n19
Huffington, Arianna, 50, 286, 302n1
Hume, David, 25, 276
Huntington, Samuel, 291
Hussiana J. Abdullah, 34, 42n16
Hypolite, 277

Ibrahim Hamza, 34, 42n16
Ilinitch, Anne Y., 40n6
Ingersoll, Ernest, 247n20
Inglehart, Ronald, 72n9
Inniss, Leslie B., 246n18
Inoguchi, Takashi, 144n26

Jackson, Bernard S., 41n9
Jameson, Fredric, 5, 39
Jaspers, Karl, 219
Jessop, Bob, 157
Johnson, D. Gale, 40n7
Jorion, Philippe, 13, 40n5
Juergensmeyer, Mark, 41n9

Kammen, Michael, 50
Kant, Immanuel, 2, 276, 282
Kariel, Henry S., 30, 146, 246n13, 282
Katzenstein, Peter J., 29, 40n4, 116, 132, 143n25
Keohane, Robert, 132, 143n25
Keynes, John Maynard, 15, 27, 149
Kipling, Rudyard, 103
Krasner, Steven D., 132, 143n25
Krueger, Anne O., 142n10
Kubler-Ross, Elisabeth, 178

Larmore, Charles, 5
Laurence, Henry, 120, 143n19
Lash, Scott, 5, 18
Lefebvre, Henri, 39, 283
Levine, Daniel H., 246n14
Lewin, Arie Y., 40n6
Lewis, Bernard, 41n9
Lim, Siong Guan, 143n22
Lippmann, Walter, 226
Lipsett Seymour Martin, 249
Locke, John, 25, 276
Luo, Yadong, 125
Lucier, V. A., 247n20
Lyotard, Jean Francois, 5, 24

Machiavelli, Niccolo, 110
Madison, James, 194, 221, 274

Makin, Tony, 143n18
Mandel, Ernest, 159
Mann, Michael, 159
Marcuse, Herbert, 5, 218
Marx, Karl, 25, 39, 227
Mauzy, Diane K. and Milne, R. S.,
    245n8
May, Brian, 42n13
Mearsheimer, John, 15
Mendoza, Enrique G., 40n5
Michaels, Walter Benn, 219,
    245n12
Mill, John Stuart, 280
Miller, Nathan, 156
Mittelman, James H., 18–19
Moon, Katherine H. S., 201–202

Naipaul, V. S., 139, 177, 232
Narayan, R. K., 5
Neubauer, Deane E., 5, 302n1, 304
Nietzsche, Friedrich, 24, 146, 229,
    277, 282
    "herd-like mentality", 31
    madman, 221
    McFadden on Nietzsche,
    246n18
    narrative and metanarrative,
    178–179
Norton, R. D., 43
Nye, Joseph S., 227

Pareto, Alfredo, 149–150
Parsons, Elsie Clews, 247n20
Patrick, Hugh, 44
Perris, Arnold, 247n20
Perry, Elizabeth J., 93
Pfaltzgraff, Jr. Robert L., 71n2
Postman, Neil, 5, 145, 231, 272

Popper, Karl, 27
Pryor, Frederick L., 142n2

Ra'Anan, Uri, 71n2
Rappaport, Roy A., 5
Robinson, Bill, 93
Rodrik, Dani, 141n1
Romm, James S., 40n1
Rorty, Richard, 5
Rosenfield, Sarah, 40n7
Rushdie, Salmon, 41n11

Sahlins, Marshall D., 5, 283–285
Said, Edward W., 38, 89–90
Sartre, Jean Paul, 21, 277, 279n31
Scheer, Robert, 42n15
Schlosser, Eric, 53–54, 72n7
Schram, Stanford, 46–47
Schultz, George, 32–33, 186
Shklar, Judith N., 5
Shusterman, Richard, 247n22
Sisci, Francesco, 141n4
Skeel, David A., 262
Skinner, Quentin, 279n31
Smith, Adam, 15, 148–149, 288–
    289
Smith, Tony, 5
Song, Xue, 72n4
Stark, Oded, 40n7
Stiglitz, Joseph, 138, 149
Strange, Susan, 18

Thucydides, 14, 44, 162
Tilly, Charles, 5
Thomas, John W., 143n22
Tucker, Bruce, 247n21
Turnbull, Phyllis, 33
Tyson, Bryan F., 246, 246n17

Urbinati, Nadia, 246n16

Vattimo, Gianni, 5
Vietnamese, and the Vietnam War, 94

Wallestein, Immanuel, 39
Waltz, Kenneth, 15
Weber, Max, 275
    iron-cage syndrome, 11, 63–64
West, Cornell, 22, 72n5

White Stephen K., 5
Williamson, Jeffrey G., 18
Wittgenstein, Ludwig von, 279n31
Witkin, Robert W., 41n12

Yaverbaum, Eric, 177
Young, Kenneth T., 141

Zahralddin-Aravena, Rafael X.,
    142n5

Subject Index

666 (the numbers), 30, 112
9/11, 36–37, 112
    post 9/11, 57, 91

Abdullah Ahmad Badawi, 98, 100,
    133, 142n9
Afghans, 267
African-Americans, 205
    Black people, 243n3
Air France v. Saks (1985), 264
Airbus Industrie and Airbus S. A. S.,
    80
airline business, 74–77
Al-Qaeda, 64–65, 113, 289
Alaska Purchase, 277
Alfred Dunhill of London v. Cuba
    (1976), 263
America and the Asian financial
    crisis, 116–122
America's political paradox,
    103–108, 280
American
    globalization, definition of, 6
    popular culture, 130, 208–247
American CEOs, 68, 163–174, 225
    American Dream, 31–32, 84,
        236–237, 242–243, 290–291
    atrocities, 281
    public space, 232–237
    hero, 267
American MNCs, 6, 15, 54–55, 68,
    157–158, 163–179, 237
Ancien Regime, 238
Ancient Greeks, 300
anti-Americanism, 110

anti-Semitism, 110, 134, 214–215
anti-white, 272
Anwar Ibrahim, 98, 244n7
    marginalization, 99–100, 142n9
Appomattox, 93
Articles of Confederation, 10
ASEAN, 91, 96
Asian
    bourses, 119–120
    Free Trade Agreement, 95
    financial crisis, 101–102,
        116–122
Australian, 284

Bharathiya Janata Party (BJP), 126
BBC World, 70
Berlin Airlift, 195
Bill of Rights, 263
Black America, 247n19
Bretton Woods system, 15, 111
British Petroleum, 78
*Brady Handgun Violence Prevention
    Act* (1993), 62, 263–264
Brown v. Board of Education of Topeka
    (1954), 112, 198
Burroughs v. United States (1934), 7
Bush, George, 95
Bush, George W., 7, 50, 133, 176,
    183–184, 187
    and moral dilemma, 36
    and the failure to act, 108

capitalism, 162–163
Chan et al. v. Korean Airlines (1989),
    264

China
   manufacturing base, 97
   People's Liberation Army
      (PLA), 97
   relations with the United States
      of America, 122–125
   FDI and Chinese markets, 140
Chinese, 189, 243, 243n3, 260
   Muslims, 110, 112–114
   philosophers, 12
   Singaporeans, 88
   Christian
   Brothers, 281
   God, 288
civil rights, 49
Civil Rights Act (1965), 198
Cold War, 10, 31, 44, 50, 74, 151,
   156, 183, 193, 195, 250, 272,
   281, 289–290
Communist Party of America, 11
Communist Party of Malaya
   (CPM), 135–136
Communist Party of Thailand
   (CPT), 135
Cronkite, Walter, 198
Congress Party of India, 127
consumer price index, 50–54
CNBC, 139
Crimean War, 281
CSPAN, 11, 108

Deng Xiaoping, 155
*Department of the Army v. Blue Fox,
   Inc* (1999), 263
Detroit Project, 56
Duke, David, 205, 269–270

Egypt, 190–191
Egyptians, 187–189

Eisenhower, Dwight D., 182, 187,
   191–192, 203–204
ETIM (East Turkestan Islamic
   Movement), 115
Eurasian, 86–87
European Coal and Steel
   Community (ECSC), 43
Exxon-Mobil, 78

Freedom of Information Act, 2
Federal Energy Regulatory
   Commission (FERC), 90
Feres v. United States (1950),
   183
*First Security National Bank v.
   United States* (1965), 262
Ford, Gerald R., 101
Frankfurt School, 224
French
   and the Panama Canal, 154
   social behavior, 252

Gandhi, Sonya, 125
Gates, Bill, 149–150, 172
German and Teutonic, 238
German Democratic Republic,
   131
Global
   gaze, 281–285
   norms, 254–261
   paradox of politics, 280
globalization
   Americanization, iii–ix, 29–34
   problem of religion, 22–26
   world phenomenon, 39–40
Goh Chok Tong, 81
Gorbachev, Mikhail, 95
Gore, Albert, 98–99
Grant, Ulysses S., 154

Greenspan, Alan, 123, 285–287
Gulf War, 236

Hampton v. Mow Sun Wong (1976),
    263
Harken Energy Corporation, 50
Human Genome Project, 250

IBRC, 15
IBRD (International Bank for
    Reconstruction and
    Development), 256
India and the United States of
    America, 125–129
Indian-Americans, 205
Indian Oil Corporation, 129
Indians, 86–87, 125–129, 189
individualism, 236–237, 208–247
Industrial Revolution, 145
international business companies
    (IBC), 9
IMF (International Monetary
    Fund), 102, 116–117, 137–138,
    160
Iraq and Iran, 109–110, 186, 220,
    240–241, 266
    fall of the Shah, 266, 295–296
    ten-year War, 265–267
Irish, 147
Islamic Association of China, 111
Israel, 100
Italian, 252

Japan, 121
    Diet, 274
    economic boom, 137
    relationship with the United
        States of America, 129–133
    salarymen, 275

Japanese, 252–253, 255
Jefferson v. United States (1950),
    183
Jemaah Islamiah, 64–65
Jews, 133, 214–215, 243, 243n3
Jim Crow laws, 66, 198
Johnson, Lyndon B., 101

Kim Il Sung, 95
Kissinger, Henry A., 181n 38, 198,
    207n23, 296–297
Korea, North, 95–96
Korea, South, 95, 117, 132, 201,
    220, 240–241
Korean, 205, 243, 243n3, 252, 267
Kumar, Sanjay, 165
Kuo-mintang, 188

Lee Kuan Yew, 76
    as Minister Mentor, 80–81,
        96–97
Lee Hsien Loong, 78–79, 86, 97
Leeson, Nick, 120–121
Louisiana Purchase, 267, 277

Mahathir Mohamad, 97–98,
    99–100, 215–216, 244–245n7
    and Jews, 99–101, 214–215
    "kampung economics", 101
Malaysia, 213–214, 216, 244n7
    "abang-adik" relationship,
        77–79
Muslims, 133
    other political relations with
        Singapore, 88–91
    religious police, 35
Manifest Destiny, 146
Mao Tse-tung, 94, 96, 155, 222
Marshall, David, 76

Maryland v. United States (1965), 262

McArthur, Douglas, 132

McCarthyism, 127, 220

McKinley, William, 154

McVeigh, Timothy, 271–272

Mexicans, 267

Metaphysics, European, 152

Military Industrial Complex, 109, 193–196, 206

    business relations, 203

    Eisenhower, 197

MNC

    American, 153, 157–158, 163–179, 225, 237

    See also American MNC.

    European, 43

modern, 151, 252–255

modernity, 5, 145–148

    crisis of, 38–40

    General Theory of Equilibrium, 152

    late modernity, 5

    optimism and progress, 250–251

    terrorism, 290–291

    traditional roles, 131

Moore, Michael, 241, 272

Monroe Doctrine, 146

Morgan, J. P., 155

Most Favored Nation (MFN), 96, 111

mullahs, 186

Muslim, 252–253

Mutual Life Insurance Company of New York v. Harris (1877), 262

Nation of Islam, 270–271

National Farmers Union Insurance Companies v. Crow Tribe of Indians (1984), 264

National Federation of Federal Employees v. United States (1999), 263

NATO (North Atlantic Treaty Organisation), 43

neoliberalism, 14, 38–39, 192–193, 272

New World Order, 95

New Zealand, 284

Nitze, Paul H., 198

Nixon, Richard M., 101, 134, 282

Nixon v. Warner Communications (1978), 263

norms

    and values, 248–279

    legal, in America, 261–265

NRA (National Rifle Association), 62

Nuclear Regulatory Commission (NRC), 90

oil, 109–110

OPEC (Organization of Petroleum Exporting Countries), 45, 89, 220

Osama bin Laden, 48

Palestinian Question, 133

Pearl Harbor, 184

People's Mojahedin Organization of Iran v. United States Department of State and Madeline K. Albright, Secretary of State (1999), 206n2

The Philippines, 117
Pillay, J. Y. M., 82
Plessy v. Ferguson (1896), 112
Portuguese, 118
post Cold War, 91
Powell, Colin, 37, 198, 207n13
producer price index, 52–54
public space and leisure, 230–232

Rameau's Nephew, 238
RAND Corporation, 44, 95, 107, 195
Rand, Ayn, 285–286
realism, and its writers, 14–15
Reliance Industries, 129
Rice, Condoleezza, 36, 108
Roe v. Wade (1973), 112
Roosevelt, Franklin D., 155–156
Douglas Robinson, 155
Eleanor Roosevelt, 222
Roosevelt, Theodore, 155, 259
Russian, 238

Saddam Hussein, 32, 69, 109, 239
Saeed Rezai v. Immigration and Naturalization Service (1995), 206n2
Shell, 78
Shinawatra, Thaksin, 112–116
Singapore, 74–91, 117, 123, 213–214, 216
Hendrickson Affair, 97
Malaysia's "whipping boy", 79
MNCs, 91
Singapore Airlines, 79–84
Special Assistance Plan schools, 86–88
scholarships, 88

Soros, George, 123, 214–215
Southeast Asia, 140–141
Sukarnoputri, Megawati, 119

Taiwan, 85, 94, 96, 187
Thailand, 116–122, 201
Thais of Chinese descent, 135
Trask, Haunani Kay, 205

United Malays National Organization (UMNO), 99
United States v. Oliver L. North (1990), 206n2
United States v. Glaxo Group (1973), 263
United States v. Sioux Nation of Indians (1980), 263
United States v. Varig Airlines (1984), 264
US Constitution
Second Amendment, 274
Sixteenth Amendment, 9

Vajpayee, 126
Vietnam, 201, 220, 240–241
Vietnam War, 236
Vietnamese, 267
Vietnamese-Americans, 205
Voting Rights Amendment Act (1976), 263

Westminster, system of parliamentary democracy, 8
White flight, 243, 243n3; *see also* 247n19
Wilson, Woodrow, 204
Wilson v. Omaha Indian Tribe (1973), 263

Wiranto, 118–119
World Bank, 69, 160
world values; *see* global norms
World Values Survey, 65, 175, 205
Worldwide Volkswagen Corporation v.
  Woodson (1980), 263

World Trade Center (New York),
  48
WTO (World Trade Organisation),
  15, 69

Yongchaiyudh, Chavalit, 117

Other Titles on Politics and International Relations

Other Titles on Politics and International Relations

Bringing the Party Back In:
How China is Governed
edited by Kjeld Erik Brødsgaard and
Zheng Yongnian
ISBN 981 210 252 3

The Enemy Within: Combating
Corruption in Asia
edited by Simon Tay and Maria Seda
ISBN 981 210 189 6

Parties and Politics: A Study of
Opposition Parties and the PAP in
Singapore (2nd edition)
by Hussin Mutalib
ISBN 981 210 408 9

Damage Control: The Chinese
Communist Party in the Jiang
Zemin Era
edited by Wang Gungwu and Zheng
Yongnian
ISBN 981 210 251 5 (paperback)
ISBN 981 210 259 0 (hardcover)

The Quest for World Order:
Perspectives of a Pragmatic
Idealist
by Tommy Koh, *edited by* Amitav
Acharya
ISBN 981 210 333 3